Lawrenceville
Press

An Introduction to Computing Using Microsoft® Works

Version 3.0 for IBM PC and Compatibles

Bruce Presley
William Freitas

First Edition published 1989
Second Edition published 1991
Copyright © 1993
by

Third Edition

ISBN   1-879233-31-2   (softcover)
ISBN   1-879233-32-0   (hardcover)

Printed in the United States of America

All orders including educational, Canadian, foreign, FPO, and APO addresses may be placed by contacting:

Lawrenceville Press, Inc.
P.O. Box 704
Pennington, NJ 08534-0704
(609) 737-1148
FAX: (609) 737-8564

This text is available in both hardcover and softcover editions.

16 15 14 13 12 11 10 9 8 7 6 5 4 3 2 1

The text is written and published by Lawrenceville Press, Inc. and is in no way connected with the Microsoft® Corporation.

Microsoft® is a registered trademark of the Microsoft Corporation.

P | PREFACE

We believe the best way to introduce students to computing is with an introductory course that gives them considerable "hands-on" the computer experience. This objective is best accomplished with an integrated software package such as Microsoft Works that teaches the student how to use a word processor, data base, and spreadsheet. We also believe that an introductory course should include a discussion of the role computers play in modern society as well as a brief history of computing. These goals are accomplished by this text which is designed to serve both the needs of students who will complete only an introductory course, as well as those who will go on to take subsequent computer courses. The emphasis of this text is on the concepts of computing and problem solving using Works so that students learn how computers can be applied to a wide range of problems. The text is written to be used either in a one or two term course by students with no previous computer experience.

Design and Features

FORMAT
Each chapter contains numerous examples and diagrams printed in a two color format to help students visualize new concepts. Works' menus are displayed in the margins for easy reference.

OBJECTIVES
An outline of the significant topics that should be emphasized is presented at the beginning of each chapter.

CONCEPTS of APPLICATION
Each of the application areas begins with an introductory section which describes the application and its uses. In this way, students are taught the purpose of the application without being overly concerned with the specific software. If the student then goes on to use another software package, he or she will fully understand the general concepts behind each application.

HANDS-ON PRACTICE
In the applications chapters each new concept is presented, discussed, and then followed by a hands-on Practice which requires the student to test newly learned skills on the computer. The Practice sections also serve as excellent reference guides to review applications commands.

CHAPTER SUMMARY
At the end of each chapter is an outline that briefly discusses the concepts covered in the chapter.

VOCABULARY	A vocabulary section which defines the new terms used is given at the end of each chapter.
REVIEW PROBLEMS	Numerous review problems are presented keyed to each section of the chapter, providing immediate reinforcement of new concepts. Answers to all review problems are included in the *Teacher's Resource Package* described below.
EXERCISES	Each of the applications chapters includes a set of exercises of varying difficulty, making them appropriate for students with a wide range of abilities. Answers to all exercises are included in the *Teacher's Resource Package* described below.
HISTORY of COMPUTING	Before learning to use the applications software, Chapter One introduces students to a history of computing and covers the vocabulary needed to understand the concepts presented in later chapters.
PROGRAMMING	Chapter Twelve offers an introduction to programming in BASIC. This introduction is sufficient to illustrate the problem-solving concepts involved in writing a computer program.
SOCIAL and ETHICAL IMPLICATIONS	Because computers play such an important role in modern society, Chapter Thirteen discusses the social and ethical consequences of living in a computerized society. Advances in computer-related technology that will impact on the student's world are also discussed. Telecommunication is explained and the Works Communications application introduced.
CAREERS in COMPUTING	It is hoped that many students will become interested in careers in computing based upon their experience in this introductory course. A section in Chapter Thirteen outlines different computer careers and the educational requirements needed to pursue them.
APPENDICES	Summaries of Works and DOS commands and keyboarding skills are presented in appendices at the end of the text for easy reference.

Teacher's Resource Package

When used with this text, the Lawrenceville Press Teacher's Resource Package provides all the additional material required to offer students an excellent introductory computer applications course. These materials, along with the text, place a strong emphasis on developing student problem-solving skills. The Package divides each of the chapters in the text into a series of lessons which contain the following features:

- **ASSIGNMENTS** - Reading and problem assignments are suggested for each lesson.

- **DISCUSSION TOPICS** - Additional material is provided which supplements the text and can be used in leading classroom discussions. Often this includes explanations of more advanced commands or concepts not covered in the text.

P

- **TRANSPARENCY MASTERS** - Most lessons contain transparency masters which often present diagrams of the different applications screens.

- **WORKSHEETS** - Included in each lesson is a worksheet containing problems which are meant to be completed in the computer lab. These problems supplement those in the text, giving students additional reinforcement of the concepts they have just learned. Many of these problems make use of the data files included on the Master Diskette described below.

- **QUIZ** - Each lesson contains a short quiz which tests recently learned skills.

- **MASTER DISKETTE** - A Master Diskette that contains files to be used in conjunction with text problems and worksheets is included in the Teacher's Resource Package. These files are especially helpful in allowing students to work with large amounts of data without first having to type it into the computer. Student diskettes can be easily made by following the directions included with the Master Diskette. The Master Diskette is supplied in both 5.25" and 3.5" formats. 10-packs of prepared student diskettes are also available.

In addition to the material in the lessons, the following features are found at the end of each chapter:

- **TESTS** - Two sets of comprehensive end of chapter tests are provided as well as a mid-term and final examination. A full set of answers and a grading key are also included. The tests are included in files on the Master Diskette so that they may be edited.

- **ANSWERS** - Complete answers are provided for the Review and Exercise problems presented in the text. Where appropriate, answers have also been included on the Master Diskette.

As an added feature, the above material is contained in a 3-ring binder. This not only enables pages to be removed for duplication but also for the insertion of additional teacher notes.

Preface to the Third Edition

The first and second editions of *An Introduction to Computing Using Microsoft Works* have established this text as the leader in its field with more than one million students having been introduced to computing using its "hands-on" approach. With this third edition we believe that we have made significant improvements in the text. These improvements have been based on the many comments we have received, and a survey of instructors who are teaching the text, as well as from our own classroom experience.

The third edition includes an additional Word Processing chapter (Chapter Four) which discusses such topics as paragraph indents, setting tabs, and footnotes. In the Data Base chapters the discussions of queries and reports have been reorganized and expanded. The spreadsheet is now presented in three rather than two chapters. The order of topic presentation has been made more logical while the discussion of difficult topics has been expanded.

Throughout the text the Practices have been rewritten to increase clarity. Additional Exercises and Reviews have been included, many of which make use of new files from the Master diskette.

Thousands of instructors have found the Teacher's Resource Package and its accompanying Master Diskette an important part of their instructional materials. The latest edition of the Package not only reflects the changes made to the text, but also includes new worksheets, new tests (two versions of each), and a quiz for each lesson.

As an additional feature the softcover edition now has an improved "lay flat" binding which keeps the text open at any page.

As teachers we know the importance of using a well written, logically organized text. With this third edition we believe that we have produced the finest introductory computer text and Teacher's Resource Package available.

Acknowledgments

The authors would like to thank the following people whose talents contributed to the production of this text.

Beth Brown for the new spreadsheet chapters and her unerring review of the rest of the text. John Borelli for converting the data base material to version 3. The quality and clarity of much of this new edition is due to their efforts and hard work. Andrew Krasnov has produced the large data bases found on the Master Diskette which allow students to work with extensive data.

For their careful review of the first edition of the text while it was being written we are especially grateful to Arlene Yolles of Ridgefield High School in Ridgefield, Connecticut, Clyde Knowlton of the Horseheads Central School District in Horseheads, New York, Pat Reisdorf of the Foxcroft School in Middleburg, Virginia, and Eric Neufer of the Hun School in Princeton, New Jersey. Many of their suggestions have been incorporated in this text.

The imaginative graphic designs were produced by Gregg Schwinn, Alan Chin-Lee, and Marge Vining. Rachel Stern and Savage Design created the new page format, and produced the computer-based layout. We very much appreciate both their effort and willingness to work under demanding deadlines.

P

Thanks are due George Elston and Bonnie Carter at Marketing Design Concepts, and Courier Printing, Inc., especially Rick Dunn who supervised the printing of the text. For her help with the Works software we wish to thank Ellen Mosner of the Microsoft Corporation.

The success of this and many of our other texts is due to the efforts of Heidi Crane, Vice President of Marketing at Lawrenceville Press. She has developed the promotional material which has been so well received by instructors around the world, and coordinated the comprehensive customer survey which led to many of the refinements in this edition. Michael Porter is responsible for the efficient service Lawrenceville Press offers in shipping orders.

A very special note of appreciation is due our colleague in the Computer Science department and friend, Ruth Wagy, who has generously shared with us materials developed in her applications courses. She has also helped test this text in her classes, and has offered many valuable suggestions on ways in which it could be improved.

Finally, we would like to thank our students, for whom and with whom this text was written. Their candid evaluation of each lesson and their refusal to accept anything less than perfect clarity in explanation have been the driving forces behind the creation of *An Introduction to Computing Using Microsoft Works*.

About the Authors

Bruce W. Presley, a graduate of Yale University, taught computer science and physics at The Lawrenceville School in Lawrenceville, New Jersey for twenty-four years where he served as the director of the Karl Corby Computer and Mathematics Center. Mr. Presley was a member of the founding committee of the Advanced Placement Computer Science examination and served as a consultant to the College Entrance Examination Board. Presently Mr. Presley, author of more than a dozen computer text books, is president of Lawrenceville Press and teaches computing applications in Boca Raton, Florida.

William R. Freitas, a graduate in computer science of Rutgers University, is director of development at Lawrenceville Press where he has co-authored several programming and applications texts as well as a number of Teacher's Resource Packages. Mr. Freitas currently teaches computing applications and Advanced Placement Computer Science in Boca Raton, Florida.

For seven years we have been privileged to teach computer science under the guidance and leadership of our close friend and colleague, Ruth Wagy. Her dedication to the highest standards of computer education have made her an inspiration to us and it is to her that we dedicate this text.

Table of Contents

Chapter Three - Manipulating Text with the Word Processor

Chapter Four - Advanced Word Processor Techniques

Chapter Five - Introducing the Works Data Base

Chapter Six - Manipulating Data with the Data Base

Chapter Seven - Reports and Advanced Data Base Techniques

Chapter Eight - Introducing the Spreadsheet

Chapter Nine - Manipulating Data with the Spreadsheet

T

Chapter Ten - Advanced Spreadsheet Techniques

Chapter Eleven - Integrations

Chapter Twelve - An Introduction to Programming in BASIC

Chapter Thirteen - Telecommunications and the Future of Computing

Appendix A - Keyboard Commands and Functions

Appendix B - DOS Commands and Making Backups

Appendix C - Keyboarding Skills

T

An Introduction to Computers

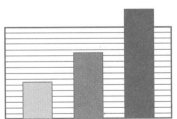

Objectives

After completing this chapter you will be able to:

1. Define what a computer is.

2. Discuss the history of computers.

3. Understand how computers work.

4. Name the components of a modern computer system.

5. Understand the advantages of using a computer.

6. Know what software and hardware are.

1

This text is about computers: their history, how they process and store data, how they can be programmed, and the role they play in modern society. We will employ a popular computer program named Microsoft Works to teach you how to use the computer to word process and produce data bases and spreadsheets. Each of these applications will be explained as we proceed.

There are three reasons for learning how to use a computer. The first and most important is to develop problem-solving skills. This is done by learning how to analyze a problem carefully, developing a step-by-step solution, and then using the computer as a tool to produce a solution.

A second reason for learning about computers is to become acquainted with their capabilities and limitations. Because you are a part of a society which is becoming increasingly computerized, learning to use a computer is probably the best way to become familiar with one.

Finally, using a computer can be fun. The intellectual challenge of controlling the operations of a computer is not only rewarding but also an invaluable skill. The techniques learned in this class can be applied to your other subjects, and to your personal and business life as well.

1.1 What is a Computer?

A computer is an electronic machine that accepts information (called "data"), processes it according to specific instructions, and provides the results as new information. The computer can store and manipulate large quantities of data at very high speed and even though it cannot think, it can make simple decisions and comparisons. For example, a computer can determine which of two numbers is larger or which of two names comes first alphabetically and then act upon that decision. Although the computer can help to solve a wide variety of problems, it is merely a machine and cannot solve problems on its own. It must be provided with instructions in the form of a computer "program."

A program is a list of instructions written in a special language that the computer understands. It tells the computer which operations to perform and in what sequence to perform them. In this text we will use a computer program called Microsoft Works and will also learn how to write our own programs in the BASIC programming language.

THE HISTORY OF COMPUTERS

Many of the advances made by science and technology are dependent upon the ability to perform complex mathematical calculations and to process large amounts of data. It is therefore not surprising that for thousands of years mathematicians, scientists, and business people have searched for "computing" machines that could perform calculations and analyze data quickly and accurately.

1.2 Ancient Counting Machines

As civilizations began to develop, they created both written languages and number systems. These number systems were not originally meant to be used in mathematical calculations, but rather were designed to record measurements like the number of sheep in flock. Roman numerals are a good example of these early number system. Few of us would want to carry out even the simplest arithmetic operations using Roman numerals. How then were calculations performed thousands of years ago?

Calculations were carried out with a device known as an *abacus* which was used in ancient Babylon, China, and throughout Europe until the late middle-ages. Many parts of the world, especially in the Orient, still make use of the abacus. The abacus works by sliding beads back and forth on a frame with the beads on the top of the frame representing fives and on the bottom ones. After a calculation is made the result is written down.

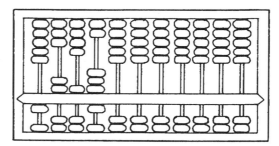

The Abacus is a calculating device used throughout the Orient

1.3 Arabic Numerals

Toward the end of the middle ages, Roman numerals were replaced by a new number system borrowed from the Arabs, therefore called Arabic numerals. This system uses ten digits and is the system we still use today. Because the Arabic system made calculations with pencil and paper easier, the abacus and other such counting devices became less common. Although calculations were now easier to perform, operations such as multiplication and division were able to be done by only those few mathematicians who were well educated.

1.4 The Pascaline

One of the earliest mechanical devices for calculating was the Pascaline, invented by the French philosopher and mathematician Blaise Pascal in 1642. At that time Pascal was employed in the recording of taxes for the French government. The task was tedious and kept him up until the early hours of the morning day after day. Being a gifted thinker, Pascal thought that the task of adding numbers should be able to be done by a mechanism that would resemble the way a clock keeps time.

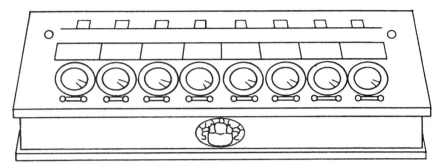

The Pascaline was a mechanical calculating device invented by Blaise Pascal in 1642

The *Pascaline* he invented was a complicated set of gears which could only be used to perform addition and not at all for multiplication or division. Unfortunately, Pascal never got the device to work properly.

1.5 The Stepped Reckoner

Later in the 17th century, Gottfried Wilhelm von Leibniz, a famous mathematician who is credited with being one of the developers of the calculus, invented a device that was supposed to be able to add and subtract, as well as multiply, divide, and extract square roots. His device, the *Stepped Reckoner*, included a cylindrical wheel called the Leibniz wheel and a moveable carriage that was used to enter the number of digits in the multiplicand.

Though both Pascal's and Leibniz's machines held great promise, they did not work well because the craftsmen of their time were unable to make machined parts that were accurate enough to carry out the inventor's design. Because of mechanically unreliable parts, the devices tended to jam and malfunction.

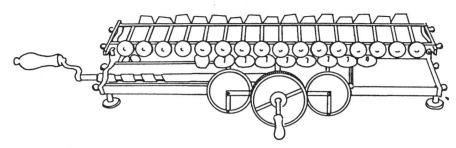

The Stepped Reckoner was another early attempt at creating a mechanical calculating device

1.6 The Punched Card

In 1810 Joseph Jacquard, a French weaver, made a revolutionary discovery. He realized that the weaving instructions for his looms could be stored on cards with holes punched in them. As the cards passed through the loom in sequence, needles passed through the holes and then picked up threads of the correct color or texture. By rearranging the cards, a weaver could change the pattern being woven without stopping the machine to change threads.

Jacquard's loom was the first device to make use of punched cards to store information

The weaving industry would seem to have little in common with the computer industry, but the idea that information could be stored by punching holes on a card was to be of great use in the later development of the computer.

1.7 Babbage's Difference and Analytical Engines

In 1822 Charles Babbage began work on the *Difference Engine*. His hope was that this device would calculate numbers to the twentieth place and then print them at forty-four digits a minute. The original purpose of this machine was to produce tables of numbers that would be used by

An Introduction to Computing Using Microsoft Works

ship's navigators. At the time navigation tables were often highly inaccurate due to calculation errors. In fact, several ships were known to have been lost at sea because of these errors. Again because of the mechanical problems that had plagued Pascal and Leibniz, the Difference Engine never worked properly.

Undaunted, Babbage later planned and began work on a considerably more advanced machine, called the *Analytical Engine*. This machine was to perform a variety of calculations by following a set of instructions, or "program", entered into it using punched cards similar to the ones used by Joseph Jacquard. During processing, the Analytical Engine was to store information in a memory unit that would allow it to make decisions and then carry out instructions based on those decisions. For example, in comparing two numbers it could be programmed to determine which was larger and then follow different sets of instructions. The Analytical Engine was no more successful than its predecessors, but its design was to serve as a model for the modern computer.

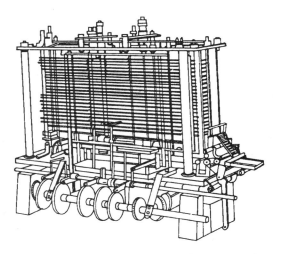

Babbage's Analytical Engine was a calculating machine which used punched cards to store information

Babbage's chief collaborator on the Analytical Engine was Lady Ada Augusta, Countess of Lovelace, the daughter of Lord Byron. Interested in mathematics, Lady Lovelace was a sponsor of the Engine and one of the first people to realize its power and significance. She also tested the device and wrote of its achievements in order to gain support for it. Because of her involvement she is often called the first programmer.

Babbage had hoped that the Analytical Engine would be able to play chess, thinking out and making brilliant moves. Lady Lovelace, however, said that the Engine could never "originate anything," meaning that she did not believe that a machine, no matter how powerful, could think. To this day her statement about computing machines remains true.

1.8 The Electronic Tabulating Machine

By the end of the 19th century, U.S. Census officials were concerned about the time it took to tabulate the count of the continuously increasing number of Americans. This counting was done every ten years, as required by the Constitution. The Census of 1880, however, took nine years to compile, making the figures highly inaccurate by the time they were published.

To solve the problem, Herman Hollerith invented a calculating machine that used electricity rather than mechanical gears. Holes representing information to be tabulated were punched in cards similar to those used in Jacquard's loom, with the location of each hole representing a specific piece of information (male, female, age, etc.). The cards were then inserted into the machine and metal pins used to open and close electrical circuits. If a circuit was closed, a counter was increased by one.

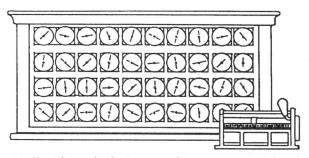

Herman Hollerith's tabulating machine, invented for the census of 1880, used electricity instead of gears to perform calculations

Hollerith's machine was immensely successful. The general count of the population, then 63 million, took only six weeks to calculate, while full statistical analysis took seven years. This may not sound like much of an improvement over the nine years of the previous census, but Hollerith's machine enabled the Census Bureau to make a far more detailed and useful study of the population than had previously been possible. Based on the success of his invention, Hollerith and some friends formed a company that sold his invention all over the world. The company eventually became known as International Business Machines (IBM).

1.9 The Electro-Mechanical Computer

By the 1930's, key-operated mechanical adding machines had been developed which used a complicated assortment of gears and levers. Scientists, engineers, and business people, however, needed machines more powerful than adding machines; machines capable of making simple decisions such as determining which of two numbers was larger and then acting upon the decision. A machine with this capability is called a computer rather than a calculator. A calculator is not a true computer because, while it can perform calculations, it can not make decisions.

The first computer-like machine is generally thought to be the *Mark I*, which was built by a team from IBM and Harvard University under the leadership of Howard Aiken. The Mark I used mechanical telephone relay switches to store information and accepted data on punched cards, processed it and then output the new data. Because it could not make decisions about the data it processed, the Mark I was not, however, a real computer but was instead a highly sophisticated calculator. It was, nevertheless, impressive, measuring over 51 feet in length and weighing 5 tons! It also had over 750,000 parts, many of them moving mechanical parts which made the Mark I not only huge but unreliable.

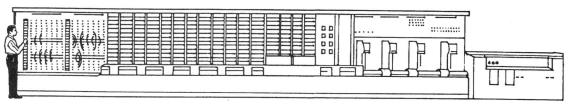

The Mark 1 weighed over 5 toms and was 51 feet long

1.10 ENIAC, *the First Electronic Computer*

In June 1943, John Mauchly and J. Prosper Eckert began work on the Electronic Numerical Integration and Calculator, or *ENIAC*. It was originally a secret military project which began during World War II to calculate the trajectory of artillery shells. Built at the University of Pennsylvania, it was not finished until 1946, after the war had ended. But the great effort put into the ENIAC was not wasted. In one of its first demonstrations ENIAC was given a problem that would have taken a team of mathematicians three days to solve. It solved the problem in twenty seconds.

ENIAC was different from the Mark I in several important ways. First, it occupied 1500 square feet, which is the same area taken up by the average three bedroom house and it weighed 30 tons. Second, it used vacuum tubes instead of relay switches. It contained over 17,000 of these tubes, which were the same kind used in radio sets. Because the tubes consumed huge amounts of electricity the computer produced a tremendous amount of heat and required special fans to cool the room where it was installed. Most importantly, because it was able to make decisions, it was the first true computer.

Because it could make decisions, ENIAC was the first true computer

ENIAC had two major weaknesses. First, it was difficult to change its instructions to allow the computer to solve different problems. It had originally been designed only to compute artillery trajectory tables, but when it needed to work on another problem it could take up to three days of wire pulling, replugging, and switch-flipping to change instructions. Second, because the tubes it contained were constantly burning out, the ENIAC was unreliable.

Today, much of the credit for the original design of the electronic computer is given to John Atanasoff, a math and physics professor at Iowa State University. Between 1939 and 1942, Atanasoff, working with graduate student Clifford Berry, developed a working digital computer on the campus at Iowa State. Unfortunately, their patent application was not handled properly, and it was not until almost 50 years later that Atanasoff received full credit for his invention, the Atanasoff Berry Computer (ABC). In 1990, he was awarded the Presidential Medal of Technology for his pioneering work, and some of his early devices were exhibited at the Smithsonian.

1.11 The Stored Program Computer

In the late 1940's, John von Neumann considered the idea of storing computer instructions in a central processing unit, or CPU. This unit would control all the functions of the computer electronically so that it would not be necessary to flip switches or pull wires to change the instructions. Now it would be possible to solve many different problems by simply typing in new instructions at a keyboard. Together with Mauchly and Eckert, von Neumann designed and built the *EDVAC* (Electronic Discrete Variable Automatic Computer) and the *EDSAC* (Electronic Discrete Storage Automatic Computer).

With the development of the concept of stored instructions or "programs," the modern computer age was ready to begin. Since then, the development of new computers has progressed rapidly, but von Neumann's concept has remained, for the most part, unchanged.

The next computer to employ von Neumann's concepts was the UNIVersal Automatic Computer, or *UNIVAC*, built by Mauchly and Eckert. The first one was sold to the U.S. Census Bureau in 1951.

Computers at this time continued to use many vacuum tubes which made them large and expensive. UNIVAC weighed 35 tons. These computers were so expensive to purchase and run that only the largest corporations and the U.S. government could afford them. Their ability to perform up to 1,000 calculations per second, however, made them popular.

1.12 The Transistor

It was the invention of the transistor that made smaller and less expensive computers possible, with increased calculating speeds of up to 10,000 calculations per second. Although the size of the computers shrank, they were still large and expensive. In the early 1960's, IBM, using ideas it had learned while working on projects for the military, introduced the first medium-sized computer named the model 650. It was still expensive, but it was capable of handling the flood of paper work produced by many government agencies and businesses. Such organizations provided a ready market for the 650, making it popular in spite of its cost.

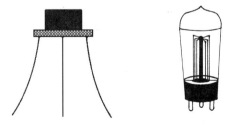

One transistor (shown larger than scale) replaced many tubes, making computers smaller, less expensive, and more reliable

These new computers also saw a change in the way data was stored. Punched cards were replaced by magnetic tape and high speed reel-to-reel tape machines. Using magnetic tape gave computers the ability to read (access) and write (store) data quickly and reliably.

Another important advance occurring at this time was the development of programming languages. Previously, computers had to be programmed by setting different switches to their On or Off positions. The first programming languages were very similar, being strings of 1's and 0's representing the status of the switches (1 for On and 0 for Off). These were called "low-level" languages. Languages such as FORTRAN (FORmula TRANslator), which was one of the first popular "high level" language, allowed programmers to write in English-like instructions that had commands such as READ and WRITE. With high level languages, it was possible to type instructions directly into the computer, eliminating the time consuming task of re-wiring.

Perhaps the most widely used high level programming language today is COBOL. COBOL was first developed by the Department of Defense in 1959 to provide a common language for use on all computers. In fact, COBOL stands for COmmon Business Oriented Language. The designer of COBOL was Grace Murray Hopper, a Commodore in the Navy at the time. Commodore Hopper was the first person to apply the term "debug" to the computer. While working on the Mark II computer in 1945, a moth flew into the circuitry, causing an electrical short which halted the computer. While removing the dead moth, she said that the program would be running again after the computer had been "debugged." Today, the process of removing errors from programs is still called debugging.

A number of new high level languages have been developed since that time: *BASIC* is a popular language used on microcomputers. You will be introduced to BASIC programming in Chapter twelve. *C* is a language designed by Bell Labs for programming large systems and is available on many computers today. Developed by the Swiss computer scientist Niklaus Wirth to teach the fundamentals of programming, *Pascal* is a language used by many schools and universities. The latest language developed by the Department of Defense is named *Ada*, after the first programmer, Ada Augusta the Countess of Lovelace.

1.13 *Integrated Circuits*

The next major technological advancement was the replacement of transistors by tiny integrated circuits or "chips." Chips are blocks of silicon with logic circuits etched into their surface. They are smaller and cheaper than transistors and can contain thousands of circuits on a single chip. Integrated circuits also give computers tremendous speed allowing them to process information at a rate of 1,000,000 calculations per second.

A typical integrated circuit chip
(approximately half an inch wide and 1.5 inches long)

One of the most important benefits of using integrated circuits is to decrease the cost and size of computers. The IBM System 360 was one of the first computers to use integrated circuits and was so popular with businesses that IBM had difficulty keeping up with the demand. Computers had come down in size and price to such a point that smaller organizations such as universities and hospitals could now afford them.

1.14 The Microprocessor

The most important advance to occur in the early 70's was the invention of the microprocessor, an entire CPU on a single chip. In 1970, Marcian Hoff, an engineer at Intel Corporation, designed the first of these chips. As a result, in 1975 the ALTAIR microcomputer was born. In 1977, working originally out of a garage, Stephen Wozniak and Steven Jobs designed and built the first Apple computer. Microcomputers were now inexpensive and therefore available to many people. Because of these advances almost anyone could own a machine that had more computing power and was faster and more reliable than either the ENIAC or UNIVAC. As a comparison, if the cost of a sports car had dropped as quickly as that of a computer, a new Porsche would now cost about one dollar.

1.15 Mainframe, Mini, and Microcomputers

There are three general size categories by which computers are classified. The choice of which size computer to use depends on what tasks are planned for it and how much data it must store.

Mainframe computers are large computer systems costing many hundreds of thousands, if not millions, of dollars. Because they are so large, mainframes can carry out many different tasks at the same time. They are used by large corporations, banks, government agencies and universities. Mainframes can calculate a payroll, keep the records for a bank, handle the reservations for an airline, or store student information for a university — tasks requiring the storage and processing of huge amounts of information.

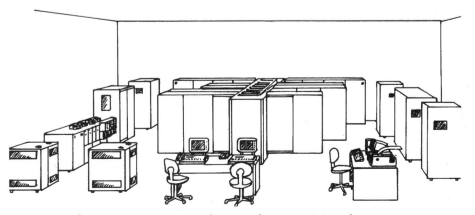

Mainframe computers are large, often requiring the own rooms

Minicomputers are smaller than mainframes, usually taking up the space of one or two small bookcases. They are also less expensive, costing from about ten thousand to about one hundred thousand dollars. Minicomputers are used by smaller businesses, schools and research institutions. Like mainframes, minicomputers can do more than one task at a time. Although minicomputers store large amounts of data, they cannot store as much as a mainframe or process it as fast.

Mini computers are smaller, but may be shared by many people at the same time

Most people using mainframe and minicomputers communicate with them by using "terminals." A terminal consists of a keyboard where commands and data are entered and monitors which display the output produced by the computer. The terminal is connected by wires to the computer, which may be located on a different floor or in a building a few blocks away. Some mainframe computers have hundreds of terminals attached and working at the same time.

Microcomputers are small and usually inexpensive. Often called "personal computers" or PC's, they can cost as little as one hundred dollars and fit on a desk top. Unlike mainframes and minicomputers, most microcomputers can only carry out one task at a time. During the past few years the processing speed and ability of microcomputers to store large quantities of data has increased at such a rapid rate that some of them now rival both mini and mainframe computers. The computer you will use is a microcomputer. In a microcomputer, the monitor and keyboard are attached to the computer allowing only one person to use it at a time.

1

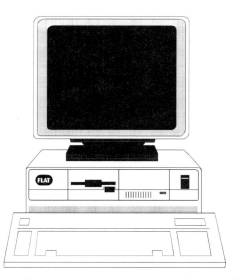

*Today's modern microcomputer combines a keyboard,
monitor, and CPU in a desktop-sized package*

1.16 How Computers Work

All computers process information, or "data." This data may be in
the form of numbers, letters, words, pictures, or symbols. In order to
process data, a computer must carry out four specific activities:

1. Input data
2. Store data while it is being processed
3. Process data according to specific instructions
4. Output the results in the form of new data

As an example of computer processing, it is possible to input a list
containing the names and addresses of one hundred thousand people
and then ask the computer to search through this data and print only the
names and addresses of those people who live in Florida. Another
example would be to ask the computer to add all integers from 1 to 1000
and print their sum (i.e., $1 + 2 + 3... + 1000 = ?$). In each of these examples,
data must be input so that it may be processed by the computer. In the
first case, the input is a list of names and addresses, while in the second,
a list of numbers. In both cases the directions the computer would follow
are given in a program.

1.17 The Components of a Computer

Computers contain four major components. Each component performs one of the four tasks we have described:

1. Input Device: a device from which the computer can accept
   data. Keyboards and disk drives are both examples of
   input devices.

2. Memory: an area inside the computer where data can be
   stored electronically.

3. Central Processing Unit (CPU): processes data and controls the flow of data between the computer's other units. It is here that the computer makes decisions.

4. Output Device: a device that displays or stores processed data. Monitors and printers are the most common visual output devices while disks drives are the most common storage devices.

The following diagram illustrates the direction in which data flows between the separate units:

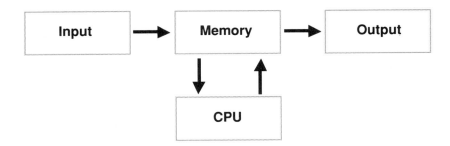

Notice that all information first flows through the CPU. Because one of the tasks of the CPU is to control the order in which tasks are completed, it is often referred to as the "brain" of the computer. This comparison with the human brain, however, has an important flaw. The CPU only executes tasks according to the instructions it has been given; it cannot think for itself.

1.18 Advantages of a Computer

Although computers cannot think, they do have some advantages over the human brain. For example, suppose you were read a list of ten numbers (input) and were asked to first, remember them (memory), second, calculate their average (process), and third, write down the average (output). In so doing, you would perform the same four tasks as a computer. Now suppose you were read 100 or 1,000 numbers and asked to calculate the average. Chances are you would get confused and tired performing all the calculations. The computer would have none of these problems. It would accurately remember all of the data and be able to quickly calculate the answers. The computer, therefore, has three important advantages over the human brain:

1. Reliable memory, with the ability to store and recall large amounts of data over long periods of time.

2. Speed, which enables it to process data quickly.

3. The ability to work 24 hours a day without rest.

Remember, however, that as reliable and fast as a computer is, it is only as "smart" as the instructions it is given by its program.

1.19 Hardware and Software

A computer requires both "hardware" and "software" to make it work. Hardware refers to the physical parts that make up a computer system and include keyboards, printers, memory units, CPU's, monitors, and disk drives. Software, on the other hand, describes the instructions or the program that is given the computer. Some software is made a permanent part of most computers, so that the tasks a computer must always be ready to perform can be carried out easily. Other software is entered into the computer only when a specific task is required. In this text we will make use of applications software written to perform a number of different tasks.

1.20 Memory

Most computers have two types of memory contained on chips, ROM and RAM. Read Only Memory or ROM contains the most basic operating instructions for the computer. It is made a permanent part of the computer and cannot be changed. The instructions in ROM enable the computer to complete simple jobs such as placing a character on the screen or checking the keyboard to see if any keys have been pressed.

Random Access Memory or RAM is temporary memory where data and instructions can be stored. Data stored here can be changed or erased. When the computer is first turned on this part of memory is empty and when turned off, any data it stores is lost. Because RAM storage is temporary, computers use disks as auxiliary memory storage. Before turning the computer off, the data stored in RAM can be saved as output on a disk so that it can be used again at a later time.

1.21 Central Processing Unit

The Central Processing Unit (CPU) directs all the activities of the computer. It can only follow instructions that it receives either from ROM or from a program stored in RAM. In following these instructions, the CPU guides the processing of information throughout the computer.

A CPU chip many times more powerful than the Mark 1 measures about 2 inches by 2 inches

The Arithmetic Logic Unit, or ALU, is the part of the CPU where the "intelligence" of the computer is located. It can perform only two operations. It can add numbers and compare numbers. Then the question is: How does the computer subtract, multiply, or divide numbers? The answer is by first turning problems like multiplication and division into addition problems. This would seem to be a very inefficient way of doing things, but it works because the ALU is so fast. For example, to solve the problem 5 x 2, the computer adds 5 two's, 2 + 2 + 2 + 2 + 2 to calculate the answer, 10. The time it takes the ALU to carry out a single addition of this type is measured in *nanoseconds* (billionths of a second). The other job of the ALU is to compare numbers and then determine whether a number is greater than, less than, or equal to another number. This ability is the basis of the computer's decision-making power.

1.22 How the Computer Follows Instructions

Memory storage, both RAM and ROM, and the CPU are made of tiny chips of silicon. These chips are so small that they must be housed in special plastic cases that have metal pins coming out of them. The pins allow the chips to be plugged into circuit boards that have their wiring printed on them.

Chips are covered by intricate circuits that have been etched into their surface and then coated with a metallic oxide that fills in the etched circuit patterns. This enables the chips to conduct electricity along the many paths of its circuits. Because there are as many as millions of circuits on a single chip, the chips are called integrated circuits.

The electrical circuits on a chip have one of two states, OFF or ON. Therefore, a system was developed that uses only two numbers, 0 and 1: 0 representing OFF and 1 representing ON. A light switch is similar to a single computer circuit. If the light is off, it represents a 0, and if on, a 1. This number system, which uses only two digits, is called the "binary" (base 2) system.

Humans find a system with ten digits, 0 to 9, easier to use primarily because we have ten fingers. The computer uses binary digits to express not only numbers, but all information, including letters of the alphabet. Because of this a special code had to be established to translate numbers, letters and characters into binary digits. This code has been standardized for computers as the American Standard Code for Information Interchange, or ASCII. In this code, each letter of the alphabet, both upper and lower case, and each symbol, digit, and special control function used by the computer is represented by a number. The name JIM, for example, is translated by the computer into the ASCII numbers 74, 73, 77. In turn these numbers are then stored by the computer in binary form:

Letter	ASCII	Binary code
J	74	01001010
I	73	01001001
M	77	01001101

An Introduction to Computing Using Microsoft Works

1.23 Bits and Bytes

Each 0 or 1 in the binary code is called a "bit" (BInary digiT) and these bits are grouped by the computer into 8 bit units called "bytes." Each ASCII code is one byte in length. Note how eight 0's and 1's are used to represent each letter in JIM in binary form.

The size of the memory of a computer is measured by the number of bytes that make up its RAM. A computer might have, for example, 64K of RAM. In computers and electronics, K represents 2^{10} which equals 1024. The letter K comes from the word *kilo*, which means 1000, and although 1024 is more than 1000, K is still used as the abbreviation. 64K of memory, therefore, is really 64×2^{10} which is 65,536 bytes.

It is possible to give a computer its instructions directly in binary code, typing in 0's and 1's using what is called "machine language." This is extremely difficult to do, which is the reason that high level programming languages have been developed. The English word instructions from these languages are translated by the computer into binary code. The software we will use in the applications chapters of this text has already been programmed making it easy for us to use.

1.24 Applications Software

One of the most useful ways in which a computer can be used is to run commercially produced "applications software." This is software written by professional programmers to perform specific applications or tasks. In this text we will use an applications program named Microsoft Works which includes three common applications: word processing, data base, and spreadsheet.

Word processing allows us to enter text from the keyboard into the computer and then manipulate it electronically. We will be able to insert and delete text, correct mistakes, move text and perform numerous other functions all on the computer screen. The text can then be printed.

Data bases allow us to store and manipulate large quantities of data using the computer. For example, a data base can store the names, addresses, grades and extra-curricular activities for all of the students in a school. It will be possible to add or delete data and produce printed reports using the data base.

Spreadsheets primarily store numeric data which can then be used in calculations. We will use a spreadsheet to store a teacher's grades and then calculate student averages. The primary advantage of a computerized spreadsheet is its ability to redo the calculations should the data it stores be changed.

One common factor shared by these three applications is their ability to store data on disk in a "file." A file is simply a collection of data stored on a disk in a form the computer can read. Unlike the computer's RAM memory, data placed in a file is not erased when the computer's power is turned off. This way, the applications program can access the information again and again.

A major advantage of Microsoft Works is that it is an "integrated" program. This means that a single program performs all three applications, allowing data stored in a file by one application to be transferred to another. Later in this course you will produce a data base file of names and addresses and then use this file in conjunction with a word processor file to produce personalized letters to everyone in the data base file.

Besides integrated programs like Works there are numerous other applications programs available. There are programs that can be used by musicians to produce musical scores and then play them on a synthesizer, programs that assist an architect in designing a building, programs that produce the special effects graphics that you see in the movies and on television, and much more. This book, for example, has been created and typeset using applications software.

As we progress in this text the usefulness of applications software will become increasingly obvious. With computers becoming more widely used, applications software is being written to assist people in almost every profession. Learning to use Works will give you an idea of how the computer and applications software can be applied to help solve many types of problems.

Chapter Summary

Man has searched for a machine to calculate and record data for thousands of years. The earliest of these devices were mechanical, requiring gears, wheels and levers, and were often unreliable. The advent of electricity brought about machines which used vacuum tubes, and were capable of performing thousands of calculations a minute. The unreliability of the vacuum tube lead to the development of the transistor and integrated circuit. Computers based on these devices were smaller, faster, more reliable and less expensive than before.

All computers have several parts in common: (1) an input device which allows data and commands to be entered into it, (2) some way of storing commands and data, (3) a Processing Unit which controls the processing, and (4) some way of returning the processed information in the form of output. In general, a computer is a machine which accepts information, processes it according to some specific instructions called a program, and then returns new information as output.

Today's microcomputer makes use of a CPU on a chip, the microprocessor which controls the actions of the computer. Based on von Neumann's concept, the computer stores both data and instruction in its memory at the same time. Memory comes in two forms, RAM chips which can be erased and used over, and ROM chips, which is permanent. Keyboards and disk drives are used to input data. Monitors and printers are used to output data. Because the contents of RAM are lost when the computer's power is turned off, disks are used to store data. The CPU contains a special device called the Arithmetic Logic Unit (ALU) which performs any math or comparison operations.

1

Vocabulary

ALU - Arithmetic Logic Unit, the part of the CPU that handles math operations.

ASCII - American Standard Code for Information Interchange, the code used for representing characters in the computer.

Bit - Binary Digit, a single 0 or 1 in a binary number.

Byte - A group of 8 bits.

CPU - Central Processing Unit, the device which electronically controls the functions of the computer.

Data - Information either entered into or produced by the computer.

Hardware - Physical devices which make up the computer and its peripherals.

Input - Data used by the computer.

K, kilobyte - Measurement of computer memory capacity, 1024 bytes.

Keyboard - Device resembling a typewriter used for inputting data into a computer.

Memory - Electronic storage used by the computer.

Microprocessor - CPU on a single chip.

Monitor - Television-like device used to display computer output.

Output - Data produced by a computer program.

Peripheral - Secondary hardware device connected to a computer such as a printer, monitor or disk drive.

Program - Series of instructions written in a special language directing the computer to perform certain tasks.

PC - Personal Computer, a small computer employing a microprocessor.

RAM - Random Access Memory, memory which the computer can both read and write.

ROM - Read Only Memory, memory from which the computer can read only.

Software - Computer programs.

Terminal - Keyboard and monitor combination used to communicate with a mainframe or minicomputer.

Reviews

Sections 1.1 - 1.10

1. What is the primary difference between a computer and a calculator?

2. What is a computer program?

3. Why did early calculating devices not work well?

4. Was Pascal's Pascaline a computer? Why or why not?

5. If successful, could Babbage's Analytical Engine been considered a computer? Why or why not?

6. a) What was the first calculating machine to make use of punched cards?
   b) What were the cards used for?

7. Why did scientists and business people want computers rather than calculators?

8. a) The Mark I was considered a calculator rather than a computer. Why?
   b) Why was the Mark I unreliable?
   c) What was the most important difference between the ENIAC and Mark I?

Sections 1.11 - 1.15

9. John von Neumann made one of the most important contributions to the development of modern computers. What was this contribution and why was it so important?

10. What made early computers so expensive?

11. What two innovations made the IBM Model 650 superior to earlier computers?

12. High level programming languages such as FORTRAN and BASIC were developed in the 1960's. Why were they important?

13. a) What is an integrated circuit?
    b) In what ways is it superior to a transistor?

14. What invention made the microcomputer possible?

15. Compare a microcomputer with ENIAC. What advantages does the microcomputer have?

16. List three jobs which could best be performed on each of the following computers:

    a) mainframe computer
    b) minicomputer
    c) microcomputer

Sections 1.16 - 1.24

17. Suppose you were to use a computer to store the names of all the students in your school and then print only those names beginning with the letter "P". Explain how each of the four activities needed to process data would be performed.

18. a) List three tasks for which a computer would be better than a human working without a computer. Tell why the computer is better.
    b) List three tasks for which a human would be better than a computer. Tell why the human is better.

19. a) What is computer hardware?
    b) What is software?

20. Which of the four major components of a computer would be used to perform each of the following tasks?

    a) display a column of grade averages
    b) calculate grade averages
    c) store electronically a set of grades
    d) type in a set of grades
    e) decide which of two grades was higher
    f) store a set of grades outside of the computer

21. What is the primary difference between the two types of memory contained in a computer?

22. How would the computer solve the problem 138 x 29?

23. Why does the computer use binary numbers?

24. How does the computer store a person's name in memory?

25. a) What is a bit?
    b) A byte?
    c) A K?

26. How many bytes of memory does a 256K computer contain?

27. What is applications software?

Chapter Two

Introducing the Word Processor

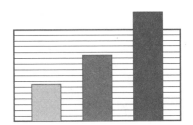

Objectives

After completing this chapter you will be able to:

1. Describe what a word processor is.

2. Describe the capabilities of a word processor.

3. Start Works and enter the Word Processor.

4. Use the Word Processor to enter and modify text in a document.

5. Select menus from the Menu bar and choose different commands from them.

6. Save a document on disk.

7. Load a previously saved document from the disk into the Word Processor.

8. Print a word processed document.

9. Exit Works properly.

2

This chapter describes what a word processor is and why it is a powerful tool for preparing documents. Directions for starting the computer, using disks, and running the Works program are given. You will use the word processor to create, edit, print, and save documents.

2.1 What is a Word Processor?

A word processor uses the computer to produce easy to read, professional-looking documents. What makes a word processor especially powerful is its ability to make changes (edit) in a document and to change the look (format) of the document in a number of different ways.

When a word processor is used, words are typed on the keyboard and transferred into the computer's memory. The document can then be edited electronically on the computer screen, and later printed. To correct a simple error or make an editing change only those words requiring changes need to be retyped. Words, phrases, and even whole paragraphs can be inserted, copied, changed, or deleted. The computer automatically adjusts the position of existing words in the document, pushing them forward or backward as needed to accommodate the changes. Editing options such as these are helpful in improving the quality of your writing — using a word processor allows the document to be continually refined until what has been written truly reflects what you wish to say.

Another useful feature of word processing is the flexibility it provides when deciding how a document is to look. Does the document look better with a half-inch margin or an inch margin? Should a paper be double spaced or single spaced? Word processed documents can be displayed in different formats on the screen and compared. When the desired format has been determined, the document may be printed.

When complete, a word processed document can be transferred from the computer's memory to a disk. The saved document can then be recalled at any time, and changes made or another copy printed. It is also possible to combine pieces of one document with another so that lengthy paragraphs and even several pages can be included in a new document without having to retype them.

2.2 *How To Use This Text*

Throughout this text new commands and procedures are introduced in a two step process. First, the command or procedure is discussed. You will be told what the command does and how to apply it, but will not use the computer at this time. Second, the discussion is followed by a section titled *Practice*. Each Practice leads you through a step-by-step example of how to use the command on the computer. You should actually perform the steps given in a Practice on the computer using Works. Practices also serve as reviews of the steps required to perform specific tasks. Because the discussion sections explain the details of what is to be demonstrated, you should read them carefully before proceeding to the Practice.

GETTING STARTED ON THE COMPUTER

You are now ready to start using the computer. This chapter will take a "hands on" the computer approach to introduce word processing and editing skills. You will learn how to turn on the computer, enter the date and time, and run the Works program. Simple "text" (characters, words, and phrases) will be entered in the word processor to demonstrate how a document may be edited, printed, and saved.

2.3 *Using Disks*

Disks will most likely be used to save any files that you create. It is important to handle the disks carefully because they store large quantities of data in a magnetic format that is vulnerable to dirt and heat. Observing the following rules will help to ensure that your disks give you trouble-free service:

1. Keep disks away from electrical and magnetic devices such as computer monitors, television sets, stereos, and any type of magnet.

2. Make sure that your disks are not exposed to either extreme cold or heat. Because they are made of plastic they are sensitive to temperature.

3. Be careful not to allow dust, dirt, or moisture to penetrate the disk by keeping it in a safe place when not in use.

4. Never touch the disk except by the edges of its jacket. Touching the disk's magnetic surface may damage it, destroying valuable data.

5. Do not bend, crush, or crimp the disk, and never place paper clips on it.

Your computer is an expensive electronic tool which should be treated carefully. A good rule to follow is never to eat or drink around the computer.

2.4 The Computer Keyboard and Word Processing

Before proceeding, take time to familiarize yourself with the computer's keyboard. Below are listed some keys which have special features when word processing. Information about additional keys will be provided as they are needed.

Cursor control "arrow" keys:

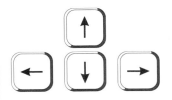

When the Word Processor screen is first displayed, a small blinking underline called the cursor (or "insertion point") appears in the upper-left corner of the Work area. The cursor can be moved around the screen, without erasing or entering text, using the *cursor control keys* which are marked with arrows (up, down, left, and right). To move the cursor down one line, press the key marked with a down-arrow. Similarly, to move the cursor up, left or right, use the key marked with the appropriate arrow. Each of these keys is a "repeat key", meaning that it will continue moving the cursor as long as it is held down. The arrow keys can only move the cursor where text has already been typed. If you attempt to move the cursor to an area of the screen which does not contain any text, the computer beeps and the cursor does not move.

Delete:

The Delete key (sometimes marked Del) is used to erase a character. Pressing Delete erases the character directly above (on) the cursor. When a character is deleted, any characters to its right are automatically moved over to fill the gap made by the deleted character.

Escape:

Esc is used to cancel (escape from) the computer's current operation. The specific effect that pressing the Escape key will have depends on the operation that is being performed.

Enter:

Enter is used to instruct Works to accept a command. In the word processor the Enter key is also used to end a paragraph or to terminate any line which does not reach the right side of the screen. When Enter is pressed the cursor moves on to the next line. Note that on some computers this key is labeled "Return" or with the symbol "↵".

Backspace:

Pressing the Backspace key (sometimes marked ←) deletes the character to the left of the cursor and moves the cursor one space to the left. Do not confuse Backspace with the left-arrow key. Both move the cursor one character to the left, but Backspace erases characters as it moves and left-arrow does not.

To insert new text the cursor is first placed using the cursor control keys where the new material is to appear, and then the new material typed. Works automatically inserts the characters you type at the current cursor position. Any text following the insertion is moved to the right to accommodate the inserted material. Deleting and inserting are powerful text editing features that allow almost any type of change to be made to a document.

2.5 Starting the Computer

Before using Works, it is first necessary to load the disk operating system (DOS) into the computer's memory. DOS contains special programs that the computer needs to run. The process of transferring DOS from disk to computer memory is called "booting." The following instructions assume that you have a computer with a hard disk. Your hard disk has been prepared so that DOS loads automatically when the computer is turned on. When booting, DOS may ask you to enter the current date and time. After DOS has booted, you will tell the computer to run the Works program. If you are using a network your directions may be slightly different. See your instructor for instructions on starting Works on your network.

•••

Practice 1

In this Practice, you will turn on the computer, enter the current date and time, and boot DOS. The Works program will then be run from the hard disk.

1) ENTER THE CURRENT DATE AND TIME AND BOOT DOS

a. Turn on both the computer and the monitor. After a few seconds, the red "in use" light on the disk drive comes on and the computer automatically loads DOS from the hard disk.

b. If you see the prompt

```
Current date is Tue  1-1-1980        <Date may be different>
Enter new date (mm-dd-yy):
```

type today's date in the form *mm-dd-yy* and then press the key marked Enter. (On your computer this key may be labeled "Return" or with the symbol "↵".) Pressing the Enter key enters whatever has been typed into the computer's memory. If you make a mistake entering the date, use the Backspace key to erase the error and type the correct date. The computer will not accept an invalid date.

c. If you see the prompt

```
Current time is 0:05.17              <Time may be different>
Enter new time:
```

type the current time in the form *hh:mm* and press the Enter key. If you make a mistake entering the time, use the Backspace key to erase the error and type the time again. The computer will not accept an invalid time.

2) START WORKS

After entering the date and time (if necessary), your computer may display several messages about the status of the machine. After the boot process is complete, you will see a line similar to:

```
C:\>
```

This is called the "DOS prompt" and it indicates that the computer is ready to accept a command from you.

2

Type

    WORKS

and press the Enter key. The Works program will run and you will see the following copyright screen:

```
┌──────────────────────────────────────────┐
│ ┌──────────────────────────────────────┐ │
│ │         Microsoft (R) Works          │ │
│ │            Version 3.0               │ │
│ │                                      │ │
│ │   (c) Copyright Microsoft Corporation,│ │
│ │      1987-1992. All rights reserved. │ │
│ │  Spelling Checker & Thesaurus (c) Copyright│
│ │  Soft-Art, 1984-1992. All rights reserved.│
│ └──────────────────────────────────────┘ │
└──────────────────────────────────────────┘
```

2.6 Using Works

Works is designed to mimic the operations performed in an office. In an office, different business documents are stored in "files" in a file cabinet. Before a file may be used, it must be taken from the cabinet and opened. In Works, each word processed document, data base, and spreadsheet is stored in a different file on a disk. (Data base and spreadsheet files are explained later in this text.) Before a previously created file may be used, it must be electronically transferred from the disk to the computer's memory. In order to create a new word processor document, a new, empty file must first be created.

After starting Works, the following screen is displayed which contains the Quick Start dialog box:

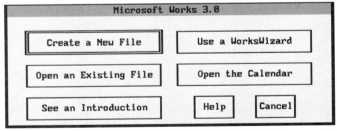

The Quick Start dialog box is displayed each time you start Works

A "dialog box" is simply a list of options from which you may choose. To select an option from a dialog box press the appropriate highlighted letter. For example, in this dialog box you may select the **Create a New File** option by typing N, or the **Open an Existing File** option by typing an O. Most dialog boxes have a "default" option — a likely choice that Works has already selected for you. In this case, the default option is **Create a New File** which is indicated by the heavier box around it. You may select the default option from any dialog box by simply pressing the Enter key.

We want to create a new Word Processor file. This option is selected by typing the highlighted letter N. Works then lists the different types of files that may be created:

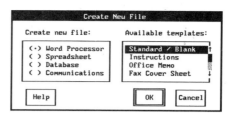

The Create New File dialog box lists the possible applications for which a file may be created

Word Processor is already selected (it is the default), so pressing Enter creates a new Word Processor file. A blank word processor screen is then displayed.

2.7 The Word Processor Screen

The Word Processor screen contains several features that will be important as you learn to use the word processor:

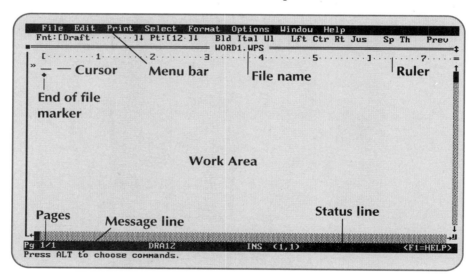

The Works Word Processor screen

Along the top of the screen is the Menu bar. Each word on the Menu bar is the name of a "menu" — a list of commands from which you may choose. Directly below the Menu bar is the Tool bar. The Tool bar provides shortcuts to some common commands and is described in the next chapter. Below the Tool bar is the Ruler. The Ruler is used to illustrate horizontal spacing and is also explained in more detail later.

Just before the bottom of the screen is the Status line. Works uses the Status line to display the number of the page you are working on, along with other information. At the bottom of the screen is the Message line which displays various messages about the command being executed. Works also uses the Message line to inform you of the actions that may be taken. The current message says that commands may be chosen by first pressing the key marked Alt. Commands are used to access Works functions and will be discussed as we proceed.

2

The file name at the top of the screen, WORD1.WPS, is a temporary name that you will change later when the file is saved. The center of the screen is called the Work area. Any text typed into the word processor appears in this area. The blinking underline in the upper-left corner of the screen is called the "cursor." It shows where characters typed into the word processor will appear.

Whenever the Word Processor screen is displayed, it is possible to enter text (characters, words, and phrases) into the file whose name is shown at the top of the Work area. Any text typed on the keyboard appears on the screen at the current position of the cursor. As we will see later, after text has been entered it is possible to make changes to it and perform several powerful operations on it. The diamond (◆) marks the end of the current document. No text may be entered after the diamond, but any number of new lines may be inserted above it.

•••

Practice 2

The following instructions assume that both DOS and Works have been loaded as described in Practice 1. You should have the Quick Start dialog box on the screen. This Practice directs you to create a new Word Processor file, enter some text into the file, and then edit it. It also demonstrates the use of the arrow and Delete keys to insert and delete characters.

1)   CREATE A NEW WORD PROCESSOR DOCUMENT

    a.   From the Quick Start dialog box, select the **Create a New File** option [*press* N]. The Create New File dialog box is displayed listing the different Works applications.

    b.   **Word Processor** is the default option and is already selected so press Enter to continue. A new, empty word processor screen is displayed. Note the Menu bar, cursor, and diamond marking the end of the document. Locate the Tool bar, Ruler, Status line, Message line, and Work area on this screen.

2)   TYPE THE FOLLOWING LINE INTO THE FILE

    Type the following, using the Shift key to generate the capital letters:

```
Hello, World!
```

    Do not press Enter.

3)   ERASE THE EXCLAMATION POINT (!)

    Press the Backspace key once to erase the character to the left of the cursor, the exclamation point (!). Works deletes the character and moves the cursor into the space formerly occupied by the erased character.

4)   MOVE THE CURSOR WITHOUT ERASING ANY TEXT

    Press the left-arrow key three times to move the cursor under the letter "r". (Be sure to use the left-arrow key, and not the Backspace.)

5)   DELETE THE LETTER "R"

    Press the Delete key once. Works deletes the character above the cursor. The screen now contains the letters "Hello, Wold" with the "l" moving over to occupy the space where the "r" was.

6) INSERT A CHARACTER

Press the r key. An "r" is inserted into the line and the "ld" characters move to the right to make room, creating "Hello, World".

7) MOVE THE CURSOR WITHOUT ERASING ANY TEXT

Press the left-arrow key until the cursor is under the "H" in "Hello". Press the left-arrow key again. The computer beeps and does not allow the cursor to be moved off the Work area.

8) DELETE ALL OF THE LETTERS

Press Delete to erase the H. Continue to press Delete until all of the letters have been deleted. Note how the remaining letters move over each time Delete is pressed.

9) TYPE THE FOLLOWING POEM, PRESSING THE ENTER KEY AT THE END OF EACH LINE:

```
Jack and Jill went up the hill,        Enter
to fetch a pail of water.              Enter
Jack fell down and broke his crown,    Enter
and Jill came tumbling after.
```

Enter is pressed at the end of each line because the lines do not reach the right side of the screen. Use the Delete and arrow keys to correct any typing errors that you may have made.

10) EDIT THE POEM

Use the Delete and arrow keys, and insert new text as necessary to make the following changes in the poem:

a) insert "BIG" and a space before the word "pail"
b) change the word "water" to "gold"
c) change the word "crown" to "arm"
d) change "came tumbling after" to "stood up and laughed"

Check - Your screen should show the edited poem similar to:

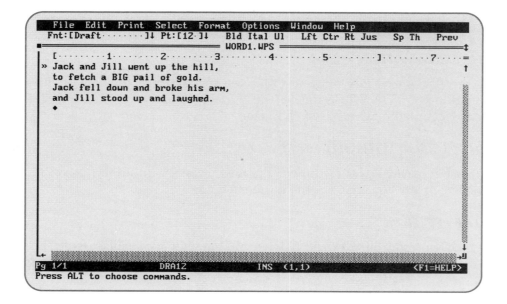

An Introduction to Computing Using Microsoft Works

2.8 Using Menus

The topmost line of the Word Processor screen is the Menu bar. Each word in the bar names a menu from which different commands may be chosen. Pressing the Alt key causes a letter in each of the menu names to be displayed in a different color (brighter or underlined on a black and white monitor):

File Edit Print Select Format Options Window Help

The Menu bar contains menus used to access different commands

Pressing the key that corresponds to the highlighted letter displays the available commands on that menu. For example, pressing the Alt key followed by F displays the File menu:

The File menu contains commands which affect files

Note: In this text we denote this sequence of keystrokes as Alt-F, meaning to hold down the Alt key and press the F. Each command on the menu also has a highlighted letter. Pressing that letter when the menu is displayed executes the command. Pressing Escape before a command selection is made removes the menu from the screen and returns the cursor to the Work area.

On the menu, several commands have three dots (. . .) following the command name (Open and Save As are examples). This means that a dialog box will appear asking for more information when this command is executed.

2.9 Saving a Document on Disk

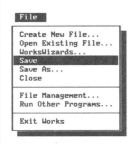

Saving documents on disk is an important part of using a word processor. Because the computer's memory can only store information while the power is on, any data in memory is lost when the computer is turned off. However, if a copy of the document is saved on disk before the power is shut off, the document can later be retrieved from the disk and loaded into memory. Unfinished documents, as well as those that might need future editing or reprinting, should always be saved.

Another important reason for saving documents is to prevent their accidental loss. A momentary power interruption can wipe everything out of the computer's memory. Even bumping the power cord can sometimes cause the memory to be cleared. It is therefore a good practice, especially when working on long or important documents, to save the document repeatedly. Then should a power failure occur, the document can be restored from the disk at the point where it was last saved. It is also important to save a document on disk before you attempt to print it because a problem involving the printer could cause the document to be lost if it has not previously been saved.

When a document is saved, a copy of what is currently stored in the computer's memory is placed on the disk. It is important to realize that the computer also retains the document in memory so that there are now two copies, one in memory and one on the disk. The copy in memory is erased when the computer is turned off, but the copy on the disk is permanent and can be recovered at any time.

Documents stored on disk are called "files," and files must be given names by which they can be identified. This name can be up to 8 characters long but may only contain letters and numbers. Special symbols such as spaces, question marks, and periods may not be used. Examples of legal file names are HOMEWORK, CHAPTER5, and 2NDMEMO. It is important to give a file a name that describes what it contains. For example, a file containing a letter to Suzy Lee is better named SUZYLEE or SUZYLETR rather than just LETTER. When a new word processor file is first saved, Works asks you to supply a name for it. Works automatically adds the extension .WPS to all word processor file names to distinguish them from files produced by other applications.

Documents are saved by selecting the Save command from the File menu. If this is the first time the file has been saved, you must enter the file's name in the following dialog box and press the Enter key:

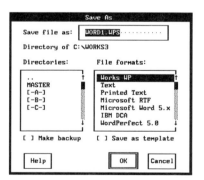

The Save command is executed from the File menu with the keystrokes Alt-F S

A copy of the document in the computer's memory is then placed on the disk, using that name.

It is important to realize that any editing changes made to a previously saved file are not stored on the disk unless the file is again saved. It is also important to realize that saving an edited document replaces the original file on the disk, erasing the original.

An Introduction to Computing Using Microsoft Works

2.10 Exiting Works

```
File
┌─────────────────────────┐
│ Create New File...      │
│ Open Existing File...   │
│ WorksWizards...         │
│ Save                    │
│ Save As...              │
│ Close                   │
├─────────────────────────┤
│ File Management...      │
│ Run Other Programs...   │
├─────────────────────────┤
│ Exit Works              │
└─────────────────────────┘
```

One of the most important procedures to learn is how to quit Works properly. Whenever you want to stop using Works, either so that another program can be run or the computer turned off, the exit procedure should be performed. If Works is not properly exited, files that you have created can be damaged or lost. Never just turn the computer off before following the exit procedure. Exiting is accomplished by selecting the Exit Works command from the File menu.

If you have created a new file, or made editing changes to a previously created file, Works informs you that any new information will be lost if you do not save the file before exiting:

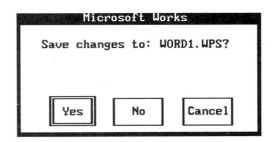

Works displays a warning if you attempt to exit without saving a new or modified file

If you wish to retain the changes, press Enter to select Yes and save the file on disk. If you do not wish to save the new version you may press N to select No and any previously saved version will remain on the disk unchanged.

● ●

Practice 3

This Practice saves the file created in Practice 2 on disk, using the name POEM.

1) *HIGHLIGHT THE MENU LETTERS*

Press Alt to highlight the menu letters on the Menu bar.

2) *DISPLAY THE FILE MENU*

Because the "F" is highlighted in File, press the F key to display the File menu.

3) *SELECT THE SAVE COMMAND*

The "S" is highlighted in Save, so press the S key to execute the Save command. Works then prompts you for the name of the file.

4) *ENTER THE NAME OF THE FILE TO BE SAVED*

The default name WORD1.WPS is shown. Type POEM on the **Save file as** line to replace the default name and press Enter.

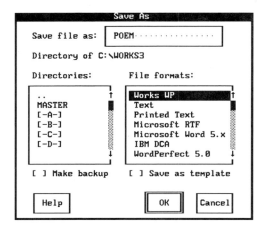

A copy of the file in memory is stored on disk using the name POEM.WPS and the dialog box removed. Note that POEM.WPS is now listed as the file name at the top of the Work area.

5) *PROPERLY EXIT WORKS*

From the File menu, select the Exit Works command [*press* Alt-F X].

The screen clears and a DOS prompt appears to inform you that Works has been exited and the computer is now ready to run a new program. Only at this point can the computer be safely turned off. If you wish to reload Works, type WORKS and press Enter.

2.11 *Word Wrap*

When using a word processor it is not necessary to stop typing to determine if the next word will fit on the end of the current line or if it must go on the next. Works determines if there is sufficient room for a word at the end of a line. If not, the word is automatically moved to the beginning of the next line in a process called "word wrap" or "wrap around."

One of the advantages of allowing Works to determine the arrangement of words on a line can be seen when deleting or inserting text. When new words are added to a line, any words to their right are moved over. If there is not enough room on the current line, those words which do not fit are moved to the next line. There may be a "domino" effect as words move from one line to the next to make room for the added text. Similarly, when deleting text, words are moved up from previous lines to accommodate the change.

Sometimes the typist rather than the computer must determine where the end of one line and the beginning of the next are located. For example, you must specify the end of a paragraph by pressing Enter, which moves the cursor to the beginning of the next line. Each time Enter is pressed again, a blank line is produced. Therefore, to end a paragraph and insert a blank line, press Enter twice and then resume typing at the beginning of the next paragraph. Enter must also be pressed to end any short lines which do not reach the right side of the screen, as in the poem you entered in Practice 3.

Practice 4

This Practice demonstrates word wrap and how paragraphs are created. A new word processor file named NEWSTORY will be created.

1) BOOT DOS AND START WORKS

Boot DOS and start Works as described in Practice 1 if you have not already done so. The Quick Start dialog box is displayed.

2) CREATE A NEW WORD PROCESSOR FILE

a. Select the **Create a New File** option from the Quick Start dialog box [*press* N].
b. Word Processor is already selected so press Enter to select the OK option and create a new word processor file.

3) ENTER THE FOLLOWING STORY

Type the story below, allowing the computer to determine the end of lines. Press Enter only at the end of a paragraph or line which does not reach the right margin, such as in the list of food. Start each paragraph with 5 spaces and each food item with 8 spaces:

```
     The Red Cross dinner dance will be held in the main
ballroom of the downtown Hilton at 7:30 PM next Saturday
night. Music for dancing will be provided by the Tom
Steves Trio. All families are invited, and tickets are
$25.00 per family.

     The menu for the evening's event will be:

        Fruit cup
        Roast Duck a l'Orange with Wild Rice stuffing
        Garden salad
        Mint parfait

     After dinner, dancing will continue until 11:30 PM.
Coffee and donuts will be served at the end of the
evening.
```

When complete, your file should be similar to:

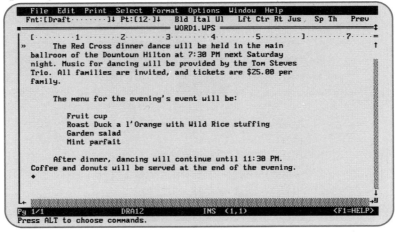

4) SAVE THE FILE USING THE NAME NEWSTORY.WPS

a. From the File menu, select the Save command [*press* Alt-F S].
b. Type the name NEWSTORY on the **Save file as** line and press Enter. Works automatically adds .WPS to the end of the file name and a copy of the file is saved on disk using the name NEWSTORY.WPS.

5) EDIT THE STORY

Use the Delete and arrow keys, and insert new text as necessary to make the following changes:

- Insert the name of your town before the words "Red Cross dinner dance." Note how the rest of the paragraph is adjusted to make room.
- The dessert has been changed from a Mint parfait to Double Chocolate Chip ice cream.
- The dance will end at 12:00 midnight and not 11:30 PM.
- The location has been changed from the downtown Hilton to the Eastside Sheraton.

6) CREATE A NEW PARAGRAPH

a. Place the cursor on the "A" which begins the sentence "All families are...".
b. Press Enter to create a new paragraph.
c. Press Enter again to create a blank line between paragraphs.
d. Press the Space bar 5 times to indent the new paragraph.
e. Add the following sentence to the end of the new paragraph:

```
Tickets are available from Mrs. Mitchell at the Red
Cross office during business hours.
```

7) ADD A HEADLINE TO THE STORY

a. Move the cursor to the very beginning of the document and add the following headline. Type 7 spaces before entering the word "DINNER":

```
       DINNER DANCE TO BE HELD AT EASTSIDE SHERATON
```

Note how the rest of the text moves to the right to make room for the headline.
b. Press Enter twice to terminate the headline and insert a blank line between it and the rest of the story.

8) SAVE THE FILE AGAIN TO RETAIN THE EDITING CHANGES

From the File menu, select the Save command [*press* Alt-F S] to save the edited NEWSTORY on disk. The old version is now erased and cannot be recovered.

Check - The completed story should be similar to:

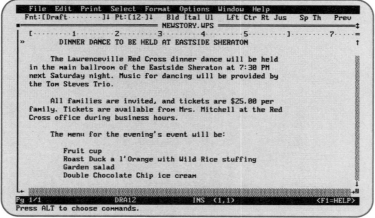

An Introduction to Computing Using Microsoft Works

9) **PROPERLY EXIT WORKS**

Select the Exit Works command from the File menu [*press* Alt-F X].

2.12 *Opening a Previously Saved File*

Before a previously saved file may be edited it must first be transferred from the disk to the computer's memory. This is accomplished by selecting **Open an Existing File** from the Quick Start dialog box. A list of previously saved files is then displayed. The list also includes additional information which will be of use later:

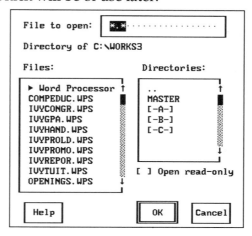

The Open Existing File dialog box lists previously created files

To select the file to be opened, the Tab key is pressed to move the cursor into the list of file names. The cursor is then placed on the desired file's name using the up- and down-arrow keys. This list is "scrollable" meaning that the list can contain more file names than can be shown on the screen at one time. Pressing the down-arrow key when the highlight is on the last file name shown in the list makes another visible. Once the file's name has been highlighted, pressing the Enter key transfers a copy of the file to the computer's memory and screen where it may then be edited. Note that you will see different files in this list depending on what has been saved on your disk.

2.13 *More About Dialog Boxes*

You already know that screens such as the one shown in the previous section are called dialog boxes. The purpose of a dialog box is to allow you to supply information that Works needs to execute a command. For example, the dialog box above is used to tell Works the name of the file to open. You used a different dialog box when saving a file. Many other Works commands have dialog boxes that are displayed when the command is executed. When a dialog box is displayed you may move the cursor from item to item with the Tab key. You may also hold down the Alt key and press the highlighted letter to select an option directly. If you display a dialog box by mistake, pressing the Escape key will remove it.

There are several different types of items which may be found in a dialog box, but most dialog boxes have certain similarities. For example, most will have several options listed at the bottom, including OK, Cancel, and Help:

```
┌────────┐  ┌────────┐  ┌────────┐
│  Help  │  │   OK   │  │ Cancel │
└────────┘  └────────┘  └────────┘
```

Because they resemble push buttons, these options are called *buttons*. The default button (OK in this example) is shown with a heavier border and may be executed by pressing Enter. Other buttons may be selected by highlighting them with the Tab key and pressing Enter, or by pressing Alt and the highlighted letter in the option name.

Another option is the list:

Files:

```
┌──────────────────────┐
│ ► Word Processor    ↑ │
│ COMPEDUC.WPS        ▓ │
│ IVYCONGR.WPS        ▓ │
│ IVYGPA.WPS          ▒ │
│ IVYHAND.WPS         ▒ │
│ IVYPROLD.WPS        ▒ │
│ IVYPROMO.WPS        ▒ │
│ IVYREPOR.WPS        ▒ │
│ IVYTUIT.WPS         ▒ │
│ OPENINGS.WPS        ↓ │
└──────────────────────┘
```

As discussed in the previous section, lists are scrollable. An item is selected from a list by highlighting it.

There are two other common elements, the radio button and the check box:

Position: **Styles:**

```
┌─────────────────────────┐    ┌──────────────────────┐
│ (•) Normal              │    │ [X] Bold             │
│ ( ) Superscript         │    │ [ ] Italic           │
│ ( ) Subscript           │    │ [ ] Underline        │
│                         │    │ [ ] Strikethrough    │
└─────────────────────────┘    └──────────────────────┘
```

Radio buttons (Normal is selected) and check boxes (Bold is selected)

Each of these is used to select an option from a group of related options. When radio buttons are used, only one option may be selected. With check boxes, any number of the listed options may be selected at the same time. These will become more apparent after you have a chance to work with more dialog boxes. Options in these boxes may be selected by pressing Alt and the highlighted letter, or by selecting the option with the Tab key.

● ●

Practice 5

In this Practice the NEWSTORY file will be transferred from the disk into the computer's memory, edited, and then re-saved in its new form. If you did not exit Works at the end of Practice 4 you should do so now by selecting the Exit Works command from the File menu.

1) BOOT DOS AND START WORKS

Boot DOS and start Works as described in Practice 1. The Quick Start dialog box is displayed.

2) EXECUTE THE OPEN COMMAND

From the Quick Start dialog box, select the **Open an Existing File** option [*press* O]. The Open Existing File dialog box is displayed.

3) MOVE THE CURSOR TO THE LIST OF FILE NAMES

a. Press Tab once. The cursor moves into the list of saved files.
b. Press Tab again. The cursor moves into the list of directories.
c. Press Tab several more times. Note how the cursor moves to each option in the dialog box.
d. Press Alt-L. The cursor jumps to the File to open box.
e. Press Alt-F. The cursor jumps to the list of file names.

4) SELECT THE FILE TO OPEN FROM THE FILES LIST

a. Press the down-arrow key. The first file name in the list is highlighted.
b. Press down-arrow 8 more times. The last file name shown in the list is highlighted.
c. Press down-arrow one more time. The list is scrolled, and a new file name made visible. Press down-arrow several more times, noting how the list scrolls.
d. Use the up- and down-arrow keys to move the cursor through the listing. Highlight NEWSTORY.WPS.
e. Press Enter to select OK. A copy of the highlighted file (NEWSTORY) is transferred from the disk into the computer's memory and displayed on the screen.

5) EDIT THE FILE

Insert and delete text where necessary to make the following changes:

*   The dinner dance will start at 7:00 PM.
*   The Schmenge Brothers Orchestra, not the Tom Steves Trio, will provide the evening's entertainment.
*   Guests will have their choice of Fruit cup or Lime sherbet for an appetizer.

6) SAVE THE MODIFIED FILE ON DISK

From the File menu, select the Save command. The modified NEWSTORY file is saved on disk, replacing the old version.

Check - When complete, the modified file should be similar to:

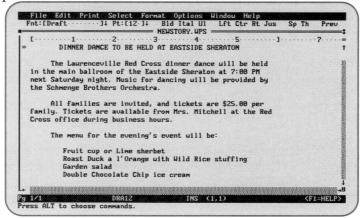

2.14 *Printing a Document*

Printing involves sending a copy of a document in the computer's memory to the printer. First, make sure that your computer is connected to a printer. Then check that the printer is turned on, is "on line," and that the paper is positioned at the top of a page. Before printing any document it should first be saved on disk so that, should an error occur and the document be erased from the computer's memory, it can be restored from the disk.

To print a document, select the Print command from the Print menu (Alt-P P). The Print dialog box is displayed where the number of copies to print and other options may be selected:

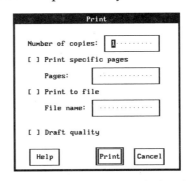

The Print command's dialog box

Because the default values are most normally used, simply press Enter to accept OK to begin printing. If more than one copy of the document is to be printed, type the number required and then press Enter. It is possible to interrupt the printing by pressing the Escape key.

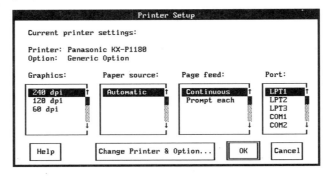

It is sometimes necessary to inform Works of the printer that you are using before printing a document. This is accomplished using the Printer Setup command from the Print menu (Alt-P S). Works uses a dialog box to display the current printer settings:

*The Printer Setup dialog box - a different printer
may be listed in yours*

The printer and model may be changed by selecting the **Change Printer & Option** button. You may have different printer options on this screen depending on the printers available. The Printer Setup procedure need only be done once and not again unless the printer is changed.

An Introduction to Computing Using Microsoft Works

Practice 6

The following Practice demonstrates how a word processor document may be printed and should only be attempted if you have a printer connected to your computer. Attempting to print without a printer attached could cause the loss of your file. Start Works if you have not already done so and open the NEWSTORY file created in the previous Practices. Step 1 should only be performed if your printer has not been selected. (Check with your instructor.)

1) SELECT WHICH PRINTER TO USE

a. From the Print menu, select the Printer Setup command [*press* Alt-P S]. A dialog box is displayed. Note the current printer settings.
b. Select the **Change Printer & Option** button [*press* Alt-C] to display the dialog box.
c. Use the arrows keys to highlight your printer.
d. If there are options for your printer, move the cursor into the options list [*press* Tab] and highlight the desired option.
e. Press Enter to select the highlighted printer and exit the dialog box.
f. Press Enter to remove the Printer Setup dialog box.

2) PRINT THE DOCUMENT ON THE PRINTER

a. From the Print menu, select the Print command [*press* Alt-P P]. The Print dialog box is displayed.
b. Press Enter to accept the default of printing 1 copy. During printing Works displays the percentage complete in the Status line. The cursor returns to the Word Processor screen when printing is complete (100%).

3) EXIT WORKS

From the File menu, select the Exit Works command (Alt-F X).

2.15 Screen Scroll

Most documents are too long to be displayed on a single screen. You saw this in the last Practice where editing changes caused the last paragraph of the NEWSTORY file to not be displayed. The Works Word Processor screen can display only a portion of a document, up to 18 lines at a time. The screen can be "scrolled" in order to bring unseen parts of the document into view. When this is done, lines of text are moved off the screen and new ones appear. The scrolled lines are not lost, just not displayed at this time.

The cursor control keys are used to move the screen window in a document. Up-arrow and down-arrow move the cursor one line at a time. The PgUp key moves the window up one screen (17 lines) and PgDn moves it down one screen. When working with long documents it can be time consuming to move the cursor in such small increments. Holding down the Ctrl key and pressing the key marked Home (Ctrl-Home) moves the cursor directly to the first character in a document. Pressing Ctrl-End moves the cursor directly to the last character in the document. Actions of the cursor control keys are summarized in the table below:

Key	Cursor Action
up-arrow	Moves up one line
PgUp	Moves up one screen, 17 lines
Ctrl-Home	Moves to the first character in document
down-arrow	Moves down one line
PgDn	Moves down one screen, 17 lines
Ctrl-End	Moves to the last character in document
left-arrow	Moves one character to the left
Ctrl-left-arrow	Moves to the beginning of previous word
Home	Moves to the beginning of line
right-arrow	Moves one character to the right
Ctrl-right-arrow	Moves to the beginning of next word
End	Moves to the end of line

Works keeps track of the position of the cursor as it is moved about the screen. The cursor position is displayed on the Status line in parentheses. For example, (1, 1) means that the cursor is in the first position (or column) on the first line on the page. (49, 8) indicates that the cursor is in the 49th position in line 8 of the current page. Normally, Works can store 60 to 65 characters on a single line, and 55 lines per page. (These options can easily be changed, as described in Chapter Three.)

•••

Practice 7

This Practice demonstrates screen scroll and cursor movement. Boot DOS and start Works if you have not already done so. A word processor file named SCROLL.WPS will be opened. Each line in SCROLL is numbered to help demonstrate screen movements.

1)   OPEN THE FILE NAMED SCROLL.WPS

a.   Select the **Open an Existing File** option from the Quick Start dialog box [*press* O]. The Open Existing File dialog box is displayed.
b.   Press Tab once to move the cursor into the list of file names.
c.   Use the up- and down-arrow keys to highlight SCROLL.WPS and press Enter.

2)   MOVE THE CURSOR TO THE BOTTOM OF THE SCREEN

Press down-arrow 17 times. As shown on the Status line, the cursor is now on line 18. Note the cursor position indicator on the Status line which reads (1, 18).

3)   SCROLL DOWN 1 LINE

Press down-arrow again. Notice that line 1 disappears off the top of the screen and line 19 appears from the bottom.

4)   SCROLL DOWN 5 LINES

a.   Press down-arrow 5 times. Note that each time down-arrow is pressed, another line scrolls off the top of the screen and the next line in the document appears from the bottom. Each time the cursor position is updated on the Status line.
b.   Press right-arrow 8 times. Notice that the cursor position indicator shows (9, 24), meaning that the cursor is in column 9 on line 24.

5) JUMP TO THE LAST LINE IN THE DOCUMENT

Hold down the Ctrl key and press the End key. The cursor moves immediately to the last line in the document, line number 80 in this file. Note the diamond marking the end of this document.

6) JUMP TO THE FIRST LINE IN THE DOCUMENT

Press Ctrl-Home. The cursor moves directly to the first line in the document. What does the cursor position indicator display?

7) MOVE DOWN ONE SCREEN

Press PgDn. The cursor immediately moves down 17 lines, and displays the last line of the previous screen, line 18, at the top of the current screen.

8) MOVE TO THE LAST LINE IN THE DOCUMENT

Press PgDn until the cursor is on the last line in the document, line 80. Press PgDn again. Works will not move the cursor past the diamond marking the end of the document.

9) LOCATE THE PAGE BREAK

a. Press PgUp once. The cursor jumps to line 52. Note the chevrons (») in the left margin next to line 55. These indicate the beginning of a new page.

b. Using the arrow keys, move the cursor above and below the chevrons several times. Note what happens on the Status line. Each time the cursor is on line 55 or higher, the page counter says Pg 2/2 and the line counter in the cursor position indicator resets (from 1,54 to 1,1).

10) JUMP TO THE END OF THE CURRENT LINE

Press End. The cursor jumps to the end of the line and the cursor position indicator changes.

11) JUMP TO THE BEGINNING OF THE CURRENT LINE

Press Home.

Check - The cursor should be at the beginning of the line. Your screen should be similar to:

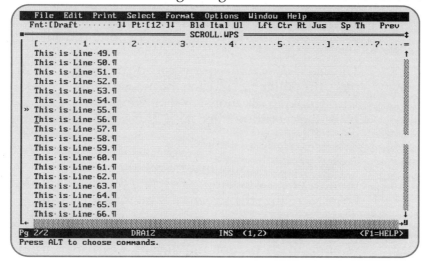

11) EXIT WORKS

From the File menu, select the Exit Works command [press Alt-F X].

2.16 Using the Mouse

Many computers come equipped with a special input device called a "mouse." If you are not using a mouse, skip this section.

The mouse may be used to perform a number of tasks

Before using the mouse, you need to learn four important words that are used to describe its actions.

Pointing:

The most basic use of the mouse is for pointing at different objects on the computer screen. When the mouse is in use, an arrow called the "mouse pointer" is displayed on the screen. (Note: on some screens the mouse pointer is displayed as a box.) Sliding the mouse along the top of the table causes the mouse pointer to move on the screen; slide the mouse to the left and the mouse pointer moves to the left on the screen, slide the mouse to the right and the pointer moves to the right.

By moving the mouse, it is possible to place the pointer on different objects on the screen. Placing the mouse pointer on an object is called "pointing." In this text, when we say to point to an object on the screen, we mean to place the pointer on it by moving the mouse.

Clicking:

When the mouse pointer is pointing to an object, it is possible to select that object by pressing the left button on the mouse and releasing it. This type of selection is called "clicking." When we say to select or click on an item, we mean to move the mouse pointer to it and then press and release the left mouse button. (Most mice have two buttons. To perform any of the tasks described in this chapter, only the left button is used.)

Double-clicking:

A special form of clicking is the "double-click." As the name implies, double-clicking requires that the mouse pointer be placed on an object and the left button pressed twice in rapid succession. Double-clicking is used to open files and select certain options from dialog boxes.

Dragging:

The last mouse technique is called "dragging." To drag an object, first place the pointer on it. Then the mouse button is pressed and held down while moving the mouse. When we say to drag an object, we mean to place the mouse pointer on it, press and hold the mouse button, and move the mouse.

Rather than using keystrokes, the mouse can be used to perform a number of tasks including selecting commands from menus and dialog boxes, scrolling the screen, and moving the cursor.

Moving the Cursor:

The cursor can be quickly placed at any location within the Work area by pointing to the location and clicking. Text can then be inserted or deleted at that point.

2

Selecting From a Menu or Dialog Box:

Moving the mouse pointer to a menu name on the Menu bar and clicking the mouse button displays the commands on that menu. For example, placing the pointer on `File` in the Menu bar and clicking displays the File menu. Commands on the displayed menu can then be selected by clicking on the desired command.

Options may be selected from dialog boxes by pointing to the option and clicking. When all the desired options have been selected, clicking on the OK or Done button removes the dialog box.

Screen Scroll:

The scroll bars below and on the right of the Word Processor screen are used to scroll through a document:

Use the scroll bars and arrows to scroll the screen with the mouse

Clicking on the down scroll-arrow moves the window down one line at a time, while clicking on the up scroll-arrow moves the window up one line. Works can move the window in larger increments by dragging the scroll box within the scroll bar. For example, dragging the box to the middle of the scroll bar causes Works to display the middle of the document. Dragging the box to the end of the scroll bar displays the end of the document. The scroll arrows can then be used to make fine adjustments to display the desired portion of the document.

Lists in dialog boxes may also be scrolled this way. For example, the **Files** list in the Open Existing File dialog box (section 2.12 above) has a vertical scroll bar that can be used to view different parts of the list.

● ●

Practice 8 - Using the Mouse

This Practice should only be performed if you are using a mouse with your computer. In this Practice the techniques used to point, click, double-click, drag, and move the cursor will be covered. Boot DOS and start Works if you have not already. The Quick Start dialog box should be displayed.

1) *OPEN THE SCROLL FILE*

   a. Place the mouse pointer on the **Open an Existing File** option in the Quick Start dialog box.
   b. Click (press and release quickly) the left mouse button. The Open Existing File dialog box is displayed.
   c. Move the pointer to the down scroll-arrow on the right of the **Files** list and click once. Note that the file names scroll within the box.
   d. Use the list's scroll bar to scroll through the file names until SCROLL.WPS is visible.
   e. Move the pointer to SCROLL.WPS and double-click on the file name (press the mouse button twice in rapid succession). The file is transferred to the computer's memory and displayed on the word processor screen.

2) *SCROLL THROUGH THE FILE USING THE SCROLL ARROWS*

   a. Point to the down scroll-arrow at the lower-right corner of the screen.
   b. Click once on the scroll-arrow. The screen window moves down one line.
   c. Continue to click on the down scroll-arrow and note how the screen scrolls.
   d. Point to the up scroll-arrow at the upper-right corner of the screen.
   e. Click on the scroll-arrow until the window displays the first line of the file.

3) SCROLL THROUGH THE FILE USING THE SCROLL BOX

a. Point to the scroll box under the up-arrow.
b. Hold down the mouse button and drag the box halfway down the screen
c. Release the mouse. The window moves to approximately the middle of the word processor file. You should be between lines 45 and 60.
d. Drag the box back to the top of the screen. The window returns to the top of the file.

4) MOVE THE CURSOR

a. Point to the first letter of the word "This" in any line.
b. Click the mouse. The cursor moves to the word. It is now possible to edit the text at this point.
c. Type your name and a space. The text is inserted at the cursor position.
d. Click on several places in the Work area and note where Works places the cursor. The cursor position indicator on the Status line is updated after each click.

5) EXIT WORKS

a. Point to the Menu bar and click on `File`. The File menu is displayed.
b. Click on the `Exit Works` command and release the button. A warning dialog box is displayed.
c. Click on **No** so that the changes are not saved. Works is exited and the DOS prompt shown.

You may now use the mouse to perform tasks in future Practices. When directed to select an option, you may use the keyboard or click on the option with the mouse.

●●

Chapter Summary

Documents ranging from research papers to business letters can be produced quickly and efficiently using a word processor. Word processing allows documents to be changed easily; text can be inserted, deleted, or modified without retyping the entire document. Formatting commands allow the appearance of text on the page to be changed. By saving the document in a file on disk, it can later be recalled, edited and printed.

The computer needs DOS (Disk Operating System) to run. This is first booted from disk into the computer's memory. After DOS has loaded, typing WORKS runs the Works program and the Quick Start dialog box is displayed. From here new files can be created and previously saved files opened.

At the top of the Works' screen is the Menu bar. Each word on the Menu bar is the name of a list of commands. Pressing the `Alt` key highlights a letter in each menu name. Typing a highlighted letter displays that menu. Each command on a menu also has a highlighted letter. Pressing the corresponding letter executes the command. Many commands display a dialog box where information is entered before executing a command. Below the Menu bar is the Tool bar which provides shortcuts to frequently used commands.

Often a dialog box contains a list. To select options from that list the Tab key or `Alt` key and a letter are used to move the cursor into the list.

The up and down-arrow keys are then used to highlight the desired option. Pressing the Enter key executes the selected command using that option. An option can be selected directly from a dialog box by holding down the Alt key and pressing the highlighted letter. A button is selected in the same manner.

This Chapter discussed the commands and procedures necessary for the production of a word processed document. The major steps in producing such a document are:

1) Boot DOS and load the Works program from the disk into the computer's memory.
2) Place the file to be word processed on the screen - either by creating a new file or opening a previously saved file from the disk.
3) Enter or edit the document.
4) Save the document on disk.
5) Print the document if necessary.
6) Properly exit Works.

A new file is created by selecting the **Create a New File** option or a previously saved file is opened by selecting the **Open an Existing File** option from the Quick Start dialog box. Saving a document is accomplished by selecting the Save command from the File menu. Selecting the Print command from the Print menu prints a document. Works is exited using the Exit Works command from the File menu.

The Works screen is like a window which displays 18 lines of a document at a time. The window may be moved through the document using the cursor control keys in a process called screen scroll. The arrow keys move the cursor one character in the direction of the arrow. Ctrl-Home moves the cursor directly to the first character in a document, and Ctrl-End to the last. Home moves the cursor to the first character in the current line, and End to the last.

Works determines if there is sufficient room for a word at the end of a line and if there is not, the word is automatically moved to the beginning of the next line in a process called "word wrap."

Works can use a mouse as a special input device. An object is selected on the screen by pointing to the object and then pressing (clicking) the mouse button. Moving the mouse pointer to a Menu name and clicking displays the commands. Clicking on a specific command selects it. Some objects are selected by double-clicking — pressing the button twice in rapid succession. The cursor can be moved within a document by pointing to the desired location and clicking. To "drag" an object, the pointer is placed on it and then the mouse button pressed and held down while moving the mouse. The scroll bars below and on the right of the Word Processor screen are used by the mouse to scroll through a document.

Alt key -Key on the lower-left side of the keyboard. Used to highlight letters in a menu and select dialog box options.

Arrow keys -Four keys that move the cursor up, down, right, and left on the screen without changing any text. The arrow keys are also used to select options from dialog boxes.

Boot -To turn on the computer and load the operating system (DOS).

Buttons -Options, listed in dialog boxes, which look like buttons.

Character -Any letter, number, or symbol which can be displayed on the computer screen.

Clicking -(mouse) Selecting an object that has been pointed to by pressing the button on the mouse.

Cursor - Blinking line on the screen which indicates where characters entered from the keyboard will be placed.

Cursor control keys - Keys used to move the cursor without having any effect on the text. PgUp, PgDn, Home, End and the arrow keys are cursor control keys.

Default - Command or option that is selected automatically by pressing Enter if no other command is chosen.

Delete key - Key that erases the character directly above the cursor.

Delete text - The removal of a character or group of characters from a document.

Dialog box - Screen used to enter information and select options required by a command.

Document - Any material that can be typed in the word processor, such as a letter, research paper, or story.

DOS - Disk Operating System programs that the computer needs to run.

Double-Clicking - (mouse) Selecting an object that has been pointed to by pressing the mouse button twice in rapid succession.

Dragging (mouse) - Placing the pointer on an object, then pressing the mouse button while moving the object to a new location.

Enter key - Key used to indicate the end of an entry, such as an option or response to a prompt, or to choose from a menu. In word processing Enter is used at the end of each paragraph.

Esc key - Key used to terminate (escape from) a command or exit a menu.

Exit Works command - File menu command used to exit Works.

File - Information created by Works which is stored on a disk. A word processor file stores a document.

File name - A name for a file stored on disk, up to eight characters in length. Works automatically adds the extension .WPS to each word processor file name.

Format - The arrangement of text on a page.

Insert text - Adding words or characters to a document.

Insertion point - See cursor.

Menu - A list of commands that are available at a particular point in a program.

Menu bar - Line at the very top of the screen showing names of available menus.

Message line - Last line on the screen, used by Works to display messages and prompts.

Mouse - A device used to position the pointer on the screen.

Pointing - (mouse) Placing the mouse pointer on an object on the screen.

Print command - Print menu command which prints the file currently on the screen.

Prompt - A message displayed on the screen by Works asking for information or actions.

2

Quick start dialog box - list of options displayed when Works is started.

Save command - File menu command used to save a document on disk.

Screen scroll - Moving through a document, the screen acts as a window showing only part (18 lines) of the document.

Scroll arrow - Arrows at ends of scroll bars used to scroll screen. (See scroll bar.)

Scroll bar - Bars on right and bottom of screen used to scroll through document.

Scroll box - Box in scroll bar that indicates current position of window in file. Box can be dragged to scroll screen.

Status line - Line at bottom of the screen used by Works to display information such as the page number and cursor position.

Text - Any character or group of characters in a document.

Tool bar - Provides shortcuts to frequently used commands.

Window - Portion of the screen used to display a document or part of a document.

Word processor - A computer application program that allows text to be entered, manipulated, and stored.

Word wrap - When the computer decides whether to keep a word on the current line, or move it to the next based on the amount of space left on the line.

Work area - Center of the word processor screen where text is typed and edited.

● ●

Reviews

Sections 2.1-2.5

1. What are three useful features that a word processor possesses?

2. How can using a word processor improve the quality of your writing?

3. Name three different businesses that could benefit from using word processors. Explain how each would benefit.

4. a) Why is it important to take good care of a disk?
    b) What should be avoided when handling or storing a disk?

5. What purpose does the Enter key serve?

6. How can the cursor be moved down 3 lines and then 10 spaces to the right?

7. What is a "repeat key"?

8. Describe the operations necessary to change the word "men" to "people" in the sentence:

    ```
    Now is the time for all good men to come to the aid of
    the party.
    ```

9. What does pressing the Enter key do when typing text in the Word Processor?

10. What is the difference between pressing the Delete key four times or the left-arrow key four times when the cursor is located in the middle of a line of text?

11. What is a dialog box?

12. When is the Quick Start dialog box displayed?

13. What is meant by a default command?

14. What is the Menu bar?

15. What is the Tool bar?

16. a) What information is displayed on the Status line?
    b) What type of messages are displayed on the Message line?

17. What is a menu and what is it used for?

18. a) How many commands does the File menu offer?
    b) What two methods may be used to select one of its commands?

19. a) How are menus selected from the Menu bar?
    b) How may you return directly from a menu to the work area without executing a command?

20. What does the diamond(◆) shown on the Word Processor screen represent?

21. What is a file?

22. Give three reasons why it is useful to save a word processor file on disk.

23. If you are working on a word processor document when the power is turned off, how can you retrieve the document if it has not been previously saved on disk?

24. a) Which of the following are legal file names?

    ```
    RICH?      LETTER2JOHN
    SINGLE     RX7 FILE
    2SHOES     JANE0194
    MYPOEMS    SUMMER
    ```

    b) What purpose do file names serve?
    c) What should be considered when selecting the file name of a word processor document?

25. When a file is saved where does it go? Is it removed from the computer's memory?

26. a) Why is it important to exit Works properly?
    b) List the steps required to exit Works starting from the Word Processor screen so that the file currently being worked on is saved.

27. What is "word wrap"?

28. What must be done to end a paragraph and start a new one?

29. a) If a previously saved file is edited will the changes be automatically made to the file on disk, or must the file be saved again?
    b) What happens to an original file if an edited version of the same file is saved?

30. What steps are used to open a previously saved file starting from the Quick Start dialog box?

31. How is a button selected in a dialog box?

32. a) Why is it important to save a document before printing it?
    b) What command is used to print a document?

33. What is "screen scroll"?

34. How is the cursor moved directly to the:
    a) end of a document?
    b) beginning of a document?

35. How can you tell exactly where in a document the cursor is located?

Section 2.16 — Mouse

36. What is "pointing" and how is it done?

37. What is "clicking" and what is it used for?

38. What steps are required to scroll to the middle of a file using the scroll box?

39. How can the cursor be moved quickly to a new location without using the arrow keys?

40. What is "dragging" and how is it performed?

Exercises

• •

1. a) Enter the following letter in a new word processor file:

```
                                      September 26, 1994




     Mrs. Margaret Livingston
     123 Main St.
     Reedsburg, WI 53959

     Dear Margaret,

         I am writing to let you know how much I am enjoying
     my new word processor. It has so many advantages over my
     old typewriter.

         One thing that I will never miss is white-out. For
     years we used it to make corrections, and it left a
     thick patch on the page.

         Now corrections are handled on the computer screen
     so that no one knows about my mistakes. Once I ended up
     retyping an eight page letter to correct the misspelling
     of the bank director's name. With my word processor it
     would have taken about 1 minute to retrieve the letter
     from a disk and make the changes on the screen. The
     revised letter could then have been printing while I got
     a cup of coffee.

         Thanks again for all your help.


                                      Sincerely,


                                      A. Secretary
```

b) Save the letter using the name MARGE.

c) Print a copy of MARGE on the printer. Check the printed copy for errors and make any necessary corrections.

d) Edit the letter as follows:

Delete the word "old" in the last line of paragraph one.
Delete the sentence "One thing that I will never miss is white-out."
Change "For years we used it" to "For years we used white-out".
Change "no one knows about my mistakes" to "my mistakes are invisible".
Replace "A. Secretary" with your name.
Add the following lines to the beginning of the third paragraph:

```
My boss likes to make several revisions of each letter
and memo that leaves the office. That means that each
has to be retyped, often several times.
```

e) Save and then print the modified letter.

2. Word processors can be used to create documents about a variety of different topics. It is interesting to think about how historical figures might have used a word processor.

a) Enter each of the following sayings into the word processor leaving a blank line between each. Name the file BENJAMIN in honor of Benjamin Franklin who wrote many famous sayings in Poor Richard's Almanac:

An apple a day keeps the doctor away.

A penny for your thoughts.

Every cloud has a silver lining.

A penny saved is a penny earned.

Early to bed, early to rise, makes a man healthy, wealthy and wise.

b) Save BENJAMIN on disk.

c) Print a copy of BENJAMIN on the printer. Check the printed copy for errors and make any necessary corrections.

d) Edit the saying on each line as follows:

Line 1: change *apple* to *orange*
Line 2: change *penny* to *dollar*
Line 3: change *silver* to *gold*
Line 4: change *penny* to *quarter* (twice)
Line 5: change *man* to *person*

e) Save the modified BENJAMIN file and print a copy.

3. You are thinking of applying to several different colleges around the country and need a letter of application.

a) Use the word processor to create a file named APPLY which contains a letter requesting information and an application from a college. You may use the following letter as a guide, substituting your own information:

```
September 28, 1994

Ivy University
Admissions Department
1 College Court
Newton, IA 63343

Dear Sirs:

I am interested in attending Ivy University. I will
graduate in 1995 and plan to major in medical
communications. I have been president of the Student
Congress for 4 years and captain of the Debate Team
for 2 years. I have varsity letters in three sports and
was a member of the All-state gymnastics and swim teams.
My current grade point average is 3.95.

Please send a course catalog and application to me at
this address:

     A. Student
     223 Main Street
     Anytown, USA 11111

Thank you very much.

Sincerely,


A. Student
```

b) Save the APPLY letter on disk.

c) Print the APPLY letter. Check the printed copy for errors and make any necessary corrections.

d) The good news is that the new grades are out and you finally got that 4.0. Change your GPA in APPLY.

e) The bad news is that you lost the recent Student Congress election. Change the file to read "3 and a half years".

f) Change the name and address of Ivy University to a school you would like to attend and print the new letter. Be sure to change the school's name in the first sentence as well.

g) Save the updated APPLY letter on disk and print a copy.

2

4. Your cousin is visiting you from out of town. Using the word processor, create, save, and print lists of directions in a file named DIRECT that your cousin can follow to go from your house to the following places:

   a) Your school. Be sure to describe what time school gets out and where your cousin should meet you.

   b) The local fast food restaurant.

   c) The closest grocery store to your house. Include a list of items that your cousin should pick up for dinner.

   d) Your video rental club. Be sure to include your membership number in the directions so that your cousin can rent some videos.

   e) Your cousin is not the brightest person in the world. Leave complete instructions describing how to use your VCR to play a video.

   f) Save DIRECT and print a copy.

5. Your school newspaper has an opening for an arts critic. Use the word processor to create a review of the last movie, concert, play, art show, or similar event that you attended in a new file named CRITIC. Save and print a copy of CRITIC.

6. A word processor can be used as a diary. Create a new file named DIARY and make a journal entry describing what you did last week. Be sure to include your plans for the upcoming weekend. Save and print a copy of your diary page.

7. Your English teacher has asked you to write an original essay entitled "How I spent my summer vacation." Use the word processor to produce a small (2 or 3 paragraph) version of this essay. Save the essay in a file named ESSAY and then print a copy of it.

8. Use the word processor to produce an advertisement for an upcoming dance or other special event. Be sure to include the date, time, and location of the event, and cost (if any). Save the file under the name ADVERT and print a copy.

9. You are enrolled in an independent study in Shakespeare and your instructor wants a schedule listing topics and due dates for your research papers. Create a file named SHAKESPR using the following memorandum as a guide, substituting your own information (use the same layout, or arrangement):

```
Memorandum

To: Kevin Dumont, English Department
From: Daniel Booksmith, student
Date: January 3, 1994
Subject: Shakespeare topics and due dates

The following schedule outlines the research paper
topics and due dates for my independent study in
Shakespeare:

Paper Topic Due Date
Hamlet  1/14
Henry V  2/4
Macbeth  2/25
Julius Caesar  3/11
Romeo and Juliet  4/1

One week before each due date I will submit an outline
containing a specific topic and a list of sources for
each paper.
```

Check you memo for errors and make any corrections, then print a copy.

10. Your science teacher has asked you to write a one page biography summarizing the life of the scientist you most admire. Include in the essay at least two references to outside sources. (Chapter four will show you how to insert footnotes into a document.) Use the word processor to write the biography and save the file on your data disk under the name SCIENCE. When complete, print a copy, review it for errors, and make any corrections.

11. a) Businesses use word processors for everything from letters and memos to advertising material. Enter the following letter, substituting your name for that of the president, and your initials for "JP":

```
                                 1 Paradise Garden
                                 Newtown, FL  33445
                                 June 10, 1994


Mr. Philip Crando, President
Italian Tours, Ltd.
14 Dunkin Drive
Key West, FL  33040

Dear Mr. Crando:

Thank you for the info you gave me during our telephone
conversation this morning, June 10, 1994. As I
```

```
explained, the head of our accounting department, Mr.
Gordon Sharp, will leave Fast Track Publishing at the
end of November, and the company would like to give him
a trip to Italy as a retirement present.

We know that Mr. Sharp would like to spend the Holiday
season traveling, and I understand you have three tours
planned for that time of the year. I look forward to
receiving the price information and brochures you said
were available.

Sincerely,


Janet Printmore
President


JP/jj
```

Check the file for errors and make any necessary corrections. Save the file as CRANDO when complete.

b) A co-worker has read the draft of your letter and proposed the following corrections:

Change the word "info" to "advice and suggestions" in the first paragraph.
Add the sentence "Your company was recommended to us as a leader in tour packages of Italy." at the end of the first paragraph.
Add the words "and his wife" after Mr. Sharp in the second paragraph.
Add a new paragraph before the closing which states "Please contact me at 555-9825 if you have any questions. Thank you."

c) Save the modified CRANDO file and print a copy.

12. You have opened a specialty store. Types of stores could include a jewelry store, clothing store, a sporting goods store, etc.

a) Use the Word Processor to create a flyer that will be sent to prospective customers announcing your grand opening. Be sure to include the name, address, and phone number of your store, as well as a list of some of the special items you will be selling. Also include the date and time of the grand opening. Save the file as OPENFLYR. Review the document and make any necessary corrections.

b) Your promotions manager has suggested a grand opening sale. At the top of the flyer add the headline, "20% OFF AT THE GRAND OPENING, FANTASTIC ITEMS AT FANTAS-TIC PRICES!" Save the updated file and print a copy.

13. Gibbons are lesser apes distantly related to man. Dr. Laura Williamson and Dr. Peter Helvetica are scientists studying the white handed gibbons on Bashibashi island. They have created a proposal for funding for their gibbon research using the word processor. Open the file named RESEARCH and make the following changes:

a) In the first paragraph in the second sentence that begins "This guide will be used...," delete the phrase "of lesser and greater apes."

b) In the same sentence insert the word "primate" before the word "studies."

c) In the last sentence of the same paragraph change the words "partial funds" to "total funding."

d) In the second sentence of the second paragraph, which begins "By studying...," insert the word "particular" between the words "unique to this" and "group."

e) In the same paragraph, before the last sentence, which begins "With this study...," insert the following sentence: `From a primate data base, behavioral statistics are easily obtained and readily comparable.`

f) Save the edited file.

g) Use the following steps to print only page 1: Select the Print command from the Print menu. Move the cursor to the **Print specific pages** option and press the Space bar. An 'X' appears next to the option. Move the cursor to the **Pages** options and type a 1. Select **Print** to print only the first page.

Chapter Three

Manipulating Text with the Word Processor

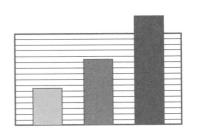

3

Objectives

After completing this chapter you will be able to:

1. Use Print Preview to see how a document will look when printed.

2. Change margins.

3. Create headers and footers for printed documents.

4. Insert and delete manual page breaks to control pagination.

5. Switch to Show All Characters mode to control the placement of text on the page.

6. Select blocks of text and apply formatting options to them.

7. Change the alignment and spacing of paragraphs.

8. Emphasize areas of text using underlining, bold, and italic characters.

9. Create superscripts and subscripts.

10. Use different fonts and sizes.

11. Set tab stops and create tables in documents using tabs.

3

hapter Two introduced the options necessary to create, edit, save, and print Word Processor documents. In this chapter formatting techniques that improve the appearance and readability of such documents are covered. Included are features that:

- control the arrangement of text on the page, such as margins, headers and footers, and pagination (how text is divided into pages).

- affect paragraphs, such as alignment (left, right, justified, and centered), spacing, and tabs.

- change the way text appears, such as bold, underline, italic, and using different fonts and sizes.

The formatting options discussed in this chapter are powerful tools, capable of manipulating text in numerous ways. After familiarizing yourself with these tools, you will understand why word processing has achieved such popularity.

3.1 Formatting Documents

Books, newspapers, and other printed materials use a variety of techniques to arrange text on a page. While you may not recognize the terms that are used to describe such techniques, you are familiar with them from publications you have seen.

Arrangements of text are called "formats." A document's format includes the size of its margins, how text lines up within those margins, the spacing between lines and paragraphs, and how the document is divided into pages. Format also includes the arrangement of text into tables composed of columns, and methods of emphasizing text such as underlined or boldface (darker) letters. This chapter describes the different ways that Works can format documents.

3.2 Previewing Documents

A powerful feature Works possesses is the ability to view a document before it is printed. This is done by selecting the Preview command from the Print menu (**Alt-P V**), and enables the user to see the overall layout of a document without actually printing it. This quick step saves time, and more importantly, paper.

Preview displays a shrunken version of the page on the screen, allowing the entire page to be viewed instead of only 18 lines:

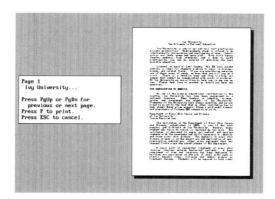

Works displays a smaller version of the page in Print Preview

While in Preview mode, the relationship between elements on the entire page can be compared. Preview enables you to decide, for example, what looks better; one inch margins or one and a half inch, left alignment or justified, a graph at the top of the page or at the bottom, and so on. Preview enables the user to determine how the elements on a page relate and work with one another, giving the opportunity to change these elements until they are positioned satisfactorily.

Selecting the Preview command displays the Preview dialog box. Normally, you will just select **Preview** to preview the document. Works then displays a smaller version of the page that the cursor is currently on, along with a message box. The message box displays the current page number and the first few words of the first paragraph. Pressing PgUp and PgDn scrolls from page to page in the document, and the message box indicates the page number. Works beeps if you have reached the last page in either direction. If the current layout is acceptable, pressing P will print the document. If changes are needed, press Escape to return to the word processor screen. There are no Preview mouse commands — you must use the keyboard to scroll and exit.

Practice 1

To demonstrate the different formatting options, the Practice sessions in this chapter use Ivy University's promotional file named IVYPROMO.WPS which is stored on your data disk. In this Practice you will open IVYPROMO and use Print Preview to scroll through the document. When directed to select an option or execute a command, you may use either the keyboard or the mouse.

1) BOOT DOS AND START WORKS

Boot DOS and start Works as described in Chapter Two. The Quick Start dialog box is displayed.

2) SELECT THE OPEN OPTION

From the Quick Start dialog box, select the **Open an Existing File** option [*press* O]. The Open Existing File dialog box is displayed.

3) MOVE THE CURSOR TO THE LIST OF FILE NAMES

Press Tab once. The cursor moves into the list of saved files.

4) SELECT THE FILE TO OPEN FROM THE FILES LIST

    a.   Use the up- and down-arrow keys to move the cursor through the listing. Mouse users should click on the scroll arrows to the immediate right of the list. Highlight IVYPROMO.WPS.

    b.   Select OK [*press* Enter]. A copy of IVYPROMO is transferred from the disk into the computer's memory and displayed on the screen.

5) PREVIEW THE FILE

    a.   From the Print menu, select the Preview command (Alt-P V). The Preview dialog box appears.

    b.   Press Enter to accept the default options and display the Preview screen. In a few seconds, the screen clears and Works displays a preview of the first page of IVYPROMO.

    c.   Press the PgDn key. The next page is displayed in Preview mode. Note the page number in the message box to the left of the previewed page.

    d.   Press PgDn again. The next page is displayed.

    e.   Press PgDn. Works beeps because this is the last page in the document.

    f.   Press PgUp to again preview page 2.

    g.   Press Escape. The preview screen is removed the document displayed. The cursor is now on the first line in page 2, the last page previewed.

3.3 Setting Margins

One way to affect the appearance of a document is by setting "margins." Margins are the blank spaces between the edges of the paper and the text. Works' default settings are 1.3 inches for the left margin, 1.2 inches for the right, and 1 inch for both the top and bottom margins on an 8.5 inch by 11 inch page:

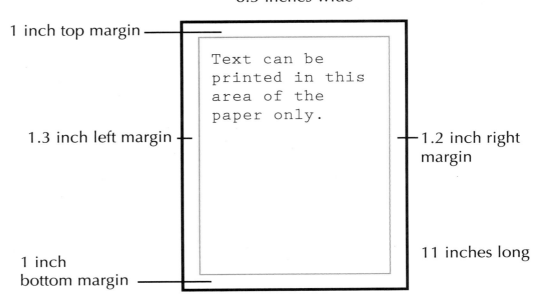

Text may only be placed between the margins in a document

Margins can be widened or narrowed as desired. Changes to the margin settings have an inverse effect on the number of characters that will fit on a line. Widening a margin decreases the amount of text that a line can contain, while narrowing a margin increases the line's capacity.

The length of a line of text that will fit across a page is determined by subtracting the size of the left and right margins from the width of the page. Using the default margins of 1.3" and 1.2" on an 8.5" page yields a line 6" long: 8.5" - 1.3" - 1.2" = 6". (Works uses the double quote as an abbreviation for inches: 8.5" means 8.5 inches).

Options for setting margins are displayed by executing the Page Setup & Margins command from the Print menu (Alt-P M). When the command is executed, a dialog box containing options which affect the document's margins is displayed. Current settings are also shown:

```
 Print
┌──────────────────────────┐
│ Print...                 │
│ Page Setup & Margins...  │
│ Preview...               │
│ Print Form Letters...    │
│ Print Labels...          │
│                          │
│ Insert Page Break        │
│ Headers & Footers...     │
│                          │
│ Printer Setup...         │
└──────────────────────────┘
```

```
┌──────────────────── Page Setup & Margins ────────────────────┐
│                                                               │
│  Top margin:     [1".......]   Bottom margin:  [1".......]    │
│                                                               │
│  Left margin:    [1.3".....]   Right margin:   [1.2".....]    │
│                                                               │
│  Page length:    [11".....]    Page width:     [8.5".....]    │
│                                                               │
│  1st page number: [1....]      [ ] Print footnotes at         │
│                                    end of document            │
│                                                               │
│  Header margin:  [0.5".....]   Footer margin:  [0.5".....]    │
│                                                               │
│  [ Help ]                       [ OK ]  [Cancel]              │
└───────────────────────────────────────────────────────────────┘
```

The Page Setup & Margins dialog box controls the margins

Top, bottom, left, and right margins each have their own entry box. For example, to change the bottom margin of a document to 0.75", the value .75 would be entered on the **Bottom margin** line and OK selected. Works will then change the document to the new margin settings. When the size of a left or right margin is changed, the screen display is adjusted to reflect the new settings. Margin settings can easily be changed to experiment with different formats. When the file is saved, it retains the current margin settings.

Using the mouse, click on the option to be changed within the dialog box and type the new value. When all changes have been made click on OK to remove the dialog box and apply the new options.

Practice 2

In this Practice margins will be set and changed for IVYPROMO. Pay attention to how each change affects the number of lines in the paragraphs and the length of those lines in reference to the ruler at the top of the screen. Start Works and open the IVYPROMO file if you have not already done so.

3

1) CHANGE THE DOCUMENT'S LEFT AND RIGHT MARGINS

a. From the Print menu, select the Page Setup & Margins command [*press* `Alt-P M`].
b. Move the cursor to the **Left Margin** option [*press* `Alt-E`].
c. Type `1.5` to set the left margin to 1.5 inches.
d. Move the cursor to the **Right Margin** option [*press* `Alt-R`].
e. Type `1.5` to set the right margin to 1.5 inches.
f. Press Enter to select OK and apply the new margins. The document now has left and right margins set at 1.5 inches and the text is reformatted on the screen. Because the margins have been increased, the number of characters on a line has been decreased.

2) PREVIEW THE DOCUMENT

From the Print menu, select the Preview command. Note how the amount of space on the right and left sides of the page is increased. Page down through several pages. The margins are the same size on each page. Press Escape to return to the word processor screen.

3) CHANGE THE DOCUMENT'S TOP AND BOTTOM MARGINS

a. From the Print menu, select the Page Setup & Margins command again.
b. Type `2.3` to set the Top margin to 2.3 inches.
c. Press Tab to move the cursor to the **Bottom margin** option and type `2.6` to set the bottom margin to 2.6 inches.
d. Press Enter to remove the dialog box and apply the new margins. Note that you will not see the results of the larger top and bottom margins on the screen — Works always displays 18 lines of text regardless of the size of those margins. However, because of the larger margins, less text can fit on a page so more pages are required. The Status line reads 1/5, indicating that the document is now 5 pages long.

4) PREVIEW THE DOCUMENT

a. From the Print menu, select the Preview command. Note how the size of the top and bottom margins has increased.

Check - Margins have been changed as shown on the preview screen:

New Top Margin

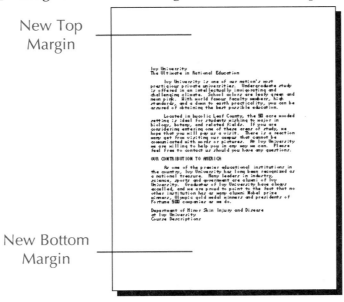

New Bottom Margin

b. Page down to the end of the document. Because less text can fit on each page there are now 5 pages in the document.

5) RESET THE MARGINS TO THE DEFAULT VALUES

    a. From the Print menu, select the Page Setup & Margins command and change the margins back to their default values:

        Top: 1   Bottom: 1
        Left: 1.3   Right: 1.2

    b. From the File menu, select the Save command to save the modified file.

3.4 Headers, Footers, and Page Numbers

Works can place one line of text at the top and bottom of each page when a document is printed. This line is often used to indicate the current page number. Text which is automatically printed at the top of each page is called a "header." Similarly, text which is printed at the bottom of each page is called a "footer." Headers and footers are created by selecting the Headers & Footers command from the Print menu (Alt-P H):

The Headers and Footers dialog box

To create a header or footer for a document, the cursor is placed at the desired option in the dialog box and the text for the header or footer typed. To remove a header or footer, the cursor is moved to the desired option and Delete pressed. When printed, the text will be centered above or below the document in the margin on each page.

It is possible to include special codes in the header or footer that will be translated when the document is printed. For example, it is possible to type the footer: Page - &P. The *&P* is a code which tells Works to print the current page number. When a document is printed with this footer, Page - 1 is printed at the bottom of page 1, Page - 2 at the bottom of page 2, and so on. It is also possible to change the alignment of the header or footer text from the default of centered. Other codes which may be included in the header or footer are shown below:

Code	Action
&D	Print current date (in the form *1/5/94*)
&F	Print file name
&N	Print current date (in the form *January 5, 1994*)
&T	Print current time
&C	Center following text (default)
&L	Left-justify following text
&R	Right-justify following text

3

Different codes may be mixed in the same header or footer. For example, the footer

```
&L My Paper   &C Page &P   &R Beth Brown
```

would print the following footer at the bottom of page 5:

```
My Paper                    Page 5                    Beth Brown
```

• •

Practice 3

In this Practice you will create a header and footer for the IVYPROMO document. Start Works and open the IVYPROMO file if you have not already done so.

1)   ENTER TEXT FOR THE HEADER AND FOOTER

    a. From the Print menu, select the Headers & Footers command [*press* `Alt-P H`]. The Headers & Footers dialog box is shown.

    b. Type `Ivy U. Promotional Information` on the **Header** line. This text will automatically be centered, the default.

    c. Move the cursor to the **Footer** option [*press* `Alt-F`].

    d. Type &L to have Works left justify any following text.

    e. Type &D to have Works print the current date. Type a space.

    f. Type &R to right justify any following text.

    g. Type `Page &P` to print the current page number. Your dialog box should be similar to:

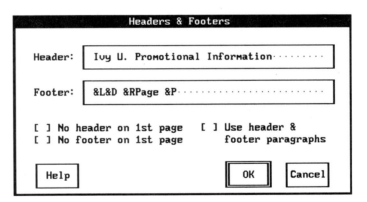

This footer will print the current date at the left side of the page, and the page number at the right. Press Enter to accept the options and remove the dialog box.

2)   PREVIEW THE DOCUMENT

From the Print menu, select the Preview command. Note the header and footer. Page down through the document. Note the header and footer positions and that the page number in the footer changes. When done, press Escape to return to the word processor screen.

Check - Each page in the document should contain the header and a footer with the current date and proper page number. Note the alignment of the text in the footer:

3) SAVE THE MODIFIED FILE

From the File menu, select the Save command to save the modified file on disk. The header and footer will be retained in the document.

3.5 Pagination

Pagination is the division of a document into page-sized sections for printing. Using the specifications for page length and margins, Works calculates the number of lines that fit on each printed page. Do not confuse screen "pages" which contain 18 lines of text with printed pages which usually contain 50 to 60 lines.

A "page break" is the location in a document where one printed page ends and another begins. Works automatically indicates page breaks at the very left side of the screen. At the position of each page break, Works places a chevron marker (»). In addition, the current page number and total number of pages in the document is shown on the Status line. For example, Pg 2/4 means that the second page in a four page document is currently displayed. You may have noticed that the page break markers and the page counter occasionally disappear when editing changes are made. This is because the change may affect the pagination of the document. Works automatically recalculates the page breaks and page counter after such changes, then displays the updated markers.

Some types of material call for starting a new page before completing the previous one: the beginning of a new chapter, a change in subject matter, or the presentation of a table or chart are three examples. You can cause the computer to advance to the next page regardless of the number of lines left on the current page by creating a "manual page break." To do this, place the cursor where the new page is to start, hold down the key marked Ctrl and press Enter (Ctrl-Enter). A dotted line is then shown across the screen and Works recalculates the pages. Manual page breaks can be removed by placing the cursor on the dotted line and pressing Delete.

3

Practice 4

This Practice demonstrates automatic and manual page breaks. Start Works and open the IVYPROMO document if you have not already done so.

1) LOCATE THE PAGE BREAK MARKERS

a. Jump to the first character in the document [*press* Ctrl-Home].
b. Scroll down the document until the page break marker (») at the end of the first page is visible.
c. Move the cursor above and below the page break marker. Note how the Status line is updated to show what page the cursor is on.
d. Scroll down the document until the page break marker at the end of the second page is visible.

2) INSERT A MANUAL PAGE BREAK

a. Move the cursor down until it reaches the first blank line directly below the second page break marker.
b. Press Ctrl-Enter. A dotted line appears across the screen to indicate the position of the manual page break.
c. Wait for Works to recalculate the page breaks. The Status line is then updated to show that the cursor is now on page 4.

Check - Both the regular and manual page breaks are visible on the current screen:

Regular page break ———

Manual page break ———

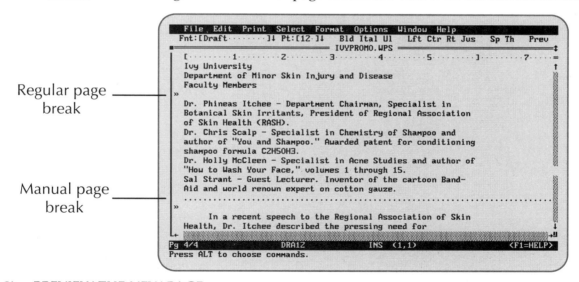

3) PREVIEW THE NEW PAGE

a. From the Print menu, select the Preview command. Move the cursor onto page 3, then page 2. Note the difference in length between page 2 and 3 — the page break causes less information to be printed on page 3.
b. Press Escape to return to the word processor screen.

4) DELETE THE MANUAL PAGE BREAK

a. Place the cursor on the manual page break dotted line marker at the end of page 3 and press Delete. The marker disappears, indicating that the manual page break has been deleted. Works recalculates the page breaks and updates the Status line.
b. From the File menu, select the Save command to save the file on disk.

3.6 The Show All Characters Command

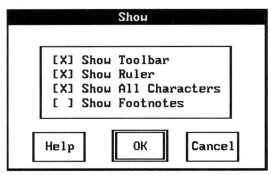

Formatting is the process of creating or changing the way a word processed document appears. As will be described below, formatting involves the placement of text in a document, including the spacing between words and lines. Often this spacing is not obvious when shown on the computer's screen. For example, an editing change might leave two spaces between a word instead of one. This would not be readily apparent on the screen. For this reason, Works includes a special option which shows normally invisible characters, such as spaces, on the screen with symbols.

To have Works display normally invisible characters, the Show command is selected from the Options menu (Alt-O H). This produces the Show dialog box:

```
┌─────────────────────────────────────────┐
│                  Show                     │
├─────────────────────────────────────────┤
│                                           │
│      ┌─────────────────────────────┐      │
│      │ [X] Show Toolbar            │      │
│      │ [X] Show Ruler              │      │
│      │ [X] Show All Characters     │      │
│      │ [ ] Show Footnotes          │      │
│      └─────────────────────────────┘      │
│                                           │
│   ┌──────┐   ┌──────┐   ┌────────┐        │
│   │ Help │   │  OK  │   │ Cancel │        │
│   └──────┘   └──────┘   └────────┘        │
└─────────────────────────────────────────┘
```

The Show dialog box — all options marked with an X are "on"

When **Show All Characters** is selected, an X is placed next to the option in the dialog box and special symbols are shown on the screen. These symbols are listed below:

Symbol	Meaning
• (raised dot)	Space character
¶	Enter character
→	Tab character (described later)

These symbols are shown on the screen as an aid in formatting and do not appear when the document is printed. To remove the symbols, execute the Show command again and turn off Show All Characters. The characters remain in the file, only the symbols are no longer displayed on the screen. It is a good practice to always use Show All Characters mode, especially when formatting and editing text.

3.7 Undo

At times you will execute a command and find that you have made a mistake. For example, you may create a format only to find that you selected the wrong options. Works supplies a way to "undo" the effects of the last command executed. Selecting the Undo command from the Edit menu (Alt-E U) reverses the effects of the previous command. Undo only works for the command just executed, and it is not possible to undo the effect of the second or third previous command.

3.8 Selecting and Deleting Blocks of Text

It is often necessary when editing to remove large amounts of text from a document. In the last chapter the Delete key was used to remove text one character at a time. This is cumbersome when the amount of text to be deleted is more than a word or two. To speed deleting, the text to be removed may first be selected. Selected text is shown on the screen "highlighted." The highlight can contain any amount of text, from a character or word to several pages.

→   Ivy·University·is·one·of·our·nation's·most·prestigious· private·universities.·Undergraduate·study·is·offered·in·an· intellectually·invigorating·and·challenging·climate.·School· colors·are·leafy·green·and·neon·pink.·With·world·famous· faculty·members,·high·standards,·and·a·down·to·earth· practicality,·you·can·be·assured·of·obtaining·the·best· possible·education.¶

A sentence is highlighted in this example

When the Delete key is pressed, all of the highlighted text is removed. This makes it easy to remove a large amount of text by moving the cursor to the beginning of the text to be deleted, highlighting it, and then pressing Delete.

Highlighting is controlled by the F8 key. Pressing F8 displays EXT (extend) on the Status line. Moving the cursor with the arrow keys then highlights text, forming a "block." When the text to be deleted has been highlighted, pressing Delete removes it from the screen. Be careful when using this technique to include only the text to be deleted in the highlight — using Show All Characters mode will help. If you delete a block by mistake, immediately executing the Undo command will replace it. Should you highlight a block and then decide not to delete it, press Escape to cancel the Extend, and then any arrow key to remove the highlight.

Using the mouse, text can be selected by moving the pointer to the beginning of the text and then dragging the mouse. A highlighted block will be created which "follows" the mouse pointer. When all of the desired text has been highlighted, the mouse button is released and the highlight remains.

3.9 Faster Block Selection

The F8 key can be used to quickly select certain blocks of text. Pressing F8 once turns selection on, displaying EXT on the Status line. Pressing F8 again highlights the entire word that the cursor is on. Pressing F8 a third time highlights the sentence that the word is in. F8 a fourth time highlights the paragraph that contains the sentence, and F8 a fifth time highlights the entire document.

First F8	Turns highlighting on
Second F8	Highlights current word
Third F8	Highlights current sentence
Fourth F8	Highlights current paragraph
Fifth F8	Highlights entire document

The size of the selection can be reduced by pressing Shift-F8. For example, if F8 had been pressed four times, an entire paragraph would be highlighted. Pressing Shift-F8 at this time reduces the highlight to the originally highlighted single sentence.

There are several mouse shortcuts for highlighting text, some of which make use of the right mouse button. Holding down the Shift key and clicking the left button produces a highlight from the current cursor position to the position of mouse pointer. Placing the pointer over a word and clicking the right button highlights the entire word, including the space after it (if there is one). There is a small vertical margin between the left edge of the screen and the beginning of the text. Clicking the left button in this margin highlights the line to the right of the mouse pointer. Clicking the right mouse button in this margin highlights the entire paragraph to the right of the pointer. The entire document may be highlighted by clicking both buttons at the same time when the pointer is in the margin. A special Practice for mouse highlighting follows Practice 5, below.

Mouse Selection Shortcuts

Action	*Highlights. . .*
Shift-click	from cursor to mouse pointer
Right button	entire word
Left button in margin	line to right of pointer
Right button in margin	paragraph to right of pointer
Both buttons in margin	entire document

Practice 5

This Practice demonstrates the selection and deletion of blocks. The Show All Characters command will be used to display special characters. Start Works if you have not already done so, and open the IVYPROMO document. You will select and delete different blocks of text. Undo will be used to restore a deleted block. Mouse users should perform this Practice and the special Mouse Practice that follows.

1)   SWITCH TO SHOW ALL CHARACTERS

  a.   From the Options menu, select the Show command [*press* Alt-O H]. The Show dialog box is displayed.
  b.   Locate the **Show All Characters** option in the dialog box. If this option is already selected, there will be an X displayed in the box next to it. If it is selected press Escape now and proceed to step 2.
  c.   Select the **Show All Characters** option [*press* Alt-L] and press Enter to remove the dialog box. Note the spaces, tabs, and paragraph markers shown in the file.

3

2) SELECT TEXT USING THE ARROW KEYS

   a. Move the cursor to the top of the document (`Ctrl-Home`).
   b. Press the `F8` key. EXT is displayed on the Status line.
   c. Press the right-arrow key. The highlight is extended to include one character.
   d. Press right-arrow five more times. The highlight is extended.
   e. Press the left-arrow. The highlight is reduced.
   f. Press the down-arrow. The highlight is extended into the next line.
   g. Press down-arrow several more times. Each time, a new line is added to the highlight.
   h. Press up-arrow several times, reducing the size of the highlight.

3) REMOVE THE HIGHLIGHT

   a. Press Escape. EXT is no longer shown on the Status line, but the highlight remains.
   b. Press any arrow key. The highlight is removed.

4) SELECT BLOCKS OF TEXT USING F8

   a. Place the cursor in the second sentence in the first paragraph, the sentence which begins "School colors. . .".
   b. Press `F8`. EXT is shown on the Status line.
   c. Press `F8` again. The current word is highlighted. Note that Works includes the space after the word in the highlight.
   d. Press `F8` a third time. The current sentence is highlighted, including the spaces after the period.
   e. Press `F8` a fourth time. The current paragraph is highlighted.
   f. Press `F8` a fifth time. The entire document is highlighted.

5) REDUCE THE HIGHLIGHT

   a. Press `Shift-F8`. The highlight is reduced from the entire document to the current paragraph.
   b. Press `Shift-F8` to reduce the highlight again. Only the "School colors" sentence is highlighted.

6) DELETE THE HIGHLIGHTED BLOCK

Press Delete. All of the highlighted text, the entire sentence, is deleted and the highlight removed.

7) DELETE AND RESTORE THE NEXT PARAGRAPH

   a. Place the cursor in the next paragraph, which begins "Located in. . .".
   b. Press `F8` four times to highlight the paragraph.
   c. Press Delete to remove the entire paragraph.
   d. From the Edit menu, select the Undo command [*press* `Alt-E  U`]. The paragraph is restored.

8) SAVE THE MODIFIED FILE

From the File menu, select the Save command. The file, without the deleted sentence, is saved on disk.

Mouse Practice

This Practice demonstrates the selection of blocks using the mouse. IVYPROMO should be open and in Show All Characters mode.

1) SELECT TEXT BY DRAGGING

   a. Place the pointer in the paragraph at the top of the document which begins "Ivy University is one. . .".
   b. Hold down the left button and drag the mouse several words to the right. A highlight is created, and each character the pointer passes over is included in the block.
   c. Release the button. The highlight remains.

2) REMOVE THE HIGHLIGHT

   Click on any text. The highlight is removed.

3) SELECT A BLOCK OF TEXT

   Place the mouse several lines below the current cursor. Hold down the Shift key and click. A block is created from the cursor to the mouse pointer

4) REDUCE THE HIGHLIGHT

   Place the mouse anywhere <u>within</u> the highlighted block. Hold down the Shift key and click. The highlight is reduced to the current mouse position.

5) SELECT BLOCKS OF TEXT

   a. Click anywhere in the text to remove the highlight.
   b. Place the pointer over a word and click the right mouse button. The entire word is highlighted, including the space after it.
   c. Place the pointer in the left margin between the edge of the screen and the beginning of the text. Click the left button. The entire line to the right of the pointer is highlighted. Click in several different places in the margin, noting how the text is highlighted.
   d. Place the pointer in the left margin next to a paragraph. Click the right mouse button. The entire paragraph is highlighted. Click the right button in several places in the margin and note how the highlight is placed.

6) HIGHLIGHT THE ENTIRE DOCUMENT

   a. Place the pointer in the left margin. Click both the left and right buttons at the same time. The entire document is highlighted. (If your entire document is not highlighted, try again being careful to press the buttons together.)
   b. Click anywhere in the document to remove the highlight.

You may use any of these techniques when directed to select blocks of text in future Practices.

3.10 Single and Double Spacing

Works can control the amount of space between lines in a paragraph. Single spacing places text on each line of the printed page while double spacing inserts a blank line between lines of text. Double spacing can make a document more readable and leaves room for notes to be written between lines, which is especially helpful when editing a document. Examples of both formats are shown below:

3

Single Space: This paragraph is single spaced. There is little room between the lines for notes or comments, but more information can be placed on each page. Most printed text, including this book, is single spaced.

Double Space: This paragraph is double spaced. Note how room

is left between each line for notes or comments.

Double spacing is used mostly for academic papers

and drafts that will be edited.

```
Format
 Plain Text
 Bold
 Underline
 Italic
 Font & Style...

 Normal Paragraph
 Left
 Center
 Right
 Justified
 Single Space
 Double Space
 Indents & Spacing...

 Tabs...
 Borders...
```

Single and double spacing are set from the Format menu, and are applied to a specific paragraph. That is, one paragraph in a document can be single spaced and the next double spaced. Single spacing is the default. To set double spacing, place the cursor in the paragraph to be double spaced and select the Double Space command from the Format menu (Alt-T D). The current paragraph is shown on the screen double spaced, leaving the paragraphs above and below unchanged. To switch back to single spacing, move the cursor to the desired paragraph and select Single Space from the Format menu (Alt-T S). Works also allows other spacing options, but these formats are rarely used. Any spacing options set are retained when the file is saved on disk.

3.11 *Paragraph Alignment*

```
Format
 Plain Text
 Bold
 Underline
 Italic
 Font & Style...

 Normal Paragraph
 Left
 Center
 Right
 Justified
 Single Space
 Double Space
 Indents & Spacing...

 Tabs...
 Borders...
```

Works provides four ways to align text in a paragraph relative to the margins: left (or unjustified), centered, right, and justified. These formats are selected by choosing the desired alignment from the Format menu.

Left alignment, the default, means that each line begins at the left hand margin. The resulting right margin is jagged. This is the format produced by a typewriter and is most often used in letters or research papers.

Center is the alignment most often used for headings and titles. It involves positioning a line so that it is equidistant from the left and right margins. Works automatically calculates the proper position of the line and then centers it.

Right alignment is the opposite of left alignment; each line extends to the right margin while the left margin is jagged.

Justified alignment creates straight paragraph borders at both margins. To justify a paragraph, the computer automatically places extra spaces between words to fill up each line. As a result the rightmost word in each line is pushed over to the right margin. Justified formats are common in newspapers and books; this textbook for example. Each of the alignments is shown next:

Left: This text is left aligned, the
          default alignment. Notice how the
          length of each line is different. The
          effect of a left aligned paragraph is
          that the right margin appears jagged.
          This format is often called "ragged
          right" for this reason.

Centered: This text is centered. Notice that each
          of the lines is placed halfway between
             the margins. Centered text is most
                 often used for titles.

Right: This text is right aligned. Each
           of the lines reaches the right margin.
          The effect of a right aligned paragraph
                is that the left margin is jagged.

Justified: This text is justified. Each of the
          lines   is   extended   to   reach   the   right
          margin. The effect of justifying a paragraph
          is that the borders on each margin appear
          straight. Note that Works increases the
          space   between   some   words   to   extend   the
          lines to the right margin.

Selecting an alignment option affects only the paragraph that the cursor is in. When an alignment is selected, the paragraph is reformatted on the screen, showing the new alignment.

• •

Practice 6

This Practice demonstrates the use of single and double spacing, and different paragraph alignment options. Start Works if you have not already done so, and open the IVYPROMO Word Processor document. You will modify the file by double spacing a paragraph, centering the two title lines, and justifying the first paragraph. Undo will be used to remove an alignment. Switch to Show All Characters if you have not already.

1) **DOUBLE SPACE THE SECOND PARAGRAPH**

 a. Move the cursor into the next paragraph, which begins "Located in. . .".
 b. From the Format menu, select the Double Space command [*press* Alt-T D]. Works double spaces the current paragraph as shown on the screen.

2) **CENTER THE FIRST TWO LINES IN THE DOCUMENT**

 a. Place the cursor at the beginning of the first line in the document, the title which reads "Ivy University".
 b. From the Format menu, select the Center command [*press* Alt-T C]. The line is centered as shown on the screen.
 c. Move the cursor onto the next line and select the Center command from the Format menu to center the second title line.

3

3) JUSTIFY THE FIRST PARAGRAPH

a. Place the cursor anywhere in the next paragraph, which begins "Ivy University is one of...".

b. From the Format menu, select the Justified command [*press* `Alt-T J`]. The paragraph is reformatted on the screen.

4) RIGHT ALIGN THE SECOND PARAGRAPH

a. Place the cursor in the next paragraph, which begins "Located in...".

b. From the Format menu, select the Right command [*press* `Alt-T R`]. The paragraph is right aligned on the screen. Note that this paragraph now has two formats — double spaced and right aligned.

5) UNDO THE LAST COMMAND

From the Edit menu, select the Undo command. The effect of the previous command (right align) is undone, and the paragraph is returned to its original state.

6) SAVE AND PREVIEW THE MODIFIED FILE

a. From the File menu, select the Save command. When IVYPROMO is next loaded, the titles will be centered, the first paragraph justified, and the second paragraph double spaced.

b. From the Print menu, select the Preview command and press Enter to preview page 1. Note how the paragraphs are aligned and spaced on the Preview.

Check - The titles should be centered, the first paragraph justified, and the second paragraph double spaced as shown on the preview screen:

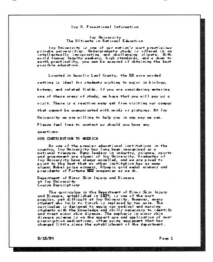

c. Press Escape to return to the word processor screen.

3.12 Formatting a Block

Often a group of paragraphs will need to have the same format. When this is the case it is not necessary to execute the formatting commands for each paragraph. Instead, the paragraphs may be highlighted as a block, and the formatting commands then selected. When executed, the format will be applied to all of the paragraphs in the block.

This is the case for most Works commands. If a block is highlighted when a command is executed, the command will affect all of the text in that block. An example is the Delete performed in a prior Practice. When the Delete key was pressed, all of the text in the highlighted block was removed. To justify an entire document you would first enter and then edit your text. Then highlight the entire document and apply the justified format by selecting the Justified command from the Format menu. The entire document is now justified.

3

3.13 *Formatting Shortcuts*

The previous section introduced formatting commands that affect paragraphs. Like all Works commands, these formats were selected by displaying a menu and choosing the desired command from the menu. For some common commands, Works has keyboard shortcuts which may be executed without displaying a menu.

Works can apply paragraph formats using keyboard shortcuts. For all of these shortcuts, the key marked `Ctrl` (Control) must be held down and a second key pressed. If a block has been highlighted, the format will be applied to every paragraph in the highlight.

Line Spacing	
`Ctrl-1`	Single spaced
`Ctrl-2`	Double spaced
Alignment	
`Ctrl-J`	Justified
`Ctrl-L`	Left
`Ctrl-R`	Right
`Ctrl-C`	Centered

For example, to justify a paragraph, place the cursor in the paragraph, hold down the `Ctrl` key, and press the J (`Ctrl-J`).

• •

Practice 7

This Practice demonstrates block formatting and keyboard formatting shortcuts. Start Works and open the IVYPROMO document if you have not already done so. Switch to Show All Characters mode if it is not already selected.

1)   *RIGHT ALIGN A PARAGRAPH USING A KEYBOARD SHORTCUT*

a.   Place the cursor anywhere in the paragraph which begins "Ivy University is one of. . .".
b.   Hold down the `Ctrl` key and press R (`Ctrl-R`), the keyboard shortcut for right alignment. The paragraph is reformatted on the screen the same as if the Right command has been used.

2)   *JUSTIFY THE BODY OF THE DOCUMENT AS A BLOCK*

a.   Place the cursor in the paragraph which begins "Ivy University is one of. . .".
b.   Start highlighting [*press* `F8`].
c.   Press `Ctrl-End` to move the cursor to the end of the document, creating a highlighted

An Introduction to Computing Using Microsoft Works

block that contains everything but the centered titles.

d. Use the keyboard shortcut to justify the block [*press* `Ctrl-J`]. The document is reformatted.

e. Press `Home` to remove the highlight and return the cursor to the top of the highlight. Note the justified paragraphs.

3) SAVE AND PREVIEW THE MODIFIED FILE

a. From the File menu, select the Save command. When IVYPROMO is next loaded, all of the body paragraphs will be justified.

b. From the Print menu, select the Preview command. Scroll through the document, noting the justified paragraphs.

c. Cancel the preview and return to the word processor screen.

3.14 Character Formats - Bold, Italic, and Underline

```
 Format 
┌──────────────────────┐
│ Plain Text           │
│ Bold                 │
│ Underline            │
│ Italic               │
│ Font & Style...      │
│                      │
│ Normal Paragraph     │
│ Left                 │
│ Center               │
│ Right                │
│ Justified            │
│ Single Space         │
│ Double Space         │
│ Indents & Spacing... │
│                      │
│ Tabs...              │
│ Borders...           │
└──────────────────────┘
```

Works' Format menu has a number of commands which affect the way that individual characters appear when printed. The most common character formats are Bold, Italic, and Underline and are used to emphasize different parts of text in a document.

The following steps are required to create emphasized text:

1. The cursor is moved to the first character of the text to be emphasized and `F8` pressed to start highlighting. (The mouse may also be used.)

2. The cursor is moved to the end of the text to be emphasized, highlighting a block.

3. The desired formatting command is executed. All highlighted characters are affected and will be emphasized when printed. The emphasized text is shown on the screen (possibly in a different color or brightness).

Because selecting the proper characters to be emphasized is important, character formatting should always be done in Show All Characters mode. Also, multiple formats may be applied to the same text. For example, a title might be bold and underlined at the same time. Examples of these character formats are shown below:

Bold: **Bold text** is printed darker than plain text so that words and phrases printed in bold stand out on the page. It is most frequently used for titles and headings.

Italic: *Italic text* is printed on a slant. Italics are most frequently used when referring to titles of publications.

Underline: <u>Underlined text</u> is used to emphasize words or phrases.

Remember, the text to be formatted must be highlighted before the format is applied.

Works has `Ctrl` key shortcuts for character formats as well:

`Ctrl-B`	Bold
`Ctrl-I`	Italic
`Ctrl-U`	Underline

To remove the emphasis, highlight the text to be changed and execute the Plain Text command from the Format menu, or use the shortcut `Ctrl-Space Bar`.

Bold, italic, and underlined text may not be differentiated from each other on your screen. However, the type of emphasis may be determined by moving the cursor to the emphasized text and checking the Status line at the bottom of the screen. A code indicating the type of emphasis is displayed: B for bold, I for Italic, and U for underlined text.

• •

Practice 8

This Practice demonstrates the use of bold, italic, and underlined text. Start Works and open the IVYPROMO file if you have not already done so. Switch to Show All Characters mode if it is not already selected.

1) HIGHLIGHT THE BLOCK TO BE BOLD

a. Move the cursor to the "I" in the first "Ivy University" title at the top of the document.
b. Begin highlighting and highlight to the end of the line.
c. From the Format menu, select the Bold command [*press* `Alt-T B`]. The highlighted text changes on the screen. Depending on your screen, the text may be shown as bold or in a different or brighter color. Note the B in the Status line indicating that this text is bold.

2) ITALICIZE THE NEXT LINE USING THE SHORTCUT

a. Move the cursor to the next line.
b. Highlight the entire line [*press* `F8` *three times*].
c. Press `Ctrl-I` to apply the Italic format using the keyboard shortcut. Note the I in the Status line indicating that this line will print in italics.

3) UNDERLINE THE FIRST LINE IN THE NEXT PARAGRAPH

a. Move the cursor to the "I" in "Ivy University is one of. . .".
b. Highlight the sentence [*press* `F8` *three times*].
c. From the Format menu, select the Underline command [*press* `Alt-T U`]. The text is shown underlined on the screen.

4) REMOVE UNDERLINING FROM PART OF THE SENTENCE

a. Move the cursor to the "i" in the "is" after "Ivy University".
b. Start highlighting.
c. Highlight to the end of the sentence, including the period.
d. Make this text plain by selecting the Plain Text command from the Format menu [*press* `Alt-T P`]. The highlighted text changes color and no formatting code is shown in the Status line. Only "Ivy University" is now underlined.

5) SAVE THE DOCUMENT

From the File menu, select the Save command to save the modified file on disk. The next time IVYPROMO is loaded, the bold, italic, and underlined text will be present.

An Introduction to Computing Using Microsoft Works

Check - The title should be in bold, the next line in italics, and the "Ivy University" in the first sentence underlined:

Ivy·University¶
The·Ultimate·in·Rational·Education¶
¶
→   Ivy·University·is·one·of·our·nation's·most·prestigious·
private·universities.·Undergraduate·study·is·offered·in·an·
intellectually·invigorating·and·challenging·climate.··With·
world·famous·faculty·members,·high·standards,·and·a·down·to·
earth·practicality,·you·can·be·assured·of·obtaining·the·best·
possible·education.¶

3.15 When to Apply Formats

Once a block has been formatted it stays that way until you change it. Any new text inserted inside the block will also have the same format. That is, a character inserted between two bold characters is automatically made bold. This leads to a very common error. Suppose you were creating a new document and wanted to have a bold, centered headline. After typing the headline, you highlight the paragraph and use the proper formatting commands to make it bold and centered. When you press Enter and begin to type the next paragraph, it is also bold and centered. In fact, all of the paragraphs that you create from this point on will be bold and centered! This is probably not what you wanted.

The problem described above can be fixed by highlighting everything but the original title and changing the format to Plain Text and Normal Paragraph, both from the Format menu. However, this problem is best avoided by following this simple rule: Type all of the material for your document first and then go back and apply the desired formatting. This will help avoid formatting errors such as this.

3.16 The Tool Bar

Directly below the Menu bar on the screen is the Tool bar:

Fnt:[Draft········]↓ Pt:[12·]↓   Bld Ital Ul   Lft Ctr Rt Jus   Sp Th   Prev

The Tool Bar allows mouse users to execute various commands

The Tool bar provides shortcuts to many commands for mouse users. One of the best uses for the Tool bar is for applying formatting commands. Three text formats and four paragraph formats may be selected by clicking on a word in the Tool bar.

Bld, Ital, Ul
Makes the currently highlighted text bold (Bld), italic (Ital), or underlined (Ul).

Lft, Ctr, Rt, Jus
Makes the current paragraph or highlighted block of paragraphs left aligned (Lft), centered (Ctr), right aligned (Rt), or justified (Jus).

The Tool bar also acts as a format indicator. For example, when the cursor is in a justified paragraph, the word **Jus** is displayed in bold letters in the Tool bar. Using the Tool bar can be quicker because no menu needs to be displayed. Other Tool bar commands will be described later.

3

●●
Mouse Practice

This Practice demonstrates the use of the Tool bar for mouse users. IVYPROMO should be open and in Show All Characters mode.

1) *CHANGE PARAGRAPH ALIGNMENTS USING THE TOOL BAR*

a. Place the cursor in the paragraph which begins "Ivy University is one of. . .". This paragraph is currently justified as indicated by the bold **Jus** in the Tool bar.
b. Click on **Ctr** in the Tool bar. The paragraph is centered. Note that Ctr is now bold in the Tool bar.
c. Click on **Lft**. The paragraph is left aligned.
d. Click on **Rt**. The paragraph is right aligned.
e. Click on **Jus**. The paragraph is again justified.

2) *CHANGE TEXT FORMATS USING THE TOOL BAR*

a. Place the cursor in the very first line, the centered title which reads "Ivy University." This text was made bold in the previous Practice, so **Bld** is bold in the Tool bar.
b. Click the right mouse button, highlighting the word "Ivy."
c. Click on **Ital** in the Tool bar. The highlighted text is made italic. Note that **Bld** and **Ital** are now bold in the Tool bar.
d. Click on **Ital** again. The italics are removed, and the text is only bold.
e. Click on **Bld**. The bold format is removed and the text is now plain.
f. Click on **Bld** again. The bold format is restored.
g. Save the file.

3.17 *Superscripts and Subscripts*

```
┌─ Format ─┐
│ Plain Text      │
│ Bold            │
│ Underline       │
│ Italic          │
│ Font & Style... │
│                 │
│ Normal Paragraph│
│ Left            │
│ Center          │
│ Right           │
│ Justified       │
│ Single Space    │
│ Double Space    │
│ Indents & Spacing...│
│                 │
│ Tabs...         │
│ Borders...      │
└─────────────────┘
```

Many times a word processed document should contain a "superscript" or "subscript." A superscript is a section of text which is raised slightly above the current line while a subscript is printed slightly below the current line. Superscripts and subscripts are most often used to indicate footnotes or other reference material in research papers or in mathematical and scientific formulas. For example:

Dr. Sulfuric[4] proved that the formula for water is H_2O.

The "4" after Dr. Sulfuric is a superscript representing a footnote reference, and the "2" in H_2O is a subscript. It is possible to emphasize more than one character in a superscript or subscript. The following line has the word "super" as a superscript and the word "sub" as a subscript:

This is a ^{super}script and this is a $_{sub}$script.

Both superscripts and subscripts are created by selecting the Font & Style command from the Format menu:

An Introduction to Computing Using Microsoft Works

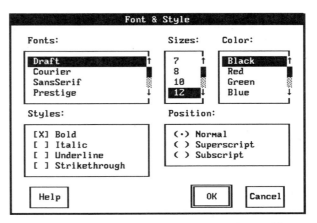

The Font & Style dialog box. Options selected here affect the highlighted text

First, the block to be formatted is highlighted and the Font & Style command executed from the Format menu (Alt-T F). The desired format option(s) is then selected from the dialog box.

Like other text formats a superscript or subscript may be indicated on the screen using different colored characters. When the cursor is placed on the emphasized text, a code is shown in the Status line: = for Subscript, + for Superscript.

Practice 9

In this Practice you will create superscripts and subscripts. Start Works and open the IVYPROMO file if you have not already done so. Switch to Show All Characters mode if it is not already selected.

1)   LOCATE THE FACULTY LIST

Scroll through IVYPROMO until the Faculty Members list is displayed. You will create the superscript and subscripts for the formula in Dr. Scalp's description — $C_2H_5OH^3$.

2)   CREATE THE FORMULA SUBSCRIPTS

a.   Place the cursor on the "2" and press F8. Press the right-arrow key once, highlighting only the "2".
b.   From the Format menu, select the Font & Style command [*press* Alt-T F]. The dialog box is shown. Note the currently selected options for font, size, etc.
c.   Press Alt-C to select **Subscript** from the Position box. The dot moves from Normal to Subscript, indicating that it is selected.
d.   Press Enter to apply the format. The dialog box is removed and Works formats the "2" on the screen.
e.   Repeat this process for the "5".

3)   CREATE THE FORMULA SUPERSCRIPTS

a.   Highlight only the "3" at the end of the formula.
b.   From the Format menu, select the Font & Style command.
c.   Select the **Superscript** option from the dialog box and press Enter. Works formats the "3".

4)   SAVE THE MODIFIED FILE

There are several other options available from the Font & Style dialog box. Two of the most important are the font and the size:

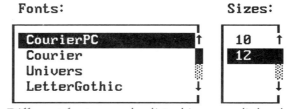

Different fonts may be listed in your dialog box

A font is a description of how characters are shaped. Many printers have the capability to print characters in a variety of different fonts. Some examples are show below:

This font is *Times-Roman*, a serif font often used in newspapers.
This is called *Helvetica*, a popular sans serif font used for headlines and titles.
This is *Courier* which resembles typewritten characters.
This font is Zapf Chancery and is modeled after calligraphy.

Available fonts differ widely from printer to printer, as do font names. One printer may have fonts named SansSerif and Serif, while another may have similar fonts named Dutch and Swiss. Other printers simply have one font, which may or may not be named.

In addition to the font, characters can also be printed in different sizes. Characters sizes are measured in "points" which are $1/72^{nd}$ of an inch. Some examples are shown below:

This is 8 point text.
This is 10 point text.
This is 14 point text.
This is 22 point text.

Again, the character sizes available vary widely from printer to printer. The larger the size, the smaller the number of characters which fit on a line, and the number of lines on a page. Works displays the current font and size on the Status line. For example, TMS12 on the Status line indicates that the current font is Times Roman and the size is 12 points. Unfortunately, different fonts and sizes are not shown on the Works screen, even in Preview mode. Therefore, the indicator on the Status line is important for determining the size and font of different sections of text.

The fonts and sizes available on your printer will most likely be different, and will change the font and size options available in the dialog box. To select a font, move the cursor into the Font list and highlight the desired font name. After the font name is selected, a Size may be selected from the list.

3

Remember, the fonts and sizes vary widely from printer to printer. You should make certain that you have selected the proper printer using the Printer Setup command (as described in Chapter Two) before changing any fonts or sizes.

Font and size may also be selected from the Tool bar using the mouse. To select a font, click on the down-arrow next to the font (`Fnt`) name in the Tool bar. A scrollable list of available fonts is then shown. After the font has been selected, clicking on the down-arrow next to the size (`Pt` for points) allows a size to be selected.

• •

Practice 10

In this Practice you will change fonts and sizes. Start Works and open the IVYPROMO file if you have not already done so. Switch to Show All Characters mode if it is not already selected.

1) CHANGE THE TITLE FONT AND SIZE

   a. Move the cursor to the first line in the document, the "Ivy University" title. The Status line indicates the current font and size for this text.
   b. Highlight the entire first line of the title.
   c. From the Format menu, select the Font & Style command. Note the current options selected for Font and Size.
   d. From the Fonts list, choose a different font. Try to pick a font with a name similar to "Helvetica," "SansSerif," or "NLQ."
   e. From the Sizes list, choose the largest available size for this font (up to 32 points).
   f. Press Enter. The font and size are changed for the highlighted text, even though it is not shown on the screen. The Status line shows the new font name and size.

2) CHANGE THE SUBTITLE FONT AND SIZE

   a. Highlight the entire next line, which begins "The Ultimate. . ."
   b. From the Format menu, select the Font & Style command.
   c. From the Font list, choose any font you wish.
   d. From the Size list, choose any size you wish.
   e. Press Enter. The font and size are changed for the highlighted text, and the Status line shows the new font name and size.
   f. Mouse users: Select a font and size from the Tool bar.

3) SAVE AND PREVIEW THE MODIFIED FILE

   a. From the File menu, select the Save command. The next time the document is opened, the titles will be in the new fonts and sizes.
   b. From the Print menu, select the Preview command. The larger size fonts are shown on the preview screen. Press **Esc** to return to the word processor screen.

3.19 Tabs and Tab Stops

Tabs are used to position text within a line or to create tables of data. Works has default "tab stops" at every half inch. Pressing the Tab key moves the cursor to the next tab stop to the right. Do not confuse tab stops with tabs themselves. Tabs are actual characters that are placed in a document using the Tab key. Tab stops are only locations specifying the length of the tab character (how far it will move the cursor).

Default tab stops are generally used for indenting text from the margin. When beginning a new paragraph, press Tab once to indent the first line half an inch before entering text. Each paragraph in the body of IVYPROMO has been formatted this way. When creating the heading of a letter, your address and the date should be aligned near the right side of the page. By using the same number of tabs, the cursor may easily be placed at the desired spot before each line is typed. While default tabs are initially set to every half inch, they can be changed to any interval desired.

Although tabs move the cursor more than one space, they are generated by a single keystroke and may be inserted into text or deleted from text the same as any other character. Pressing the Tab key does not actually insert the number of individual space characters needed to move the cursor to the next tab stop. Instead, a code is placed in the text which tells Works to move to the next tab stop. When Show All Characters has been selected, this code is displayed on the screen as an arrow (→). Deleting a tab requires that only the code be deleted, and the text will automatically be moved to the left to fill the space created by removing the tab.

It is possible to insert a Tab into a previously entered line of text. After a line has been typed, positioning the cursor in the line and pressing Tab will move the characters to the right of the tab to the next tab stop.

3.20 Opening and Closing Files

```
 File 

 Create New File...
 Open Existing File...
 WorksWizards...
 Save
 Save As...
 Close

 File Management...
 Run Other Programs...

 Exit Works
```

You will often need to work on more than one file after booting Works. When this is the case, the current file that you are working on should be saved, and then "closed." Closing a file means that it is removed from the computer's memory and no further editing changes may be made. Selecting the Close command from the File menu (Alt - F C) closes the currently displayed file and clears the screen. If you attempt to close a file which has been edited but not saved, Works warns you before preceding:

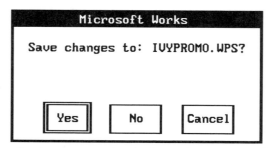

Works displays a warning before closing a modified file

If you wish to save the changes before closing, accept the **Yes** default. If instead you wish to close the file without saving the edited version, select the **No** option. Select **Cancel** to return to the word processor.

An Introduction to Computing Using Microsoft Works

3

Once the file has been closed, you may wish to open a previously saved file. This is done by executing the Open Existing File command from the File menu (Alt-F O). The Open Existing File dialog box is then displayed, allowing you to select from a list of previously saved files. If you instead wish to start work on a new file, the Create New File command from the File menu creates a new, empty word processor file. It is a good practice to close any open files before using the Open or New commands. Closing a file removes it from the computer's memory, and protects the file from being accidentally erased by a power failure.

●●●

Practice 11

This Practice demonstrates how to use the Close and Create New File commands, and work with tabs. The Show All Characters command will be used to display formatting characters. IVYPROMO should be open from the last Practice.

1) CLOSE THE IVYPROMO FILE

From the File menu, select the Close command [*press* Alt-F C]. The file is removed from memory and the screen clears. The File menu is displayed.

2) CREATE A NEW WORD PROCESSOR FILE

a. From the File menu, select the Create New File command. The Create New File dialog box is displayed.
b. Press Enter to create a new word processor file.
c. If it not already, switch to Show All Characters mode.

3) ENTER TEXT AND INSERT THREE TABS

a. Type: This is a test.
b. Press Home to return to the first character in the line.
c. Press the Tab key. A tab character is inserted and an arrow is shown. The line is indented to the first tab stop at 0.5" inches.
d. Press the Tab key 2 more times. Because you have placed three tabs into the document, three arrows are shown. The line is indented 1.5 inches (three default 0.5" tabs = 1.5").

4) DELETE THE TABS

a. Press the Home key to return to the beginning of the line.
b. Press the Delete key. A tab is deleted, and the arrow marker removed. The line is now indented only 1 inch (two 0.5" tabs).
c. Press Delete 2 times to remove the tabs. The arrow markers disappear. By deleting these markers you have not affected the tab stops in any way, only removed the tab characters from this line.

5) CLOSE THE FILE

a. From the File menu, select the Close command.
b. Because the file has been changed, Works displays the warning:

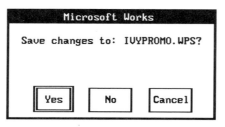

Select **No** to close the file without saving. The File menu is displayed.

   c.   Select Open Existing File and open the IVYPROMO document. Note how the paragraphs in IVYPROMO are indented with tabs.

3.21 The Ruler

Directly above the work area is a Ruler that is used to measure distances from the left side of the page. This Ruler gauges the placement of horizontal formatting features including tabs and margins. The square brackets mark the left ([ ) and right ( ]) margins. Each dot on the Ruler represents one tenth of an inch. The numbers represent the number of inches from the left margin; the 1 is one inch from the margin, the 2 is two inches, and so on.

The Ruler

3.22 Setting Individual Tab Stops

In addition to the defaults, Works allows individual tab stops to be set anywhere on the line. These differ from default tab stops in that, rather than appearing at regular intervals, individual tab stops may be inserted anywhere on the line.

It is also possible to remove tab stops. Works can remove a specific stop or every tab stop in a document, including the defaults. Setting an individual tab stop automatically removes any default stops to its left. That is, setting an individual tab stop at 1.4 inches removes the default stops at .5 and 1.0 inches. The stop at 1.5 inches is not affected.

There are several different types of tab stops. The default tab stop alignment is left aligned, meaning that text entered at that stop will be aligned at the stop's left. Left-aligned stops are marked with an L on the Ruler. It is also possible to create right, center and decimal aligned tab stops which are marked with an R, C, and D respectively. A right tab aligns the end of the text at the stop, while a center tab centers the text equidistant over the stop. Decimal tabs are used with numbers and align the numbers with the decimal point at the stop. Examples of each stop are shown on the next page with the corresponding Ruler:

An Introduction to Computing Using Microsoft Works

```
[··L······1·········2······R·3······C·4·········5··D····]·
  →  Left·Stop→          Right→      Centered→    Decimal¶
  →  Name→                 Amy→      Eppelman→     12.34¶
  →  Address→     Philadelphia→           PA→    123.567¶
  →  Phone→           123-4567→        (215)→      123.4¶
```

The tab stops are indicated by letters on the Ruler

Individual tab stops are set using the Tabs command from the Format menu (Alt-F T). When executed, the Tabs command displays a dialog box where the position and alignment of the stop are specified:

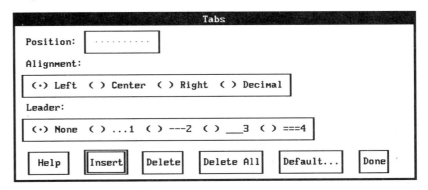

Tabs dialog box

To create a new stop, the distance of the stop from the left side of the page is entered on the Position line. Pressing Enter **Insert**s a new left-aligned stop (the default) at that position and an "L" is shown on the Ruler. When **Done** is selected the dialog box is removed and any previously entered tabs are adjusted to the new stop position. Creating a stop with a different alignment requires that the desired option be chosen from the Alignment box before **Insert** is selected. For example, to create a centered stop at 5 inches, type 5 as the Position and select **Center** from the Alignment box.

To delete a stop, type its position and select **Delete**. If you don't know the position of the stop, hold down the Ctrl key and use the left- and right-arrow keys to move the highlight along the Ruler until it is on the tab stop and then select **Delete**. **Delete All** removes all the tab stops set for that paragraph.

Any number of tab stops may be set or cleared at one time. When complete, selecting **Done** removes the dialog box, updates the Ruler, and returns the cursor to the work area. Any tab stops set or cleared are retained when the file is saved on disk, so that the next time it is loaded, the file will have the same stops.

It is important to realize that tab stops are a paragraph format, like Centered or Justified. That is, when tab stops are created, they are set for the current paragraph only. Any paragraphs before or after are not affected. This makes it possible for different paragraphs to have different sets of tab stops. As the cursor is moved through the text, the Ruler is updated to show the tab stops set for the current paragraph. Like all formatting commands, the same group of tab stops may be applied to a number of paragraphs by highlighting first, and then setting the stops.

Practice 12

In this Practice you will set and delete tab stops, creating a formatted table. Start Works and open the IVYPROMO document if you have not already done so. Display the document in Show All Characters mode if it is not already.

1) LOCATE THE STUDENT DIVERSITY TABLE

a. Move the cursor to the last character in the document.
b. Scroll up several lines to the Student Diversity table. This is a table which has been entered using tabs. There is a single tab between each column — one tab between "Area" and "Students," another between "Students" and "Percentage," and so on for the entire table. However, because tab *stops* have not yet been set, this table is not easy to read.

2) ADD A LINE TO THE UNFORMATTED TABLE

a. You will add a line to the table. Place the cursor at the end of the South America line, after 10.47%.
b. Press Enter. A new line is added to the table.
c. Press the Tab key once to indent the line. Type `Other` as the area.
d. Press Tab again and type `49` as the number of students.
e. Press Tab and type `0.89%` as the percent. Each of the lines in this table was entered similarly. The table should be similar to:

```
 File  Edit  Print  Select  Format  Options  Window  Help
 Fnt:[Draft·······]↓ Pt:[12·]↓   Bld Ital Ul    Lft Ctr Rt Jus   Sp Th    Prev
═══════════════════════════ IVYPROMO.WPS ═════════════════════════════════╤
 [······L·1····2·········3·········4········5·········]········7····=
 →      Ivy·University·prides·itself·on·having·a·diverse·                    ↑
 student·body.·Our·students·come·from·around·the·country·and·
 the·world·to·study·here.·The·following·table·shows·the·
 national·breakdown·of·our·students:¶
 ¶
 →        Area→  Students→ Percentage¶
 ¶
 →        Africa→213→ 3.87%¶
 →        Asia→  471→ 8.56%¶
 →        Europe→689→ 12.52%¶
 →        North·America→   3,503→    63.68%¶
 →        South·America→   576→ 10.47%¶
 →        Other→ 49→  0.89%¶
 →        →  5,501→    100.00%¶
 →      ¶
 In·Conclusion¶
 ¶
 →      We·hope·that·you·have·enjoyed·this·brief·description·of·           ↓
 L←                                                                        ↲
 Pg 3/3              DRA12              INS (28,46)              <F1=HELP>
 Press ALT to choose commands.
```

3) HIGHLIGHT THE TABLE

a. We wish to set three tab stops that will be the same for the entire table. So that we only have to enter the tab stops once, we will highlight the table first. Then any tab stops created affect the entire highlighted block of text. Place the cursor anywhere in the first line of the table, the title which says "Area Students Percentage."
b. Highlight to the end of the table. When the highlight is in the last line of the table (5,501), stop highlighting. Any tab stops now set will affect each highlighted line in the table.

An Introduction to Computing Using Microsoft Works

4) SET THE FIRST TAB STOP FOR THE TABLE

a. The first column of the table should be left aligned at 0.75 inches. From the Format menu, select the Tabs command [*press* `Alt-T T`]. The Tabs dialog is displayed.

b. Type `0.75` and press Enter to Insert the tab stop. An "L" is shown on the Ruler at the 0.75 position.

c. Press `Alt-D` to select **Done**. The table is re-formatted on screen with each line starting at 0.75".

5) SET THE SECOND AND THIRD TAB STOPS

a. The second column of the table should be right aligned at 3 inches. From the Format menu, select the Tabs command.

b. Type `3` as the Position.

c. Press `Alt-R` to select **Right** as the Alignment.

d. Press Enter to Insert the stop. An "R" is shown on the Ruler.

e. The last column is decimal aligned at 4.25 inches. Type `4.25` as the position, select **Decimal** (`Alt-E`) as the Alignment, and press Enter.

f. Press `Alt-D` to select **Done**. The table is now complete, and easy to read. Note the alignment of Percentage in the title. Because this is a decimal tab, the text is right aligned at the decimal position.

Check - Your table and Ruler should be similar to:

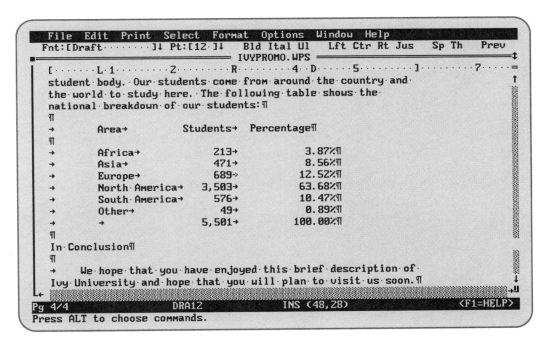

6) SAVE AND PRINT THE MODIFIED FILE

a. From the File menu, select the Save command to save the modified file. A copy of the file in memory is stored on disk. The next time it is opened, IVYPROMO will have the tab stops set.

b. From the Print menu, select the Print command and print the document. Note on the printed copy all of the formatting options created in this chapter: headers, footers, paragraph formats, text formats, fonts and styles, tab stops, etc.

c. From the File menu, select Close to close IVYPROMO.

d. From the File menu, select Exit Works to leave Works and return to the DOS prompt.

This chapter explained how text in a Word Processor document can be formatted to improve its appearance and readability. The Preview command from the Print menu allows a document to be viewed before printing.

Margins are the blank spaces between the edges of the paper and text. Works' default margin settings can be changed using the Page Setup & Margins command from the Print menu. When a margin is changed it affects all of the document from the first page to the end of the document. A header is a line printed at the top of each page, and a footer at the bottom of each page. Both are created by selecting the Headers & Footers command from the Print menu. Page numbers can be printed in either headers or footers.

Pagination is the division of a document into page-sized sections for printing. Works automatically displays the position of page breaks with chevrons, allowing you to determine how text will be divided when printed. Works keeps track of the current page and number of pages in a document, and displays this on the Status line. After an editing change, Works recalculates the position of the page breaks. Manual page breaks may be inserted when it is necessary to end the current page.

Most formatting is best done with the Show All Characters command from the Options menu turned on. When selected, this command uses special symbols to mark the position of normally invisible characters such as spaces, Tabs and Enters (paragraphs).

To "undo" the effects of the last command executed the Undo command is selected from the Edit menu.

Blocks of text are highlighted either by using the F8 key or the mouse. These blocks can be deleted using the delete key or formatted using any of the format commands.

Single and double spacing are set by selecting the Single Space or Double Space command from the Format menu. When line spacing is set it affects all text in the current paragraph, or in a selected block.

Works provides four ways to align text using the Format menu commands: Left, Right, Center and Justified. Left alignment creates a straight left hand border and a jagged right hand border. Right alignment is the opposite, creating a straight right hand border and a jagged left hand border. Centering positions a line equidistant from the left and right margins. Justified alignment creates straight borders at both margins.

Text may be made bold, italic or underlined using the appropriate commands from the Format menu. The Font & Style command from the Format menu allows superscripts and subscripts to be created. All of these text formats affect only the text in a block, which must be selected before the command is executed.

3

A superscript is a section of text which is raised slightly above the current line while a subscript is printed slightly below the current line. Both superscripts and subscripts are created by selecting the Font & Style command from the Format menu. The Font & Style command is also used to select the font and size of print.

Tables can be created in a document using tabs. Works has default tab stops at every half inch. Individual tab stops may be set and cleared selecting the Tabs command from the Format menu. Tab stops may be set as Left, Center, Right, or Decimal. The Ruler located directly above the work area is used to measure distances from the left side of the page. It is used to gauge the placement of horizontal formatting features including tabs and margins.

● ●

Vocabulary

Block - A highlighted section of text which may contain anything from a single letter to a paragraph or several pages. Once highlighted, operations such as Copy and Move may be performed on the block, or text formats such as bold applied.

Bold - Darker letters, used for emphasis.

Centered - Text positioned evenly between the left and right margins.

Close - To remove a file from the work area when it is no longer needed.

Double Space - Leaving a blank line between each line of text when a document is printed.

Font - Description of how characters are shaped.

Footer - Line which is printed at the bottom of each page.

Format - The way that text appears on a page, including options such as margins, emphasized text, and headers and footers.

Format menu - Menu from which formatting options such as bold, italic, centered and justified are set.

Header - Line which is printed at the top of each page.

Italic - Text printed on a slant.

Justified - Paragraph format in which each line of text is made to extend from the left margin to the right by adding extra space between words.

Left aligned - Default paragraph format where text is even with the left hand margin, while the right side is ragged.

Margin - Blank spaces on a printed page which surround text.

Pagination - The computer calculates and displays markers showing where text will be broken into pages when printed.

Paragraph alignment - How text is printed in relation to the margins: left (default), right, centered or justified.

Paragraph format - Use of options affecting a paragraph including alignment, spacing, tabs, indents and margins.

Points - Units for measuring character sizes.

Preview command - Enables the user to see the overall layout of a document without printing it.

Right alignment - Paragraph format where text is set even with the right hand margin, while the left side is ragged.

Ruler - Line at the top of the Work area showing placement of tab stops, indents and margins.

Show All Characters command - Causes markers to be displayed in the text at the position of normally invisible characters such as spaces, Tabs or Enters. Markers are not printed.

Show All Characters marker - Marker displayed by the Show All Characters command to indicate the placement of a normally invisible character: • (raised dot) for space, ↵ for Enter, and → for Tab.

Single space - Places text on each line of a printed page.

Subscript - Text printed slightly below the normal line.

Superscript - Text printed slightly above the normal line.

Tab stop - Position(s), shown on the Ruler, where the cursor jumps to when the Tab key is pressed. Used to create columns or indent text.

Text format - How the letters making up the text are printed: bold, underlined, italic, superscript, subscript or plain.

Tool bar - Provides shortcuts to many commands when using a mouse.

Undo command - Undoes the effects of the last command executed.

Unjustified - Left-aligned text, with the right side jagged.

• •

Reviews

Sections 3.1 - 3.5

1. a) What is meant by formatting text?
   b) List five publications in which you have seen formatted text and describe the formats used.

2. What does the Preview command from the Print menu display and why is it useful?

3. a) List the steps required to change the margins of a document so that the left margin is at 2 inches and the right margin at 3 inches.
   b) How long is a line of text after these margins have been set? (Assume an 8.5 x 11 inch page of paper.)
   c) When working on the word processor screen, how can you tell where the margins have been set?

4. Explain the steps required to print the header "My Summer Vacation" at the top and a footer containing the current date and page number at the bottom of each page of a document.

5. a) What is meant by pagination?
   b) How is pagination indicated on the word processor screen?
   c) Explain two situations when you might want to control the pagination in a document.

6. What is a "page break" and how is one indicated on the Works' screen?

7. What is a "manual page break" and how is one created?

8. What normally invisible characters are displayed on the screen when the Show All Characters option is selected?

9. How can the effects of the last command executed by undone?

10. a) What is meant by a block of text?
    b) How can you tell which text is included in a block on the word processor screen?

11. a) List the steps required to delete the second paragraph in a five paragraph document.
    b) Why is it usually best to delete text with the Show All Characters option selected?

12. What is the result of pressing the F8 key three times?

13. What is the easiest way to delete a line of text?

14. a) Why might you want text to be double spaced?
    b) List the steps required to double space only the second paragraph in a document that contains five paragraphs.
    c) Will the second paragraph appear double spaced on the screen?

15. What is meant by justified text?

16. a) What is meant by centered text?
    b) What type of text is usually centered?

17. a) What is meant by text that is left aligned?
    b) What type of document is usually formatted using left alignment?

18. What sequence of steps must be executed to justify an entire document?

Sections 3.14 - 3.18

19. List the steps required to bold the first line of text and underline the second line in a word processed document.

20. Looking at the screen how is it possible to determine which text will print bold, italic or underlined?

21. After creating a document title which is both centered and bold, you discover that you have also accidentally centered and bolded the first two paragraphs. How do you remove these formats from the paragraphs?

22. Mouse users: How would you use the Tool bar to justify the first paragraph in a document?

23. What is the difference between a superscript and a subscript?

24. What is a font? Name three fonts.

25. What is the size of characters measured in?

26. How can you tell the font and size of characters on the screen?

27. What does closing a file do?

28. a) What are tabs used for?
    b) What are default tabs?
    c) How are tabs deleted?

29. What is the screen Ruler and what is it used for?

30. a) List the steps required to set tabs at 1.2 and 2.4 inches.
    b) When working on the word processor screen, how can you tell where tabs stops have been set?
    c) How can you tell where tabs have been entered in the text?

31. How is a tab stop deleted?

32. What is the best method for setting the tab stops in four continuous paragraphs to the same values?

3 | Exercises

● ●

1. Open the file named COMPEDUC.WPS on your data disk and make the following changes as noted below:

Justify all paragraphs

```
Computers in Education
```
Center and bold title

```
Over the past ten years it has become obvious that
computers will play an increasingly important role in
education. The invention of the microcomputer has made it
possible for schools to purchase large numbers of
computers at affordable prices. Now that computers are
available for student use, educators have been discussing
how they should be used. Below are a few examples of how
schools are using their computers.
```

```
Computer Aided Instruction
```
Bold subtitle

Underline 2nd sentence

```
Computer programs have become available which instruct
students in different academic disciplines. These
programs have been especially effective in instructing
students in languages and mathematics. When used with
elementary school students, computer aided instruction
(CAI) has been found to keep students interested in a
subject while entertaining them at the same time. This is
especially true of programs that employ multi-media —
integrating the computer with devices such as CD players,
and video disks. Mrs. Groves, a teacher at West Lawrence
Elementary School, said, "When used as part of a complete
learning system, computers help reinforce skills learned
in the classroom."
```

```
Applications Programs
```
Bold subtitle

```
Many students are now taking courses which introduce them
to applications software. They are taught how to use word
processing, data base, and spreadsheet software. Most
students find that knowing how to use such software can
help them in their other courses. Mr. Ronald Johnson of
Ivy University said, "Our students are especially
interested in learning how to use integrated software
like ClarisWorks and Microsoft Works."
```

```
Writing Programs
```
Bold subtitle

```
Students who would like to pursue careers in computing
often elect to take courses which teach them how to write
computer programs. The languages most often learned are
BASIC and Pascal. Besides learning to program, these
courses teach valuable problem-solving skills.
```
Italicize "BASIC" and "Pascal"

```
Lawrence Township Computer Usage        Bold subtitle

The following table shows the number of computers in
Lawrence Township schools and percentage by manufacturer:

Manufacturer    Number      Percent
Apple II   35   7.6%
Commodore  19   4.1%
IBM and clones 187   40.6%
Macintosh 212   46.0%
Other       8   1.7%
```

a) Insert a right aligned footer which prints the current time.

b) Increase the size of the document's title.

c) Change the font of the subtitles of each section.

d) Format the table at the bottom of the document with the following tab stops:

    2.25" Right aligned tab stop (for the number of computers)
    3.1" Decimal aligned tab stop (for the percentage of computers)

e) Make the column titles in the table bold.

f) Save the modified file, and print a copy.

2. The file named OPENINGS.WPS on your data disk contains several lines which could be used
    to start a short story.

    a) Choose one of the lines, delete the rest using blocks, and then write a paragraph using the
        opening line.

    b) Justify and double space the paragraph.

    c) Insert a bold and enlarged title.

    d) Create a centered header with your name.

    e) Save the story then print a copy.

3. The SuperSub store has just opened a new store in this area. They are creating a flyer and need
    your help to improve its appearance. Open the SUPERSUB.WPS file.

    a) Center and bold the flyer's heading.

    b) Change the font for the heading and increase its size.

    c) Make all occurrences of the word "SUPER" in SUPERSUB a superscript. Make all
        occurrences of the word "SUB" in SUPERSUB a subscript.

d) Bold each occurrence of the word SUPERSUB.

e) Justify the entire body of the advertisement.

f) Change the font of all the occurrences of the word "FREE" so it stands out.

g) Insert a superscripted asterisk (*) after the word "FREE!" in the first paragraph. At the very bottom of the flyer in a small font size, create a new paragraph:

   `*Availability and number of customers may make the offer null and void. No refunds, rainchecks, or apologies.`

h) Save SUPERSUB on disk and then print a copy of the file.

4. In Chapter Two, Exercise 5 you wrote a review of a recent movie or concert in a file named CRITIC.WPS.

a) Open CRITIC and insert a bold, centered headline which has the name of the event you reviewed.

b) Italicize any titles in the review, such as the title of a movie, an album or song title, etc.

c) The paper's editors like all submissions to be doubled spaced. Format your review to conform with their wishes.

d) Add the centered header "CRITIC'S CHOICE".

e) Justify the text in the review so that it looks more like a newspaper article.

f) Save the modified review and print a copy.

5. Tables make information easier to read and understand. It is a simple process to create tables in documents using the Tab key.

a) Create a new word processing file and enter the following table, separating the opponent column from the record column with a single tab character:

Opponent	Record
Audubon	7-4
Cherry Hill East	7-4
Cherry Hill West	4-7
Collingswood	2-8
Gulf Stream	6-5
Haddon Heights	10-1
Pine Crest	1-10

b) Format the table by setting a right aligned tab stop at 3.5".

c) Make the column titles bold.

d) Insert a centered tab stop at 4.7" for the entire table and add a third column as shown below:

Division

I

IV

II

III

IV

V

I

e) Save the document as TABLE and print a copy. Your table should be similar to:

Opponent	Record	Division
Audubon	7-4	I
Cherry Hill East	7-4	IV
Cherry Hill West	4-7	IA
Collingswood	2-8	III
Gulf Stream	6-5	IV
Haddon Heights	10-1	V
Pine Crest	1-10	I

6. In Chapter Two, Exercise 3 you created a file named APPLY.WPS which contained an application letter for a college. Open the APPLY.WPS file and follow the directions below to create the following table with tabs for the application letter:

a) Insert two blank lines at the end of the body of the letter, just before the closing.

b) Using single tab characters to separate each column, enter the table below:

Year	Semester	GPA	Special Activities
1992	Fall	3.9	Captain of Debate Team
1992	Spring	3.6	All state swim team
1992	Summer	3.95	President of Student Body
1993	Fall	4.0	All state gymnastics team

c) Set the following tab stops for the entire table:

At 1.75" insert a centered tab stop for the Semester column
At 2.75" insert a decimal aligned tab stop for the GPA column
At 3.5" insert a left aligned tab stop for the Special Activities column

d) Make the column titles bold.

e) Change the body of the letter only to double spaced.

f) Save and print a copy of the modified letter.

An Introduction to Computing Using Microsoft Works

3

7. Red Barn petting zoo needs to have a listing of their farm animals. In a new file, type the following table, separating each column with a single tab:

Name	**Color**	**Gender**	**Type**
Betsey	Black/White	F	Gernsey Cow
Bluebell	Brown	F	Ayrshire Cow
Lucy	Brown	F	Morgan Riding Horse
Sandy	Tan/White	F	Mustang Horse
Toby	White	F	Shetland Pony
Harriot	Red	F	Shetland Pony
SusieQ	Red	F	Jersey Red Hen
Harry	Red	M	Maine Red Rooster
Marylou	White	F	Long Island Duck
Larry	White	M	Long Island Duck

a) Set the following tab stops for the entire table:

At 1.4" insert a left aligned tab stop for the Color column
At 2.7" insert a center aligned tab stop for the Gender column
At 3.4" insert a left aligned tab stop for the Type column

b) Bold the column headings.

c) Insert a bold, centered title above of the table which reads: Red Barn Farm Animal Inventory.

d) Change the bottom, left, and right page margins to .75".

e) At 5.5" insert a left aligned stop for the entire table. Add the following column to the end of the table:

Location

Farm Stall A1
Farm Stall A2
Farm Stall A3
Farm Stall B1
Farm Stall B2
Farm Stall B3
Barn Yard
Barn Yard
Farm Pond
Farm Pond

f) Save the file as REDBARN, and print it out.

8. The Ivy University literary magazine would like to print the essay you wrote for Chapter Two, Exercise 7. Open the ESSAY.WPS file and make the following changes:

a) Insert a bold, centered title describing your essay.

b) The body of the essay should be double spaced.

c) Create a header showing your name left aligned, and the file name right aligned.

d) Insert a footer which prints the page number.

e) The margins of the paper should be .75 inches on the top and bottom, and 1 inch on the left and right.

f) Save the modified file and print a copy for the magazine.

9. The memo you wrote in Chapter Two, Exercise 9 needs to be formatted. Open SHAKESPR.WPS and make the following changes:

a) Insert a centered header showing the course title: Independent Study of Shakespeare.

b) Make the word "Memorandum" bold and italic.

c) Underline the words "To," "From," "Date," and "Subject."

d) Edit the listing of research papers so that there is a single tab before each paper topic and each due date. Delete any spaces that were previously used to separate the columns.

e) Italicize the Paper topic and Due date titles.

f) Set the following tab stops for the entire table:

Centered at 2 inches for the paper topic
Right aligned at 4 inches for the due date

g) Preview the document. The tabs stops could be improved, so they will be changed in the next step.

h) Delete the previous tab stops and create new ones for the entire table:

Right aligned at 2 inches
Left aligned at 4 inches

Preview the document again, noting the changes to the table.

i) Change the tab stops for the entire table to:

Left aligned at 1"
Right aligned at 3.5 inches

j) Preview the document. These stops are acceptable. Insert a blank line between the column titles and the column information.

k) Save the modified memo and print a copy.

3

10. Open the SCIENCE.WPS file, which contains the biography you wrote in Chapter Two, Exercise 10 and make the following changes:

   a) Insert a right aligned header showing your name.

   b) Insert a footer showing the date.

   c) Change the top and bottom margins to .75 inches, and the left and right margins to 1 inch.

   d) Center, bold, and underlined the title of your paper.

   e) Double space the body of the biography.

   f) Save the modified file, and print out a copy.

11. In Chapter Two, Exercise 8 you created an advertisement for an upcoming event in a file named ADVERT.WPS.

   a) Open the ADVERT file and use formatting options such as tabs, centering, and different fonts, sizes, and styles to make the advertisement more attractive.

   b) Insert a footer to the file that has the current date left aligned, and the file name right aligned.

   c) Save and print the modified file.

12. The Gibbon Research Proposal you corrected in Chapter Two, Exercise 13 needs further refinement before it is finished. Open the RESEARCH.WPS file and make the following changes:

   a) Center the paragraphs from "A PROPOSAL FOR RESEARCH" to "University of Eastern Florida."

   b) Make the first three sentences of the Proposal bold:

   A PROPOSAL FOR RESEARCH
   BEHAVIORAL STUDIES OF THE
   WHITE HANDED GIBBONS ON BASHIBASHI ISLAND

   c) Change the left and right margins to 1 inch.

   d) Insert a left aligned footer which prints "Page" followed by the page number.

   e) The following lines are to be printed at the top of each page:

   L. Williamson and P. Helvetica
   To. - Archaeological Center
   Proposal - Development of behavioral guide...

   Locate the two occurrences of this page heading and insert a manual page break before each.

f) Underline the headings Summary, Purpose and Description, White-handed Gibbons, and Computerized Guide.

g) Create the following table on the bottom of page two, inserting a single tab before the first column and between each of the columns:

Name	Hours	Name	Hours
Aardvark	242	Magenta	76
Apollo	193	Saffron	187
Athena	385	Sunlight	28
Avant Garde	49	Trickery	357
Ballerina	142	Vanguard	274
Emerald	125	White face	757
Eric the Red	112	White streak	91

h) Set the following tab stops for the entire table:

Left aligned at 1 inch
Right aligned at 2.75 inches
Left aligned at 4 inches
Right aligned at 5.75 inches

i) Make the column titles bold, and separate the titles from the table with a single blank line as shown in the table above.

j) Insert a title at the top of the table which reads: Total Observation Hours for the Gibbon Community on Bashibashi Island. Make the title bold, centered, and a larger size than the rest of the table.

k) Below the table insert the following notes:

Research conducted:
51 Weeks
68 Hours/Week
3468 Total Hours

l) The formatting of budget table on page 3 needs to be improved. Set a decimal aligned tab stop at 5" so the budget amounts will line up.

m) Save the modified file and print a copy.

13. The Store Opening you announced in Chapter Two, Exercise 12 needs some examples of the inventory you carry. Open the OPENFLYR.WPS file and make the following changes:

a) Using tabs, create an inventory table on the bottom of your announcement. Use a single tab before the Item, Description, and Price columns, for example:

Item	Description	Price

b) Underline the column headings and complete the table. Your table should be similar to the following pet store example:

Item	Description	Price
Parrot Feed	20 lb. Premium Mix	$15.00
Hay	Pangola Bale	$9.00
Cat Food	Case Science Diet Canned	$24.00
Collar	Nylon per foot	$2.50
Aquarium	20 gallon	$45.00
Book	How To Care for Rabbits	$9.50

c) Set the following tab stops for the entire table (including column titles):

At 1" insert a center aligned tab stop for the Item column
At 2" insert a left aligned tab stop for the Description column
At 5.5" insert a decimal aligned tab stop for the Price column

d) Center, bold, and increase the size of the letter's heading which contains your store's name, address, and phone number.

e) Make the announcement of the sale centered, larger, and a different font.

f) Bold and underline the date and time of the grand opening.

g) Double space the body of the announcement.

h) Save the file and print a copy of the modified announcement.

14. CityZoo keeps a listing of their animals in the word processor. Open the CITYZOO.WPS file and make the following changes:

a) Change the left and right margins to .5 inches.

b) Set the following tab stops for the entire table (including column titles):

At 2.6" insert a center aligned tab stop for the Number/Gender column
At 3.5" insert a left aligned tab stop for the Type column
At 4" insert a left aligned tab stop for the Location column
At 6.7" insert a right aligned tab stop for the Staff column

c) Make all the column titles in the table bold.

d) Make the title, CityZoo Catalogue, larger and a different font.

e) Insert the following footer to the animal listing:

Dr. Yolanda Delgado - President of CityZoo

f) Below the listing add the following legend with one tab before each letter, as shown:

Animal Type
M - Mammal
R - Reptile
B - Bird
I - Insect
F - Fish

g) Save the modified catalogue, and print a copy.

15. You are to create a two-page newsletter on any topic that you wish. The newsletter must contain the following features:

At least 4 different stories.	A page header which shows the page number.
Two advertisements.	Bold, centered headlines.
Justified paragraphs.	Correct spelling.

At least 1 superscript footnote. Place the footnote references on the last page.
Consider using tabs to create more than one column per page (like a newspaper). Note that text in columns cannot be justified.

An example newsletter design is shown below:

I.U. News   Page 1

Ivy University News - "All the News that Fits"

We Win!

Dateline Kansas City: Today the Ivy University Roaring Tigerlilies again proved that they were a force to be reckoned with as they bested the Overbrook Rams 2-1. Overbrook took the lead early on but was soon shut down by the mighty Tigerlily defense. Not to be outdone, our offense then returned with two unanswered screamers that left the Rams in total disarray. This win gives the 'Lilies a 6-0 record. Coach Riley said that "The team has never, ever, ever played better." Talk of a possible State Championship has been heard. For complete details and a rundown of other scores please see the Sports section.

Steves' Election Bid Fails

In a surprising come-from-behind victory, dark-horse candidate J.T. Willbury today defeated incumbent Tom Steves in the Student Congress presidential race. Steves, a 3 and a half year veteran, lost by a huge margin to the newcomer Willbury. Reached at his plush offices Steves had "no comment" about the election but said that he plans to continue in his roles as debate club president and captain of the swim team. The final tally was:

Candidate	Votes
Steves	57
Willbury	3,461
Undecided	289

Editorial Comment - *by Dana A. Clarke*

It comes as no surprise to those who have followed this year's Student Congress elections that Tom Steves was not re-elected. What is surprising is the actual number of people who realized that for the last 3 and a half years this guy has been sandbagging it. If ever there was a case for impeachment, this was it. The well-oiled political machine that passed as Steves' campaign staff was a joke. His grandiose plans to have the cafeteria serve chocolate milk never materialized, nor did the student trip to the Bahamas. Those of us   (continued, next page)

---

a) Make the titles of the article slightly larger than the body.

b) Italicize any titles of books, magazines, songs, team names, etc. that appear in any of your articles.

c) If you use any tables be sure to use tabs to align the information in them.

d) Save the file as NEWSLETR, and print it out.

Chapter Four

Advanced Word Processor Techniques

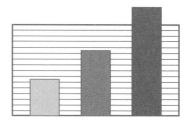

Objectives

After completing this chapter you will be able to:

1. Move and copy blocks of text.

2. Use the Search and Replace commands.

3. Jump to specific pages in a document with the Go To page command.

4. Use the spelling checker to proof a document.

5. Use the thesaurus to suggest synonyms for words in a document.

6. Create indents for paragraphs.

7. Use hanging indents to create bulleted lists.

8. Create and edit footnotes, and control their placement in a document.

9. Have Works count the number of words in a document.

10. Insert special time and date markers to create a "time stamp" for a document.

11. Insert pictures into a document and change their size.

4

This chapter deals with some of the advanced capabilities of the Works word processor. Several, like the spelling checker, are useful in everyday work. Others make special purpose jobs easy. It is not expected that you will have an immediate use for all of the commands in this chapter. However, as you begin to use Works for longer and more detailed projects they will undoubtedly become more useful.

4.1 Moving a Block

One of the most powerful editing tools that a word processor provides is the ability to move a highlighted block of text from one area of a document to another. For example, a paragraph can be moved from one page and placed on the next. Text as small as a single character or word or as large as an entire page or even a group of pages can be moved. Works automatically closes the space that formerly held the moved text and opens new space to receive it, rearranging the rest of the document to accommodate the change.

Moving a block of text is a three step process:

1. Place the cursor on the first character to be moved and highlight the block (either using the F8 key or the mouse).
2. Execute the Move command from the Edit menu. MOVE appears on the Status line to indicate that a Move is being performed.
3. Place the cursor at the new location where the block is to be moved and press Enter.

When Enter is pressed the highlighted text is moved from its old position to the position of the cursor. It is best to select the block to be moved with the **Show All Characters** option on, making it easy to include any space, Tab, or paragraph markers that are to be moved in the highlight.

4.2 Copying a Block

Works can also copy blocks of text. While the Move command deletes a block from its original position and reproduces it in another location, Copy retains the original and creates an exact duplicate in a new location.

The procedure for copying is similar to that for moving blocks. To copy a block of text, the block is highlighted and the Copy command executed from the Edit menu. The cursor is then moved to the position where the copy is to be placed and Enter pressed. During the Copy procedure, COPY is shown on the Status line to inform you that text is being copied.

The Edit menu also has a Delete command which removes a high-lighted block from the document. This command has the same effect as highlighting a block and pressing the Delete key.

Practice 1

This Practice demonstrates the use of block move and copy commands. A block consisting of a sentence will be moved, and then an entire paragraph copied.

Previous Practices have given the keyboard commands required to execute a command (for example, Alt-E M). By now you should be familiar with the process of displaying menus and selecting commands. The rest of the Practices will simply say "From the Edit menu, select the Move command." You may then display the menu and select the command using either the keyboard or the mouse.

1) START WORKS AND OPEN IVYPROMO

a. Boot DOS and start Works as described in Chapter Two. The Quick Start dialog box is displayed.
b. From the Quick Start dialog box, select the **Open an Existing File** option. The Open Existing File dialog box is displayed.
c. Move the cursor to the list of file names and highlight IVYPROMO.WPS.
d. Select OK. A copy of IVYPROMO is transferred from the disk into the computer's memory and displayed on the screen.

2) HIGHLIGHT THE BLOCK TO BE MOVED

a. From the Options menu, select the Show command and switch to **Show All Characters** mode if you have not already done so. You will move a sentence from the second paragraph to the first.
b. Place the cursor in the sentence which begins "There is a . . ." in the second paragraph.
c. Highlight the sentence, using either F8 or the mouse, being sure to include the space after the period.

3) ISSUE THE MOVE COMMAND

a. From the Edit menu, select the Move command. MOVE is shown on the Status line.
b. Works displays the prompt

```
Select new location and press ENTER. Press ESC to cancel.
```

on the Message line. Move the cursor to the "W" that begins the sentence "With world famous . . ." in the first paragraph.

   c.   Press Enter. The sentence is moved from one paragraph to another.

4) HIGHLIGHT THE BLOCK TO BE COPIED

   a.   You will produce a copy of the first paragraph at the end of the document. Make sure that the cursor is in the first paragraph, which begins "Ivy University is . . .".

   b.   Highlight the entire paragraph.

5) ISSUE THE COPY COMMAND

   a.   From the Edit menu, select the Copy command. COPY is displayed on the Status line and

     `Select new location and press ENTER. Press ESC to cancel.`

     is shown on the Message Line.

   b.   Press `Ctrl-End` to move the cursor on the last line in the document.

   c.   Press Enter to copy the block. A copy of the first paragraph is placed at the cursor position.

   d.   Jump back to the top of the document by pressing `Ctrl-Home` and verify that the original paragraph is still there.

6) SAVE THE MODIFIED FILE

From the File menu, select the Save command. Your file should be similar to:

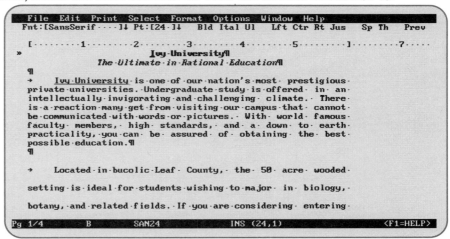

<u>Check</u> - The sentence about visiting the school should be moved from the second paragraph to the first and a copy of the first paragraph placed at the bottom of the document.

4.3 *Searching For Text in a Document*

The Search command operates differently than the other commands you have studied so far. Executed from the Select menu, Search does not involve entering text or editing it. Instead, the computer scans a document looking for a particular combination of letters called the "Search for text." This text may be a single letter, a word, or a phrase and is entered at the **Search for** option in the following dialog box:

```
┌─────────────────────────────────────────┐
│                  Search                   │
├───────────────────────────────────────────┤
│   Search for:  ┌──────────────────────┐   │
│                │ . . . . . . . . . . .│   │
│                └──────────────────────┘   │
│   [ ] Match whole word                    │
│   [ ] Match upper/lower case              │
│                                           │
│   ┌──────┐      ┌──────┐   ┌────────┐     │
│   │ Help │      │  OK  │   │ Cancel │     │
│   └──────┘      └──────┘   └────────┘     │
└─────────────────────────────────────────┘
```

The Search command's dialog box

Starting from the current cursor position, the computer moves through the document looking for a sequence of letters that matches the search text. If a match is found the scanning stops, allowing the document to be read or edited. The search can then be repeated until all occurrences of the **Search for** text have been found. Search is useful when trying to locate a specific word or passage in a large document.

Note that Search begins its search at the current cursor position. To search the entire document the cursor must first be moved to the beginning of the file (Ctrl-Home) before executing the Search command. When entering new **Search for** text, any old **Search for** text is automatically removed from the dialog box when the new text is typed.

Search has a number of different options. Normally, Works ignores case differences (i.e., uppercase and lowercase) during a search. If the **Search for** text is Dog Works will find dog, Dog, DOG, etc. The **Match upper/lower case** option tells Works to find only text with the same capitalization as the **Search for** text. For example, a **Match upper/lower case** search for CAT will not find Cat or cat.

It is important to realize that a match is also considered to be found when the **Search for** text is located within another word. For example, specifying a **Search for** text of the will not only find "the" but also they, theory, another, etc. Such false finds can be eliminated by using the **Match whole word** option. When selected, this option only finds occurrences of the **Search for** text when it is not part of another word.

Many times you will want to continue to search for the same text. While it is possible to execute the Search command again, Works provides a shortcut by using the F7 key. Pressing F7 repeats the last Search command performed, using the same **Search for** text and options.

4.4 The Go To Page Command

```
┌─────────────┐
│   Select    │
├─────────────┤
│  Text       │
│  All        │
├─────────────┤
│  Go To...   │
│  Search...  │
│  Replace... │
└─────────────┘
```

Often you know that the text you wish to locate is on a certain page. The Go To command from the Select menu allows you to move the cursor directly to the top of any page in the document. This is much quicker than using the cursor control keys or mouse when the document is long. Once you have jumped to the desired page, the Search command, arrow keys, or mouse can be used to place the cursor at the desired position on that page. A benefit of this command is that it limits the amount of text that is checked by the Search command, making the Search quicker. For

An Introduction to Computing Using Microsoft Works

example, if you wish to locate the occurrence of some text which is on page 15 or later, you can use Go To to jump to page 15 and then execute the Search command.

• •

Practice 2

This Practice demonstrates the Search command. If you have not already done so, start Works and open IVYPROMO. You will search for every occurrence of the word "bandage."

1) EXECUTE THE SEARCH COMMAND

a. Make sure that the cursor is at the top of the document by pressing Ctrl-Home.
b. From the Select menu, select the Search command. A dialog box is displayed.

2) ENTER THE SEARCH FOR TEXT

Type the word bandage and select OK. There is a slight pause as Works searches the document. The first "bandage" found is in the course description for class 101.

3) REPEAT THE SEARCH USING THE SAME SEARCH TEXT

a. From the Select menu, select the Search command again. Note that the old Search for text is shown in the dialog box.
b. Select OK to repeat the search using the same Search for text. The cursor moves to the next occurrence of bandage.

4) FIND THE REST OF THE OCCURRENCES OF BANDAGE

a. Press the F7 key. Works repeats the Search and moves to the next "bandage."
b. Press F7 until all occurrences of "bandage" have been found. How many did you find?
c. When all occurrences of the Search for text have been found, Works displays the following message:

Select OK to continue.

5) JUMP TO DIFFERENT PAGES USING GO TO

a. From the Select menu, execute the Go To command. The Go To dialog box is displayed:

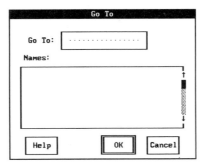

Type a 2 and select OK. The cursor jumps to the first character in the first line on page 2.

b.   Execute the Go To command again. Type a 1 for the page and select OK. The cursor jumps directly to the top of the document.

4.5 Replacing Text

The Replace command from the Select menu locates text in a document, just as the Search command does, but then replaces it with another piece of text that you supply. This makes it easy to create different versions of the same document that have some specified differences. For example, Works could be used to create a letter requesting a college interview with Ivy University. After printing the letter, Replace could be used to change every occurrence of "Ivy University" in the letter to "Trenton State" and then to "New Brunswick College" and so on. Thus all the letters needed could be easily created without having to type each one separately; the master letter is typed once and the name of the school is changed using Replace.

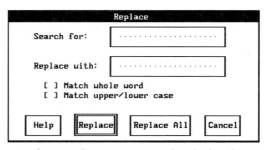

The Replace command's dialog box

The Replace command can be dangerous. If the **Search for** text is not clearly defined, unwanted replacements may be made. For example, specifying a **Search for** text of the will not only replace every occurrence of "the", but also any word that contains the, such as they, theory, another, etc. One way to avoid unwanted replacements is to define the **Search for** text very carefully. For example, specifying the followed by a space as the **Search for** text will avoid the replacements described above. Another way is to use the **Match whole word** option. When selected, this option only replaces occurrences of the **Search for** text when it is not part of another word.

Like the Search command, Replace starts its search from the current cursor position and can be made to replace only exact uppercase and lowercase matches. Replace also has the option of replacing all occurrences with the new text, or one at a time, prompting you to verify that each change should be made. It is usually advisable to verify each replacement before it is made, thereby avoiding unwanted changes. When entering new **Search for** and **Replace with** text, any old text will automatically be deleted when the new text is entered.

An Introduction to Computing Using Microsoft Works

Practice 3

Ivy University is considering updating its image by changing its name. This Practice will use the Replace command to change each occurrence of "Ivy University" to "Modern College" in the IVYPROMO file. This will allow the school's administration to see how the document looks with the new name. If you have not already done so, start Works and open the IVYPROMO file.

1) EXECUTE THE REPLACE COMMAND

a. Move the cursor to the beginning of the document by pressing `Ctrl-Home`.
b. From the Select menu, execute the Replace command. The Replace dialog box is shown.
c. Type `Ivy University` for the **Search for** text, replacing any old text that may remain from a previous Search.
d. Move the cursor to the **Replace with** option and type `Modern College`.
e. Select the **Replace** option.

2) REPLACE EACH OCCURRENCE

a. Works moves the cursor to the first occurrence of Ivy University and displays the message:

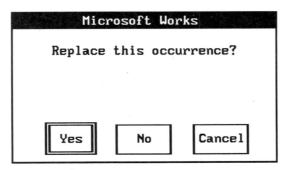

Select **Yes** to replace it with Modern College.
b. Works moves the cursor to the next occurrence of Ivy University. Select **Yes** to replace it with Modern College.
c. Repeat part (b) for each occurrence of Ivy University. When Works has completed the Replace command, it will leave the cursor at the position where the last replacement was made and display the message:

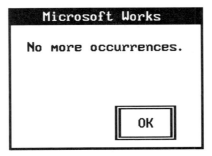

All occurrences of Ivy University have now been changed to Modern College. Select OK to continue.

Check - Scroll through the document to verify that each occurrence of Ivy University has been changed to Modern College.

3) CLOSE THE MODIFIED FILE

a. The university has decided that it does not like the name change. From the File menu, select the Close command.
b. Works displays the warning "Save changes to IVYPROMO.WPS?" Select **No** to close the file and abandon the changes.
c. From the File menu, select the Open command and open IVYPROMO again. Note that the changes were not saved.

4.6 Using the Spelling Checker

One of the most useful features of modern word processors is the ability to have the computer check the spelling of the words in a document. In Works, this is accomplished by selecting the Check Spelling command from the Options menu. When this command is executed, Works starts at the current cursor position and compares each word in the document to a dictionary file. Words not found in Work's dictionary are displayed in a dialog box. From this box you have the option of typing a correction or having Works produce a list of suggested spellings from which you may select:

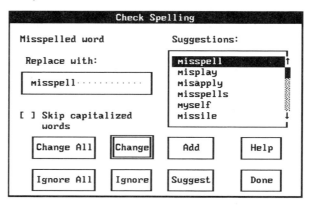

The Check Spelling command's dialog box

Remember, to use the keyboard to select an option such as **Ignore** or **Suggest** from the above dialog box, you must hold down the Alt key and press the highlighted letter. For example, to select **Ignore**, press Alt-I. Mouse users can click on the desired option button.

Because the dictionary file cannot contain every word in the English language, it is possible that Check Spelling may come across a word that it does not have in its dictionary. This is especially true for proper nouns like names and places. When Works does not know a word you have three options. If the word is spelled correctly you can tell Works to ignore it and proceed to the next misspelled word. If the word is one that you will use often, such as your name, you can have Works add the word to its dictionary. Once added, such words are no longer considered misspelled when they appear in a document. Finally, you can select a new spelling from Works' suggestions or type your own correction.

Mouse users can click on **Sp** on the Tool bar to execute the Check Spelling command. When the dialog box is displayed, simply click on the desired option button to select it.

4 Practice 4

Ivy University is about to print 50,000 copies of its promotional file for distribution around the country. This Practice will use the Check Spelling command to verify the spelling in the document before sending it to the print shop. If you have not already done so, start Works and open the IVYPROMO file.

1) EXECUTE THE CHECK SPELLING COMMAND

a. Make sure that the cursor is at the very top of the file by pressing Ctrl-Home.
b. From the Options menu, select the Check Spelling command to start the spelling check. There is a pause as Works checks the spelling. Works finds a questionable word in the course description section and displays it in the dialog box.

2) IGNORE THE MISSPELLED WORD

Because "today's" is spelled correctly, select the **Ignore** option [*press* Alt-I]. Works continues to check for misspellings.

3) CORRECT THE MISSPELLED WORD

a. Works finds the word "proffessional". Have Works suggest a spelling by selecting the **Suggest** option. Works checks its dictionary and displays the most likely spellings in the Suggestions list. The highlighted word in the Suggestions list is also shown as the **Replace with** option.
b. Because it is correct, accept the suggested spelling of "professional" and have it replace the misspelled word in the file by selecting the **Change** option. Works updates the file and continues to check the spelling.

4) CORRECT THE NEXT MISSPELLED WORD

a. Have Works **Suggest** a spelling for "Feild". Works checks the dictionary and displays the most likely spelling as the **Replace with** option.
b. Because the suggestion is not the one we want, scroll through the list of suggested spellings. Highlight the correct spelling, "Field".
c. Select the **Change** option to replace the misspelled word with the highlighted spelling from the Suggestions list. Works then continues to check the spelling.

5) IGNORE THE NAMES AND FORMULA

a. Ignore the spelling of any proper names and the chemical formula by selecting **Ignore**.
b. When the spelling check is finished, Works displays the following message:

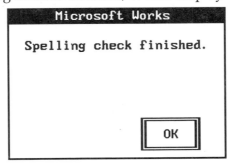

Select OK to return to the word processor screen.

6) SAVE THE CORRECTED FILE

4.7 Using the Thesaurus

Using a thesaurus can help make your writing more interesting. Works contains a built-in thesaurus that finds synonyms for many words and phrases. To use the thesaurus, select a word by placing the cursor on it and execute the Thesaurus command from the Options menu. Works then lists definitions for the selected word and suggested synonyms:

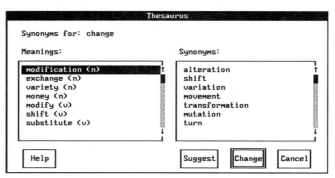

Because a single word can have different definitions, Works provides a list of meanings, identified by their parts of speech (*n* for noun, *v* for verb, *a* for adjective, and *o* for other). Highlighting different meanings changes the list of synonyms. Selecting **Change** replaces the word in the document with the highlighted meaning or synonym. Selecting **Cancel** removes the dialog box, leaving the word unchanged.

Works can be asked to find additional synonyms by highlighting a synonym in the list and choosing **Suggest**. Additional synonyms may then be found for those new synonyms, and so on.

Like the dictionary, Works uses a file for its thesaurus which cannot contain every possible word. If Works cannot find any synonyms for the selected word but finds a word which it believes is related to the selected word, it displays the word. For example, Works displays "universe" when asked for a synonym of "university" and indicates that it is a similar word. Selecting **Suggest** then displays a list of synonyms for universe. If Works cannot find any similar words, it displays the message:

Because a misspelled word will not be found, it is a good practice to spell check a document before using the thesaurus.

It is important to realize that the Thesaurus will only replace the highlighted word or phrase. For example, the word "change" might appear five times in a document. However, only the highlighted one will be replaced with the selected synonym. (If you wish to replace more than one, it is possible to use the Replace command and enter the synonym as the **Replace With** text.) After using the thesaurus to change words, you must save the file in order make the changes permanent.

Mouse users can execute the Thesaurus from the Tool bar by clicking on **Th**. When the dialog box is displayed, options are selected by clicking on the desired button.

• •

Practice 5

In this Practice you will use the thesaurus to suggest synonyms for two words. Start Works and open the IVYPROMO document if you have not already done so.

1) LOCATE THE WORD TO BE CHANGED

a. Using the Search command, search for the word "major". *F7*
b. There are several occurrences. Place the cursor in the "major" in the sentence which begins "A major part of successful treatment. . ." in the second paragraph of the course descriptions.

2) EXECUTE THE THESAURUS COMMAND

From the Options menu, select the Thesaurus command. Works highlights the word "major" and displays the Thesaurus dialog box:

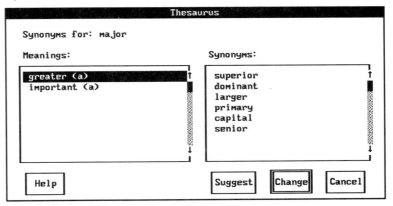

3) SELECT THE DESIRED MEANING

The definition of major that is being used in the sentence is most similar to "important." Highlight "important" to display a new list of synonyms.

4) SELECT THE DESIRED SYNONYM AND REPLACE THE WORD

a. From the list of synonyms for important, highlight "significant."
b. Select **Change**. Works replaces "major" with "significant" in the document and removes the dialog box.

5) CHANGE THE WORD "COMMON"

a. Place the cursor in the word "common" in the description for course 101.
b. From the Options menu, select the Thesaurus command. "Common" has many different meanings.
c. Select the meaning "ordinary" to get a list of synonyms.
d. Select the meaning "prevalent" to get another list of synonyms.
e. Select "universal" from the list of synonyms for prevalent.
f. Select **Change**. Common is changed to universal in the file.

6) SAVE THE MODIFIED FILE

The file must be saved to make the changes permanent. From the File menu, select Save to save the modified file on disk.

4.8 Indents

It is important to realize that margins are set for the entire document, and may not change from paragraph to paragraph or page to page. However, it is possible to alter the width of the lines in a specific paragraph by using "indents."

Indents make the margins of a paragraph appear to be larger. The default indent is 0", meaning that lines of text in a paragraph will extend from the left to the right margin. It is possible to set off a paragraph (such as a long quotation) from the rest of the text by specifying left and right indents. This causes the paragraph to have a smaller line length. For example, it is possible to set the left and right indents to 1 inch. Should this be done, the length of the current line would be 4 inches; the normal 6 inch line (8.5" - 1.3" - 1.2") minus the amount of the indent (1" on the left and 1" on the right). The resulting text would be similar to:

```
This is a normal paragraph. Each full
line extends from the left margin to the
right margin.

        This paragraph is indented.
        The lines extend from the left
        to the right indent, making
        for a smaller line length.
```

It is also possible to have paragraphs with only a left or only a right indent. Indents are set by selecting the Indents & Spacing command from the Format menu:

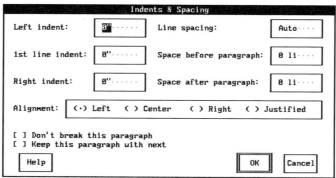

Indents are set using this dialog box

It is possible to set just a left or right indent, or both by moving the cursor to the desired option and typing the length of the indent. Setting an indent from this menu affects only the paragraph which contains the cursor. When the cursor is moved to an indented paragraph, the markers on the Ruler ([,]) automatically move to show the size of the indent.

Practice 6

In this Practice you will set and change paragraph indents. Start Works and open IVYPROMO if you have not already done so.

1) CREATE 1 INCH PARAGRAPH INDENTS

a. Move the cursor to the paragraph which begins "The modern world around us . . .", the quote below the faculty listing.
b. From the Format menu, select the Indents & Spacing command. A dialog box is displayed.
c. Type 1 for the **Left indent** option.
d. Move the cursor to the **Right indent** option.
e. Type 1 for the right indent.
f. Select OK to remove the dialog box and apply the indents. The quote now has left and right indents of 1 inch and the text is reformatted on the screen. The rest of the document is unchanged. Note the positions in the markers ([,]) on the Ruler.

2) CHANGE THE INDENTS

a. Make sure that the cursor is still in the quotation paragraph.
b. From the Format menu, select the Indents & Spacing command.
c. Type .5 for the **Left indent**.
d. Type .75 for the **Right indent**.
e. Select OK to apply the indents. The paragraph is reformatted and the positions in the markers on the Ruler are changed.
f. Move the cursor out of the quote paragraph. Note how the position of the markers on the Ruler is changed.

3) SAVE THE MODIFIED FILE ON DISK

Check - Your screen should be similar to:

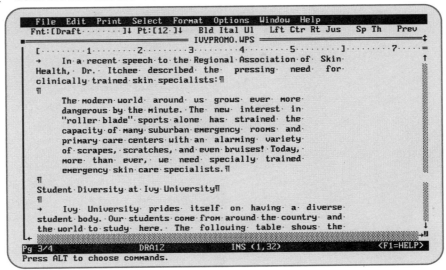

4.9 *Hanging Indents and Bulleted Lists*

Indents are most commonly used for setting off long blocks of text, quotes (as in the last Practice), outlines, and in bibliography entries. An indented block of text often draws attention to itself while adding to the overall appearance of the page.

A special type of indent is the "hanging" indent. As the name implies, the first line of this indent hangs out to the left over the lines below it. Hanging indents are useful when preparing lists, creating outlines, or including a standard bibliography in a research paper. Below is an example bibliography entry, using the hanging indent format:

Canine, Butch S. *My Life as a Dog: A True-Life Story*. New York: Sirius Press, 1992.

Note that the first line, which contains the author's name, sticks out from the rest of the bibliography entry. The rest of the paragraph hangs below the first line.

A hanging indent is created using the Format menu's Indents & Spacing command and entering the desired measurements in the dialog box. In the **Left indent** option, type the measurement that represents the indent for the main part of the paragraph. In the **1st line indent** box, type a negative measurement (preceded by a minus sign, "-"). The negative number extends the first line of the paragraph out toward the left margin, creating the "hanging" effect:

```
               <——— Negative 1st line indent
      0····¦····[·········2········3········4········5·]··
                  Canine,·Butch·S.·My·Life·as·a·Dog:·A·True-Life·
Left indent ———> Story.·New·York:·Sirius·Press,·1992.¶
```
                                                    Right indent

A negative first line indent creates the hanging effect

The first line indent is shown on the Ruler as a vertical bar (|).

A special use for the hanging indent is in the creation of "bulleted lists." A bulleted list is a unique way to vertically list separate items, sentences, or paragraphs using a special symbol or character to introduce each line. The following is an example of a bulleted list:

Today's Lunch Specials

* *Pizza Bianca* - A delicate blend of four imported cheeses mixed with fresh Italian herbs on a thin, crispy crust.
* *Insalata di Pollo* - Oak grilled chicken breast served with fresh salad greens, mozzarella, roasted peppers, and olives in a light vinaigrette.
* *Veal Chop* - Mesquite grilled with mushrooms.

In a bulleted list each item is a separate paragraph, formatted with a hanging indent. After creating the hanging indent, a bullet character, such as an asterisk or a lowercase "o", is added to draw attention to each item of the list. A Tab is used after the bullet to align the first line of text with the rest of the hanging indent:

*→*Pizza Bianca* - A delicate blend of four imported cheeses mixed with fresh Italian herbs on a thin, crispy crust.¶ —— Enter

Tab

*→*Insalata di Pollo* - Oak grilled chicken breast served with fresh salad greens, mozzarella, roasted peppers, and olives in a light vinaigrette.¶

*→*Veal Chop* - Mesquite grilled with mushrooms.¶

Remember that bulleted lists do not show any order of importance within the list; everything is equally important. Numbered lists, on the other hand, show a priority of importance and should be used, for example, when listing steps in a recipe.

Hanging indents are also used to create numbered lists, which should be used when order is important. The following recipe is an example of a numbered list created with a hanging indent:

1. Pour chicken broth into saucepan and bring to a boil.
2. Add noodles and cook for 5-7 minutes, stirring occasionally.
3. Reduce heat and add chicken chunks. Let simmer for 3-4 minutes.
4. Serve immediately with crackers.

Numbers are used as the "bullets" for this recipe because each step logically follows the previous one. If the noodles were added first, for example, they would probably burn in the bottom of the saucepan, ruining a potentially great supper!

• ◆

Practice 7

In this Practice you will create a hanging indent and a bulleted list in the course description of IVYPROMO. Start Works and open IVYPROMO if you have not already done so.

1) SCROLL TO THE COURSE DESCRIPTIONS

Scroll to the course descriptions and place the cursor in the paragraph describing course 101, which begins "A comprehensive survey . . .".

2) SET LEFT AND RIGHT INDENTS

a. From the Format menu, select Indents & Spacing.
b. Type .75 for the **Left indent** and .25 for the **Right indent**.
c. Select OK to apply the indents. Notice how the paragraph is indented to .75 inch on the left and .25 inches on the right.

3) CREATE THE HANGING INDENT

a. With the cursor in the same paragraph, execute the Indents & Spacing command again.

b. Type - . 5 in the **1st line indent** box. This causes the left indent to be reduced by one half inch for the first line only.

c. Select OK to apply the new indent options. Note how the first line indent is changed: the first line hangs to the left of the rest of the indented paragraph. The first lined indent marker (|) is shown on the Ruler.

4) ADD THE BULLET

a. Move the cursor to the first character in the current paragraph, the "A" in "A comprehensive survey . . .".

b. Type an asterisk (*) to act as the bullet.

c. The bullet must be separated from the first word in the paragraph. Press the Tab key to insert a tab between the bullet and the "A". This aligns the text in the first line with the rest of the indented paragraph. The course description paragraph is now a bulleted list.

Check - Your course description should be similar to:

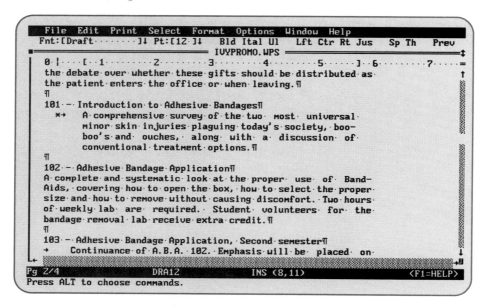

5) BULLET THE NEXT COURSE DESCRIPTION

a. Place the cursor in the paragraph describing course 102, which begins "A complete and systematic . . .".

b. Using the Indents & Spacing command, set a **Left indent** of .75, a **1st line indent** of -.5, and a **Right indent** of .25.

c. At the beginning of the paragraph, type an asterisk for the bullet, and then press Tab to realign the text. The course description for 102 now has the same format as course 101.

6) SAVE THE MODIFIED FILE

Save the file. The new hanging indent and bulleted course descriptions will be retained in the document.

An Introduction to Computing Using Microsoft Works

4.10 Shortcuts for Setting Indents

Creating indents and bulleted lists becomes much easier and faster when you learn the shortcut keys that Works has included. For example, to quickly create an indented or "nested" paragraph, simply place the cursor in the desired paragraph and press Ctrl-N (the "N" stands for "nested"). To quickly set a hanging indent, position the cursor and press Ctrl-H ("H" for hanging). A bullet can then be added to the paragraph if desired.

These commands are very useful for creating outlines and similar lists because each time they are executed, the amount of the indent is increased. For example, the first time Ctrl-N is pressed, the left indent is set to 0.5". Pressing Ctrl-N again in the same paragraph increases the indent to 1".

To undo a nested or hanging indent one level, press Ctrl-M or Ctrl-G respectively. Indenting short-cuts are summarized below:

To Create	Press	To Undo
Nested indent	Ctrl-N	Ctrl-M
Hanging indent	Ctrl-H	Ctrl-G

To remove all indents, simply select the Normal Paragraph command from the Format menu (Alt-T N).

• •

Practice 8

In this Practice you will use Control key shortcuts to create hanging indents and bulleted lists. Start Works and open IVYPROMO if you have not already done so.

1) CREATE A NESTED INDENT USING SHORTCUTS

a. Place the cursor in the course description paragraph for course 103, which begins "Continuance of . . .".
b. Press Ctrl-N. The paragraph is indented by .5 inches on the left. Note the position of the left indent marker in the Ruler.
c. Press Ctrl-N again. The left indent in increased by .5 inches to 1 inch.
d. Press Ctrl-N a third time. The indent in increased to 1.5 inches.
e. We would like to "un-nest" the indent by one level. Press Ctrl-M. The left indent is reduced by .5 inches to 1 inch.

2) REMOVE THE INDENT

From the Format menu, select the Normal Paragraph command. All indents are removed from the paragraph.

3) CREATE THE HANGING INDENT

a. With the cursor in the same paragraph, press Ctrl-H. A hanging indent is created with the left indent set to .5 inch and the first line indent to -.5. Note the markers on the Ruler showing the first line (|) and left ([ ) indents.
b. Place the cursor on the first character in the description and type an asterisk (*).

c. Type a tab to separate the bullet from the rest of the text.

d. Repeat parts (a) through (c) for each of the remaining course descriptions.

4) SAVE THE MODIFIED FILE

Save the file. The course descriptions are now bulleted lists created with a hanging indent.

<u>Check</u> - Your course descriptions should be similar to:

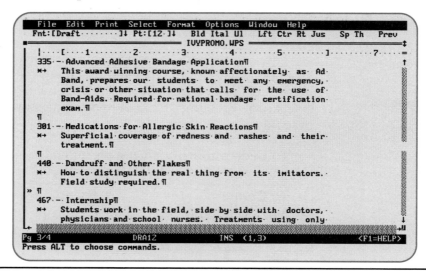

4.11 Creating Footnotes

A footnote is a reference to another document. Research papers and reports often require the use of footnotes to identify reference sources. Creating footnotes in Works is easy using the Footnote command from the Edit menu. Selecting Footnote creates a footnote reference at the current cursor position. Works allows you to choose between a numbered footnote and one indicated by a character marker:

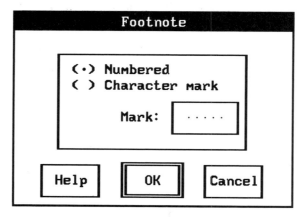

The Footnote dialog box

Numbered is the most common option. When OK is selected, Works displays a small window identified as "FOOTNOTES" at the bottom of the screen:

4

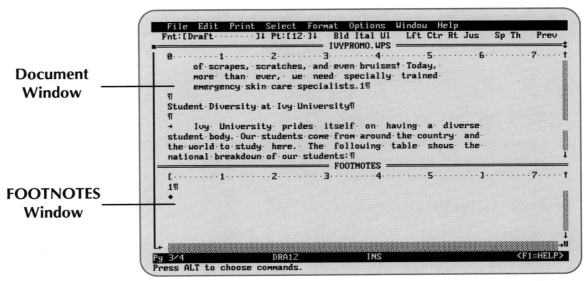

Document Window

FOOTNOTES Window

The FOOTNOTES window is split along the bottom of the document

The footnote number is automatically shown in both the FOOTNOTES window and the text. Appropriate information for this footnote is then entered in the FOOTNOTES window. All of the commands you have learned so far, such as formatting, spell checking, and the thesaurus may be used in this window.

Pressing the F6 key returns the cursor to the document. Both the text and the FOOTNOTES window will still be shown. F6 again returns the cursor to the FOOTNOTES window. Mouse users can simply click in the desired window to place the cursor.

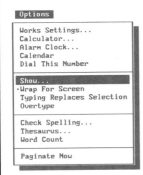

To remove the FOOTNOTES window, use the Show command from the Options menu and turn off the **Show Footnotes** option. Any previously created footnotes are not erased by this; the FOOTNOTES window is only hidden and may be displayed again with the Show command.

Works automatically places and maintains the footnote numbers — Works will renumber any moved, copied, or new footnote. To delete a footnote place the cursor on the footnote number in the text and press the Delete key. Works eliminates the footnote reference from the FOOT-NOTES window and automatically renumbers any remaining footnotes. After adding or changing a footnote, the document must be saved to make the change permanent.

In Works, the footnotes you create can be printed at the bottom of the page on which the reference occurs, or all footnotes may be printed together at the end of the document. These options will be described after the following Practice.

In this Practice you will create a footnote. Start Works and open IVYPROMO if you have not already done so.

1) LOCATE THE TEXT TO FOOTNOTE

The quote by Dr. Itchee in the Faculty description (located below the course descriptions) was previously printed in another document and needs to be properly referenced. Place the cursor at the end of the quote, just after "skin care specialists."

2) EXECUTE THE FOOTNOTE COMMAND

a. From the Edit menu, select the Footnote command.
b. Select **Numbered**. Works opens the FOOTNOTES window where the footnote text will be entered. Note the "1" in the FOOTNOTES window. This indicates that the text that you will type is for the first footnote in this document.

3) ENTER THE FOOTNOTE TEXT

Type the following text:

```
Dr. Phineas Itchee, "Keynote Address," 15th Annual RASH
Regional Conference Proceedings, June, 1993, p. 17.
```

4) FORMAT THE FOOTNOTE TEXT

a. In the footnote, highlight the section of text which reads "15th Annual RASH Regional Conference Proceedings."
b. Because this is a title, we will underline it. From the Format menu, select Underline. The title is underlined.
c. Highlight the "th" in "15th."
d. From the Format menu, select the Font & Style command and make this text **Superscript**.

5) SWITCH BETWEEN THE FOOTNOTES WINDOW AND DOCUMENT

a. Press F 6. The cursor jumps back into the document. If it is not currently visible, scroll to the end of the quote. Note the superscript "1" that Works has placed at the end of the quote.
b. Press F 6 again. The cursor returns to the FOOTNOTES window.
c. From the Options menu, select the Show command. A dialog box is displayed. Note that **Show Footnotes** is currently selected.
d. Select **Show Footnotes**, turning this option off, and OK. The FOOTNOTES window is removed from the screen.

6) SAVE THE DOCUMENT

To store the footnote with the document, the file must be saved. From the File menu, select the Save command. The document, with footnote added, is saved on disk.

7) PREVIEW THE DOCUMENT

a. From the Print menu, select the Preview command. A Preview of the document is shown.
b. If it is not already, scroll the preview screen to display the page with the quote. Note the footnote at the bottom of the page, and how it is separated from the text by a short underline.
c. Press Escape to return to the Word Processor screen.

4.12 Editing Footnotes

Sometimes it is necessary to change a footnote's information. The **Show Footnotes** option of the Show command controls the display of the FOOTNOTES window. (If no footnotes have been created, this option is unavailable.) Once the cursor is inside the FOOTNOTES window all formatting and editing commands may be used.

A long document may have dozens of footnotes, making it difficult to locate the desired footnote text in the small FOOTNOTES window. Works always keeps the footnotes in order, so it is easy to scroll to the appropriate footnote. Additionally, it is possible to use the Search command while in the FOOTNOTES window to locate the footnote number or another piece of related text.

4.13 Footnote Options

When printing a document with footnotes, Works can print the footnotes at the bottom of each page, or all footnotes can be printed at the document's end (endnotes). This option is controlled using the Page Setup & Margins command from the Print menu:

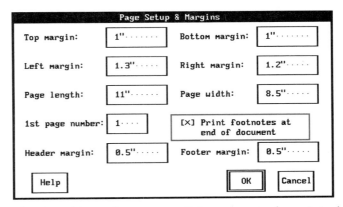

Selecting this option cause all footnotes to be printed at the end of the document

When the **Print footnotes at end of document** option is selected, all of the footnotes will be printed after the last line in the document. If you wish to have the footnotes start on a separate page, make the last character in the document a manual page break (Ctrl-Enter).

In this Practice you will change the footnote options and view the document. Start Works and open the IVYPROMO document if you have not already done so.

1)   DISPLAY THE FOOTNOTES WINDOW

    a.   From the Options menu, select the Show command. Note that **Show Footnotes** is currently not selected.

    b.   Select **Show Footnotes**, turning this option on, and OK. The FOOTNOTES window is displayed on the screen.

2)   EDIT THE FOOTNOTE

    a.   Press F6 to place the cursor in the FOOTNOTES window.

    b.   The first line of our footnote needs to be indented one half inch. To do this, from the Format menu, select the Indents & Spacing command.

    c.   Create a .5 inch **1st line indent** for the footnote.

    d.   Using the Show command, close the FOOTNOTES window.

3)   SET THE FOOTNOTES OPTION TO END OF DOCUMENT

    a.   From the Print menu, select the Page Setup & Margins command. The dialog box is displayed.

    b.   Select the **Print footnotes at end of document** option.

    c.   Select OK to accept the options and return to the document.

4)   PREVIEW THE PAGE WITH THE FOOTNOTE

    a.   From the Print menu, select the Preview command and view the document. Scroll to the last page of the document and note the positioning of the footnote.

    b.   Press Escape to cancel the preview and return to the document.

5)   ADD A MANUAL PAGE BREAK AND TITLE

    a.   Move the cursor to the last character in the document.

    b.   Press Ctrl-Enter to create a manual page break. A dotted line is shown across the screen.

    c.   Type the title References and press Enter.

    d.   Make the title centered and bold.

6)   SAVE THE DOCUMENT

7)   PRINT THE DOCUMENT

    a.   From the Print menu, select the Print command and print a copy of the entire document. Note how the footnote is printed at the end of the document.

    b.   From the Print menu, select the Page Setup & Margins command. Turn off the **Print footnotes at end of document** option.

    c.   Using the Print command, print only page 3. The footnote is again printed at the bottom of the page.

8)   EDIT AND SAVE THE MODIFIED DOCUMENT

    a.   Because the document again has footnotes, the endnote title created in step 5 needs to be removed. At the very end of the document, delete the "References" title and manual page break.

    b.   Save the modified file.

4.14 Word Count

Works has a Word Count feature that journalists and desktop publishers will find useful when "writing for space" — writing to fill a precise amount of newspaper or publication space. Students may use this command to determine if an assignment meets the required number of words. Selecting the Word Count command from the Options menu displays the number of words in the current document:

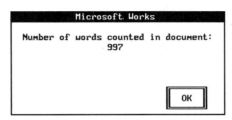

The Word Count dialog box

Any text in a header or footer is ignored and not counted. Footnote text, however, is counted and will be included in the total.

Works can also be told to count the words in a portion of the current document. Simply highlight the section to be counted, and then execute the Word Count command. Works indicates whether the words counted are "in selection" or "in document."

4.15 Time Stamping Files

Many of the commands in this chapter are designed to be most useful when working with longer documents. It is expected that such documents will go through many different drafts and revisions, and it can be difficult to keep track of the most current version, especially after the document has been printed. One way keep track of document revisions is to "time stamp" a file by including the current date, time, and file name in the file. That way, when referring to a printed copy, it is easy to determine if it is the most current version or not.

Works provides an easy way to time stamp a document using the Insert Special Character command from the Edit menu:

The Insert Special Character dialog box

When selected, each option inserts a marker that is replaced by the actual information when the document is printed. For example, selecting **Print date** inserts the marker `*date*` at the cursor position, and **Print time** inserts `*time*`. The markers are replaced by the current date and time (as read from the system clock) on the printed copy. For example, the markers

```
*date* *time*
```

might print as:

```
6/27/93   8:35 PM
```

The date and time markers are not composed of separate characters, but instead are really just placeholders for the actual current date and time. Works treats each inserted marker as a single character. Each time the file is printed, Works checks the system clock and prints the current date and time.

Placing the time stamp in the header or footer is even better, because the information then appears on each printed page. Just as &P in a header or footer printed the page number, the following characters may also be used:

&D	Print current date
&T	Print current time
&F	Print file name

● ●

Practice 11

In this Practice you will use Word Count to determine the number of words in the promotional file and add a time stamp to the document's header. Start Works if you have not already done so and open the IVYPROMO file.

1) EXECUTE THE WORD COUNT COMMAND

   a. We want to count the words in the entire document, so make certain that no text is highlighted.
   b. From the Options menu, select the Word Count command. Works performs the necessary calculations and displays the word count in a dialog box. How many words are there in your document?   *1004*
   c. Select OK to continue.

2) INSERT THE DATE AND TIME IN THE HEADER

   a. From the Print menu, select the Headers & Footers command. The header, created in Chapter Three, appears.
   b. Place the cursor at the far left of the header.
   c. Type &D to have Works print the date.
   d. Type a space to separate the date and time.
   e. Type &T and a space to have Works print the time.
   f. Select OK to apply the updated header.

3) DEMONSTRATE HOW THE TIME STAMP IS UPDATED

The date and time "time stamps" will be updated each time the document is printed. Using the Print command, print a copy of page 1 only. Retrieve the printout and note the time printed in the header.

4) SAVE AND CLOSE THE MODIFIED FILE

4.16 Adding Pictures

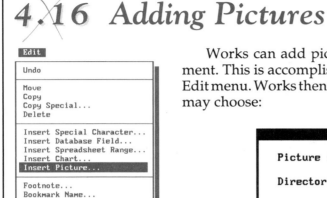

Works can add pictures or "graphics" to a word processed document. This is accomplished using the Insert Picture command from the Edit menu. Works then displays a list of existing pictures from which you may choose:

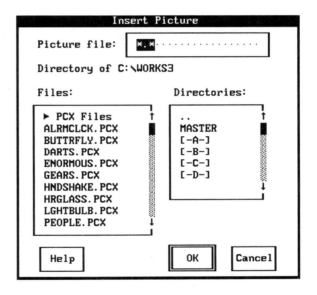

Each of the files listed in the Insert Picture dialog box contains a graphic

Highlighting a picture name and selecting OK places a marker at the current cursor location showing the name of the selected picture file. When printed or previewed, this marker is replaced by the actual picture (similar to the date and time markers described earlier). Pictures can be used for a variety of different purposes: decorative art, technical diagrams, company logos, etc.

It is important to realize that Works cannot create pictures such as these, only print them. A picture must already exist in a file for Works to use it. Pictures are created using special drawing programs and saved in a file the same way that Works creates word processed documents and saves them in files. More information about computer graphics and their creation and use is given in Chapter Thirteen.

In this Practice you will insert a picture into a document. Start Works if you have not already done so.

1) OPEN AND EDIT THE FAX DOCUMENT

a. From the File menu, use the Open Existing File command to open the file named FAX. This is the cover sheet for a fax.
b. Type your name on the TO line and your phone number on the PHONE line.

2) POSITION THE CURSOR

One of the most common uses for pictures is in company logos and letterheads. We will add a logo to this document. Move the cursor to the very beginning of the file.

3) INSERT THE PICTURE

a. From the Edit menu, select the Insert Picture command. A list of available picture files is displayed.
b. Highlight the file named ENORMOUS.PCX and select OK. A marker is inserted into the document:

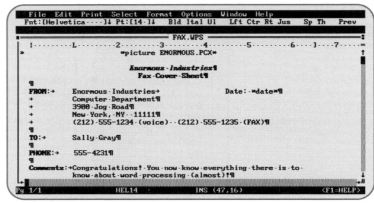

4) SAVE AND PREVIEW THE DOCUMENT

a. Save the modified file.
b. From the Print menu, select the Preview command to see the actual graphic.

4.17 Modifying Pictures

Once the picture has been inserted, it can be modified in various ways using the Picture command from the Format menu:

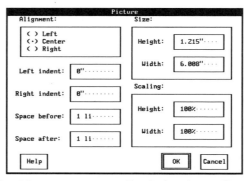

The Picture command's dialog box allows an inserted picture to be changed

An Introduction to Computing Using Microsoft Works

4

The Picture command is only available when the cursor in on a picture marker. (Normally, this position in the menu is the Indents & Spacing command.) This is an example of Works' "smart menus" — Works will sometimes alter the commands in a menu based on what it determines are your current needs. This saves space in the menu and makes Works easier to use.

The most common operation is to change the size of a picture. Works can do this in two ways, either by giving the exact **Size** of the graphic or specifying a percentage to expand (or reduce) the picture by in the **Scaling** boxes. Note that for both options a **Height** and a **Width** may be specified. Works can also change the **Alignment** of a picture and the amount of blank space around it.

Practice 13

In this Practice you will modify the picture inserted in the last Practice. Start Works and open FAX if you have not already done so.

1)   SELECT THE PICTURE COMMAND

a.   Move the cursor off of the picture marker.

b.   Display the Format menu. Note the Indents & Spacing command. Press Escape to remove the menu.

c.   Move the cursor onto the picture marker and display the Format menu again. The Indents & Spacing command has been replaced by the Picture command.

d.   Select the Picture command to display the dialog box.

2)   CHANGE THE SCALING

a.   Reduce the width by one half by moving the cursor to the Width box in the **Scaling** option and typing 50. (50% is one half.)

b.   Select OK.

c.   Use the Preview command to preview the modified picture. The picture is now half as wide but still the same height. Press Escape to return to the word processor screen.

3)   CHANGE THE SIZE

a.   From the Format menu, select the Picture command.

b.   In the Size box, change the **Height** to 3 inches and select OK.

c.   Preview the document. The picture is now half as wide but almost 3 times as tall. Press Escape to return to the word processor screen.

4)   RESTORE THE PICTURE

a.   From the Format menu, select the Picture command.

b.   In the Scaling box, change the **Height** to 100 percent and the **Width** to 100 percent. This restores the picture to its original height and width.

5)   SAVE AND PRINT THE DOCUMENT

a.   Save the document. The next time FAX is opened the picture will be present.

b.   Print a copy of the document. Note the graphic, and how today's date is printed because of the *date* marker.

c.   From the File menu, select Exit to quit Works.

4.18 Where can you go from here?

These last three chapters have introduced you to the concepts of Word Processing. You can now create, edit, format, and print word processed documents using Works. Later in this text you will learn how to integrate charts in a document and produce personalized form letters. Works has several other word processing options that you may wish to learn about. The best place to begin is by reading the Word Processor sections of the Works manual supplied by Microsoft.

For many people, the ability to word process justifies the expense of purchasing a personal computer. There are dozens of different word processing programs available, some of which have options and features not included in Works. Three of the more popular packages are Microsoft Word, WordStar, and WordPerfect. Because you have learned how to use the Works word processor, you will easily be able to learn and use another program such as the ones listed above. Word processing is a valuable skill, not only for school work but in your personal and professional life as well.

Chapter Summary

Blocks are highlighted sections of text created using the F 8 key or by dragging the mouse. Blocks may be deleted, moved or copied. To Move a block of text from one location within a document to another the block is highlighted, the Move command from the Edit menu executed, the cursor moved to the new location, and the Enter key pressed. To Copy a block of text so that it appears both at its original location and at a new location the above procedure is used except the Copy command rather than Move command selected. A block may be deleted by executing the Delete command from the Edit menu

The Search command from the Select menu allows a document to be searched for a particular combination of characters called the **Search for** text. To replace text in a document with different text the Replace command from the Select menu is executed. Both commands start their searches from the current cursor position. The cursor can be moved to the first character on any page with the Go To page command from the Select menu.

Two of the most powerful features of the Works Word Processor are the Spelling and Thesaurus commands, both in the Options menu. Spelling compares the words in the document to a dictionary file. If a word is found which is not in the file, Works can replace it with a suggested word or will allow you to type a correction. Thesaurus lists synonyms for a highlighted word, and then allows the word to be replaced with one of the synonyms.

It is possible to alter the width of the lines in a specific paragraph creating an "indent" using the Indents & Spacing command from the Format menu. It is also possible to create paragraphs with only a left or

4

right indent. A "hanging indent" has the first line of an indent hang out to the left over the lines below it. Bulleted lists are produced in this way.

Footnotes are created using the Footnote command from the Edit menu. The text for a footnote is entered in the FOOTNOTES window. Footnotes may be printed at the bottom of the page on which the reference occurs, or all the footnotes may be printed together at the end of a document.

Selecting the Word Count command from the Options menu displays the number of words in the current document. To keep track of document revisions a "time stamp" which includes the current date, time, and file name may be included in a document using the Insert Special Character command from the Edit menu, or by placing codes in the header or footer.

Works can add pictures or "graphics" to a document using the Insert Picture command from the Edit menu. Once a picture has been inserted, it can be modified using the Picture command from the Format menu.

● ●

Vocabulary

Block - A highlighted section of text which may contain anything from a single character to an entire document. Once highlighted, operations such as Copy and Move may be performed on the block or text formats applied.

Bulleted list - A list where each item is set off by a special symbol or character.

Check Spelling command - Checks the spelling of a document and offers suggestions to words not found in the Works dictionary file.

Copy command - Copies a highlighted block and places it in a new location without removing the text from its originally location.

Footnote - Reference to another document.

FOOTNOTES window - Window at the bottom of the word processor screen where footnote text is entered.

Go To command - Used to jump the cursor directly to the top of a specified page.

Hanging indent - First line of an indent which hangs out to the left over the lines below it.

Indent - Paragraph formatting option which increases the left or right margin.

Insert Picture command - Displays a list of existing pictures which may be chosen.

Move text - Removes a highlighted block from its current position and places it in a new one.

Picture command - Allows a picture within a document to be modified.

Replace command - The computer replaces one specified section of text with another.

Search command - The computer searches a document for specified text.

Search for text - Text entered by the user to be found or replaced.

Synonym - A word having a meaning that is the same or nearly the same as that of another word.

Thesaurus command - Lists words with similar meanings (synonyms) for a highlighted word.

Time stamp - A line in a document that contains the current date, time, or file name.

Word Count command - Displays the number of words in a document.

Sections 4.1 - 4.5

1. a) What is meant by "moving" a block of text?
    b) List the steps required to move the second paragraph in a document to a point directly after the fourth paragraph.

2. a) What is meant by "copying" a block of text?
    b) What is the difference between moving and copying a block of text?

3. a) What is meant by searching for text?
    b) Give three examples where you might use the Search command.

4. List the steps required to find each location of the name "Judith Habersham" in a document.

5. In a search for the word "hat" how can you avoid finding the word "that"?

6. a) What is the Replace command used for?
    b) Give three examples where the Replace command might be used.

7. Why is it usually inadvisable to use the Replace All option of the Replace command?

Sections 4.6 - 4.13

8. a) Explain what steps must be taken to have Works check the spelling of a document starting from the beginning.
    b) What does Works do when it finds what it considers a spelling error?
    c) Is it possible that Works might indicate an error when a word is spelled correctly?

9. a) What is a thesaurus?
    b) What words might the Thesaurus command produce for the word "house"?

10. What is an indent and when might one be used?

11. List the steps needed to produce a left and right indent of 0.5".

12. Explain how a hanging indent of 0.3" can be created for the indent created in Review 11.

13. a) What is a footnote used for?
    b) List the steps needed to produce a numbered footnote.

14. If the FOOTNOTES window is currently closed, explain how to open it and make a correction to a footnote.

15. Footnotes may either be printed at the bottom of the page on which the reference occurs, or all footnotes printed together at the end of a document. Explain how needed to print footnotes in either location.

16. Explain how to display the number of words in a document.

17. What is a "time stamp" and what it is used for?

18. What steps must be taken to insert a picture into a document?

19. How can the size of a picture inserted into a document be increased?

Exercises

1. The file on your data disk named PARTY.WPS gives directions to a party, but the steps are listed out of order. Use the Move command to place the directions in proper order. Save the modified file and print a copy.

2. The Copy command is useful when text must be repeated in a document.

   a) Use the Copy command to create a file called MYNAME which contains your name 50 times, each on a separate line. Consider copying a block with more than 1 line.

   b) At the end of the file, use the Insert Special Character command to have Works print the current date and time.

   c) Create a header with your name left aligned and the name of the file right aligned.

   d) Save MYNAME and print it.

3. Bulleted lists can be very useful in making things stand out. Open NEWSTORY.WPS and make the following changes:

   a) Create bullets for the menu items as shown below:

       * Fruit cup or Lime sherbet
       * Roast Duck a l'Orange with Wild Rice stuffing
       * Garden salad
       * Double Chocolate Chip ice cream

   b) Use the Check Spelling command to check the spelling in the story, and make any corrections.

   c) In the last paragraph change the Left and Right indents to .5".

   d) Save and print the modified NEWSTORY file.

4. The research proposal you worked on in Chapter Three, Exercise 12 needs further refinement. Open RESEARCH.WPS and make the following changes:

   a) On page two of the proposal is a numbered list (1-3) that outlines the phases of the development of a computerized guide to be used by the study. Create hanging indents for these phases using the following table:

Indent	Measurement
Left indent	.75"
1st line indent	-.5"
Right indent	.75"

   b) Have Works check the spelling in the proposal, and make any necessary corrections.

c) Use the Search command to find the word *incalculable*. Replace it with a synonym by using the Thesaurus.

d) Replace all occurrences of Archaeological with Anthropological and all occurrences of Archaeology with Anthropology.

e) Locate the sentence which begins "Years two through ..." Move the entire sentence to its new location below phase 3. Separate the two paragraphs with a blank line.

f) Have Works count the number of words in the document and enter the following line at the end of the document: `Total number of words is <total>`. Replace *<total>* with the actual number of words.

g) Save and print the modified proposal.

5. The scientist's biography you worked on in Chapter Three, Exercise 10 needs to be refined. Open SCIENCE.WPS and make the following changes:

a) The biography you wrote contains at least two references to outside sources. Create proper footnotes for these references using the Footnote command.

b) Have Works check the spelling in the biography, and make any necessary corrections.

c) Use the Thesaurus to change three words you feel could be improved. Italicize these words.

d) Save and print the modified biography.

6. In Chapter Two, Exercise 5 you were asked to create a review of the latest movie, concert, or similar event that you attended. Open CRITIC.WPS and make the following changes:

a) The school newspaper needs to know that they are getting the most recent copy of your review. Have Works print the current date and time on the last line of the review.

b) Create Left and Right indents of .75" for the first and third paragraphs of your review.

c) Have Works check the spelling in the review, and make any necessary corrections.

d) Have Works count the number of words in the document and enter the following line at the end of the document: `Total number of words in article is <total>`. Replace *<total>* with the actual number of words.

e) Preview the article. Return to the Work area screen and correct any errors if necessary.

f) Save and print the modified review.

7. In Chapter Two, Exercise 4 you created a file that contained directions to a number of different places. Unfortunately, your cousin is having a hard time reading and following these directions. Open DIRECT.WPS and make the following changes:

a) Have Works check the spelling, and make any necessary corrections.

b)   Separate the directions into individual lettered steps and use hanging indents to make them easier to read. Create Left and Right indents at .75" and a 1st line indent at -.5". Use the following example as a guide:

Directions to Gargantuan Gulch:

    a.   Go South on Sibley Avenue until you come to a stop sign. Turn right.

    b.   After about one mile you will cross a bridge. Gargantuan Gulch will be on your left.

c)   Use the Insert Special Character command to insert the current date and time in the first line of the document.

d)   Preview the directions. Return to the Work area screen and correct any errors if necessary.

e)   Save and print the modified directions.

8.   In Chapter Three, Exercise 6 you modified a college application letter. Open APPLY.WPS and make the following changes:

a)   Replace all occurrences of the school's name with New Brunswick College.

b)   Have Works check the spelling, and make any necessary corrections.

c)   Because the college requires that application letters be at least 50 words in length, add a sentence at the bottom of the letter which indicates the actual number of words in the letter.

d)   Save and print the modified letter.

9.   The file on your data disk named COMPEDUC.WPS contains information about computers in education. Open this file and make the following changes:

a)   This document contains information to be presented at the Conference of American Education. Create a header with the conference name left aligned and the current date right aligned.

b)   Change the Left margin to .75" and the Right margin to .5".

c)   Change the Right and Left indents to .5" for the paragraph which begins "Computer programs have become..."

d)   Move the entire last section concerning Computer Usage (including the subtitle and table) to its new location after the indented paragraph. The section titled Lawrence Township Computer Usage should now be the third section of the document. Be sure each section is separated by a blank line.

e)   Preview the document. Return to the Work area and correct any errors if necessary.

f)   Save and print the modified document.

4

10. Using the flyer you designed in Chapter Three, Exercise 13 make the following changes to create a more effective selling tool. Open OPENFLYR.WPS and make the following changes:

   a) Have Works check the spelling, and make any necessary corrections.

   b) To make the flyer look more exciting, create right and left indents of .75" for each paragraph.

   c) The word "Item" in the inventory table is unsatisfactory. Replace it with a more descriptive word from the Thesaurus.

   d) The print shop that prints the flyers charges by the word. Insert a manual page break at the bottom of the flyer. Copy the name, address, and phone number of your store to the top of the new page and include a sentence that indicates the total number of words in the flyer.

   e) Save and print the modified letter.

11. Ivy University is launching a new campaign to attract students. The IVYPROMO.WPS file on your data disk contains a promotional advertisement for Ivy University. Open this file and make the following changes:

   a) Insert markers that will have Works print the current date and time at the very end of the document.

   b) Ivy's English department has pointed out that the term "A huge" is too informal to be used in this important document. Search for "huge" and then replace it with a more descriptive word from the Thesaurus.

   c) Create hanging indents for the list of faculty members of the Department of Minor Skin Injury and Disease. Make the Left and Right indents .5" and the 1st line indent -.25" for all faculty members.

   d) Aside from Dr. Itchee, two other faculty members have published works, Dr. McCleen and Dr. Scalp. Find their names on the faculty list and create the following footnotes for their works:

   > Dr. Chris Scalp, *You and Shampoo*, Pennington, NJ: Lawrenceville Press Inc., 1989, p. 114.
   > Dr. Holly McCleen, *How to Wash Your Face Vol. I-XV*, New York: Maple, Snow & Daughters Inc., 1991.

   e) Create a .5 inch left indent for both footnote references.

   f) Save and print the modified promotional advertisement.

12. In Chapter Three, Exercise 3 you assisted in the design of a flyer for the SuperSub store opening. Open SUPERSUB.WPS and make the following changes:

   a) Replace all occurrences of "best" with "greatest".

   b) Insert the following sentences below the paragraph which begins: "Lemonade isn't the only thing ...". Be sure to press Enter after each dessert.

Here are some of Nanny's favorites:

Pure Chocolate Dream Cream Pie with chocolate crust and fudge frosting.
New York Cheese Cake with bits of cream cheese, raspberries in syrup, and chocolate shavings.
Fresh Strawberry Pie on a graham cracker crust topped with whole straw-berries and homemade vanilla ice cream.

c) Create a bulleted list of the desserts. Use Left and Right indents of .75" and then use -.5" for the 1st line indent. Use an asterisk for the bullet character.

d) Italicize every capitalized word in the list of desserts.

e) The print shop that prints the flyers charges by the word. Insert a sentence at the bottom of the flyer which states how many words are in the flyer.

f) Save and print a copy of the modified file.

13. CityZoo needs more work done on the animal inventory you created for them in Chapter Three, Exercise 14. Open CITYZOO.WPS and make the following changes:

a) The Staff column should include the caretaker's name for each animal. Copy each staff member's name into the proper location for the remainder of the list.

b) The heading "Location" is not very descriptive. Replace it with a more descriptive name from the Thesaurus.

c) Scroll down to the bottom of the catalog and insert two blank lines. Then copy the title of the catalog and insert it at the bottom of the page. Under the title, enter the address and phone number of the zoo, and then center the four lines:

2323 Big Cat Bend
Long Boat Key, FL 33548
(555) CITY-ZOO or 248-9066

d) The zoo stores their catalog on a computer and is charged a storage fee for every word. Insert a sentence at the bottom of the document which states how many words are in the catalog.

e) Save, preview, and print a copy of the modified file.

Chapter Five

Introducing the Data Base

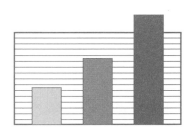

File - Create New File

File - Save

Print - Preview

Print - Print

Edit - Insert Line

Edit - Delete Line

Edit - Move Field

Format - Field Size

5

Objectives

After completing this chapter you will be able to:

1. Describe what a data base is.

2. Give examples of manual (non-computerized) and computerized data bases.

3. Describe common data base operations.

4. Explain why a computer is useful for manipulating a data base.

5. Define what records, fields, and entries are.

6. Plan and design a form for a computerized data base using appropriate field names.

7. Create a data base form using Works.

8. Preview, save, and print a data base form.

9. Modify a data base form.

5

This chapter provides an introduction to data bases and describes how they organize and store information. Specific tasks that are performed using a data base are covered as examples. Specialized terms that describe the operations and structure of a data base are defined. Attention is given not only to understanding what a data base is, but also to the planning and design considerations that make them more efficient and easy to use. This chapter also explains the step-by-step process of creating and modifying a data base, from paper and pencil sketches to computerized printouts.

Using Works, you will create, save, print, and modify a data base. Because a knowledge of data base concepts and terminology is required, it is important to thoroughly understand the material in this chapter before proceeding to the next.

5.1 What is a Data Base?

A data base is simply a group of related pieces of information. You are familiar with several different manual (non-computerized) data bases: the card catalog in a library, a recipe file box, an office "Rolodex" file for phone numbers, and a file cabinet storing a school's student records. These are all examples of data bases. Each item in a data base is related to each of the others in some way. For example, each card in a card catalog records information about a specific book in a library.

One way to think of a data base is as a collection of forms, each storing the same type of information. An example of such a form would be a card in a library's card catalog which stores the reference number, title, author, and publisher data for a single book:

University Card Catalog

Number: SP125

Title: Patchwork Quilts Through the Ages
Author: Dr. Rosey Greer
Published: Scrapwork Press, New Haven, CT, 1982

```
┌──────────────────────────────────────────────────────┐
│              University Card Catalog                    │
│                                                         │
│  Number: EP356                                          │
│                                                         │
│  Title: Trees and Their Furry Friends                   │
│  Author: Russell Fallenleaf                             │
│  Published: Redwood Publishing Co., Wauwau, WY, 1993    │
│                                                         │
└──────────────────────────────────────────────────────┘
```

Although they store data for different books, card catalog cards have the same format

Each card is organized so that the different pieces of information appear at the same locations. A book's reference number is in the upper-left corner, title on the first line of the card, author on the second line, and so on for every card in the catalog. A consistent design makes it easy for your eyes to pick out needed information when scanning through a stack of cards.

5.2 *Computerized Data Bases*

As you have discovered from using the word processor, the computer is a powerful tool for storing and manipulating information. The speed and storage capabilities of the computer make it an ideal tool for managing large amounts of information in the form of data bases.

Today almost all businesses and organizations use computer data bases in some way. A data base can be used by a bank to store the account information of its depositors or by a school to store student records. Department and grocery stores keep track of the different items they have for sale, their prices, and how many of each are in stock in a computer data base. The size of such data bases can become very large. A major advantage of using a computer is its ability to search through a large data base for a specific piece of information in a very short amount of time. In addition, because the computer can store information about thousands of items on a small disk, the amount of space needed to store a large data base is substantially reduced.

Computerized data bases can be used to organize information about virtually any area of knowledge: agriculture, biology, education, law, medicine, economics, and more. It is even possible to have a data base which stores information about other data bases. Any information that can be stored in a list or on individual forms can be put into a data base. Governments maintain thousands of computer data bases with information ranging from births and deaths to taxes. Many historians refer to our present time as the "Information Age" primarily because of the ability computers and data bases have given us to store and manipulate huge amounts of information. Clearly then, because data bases are becoming more important to the world in which we live, it is increasingly necessary to learn what they are and how to use them.

5.3 Data Base Terminology

Like the documents produced by the word processor, the information in a computer data base is stored on disk in a file. A data base file has its own unique structure and differs from a word processor file or a file for some other application. Information on a single item in a data base is called a "record." For example, the catalog card for *Patchwork Quilts Through the Ages* could be thought of as a single record which is different from the record or card for any other book. A data base file, therefore, is a collection of related records. In Works, up to 32,000 records may be stored in a single data base file.

Information within a record is separated into "fields." Author, title, and reference number are three separate fields in a single catalog card record. It is important to note that each record in a data base has the same fields, but that the data stored in each field differs from record to record. For example, in the card catalog, each card has a place for a reference number, title, author's name, etc., but no two cards have the same reference number. The order and placement of fields in a record is called a "form."

The data stored in an individual field in a single record is called an "entry." For example, in the card catalog, *Author* is a field; a place for an author's name appears in each record. *Rosey Greer* is an entry, the author of a specific book. It is important to remember that each record in a data base contains the same fields, but different entries.

Naturally, the size of a record depends on the number of fields it contains. It is not uncommon for a record to have as few as two fields, such as a name and phone number. On the other hand, large business or scientific data bases may contain hundreds of fields in each record. In Works, each record may contain up to 256 fields. The following diagram shows the differences between a record, field, and entry using the card catalog as an example:

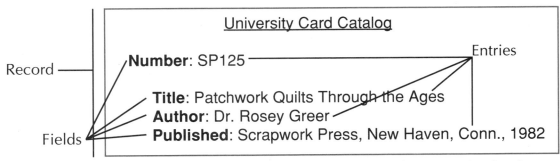

A record contains all the information for a single item in the data base

5.4 Creating a New Data Base

To create a new Works data base, DOS is booted and Works started as described in Chapter Two. The **Create a New File** option is selected from the Quick Start dialog box to display the Create New File dialog box. **Database** is then selected to display a blank data base form:

Menu bar

Toolbar

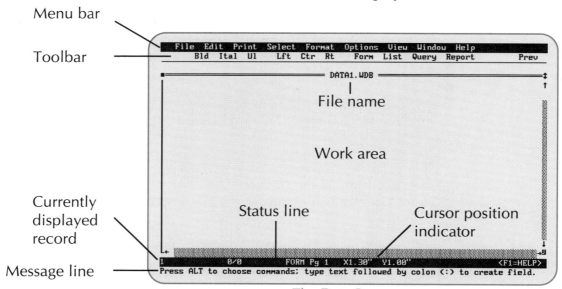

File name

Work area

Currently
displayed
record

Status line

Cursor position
indicator

Message line

The Data Base screen

The layout of the data base screen is very similar to the word processor screen, containing the Menu bar, Tool bar, file name, and Message and Status lines. Included on the Status line is the number of the record currently displayed, the total number of records in the data base, and the cursor position. Cursor position is expressed by X and Y coordinates, with X corresponding to horizontal positioning in inches from the left margin, and Y to vertical positioning in inches from the top margin. For example, the position X2.20" Y4.50" indicates that the cursor is 2.20 inches from the left edge of the page and 4.50 inches from the top. The name, width, and placement of each field in the data base are determined on this screen.

5.5 Using Labels in Forms

It is possible to include labels in a data base form. Labels are text that can be used as titles to identify a form, or to give added information concerning a specific field. For example, the following labels could act as titles for data bases: Store Inventory, Class Members, Pete's Addresses, Mega Music Customer Mailing List, etc..

Labels can be used to clarify a field name or give added information concerning an entry, but are not part of the field name. For example, the label (Y for Yes, N for No) positioned next to the Paid field in the example below tells the entry person to only type Y or N in the field:

5

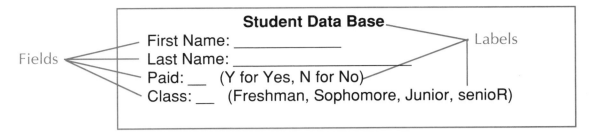

By only entering one letter, the risk of typographical errors is reduced, while speed and efficiency is increased.

To create a label, the cursor is first placed in the desired position on the screen. Then, the label text is typed, and Enter pressed. Labels can be deleted by placing the cursor on the desired label and selecting Delete Label from the Edit menu. Works then removes the unwanted label from the form.

5.6 *Saving a Data Base on Disk*

Executing the Save command from the File menu saves the current data base in a file on disk. Works uses the extension .WDB to indicate data base file names. When a data base is saved, a copy of each of the records currently in the computer's memory is made on disk. Once a file has been saved, it may be Opened later and the data stored in it displayed, printed, or changed. It is important to periodically save a data base when it is being worked on so that, should an accident such as a power failure occur, it would be possible to recover the file from the disk. After it has been saved, the file should be closed if it is no longer needed by selecting the Close command from the File menu.

● ◆

Practice 1

In this Practice you will create a new data base file, and place labels using the cursor position indicator. You will also delete unwanted labels.

1)   START WORKS AND CREATE A NEW FILE

   a.   Boot DOS and start Works as described in Chapter Two. The Quick Start dialog box is displayed.
   b.   From the Quick Start dialog box, select the **Create a New File** option. The Create New File dialog box is displayed. Select **Database** to display the blank data base form.
   c.   Note the locations of the Menu bar, Tool bar, file name, and the Message and Status lines. Also note the record number indicating the record currently displayed, the total number of records in the data base, and the cursor position indicator, all located on the Status line.

2)   USE THE CURSOR POSITION INDICATOR

   a.   Notice that the cursor position indicator reads X1.30" Y1.00", meaning that it is 1.3 inches from the left side of the page and 1 inch down. These numbers reflect Work's default margin settings of 1 inch at the top and 1.3 inches on the left.
   b.   Using the arrow keys or the mouse, move the cursor to X1.30" Y3.83". Which part of the screen is the cursor at now?

c. Press right-arrow seven times and up-arrow seven times. Notice how the cursor position indicator reflects the change each time the arrow key is pressed. The cursor position indicator should now read X2.00" Y2.67".

3) PLACE A TITLE LABEL ONTO THE FORM

a. Using the cursor position indicator, place the cursor at X2.90" Y1.00".
b. Type the label Student Data Base and press Enter. Note that the label also appears on the Formula line. This title will appear on all the records in the data base.
c. Move the cursor to X6.40" Y3.67" and enter: Right-hand side
d. Move the cursor to X1.40" Y3.50" and enter: Left-hand side

Check: Your screen should be similar to:

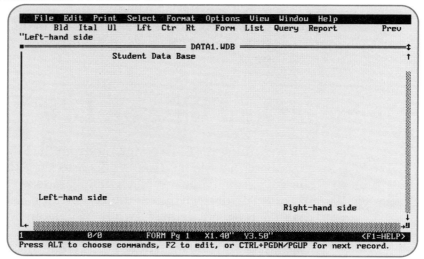

4) DELETE THE CORNER LABELS

a. Place the cursor on the Right-hand side label and notice the width of the cursor. Press up-arrow and down-arrow several times. The width of the cursor changes depending on whether or not it is on a label. When on the label, the label is shown on the Formula line.
b. From the Edit menu, select the Delete Label command to remove the label from the form.
c. Place the cursor on Left-hand side. Press the Delete key and then Enter to remove the label from the form. The title Student Data Base should be the only label on the screen.

5) SAVE THE NEW DATA BASE

a. From the File menu, select the Save command to display the dialog box.
b. Type the new name of the data base file, STUDENT, and select OK to save the file. The present form is saved on disk.

5.7 A Simple Data Base

To review what has been discussed so far, let us look at the manual system currently used by Ivy University to record student data. Each record currently uses the following form on paper:

```
Name:
Address:
Date Admitted:
GPA:
Tuition Paid:
```

All of the information above for a single student is considered to be a record. Each record contains five specific topics, or fields, which display information about each student. These fields are defined below by describing the information they store:

Name: Student's name.

Address: Student's school (dorm) address.

Date Admitted: Date the student was admitted to the University.

GPA: Stores the student's Grade Point Average on a scale from 0.0 to 4.0.

Tuition Paid: Whether or not the student has paid the tuition for this semester. To save space, a code of Y represents Yes and N represents No.

Here are sample records for three I.U. students:

```
Name: Matilda Rose
Address: 435 Frelinghuysen Hall
Date Admitted: 2/14/91
GPA: 3.4
Tuition Paid: Y
```

```
Name: Sam Adams
Address: 121 Carey Quadrangle
Date Admitted: 3/12/92
GPA: 1.5
Tuition Paid: N
```

```
Name: Roberta Poisson
Address: 8P Corwin Place
Date Admitted: 6/27/93
GPA: 4.0
Tuition Paid: N
```

Notice how each of the records has the same form containing the same fields, but that the entries differ from record to record. It is also possible for a record to have "empty" entries; that is, a field which does not yet store any data. As an example, when new students enroll they have no value for their GPA, so that field is left blank. When their first semester is over, their record may be updated and the new GPA value stored in the field.

5.8 Common Data Base Operations

Data bases become useful when *searching*, *querying*, *reporting*, and *sorting* operations can be performed on them. The power of a computerized data base is that these operations may be performed on large quantities of data very quickly.

Searching:

The simplest data base operation is the "search." When users search a data base, they ask the computer to locate the first record which contains some specific text, either a letter, number, word, or group of words. Each record in the data base is checked, starting from the first, to see if it contains the requested information in any of its fields. If it does, the cursor jumps to that field. Subsequent searches locate the next field containing the desired text until no fields can be found.

Search is limited because it locates any field that contains the search text. For example, asking Works to search for "5" in the three student records above will first locate the 5 in the Address field of Matilda Rose's record. On the next search it locates the 5 in the GPA field of Sam Adams' record.

Querying:

More powerful than searching is the Query which allows you to display all records which meet certain criteria. Criteria are conditions such as 'greater than' or 'not equal to' that can be applied to specific fields. For example, using the proper criteria it is possible to display only records which have 4.0 in the GPA field, or all students who were admitted between 5/1/94 and 5/16/94. Criteria can be joined together making complex conditions which limit the number of records displayed. This makes querying a powerful tool for gathering specific information from a large data base. Some example criteria are:

Which students are from Maine?
Show all students with the Last Name "Lee".
Show all students with a GPA less than 2.0 who were admitted before 1/1/92.

It should be obvious that a data base can only be queried for information that it stores in its records. That is, it would be impossible to search Ivy's student data base to determine the average rainfall in New Jersey because this involves asking the data base for information it does not store.

Reports:

Information taken from a data base is called a "report" and consists of data from specific records and fields. Reports can contain many pieces of data, or just one. For example, there may be hundreds of students from Maine, but Roberta Poisson has only one value for her current GPA. Reports generated with Works can contain titles and calculate totals, subtotals, and averages. Reports can also make use of formatting options such as bold or centered text as in the Word Processor. Reports may be printed on paper or displayed on the screen.

5

Reports can differ based on the person who is using them. Different reports may contain different information, or the same information in a different order. For example, the university's business department may need to have a report which includes the tuition paid information, but is probably not interested in the student's GPA. Chapter Seven explains how a Works data base report is designed and printed.

Placing records in a specific order is called "sorting." It is easier to locate specific information in a data base if the records are arranged in order based on the data stored in a specific field. In a student data base, it would be easier to search for a specific student's information if the records were ordered alphabetically by last name. To find Roberta Poisson's grade point average, for example, it would not be necessary to look at every record in the file, but to simply go directly to the name "Poisson." Reports are also easier to read and understand when the information presented is in logical order.

A sort is performed based on the entries stored in one field called the "key field" which is chosen by the user. When a data base is sorted, the position of a record in the file is changed based on the data stored in its key field. In the student records example above, the key field is the name field, so the records appear in order by name. When Works performs a sort, it has been programmed to know that the character "A" is less than "B" and that 1 is less than 2 and so on. If the key field is a date field, the data base knows that 1/1/94 comes before 6/27/94, etc. This is called chronological order. Here are the three student records sorted by date admitted:

Name: Matilda Rose
Address: 435 Frelinghuysen Hall
Date Admitted: 2/14/91
GPA: 3.4
Tuition Paid: Y

Name: Sam Adams
Address: 121 Carey Quadrangle
Date Admitted: 3/12/92
GPA: 1.5
Tuition Paid: N

Name: Roberta Poisson
Address: 8P Corwin Place
Date Admitted: 6/27/93
GPA: 4.0
Tuition Paid: N

A computer data base file can be easily sorted on different key fields as the need arises. One report may need the data ordered by last name, and another by GPA or admit date. Here are the same three student records sorted in descending order (high to low) by GPA:

Name: Roberta Poisson
Address: 8P Corwin Place
Date Admitted: 6/27/93
GPA: 4.0
Tuition Paid: N

Name: Matilda Rose
Address: 435 Frelinghuysen Hall
Date Admitted: 2/14/91
GPA: 3.4
Tuition Paid: Y

Name: Sam Adams
Address: 121 Carey Quadrangle
Date Admitted: 3/12/92
GPA: 1.5
Tuition Paid: N

In a computer data base, the records may be sorted quickly using any field as the key field because the information is stored in the computer's memory and not on paper forms. Sorting is often not possible in a manual data base without a large amount of work. For this reason most libraries must maintain two separate manual card catalogs to have their books listed by both author and subject, which often leads to errors, mis-filed cards, etc.

Libraries must maintain two separate manual card catalogs to have their records sorted by both title and subject

Modifying:

From time to time, data base files must be modified to be kept current: old information removed, outdated information updated, and new information added. At the end of each school year, Ivy must remove any graduating seniors from its student data base. This involves "deleting" certain records from the data base file. New GPAs must be calculated for the remaining students and placed in the GPA field. Changing the information stored in a field is called "updating" the file. Finally, the names and related data of any new students who have been accepted must be added to the file in new records.

A definite advantage of a computerized data base is the ease in which it may be modified. Like the Word Processor, changes made to a data base file can be made on the screen and stored electronically. When all of the desired changes have been made, the modified data base can be saved on disk for future use. A change to a manual data base would

An Introduction to Computing Using Microsoft Works

5

require that the appropriate record be located and then physically changed, either by using an eraser or by rewriting the information onto a new form.

Practice 2

In this Practice you will manually sort the three student records in the I.U. Student data base of Section 5.7. On a piece of paper list the records:

a. In alphabetical order according to last name.
b. In descending order according to the month of admission.
c. In alphabetical order based on tuition paid.

5.9 *Planning a Data Base*

A great deal of time and thought should go into the planning of a data base before it is created. Carefully planning a data base will save time and eliminate frustration later. Below are listed three important steps for planning a data base.

Steps for Planning a Data Base

1. Determine what data should be stored in each record. This is best accomplished by examining the needs of the different users of the data base. Start by creating a general list on paper of the data available. Eliminate any information that is not directly related to the overall purpose of the data base.

2. Examine the specific operations to be performed on the data base. Do the operations require any information that is missing from the current list? For example, will there be a need to separate the first name from the last? Is there a need for a complete mailing address or will a street address or phone number be enough? Make any changes required to the list produced in step 1.

3. Create a list of fields and field names using the list from step 2. Use this list to create a description of the data stored in the different fields, their types (character, numeric, date, etc.), and the operations performed with them. Sketch a sample form for a single record on paper.

In step 2, it is helpful to create examples of the reports that may be needed by sketching them on paper. This makes it easy to see what information is required by each report.

Careful planning requires information about both the user(s) of the data base and the operations that will be performed on it. Data base designers often spend a great deal of time talking to the user(s) of a proposed data base and analyzing their needs before making any decisions about fields, forms, reports, etc. It is also important to realize that most data bases are accessed by more than one user, each of whom has different requirements and will perform different operations. The time spent planning makes it easier for each user to get the fullest use from the information stored in the data base and avoids having to later make major modifications to the data base. Sketching sample forms and reports on paper helps to define the data base and shows where potential errors may occur. Only after the design has been checked by hand should the computer be used to actually create the data base.

5.10 Planning Records and Fields

The two most important questions when designing a data base are "What information should be stored?" and "What operations will be performed on that information?" Deciding what information to store depends on what the data base will be used for. A student data base would not contain any information about salaries or how many desks are in certain classrooms, only information that is directly related to the students.

Using the manual student data base described in Section 5.7, we will now prepare to computerize the records by following the steps explained above in Section 5.9. Each record in a student data base would probably contain the following fields at a minimum:

```
Student Name
Address
Date student was admitted
Current GPA
Has tuition been paid?
```

It is important to realize that each record stores all of the information above for a single student, and that the data base will contain one record for each student enrolled in the University.

Next, the operations performed on the data base should be considered. Ivy University keeps its student records in order by last name. So that the records may be sorted based on the last name only, two separate fields have to be created to store the student name — a first name field and a last name field:

```
First Name
Last Name
Address
Date student was admitted
Current GPA
Has tuition been paid?
```

Finally, the administration would like to be able to send warning letters to each student who has a low GPA. In order to use the data base to produce complete mailing labels, the address field must be expanded to include separate fields for a city, state, and zip code:

An Introduction to Computing Using Microsoft Works

5

```
First Name
Last Name
Street address
City
State
Zip code
Date student was admitted
Current GPA
Has tuition been paid?
```

Several problems have been avoided by carefully considering the uses for this data base before it is created. For example, the ability to have the computer produce mailing labels is a valuable asset to the users of the student data base. Had this not been planned for, a great deal of work would have to be done either to later modify the data base or to create some manual system for recording student addresses. Storing a complete student mailing address in separate fields allows the university to more fully use the power of the computer data base.

5.11 Choosing Field Names

Each field must have a distinct name to distinguish it from the other fields in a record. A well chosen field name describes the data stored in that field, making it easy to determine its use. Below are good examples of field names for the student record data base:

Data	Field name
First Name	`First Name:`
Last Name	`Last Name:`
Street address	`Address:`
City	`City:`
State	`State:`
Zip code	`Zip:`
Date student was admitted	`Admit Date:`
Current GPA	`GPA:`
Has tuition been paid?	`Paid:`

Avoid using numbers or symbols (1, #, @, *) as the first character in a field name of any type. Works may not recognize these characters and will display an error message when trying to perform different operations later. Use field names that are concise and informative and show some relationship to what should be entered. For example, the field name "Person" is too vague and does not convey the fact that the *name* of the person should be entered. Instead, a field name such as "Customer" or "Name" should be used.

Most computer data bases have a limit on the number of characters in a field name. Choosing the shortest possible name which accurately describes the contents of the field is therefore important. This is why the name Address rather than Street Address was chosen to represent the street address field. In general, a name of ten characters or less should be able to describe the data stored in any field. However, should it be required, Works allows up to 15 characters per field name, including spaces and punctuation marks. Works requires that each field name end with a colon (:) which is not counted as one of the 15 characters.

Practice 3

Mega Music, a national retail store that specializes in compact discs, cassette tapes, music videos, and other accessories, has hired you to computerize their customer mailing list. On a piece of paper, write appropriate field names for each of the categories below:

Customer name	Date of sale
Street address	Account number
City	Number of items purchased
State	How they paid for purchase
Zip code	What type of music they like
Male or female	Why purchased (gift, personal, work, etc.)

5.12 Form Design

The order and location in which the different fields appear in a record is called the "form." A form also includes the amount of space that each field has when displayed on the screen.

Similar to determining field names, it is also a good idea to draw a quick sketch of the general layout of the form on paper. On paper you can get a view of your form and decide the order and positioning of fields, titles, labels, etc. Group related fields together (like parts of an address) and place more important and frequently used fields first. As you become more experienced with the data base, you can include lines, boxes, and other special effects to give the form a more polished look.

Remember, careful planning beforehand can save you time and aggravation later. Adding and deleting fields at random can make the records a "hodgepodge" of data, limiting the usefulness of the data base, so take special care when planning the form.

Practice 4

In this Practice you will sketch six different form layouts for two data bases, Mega Music's customer list and Ivy University's student enrollment.

a. Mega Music liked your preliminary ideas on the contents of their customer data base done in the previous Practice, and now wants to see some of your ideas on form setup. Using the field names you created in Practice 3, sketch three different form layouts on the same piece of paper, experimenting with different field groupings, orders, and layouts.

b. Ivy University also wants you to computerize their student data base, but wants to see some examples first. Sketch three different form layouts using the fields supplied in Section 5.11.

An Introduction to Computing Using Microsoft Works

5.13 Field Types and Widths

Fields are classified by the type of data that they store. There are three basic field types in a computerized data base: character, numeric, and time/date. Character fields contain text while numeric fields contain only numbers (values). Character fields are unique in that they can include both text and digits together. For example, even though the address 7183 City View Avenue contains digits, Works interprets it as a character field because it contains both text and digits. This may occur in other examples such as product or part numbers (0934BF, 100-6, JB-23), abbreviations (6 ft 4 in, 6' 4", 32nd), telephone numbers (413-555-3699), and zip codes with four digit extensions (13090-3949). At Ivy University the name and address for each student are stored in character fields while grade point averages (GPA) are stored in numeric fields. Remember, if numbers are entered into a character field, Works interprets them as text and mathematical calculations cannot be applied.

In addition to character and numeric data, Works allows dates and times to be stored in fields. Dates are displayed in either long form (April 7, 1994) or short form (4/7/94). Times may be displayed in 24-hour form (14:30) or 12-hour form (2:30 PM). Seconds may also be shown (2:30:15 PM). Data stored in time/date fields may be used in calculations and will be explained further in Chapter Six. At Ivy University, the student's admission date is stored in a Date field.

Field width (or size) must also be determined when creating a form. Field width refers to the space adjacent to the field name where data for that field is entered. It is important to allow enough space for the data in order to create a neat, readable, organized form. The width of a field can be between 1 and 256 characters.

• •

Practice 5

In this Practice you will continue to plan the data bases for Mega Music and Ivy University by determining field types and widths for each of the forms you sketched in Practice 4. On the same piece of paper, write the correct field type and an appropriate field width next to each field name. Follow this example:

First Name: (15, Character)

5.14 Creating the Data Base Form

We will design a form for the Ivy University student data base. Each record stores the data for one student using the field names listed on the next page:

Field name	Data	Type	Width
First Name:	student's first name	character	13
Last Name:	student's last name	character	15
Address:	street address	character	21
City:	city	character	18
State:	state	character	2
Zip:	zip code	character	6
Admit Date:	date student admitted	time/date	9
GPA:	grade point average	numeric	4
Paid:	paid tuition bill? (Y or N)	character	1

The first step in creating a new data base is to enter the field names at the proper positions on the screen. It is important to place related fields next to each other so that the form is easier to use and understand. As an example, the field for the student's last name should be placed next to the field for the first name. Other fields that should be grouped together are Address, City, State, and Zip.

To create a form, the cursor is moved to the desired position on the screen and the field name typed, followed by a colon (:). Pressing the Enter key enters the field onto the form and displays a dialog box with a default field width (the space reserved to display the data) of 20 characters:

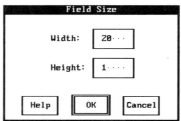

A field's width is entered in the Field Size dialog box

This width can be increased or decreased, or the default width can be accepted. The cursor is then positioned and the next field name entered. When the form is complete, it is ready to accept the data for the first record.

Practice 6

In this Practice you will create a form for the Ivy University student data base by entering field names on the Form screen. Start Works and open STUDENT.WDB if you have not already done so.

1) PLACE THE FIRST NAME FIELD ONTO THE FORM

a. Move the cursor to X1.30" Y1.17".
b. Type First Name: and press Enter to place the field onto the form at the current cursor position. The Field Size dialog box is displayed.
c. Type 13 and press Enter. The First Name field will now display up to 13 characters.

2) PLACE THE LAST NAME FIELD ONTO THE FORM

a. Position the cursor to the right of the First Name field at X4.30" Y1.17".
b. Type Last Name: and press Enter to place the field onto the form at the current position.
c. Enter 15 for the field width.

Check - Your screen should show the two fields and the title:

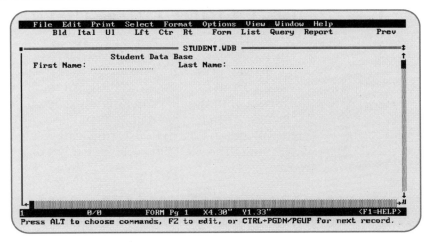

3) COMPLETE THE FORM BY ENTERING THE REST OF THE FIELDS

Next, the field for the address should be placed on the form. Using the steps described above, complete the record form by adding the rest of the fields exactly as shown in the table below. Remember to position the cursor before typing the field name.

Use the chart below to set each field's width:

Cursor Position	Field Name	Width
X1.30" Y1.33"	Address:	21
X1.30" Y1.50"	City:	18
X3.90" Y1.50"	State:	2
X1.30" Y1.67"	Zip:	6
X1.30" Y1.83"	Admit Date:	9
X1.30" Y2.00"	GPA:	4
X1.30" Y2.17"	Paid:	1

The form is now complete and record 1 is ready to accept data.

4) SAVE THE MODIFIED DATA BASE

From the File menu, select the Save command to save the STUDENT data base.

Check - Your form should be similar to:

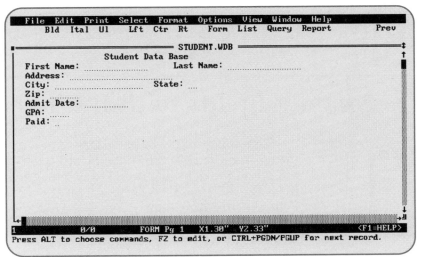

5.15 Printing a Data Base Form

After you have entered the field names and widths into the data base, you can print a copy of the form. Before actually printing, it is a good idea to choose Print Preview from the Print menu to get a miniature view of the layout of the page. Print Preview gives a good idea of what the form looks like when it is printed and enables you to make any final changes before printing. To print the form, Print is selected from the Print menu, displaying the dialog box. Selecting **Print** prints the currently displayed record.

●●

Practice 7

In this Practice you will preview the layout of the STUDENT data base using Preview from the Print menu. You will then print a copy of the form. Start Works and open STUDENT.WDB if you have not already done so.

1) PREVIEW THE DATA BASE FORM

Select Preview from the Print menu and select Preview to view the data base form. Note the overall layout of the form. Will this form be easy to use? Are the fields organized logically and thoughtfully? Press Escape to return to the form.

2) PRINT THE DATA BASE FORM

From the Print menu, select the Print command and print a copy of the STUDENT data base form.

5.16 Inserting and Deleting Lines in a Form

Sometimes blank lines need to added to a form to help create a more polished and organized look. Likewise, blank lines may have to be deleted from a data base form. A blank line can be inserted at the current cursor position using the Insert Line command from the Edit menu. A blank line can be deleted by positioning the cursor on the line that needs to be removed and then selecting Delete Line from the Edit menu. Works removes the line and moves everything below the cursor up one line. Note that a line cannot be deleted if it contains a field or a label

5.17 Moving Fields within a Form

Sometimes it may be necessary to move fields within a form due to the addition or deletion of fields, etc. To accomplish this, the cursor is placed on the field that needs to be moved, and Move Field is selected from the Edit menu. The word MOVE is shown on the Status line. Following the directions given on the Message line, the cursor is moved to the new position in the form and Enter pressed. The field name is moved and is ready to accept data in its new position.

5

Practice 8

In this Practice you will insert blank lines and move fields in the STUDENT data base file. Start Works and open STUDENT.WDB if you have not already done so.

1) INSERT BLANK LINES

a. The data base title needs to be set apart from the rest of the form. Place the cursor on the line containing the field "First Name" and from the Edit menu, select the Insert Line command. A blank line now separates the title from the rest of the form.

b. Place the cursor on the line containing the field "Admit date" and from the Edit menu, select the Insert Line command. The form is now separated into two distinct groupings of information: personal and academic.

2) MOVE THE ZIP FIELD

Place the cursor on the Zip field, and from the Edit menu select the Move Field command. Notice the word MOVE appears on the Status line and instructions are given on the Message line. Move the cursor to the field's new location, X5.20" Y1.67" and press Enter. Zip is now located to the right of the State field.

3) DELETE A LINE

Place the cursor on the line below the City field and select Delete Line from the Edit menu. There should now be only one blank line separating the student's personal and academic information. From the File menu, select the Save command to save the file.

<u>Check</u> - Your form should be similar to:

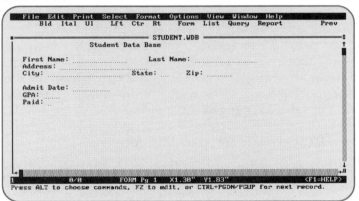

5.18 Modifying Labels

Once labels are entered onto a form, they can be changed or deleted. To edit a label, the cursor is first placed on the label and F2 pressed to enter editing mode. The word EDIT appears on the Status line. After using the arrow keys to position the cursor where the changes need to be made, the corrections are then typed, and Enter pressed. Deleting labels can be accomplished by placing the cursor on the desired label and selecting Delete Label from the Edit menu.

Works begins each label with a double quote ("). This can be seem in the Formula line when the cursor is on a label. When editing, be sure not to delete the quote, or insert any characters before it.

5.19 *Changing Field Widths*

The width of each field (the amount of space it takes up on the screen) may be changed from its current value. The Field Size command from the Format menu enables you to specify the numbers of characters to display for the current field. It is important to note that changing a field width has no effect on the data stored in the field, only its appearance on the screen. Remember, the cursor must be on the entry, not the field name, to activate this command. If the cursor is not on the entry, the command appears gray in the menu, signifying that it cannot be executed at that time.

• •

Practice 9

In this Practice you will modify the STUDENT data base file by adding and editing labels, and changing field widths. Open STUDENT.WDB if you have not already done so.

1) ADD A LABEL

To make entering data easier and quicker, add a label to the right of the Paid field at X2.10" Y2.33". Type (Y for Yes, N for No) and press Enter.

2) MAKE CHANGES TO THE TITLE LABEL

a. The form's title needs to read "Ivy University Student Data Base." Place the cursor on the title label and press F2 to enter editing mode. Notice the word EDIT appears on the Status line, and that a cursor is blinking on the Formula line next to the words Data Base.

b. Using the arrow keys, move the cursor to the beginning of the title, on the "S" in the word "Student." Type Ivy University and a space. Press Enter to make the changes permanent. The label is changed on the form.

3) INCREASE THE FIELD WIDTH OF ADDRESS

a. To increase the width of the Address field, place the cursor on the field entry space to the right of the field name (the dotted line).

b. From the Format menu, select the Field Size command to display the dialog box.

c. Type 30 and select OK to change the field size. The Address field can now display up to 30 characters.

Check - Your form should be similar to:

5

```
 File  Edit  Print  Select  Format  Options  View  Window  Help
     Bld   Ital  Ul      Lft  Ctr  Rt      Form  List  Query  Report              Prev
 ════════════════════════════ STUDENT.WDB ═══════════════════════════
                    Ivy University Student Data Base

    First Name: ..............     Last Name: ..............
    Address: ...................................
    City: ..................   State: ...   Zip: .........

    Admit Date: ..........
    GPA: ......
    Paid: .. (Y for Yes, N for No)




 1          0/0          FORM Pg 1    X5.30"  Y1.50"                    <F1=HELP>
 Press ALT to choose commands, FZ to edit, or CTRL+PGDN/PGUP for next record.
```

4) SAVE AND PRINT THE MODIFIED FILE

a.   From the File menu, select the Save command to save the data base file. The next time STUDENT is opened, the new labels will appear.

b.   Print a copy of the form by selecting Print from the Print menu.

c.   From the File menu, select the Close command to close STUDENT.

• •

Chapter Summary

A computerized data base is an organized collection of related information that is stored on disk in a file. The speed and storage capabilities of the computer make it an ideal tool for managing large amounts of information in the form of data bases. Data bases are used by many organizations (businesses, governmental agencies, educational institutions, etc.) and may become very large. They can be used to organize information about almost any area of knowledge.

Information in a data base is divided into records, each of which stores a complete set of data about a specific item. Different pieces of data within a record are called fields and the data entered into a field is called an entry.

To create a new Works data base the **Create a New File** option is selected from the Quick Start dialog box and **Database** selected from the dialog box. A blank data base form is then displayed. The arrangement of the fields within a record is called a form.

Labels can be included in a form. These are text that can be used as titles or to give information. Works assumes that any next not ending with a colon (:) is a label.

Data bases become useful when searching and sorting operations can be performed on them. When a search is performed the user asks to see the first record which contains specific information. The computer then searches each record until a field containing the sought information is located. A subsequent search locates the next occurrence of the information.

Records in a data base can also be queried. Unlike a search, a query allows the search to be limited to specific fields, and can apply criteria such as 'equal to' or 'greater than'.

Information taken from a data base is called a report. Reports may include many pieces of data, or just one. Work's reports can contain titles, calculate totals, and make use of formatting options.

Placing the records in a data base in order is called sorting. A sort is performed based on the value of one field called the "key field." When a data base is sorted, the position of a record in the file is changed based on the value stored in its key field. For example, sorting on a name field in a data base arranges the records in alphabetical order based on names.

A data base may be modified: old information removed, outdated information updated and new information added. Removing records from a data base is called deleting from the file. Changing information stored in a field is called updating the file.

Before a data base is created, a great deal of planning should go into its design. Who will use the data base and how they will use it should be considered as part of the planning process. Choosing appropriate fields, field names, types and field lengths makes a data base complete and easy to use. A hastily designed data base usually requires a large amount of work to reorganize it after it has been created.

The order in which the different fields appear in a record as well as the space allocated to each field is called the form. In a well designed data base the form should have to be changed infrequently.

There are three basic field types: character, numeric, and time/date. Character fields contain text while numeric fields contain only numbers (values). Time/date fields store times or dates in either long or short form.

The field width for each field must be determined when creating a form. This is the space where data for each field is entered.

Blank lines may be added to a form using the Insert Line command from the Edit menu. Fields may be moved within a record using the Move Field command from the Edit menu. The width of a field can be changed by moving the cursor to the field's entry location and the Field Size command from the Format menu executed.

Vocabulary

Character field - A field which stores only characters such as a name or address.

Chronological order - Ordering based on date.

Data base - A collection of related information.

Data base file - A file on disk which is created by the data base application and which stores a computerized data base.

Entry - The information stored in one field in one record.

5

Field - Specific piece of information stored in each record, such as Last Name.

Field name - Name by which the computer identifies the different pieces of information in a record.

Field type - Determines the type of data (character, numeric, time/date) a field stores.

Form - The arrangement, length and order of the fields in a data base record.

Key Field - Field which stores the data used when determining the order during a sort.

Label - Text that can be used in a form as titles or to give added information.

Modify - To change the contents of a record or entry.

Numeric field - A field which contains only numbers.

Query - Limiting the number of records that are displayed using criteria that displayed records must meet. A query is based on criteria which refer to specific fields and contain comparisons such as 'less than' or 'not equal to'.

Record - A complete collection of data for one item.

Report - Information extracted from a data base, usually printed on paper.

Search - Operation where the computer searches through the fields in a data base, displaying the first field to contain a specified text.

Sort - Places the records stored in a data base in order based on the value stored in one field.

Time/date field - A field which stores a time or date.

Update - See Modify.

• •

Reviews

Sections 5.1 - 5.7

1. Why do historians refer to our present time as the Information Age?

2. a) What is a data base?
   b) What is a record?
   c) What is a field?
   d) What is an entry?

3. What capabilities of the computer make it an ideal tool for managing data bases?

4. What determines the size of a single record in a data base?

5. Can the following be considered to be data bases? Why or why not?

   a) a phone book
   b) just the yellow pages in a phone book
   c) patient files in a doctor's office
   d) a grocery list
   e) a school yearbook

6. The following information is found in the white pages of a phone book:

```
. . .
Capeletti, Rod       712 Adams Ave.      212-0987
Caputti, Jane        80 Scarlet Ct.      123-4567
Caputti, Jane N.     255 Camden Ave.     555-1234
Caputti, M.          77 Sunset Strip     911-1111
. . .
```

    a) What information would constitute a single record?
    b) Describe the separate fields in such a record.
    c) What information does each field store?

7. List five governmental agencies that might use a computerized data base. Explain what each agency would store.

8. List the steps required to create a new data base.

9. Explain how labels may be used in a data base form.

Sections 5.8 - 5.11

10. a) What does it mean to search a data base?
    b) Give 3 examples of searches that could be performed on a student data base.

11. What is the difference between searching and querying a data base?

12. Which of the following operations constitute a search and which a query of a data base?

    a) Which records contain the name George?
    b) Which students have not paid their tuition?
    c) Which students were expelled last year?
    d) Show all records containing a 35.
    e) List all students who are over 21 years old.

13. What fields other than Name and GPA could the records in the I.U. student data base be sorted on? Give a reason for having the data base sorted this way.

14. What field are the records in a phone book sorted on?

15. a) What is a report?
    b) Describe two different reports that could be generated using the student records described in Section 5.7.

16. Answer the following questions based on the three sample student records given in Section 5.7:

    a) How many students have not paid their tuition?
    b) Which students were admitted before 1988?
    c) What are the names of the students with a GPA below 2.0?
    d) How many students live in the Carey Quadrangle?

17. Why is it important to plan a data base before using the computer?

18. a) What should be considered when choosing a field name?
    b) What is the maximum length Works allows a field name to be?

19. Why might it be better to store the first name and last name of students in separate fields rather than in the same field in the Ivy student data base?

20. a) What is a data base form?
    b) Can the design of a form be changed after a data base has been produced on the computer?

21. a) What is the difference between character and numeric fields?
    b) What is a date field?

22. How many character, numeric and date fields are there in a single student record shown in Section 5.7?

23. Is it possible to enter data in to certain fields and leave others empty in the same record?

24. Show what the form for your student record might look like.

25. Choose appropriate field names and types for the following data:

    a) a person's name.
    b) a phone number.
    c) the color of a car.
    d) an item's price.
    e) whether an item is on sale or not.
    f) the day a person was born.

26. a) What information should be stored in a computerized data base listing the cars for sale at an automobile dealership?
    b) Describe a record from such a data base, including the information to be stored in each of its fields.
    c) Using appropriate field names design a form for the data base.

27. How is a blank line inserted into a form?

28. List the steps required to move a field within a form.

29. List the steps required to change the width of a field.

Exercises

1. Many people use a computerized data base in place of an address book.

    a) On a piece of paper create a list of data categories for your address book. Be sure to include the full name, complete mailing address, and phone number for each entry.

    b) It would be a good idea to store birthdays in your data base. Add this field to your list of categories.

    c) Using your categories, create a list of field names, showing types and widths for each.

    d) Design several thumbnail sketches of the form experimenting with order, groupings, and spacing. Be sure to include a title label for the form.

    e) Pick the best form from part (d). Using Works, create the form in a new data base on the computer. Next to each field on the thumbnail sketch, indicate the field's X,Y coordinate.

    f) Save the data base using the name ADDRESS.WDB.

    g) Preview the form and make any changes required. When the form is complete, print a copy.

2. Everybody wants to be an author. You will list some books that your friends might write in a data base. For example, a friend who likes to talk on the phone may write a book entitled *Is There Life Beyond The Telephone?* The purpose of this data base is to create a catalog of your friends and their works which will then be sent to different publishers.

    a) On a piece of paper create a list of data categories for your author catalog.

    b) Publishers who read this catalog will want a phone number and a complete mailing address (address, city, state, zip code) where they can contact the author. Make sure that these categories are included in the list created above along with the author's name and the title of the work.

    c) Using your categories, create a list of field names, showing types and widths for each.

    d) Design several thumbnail sketches of the form experimenting with order, groupings, and spacing. Be sure to include a title and labels for any fields that need clarification.

    e) Pick the best form from part (d). Using Works, create the form in a new data base on the computer. Next to each field on the thumbnail sketch, indicate the field's X,Y coordinate.

    f) Save the data base form using the name CATALOG.WDB.

    g) Add a new field that designates the subject area of each publication. Examples of subject areas include fiction, science fiction, non-fiction, education, humor, drama, romance, western, etc. To save time and eliminate errors, this field should store an abbreviation such as F for fiction, E for education, etc. Be sure to include a label describing what the abbreviations stand for.

5

h) Save the modified CATALOG.

i) Preview the form and make any changes required. When the form is complete, print a copy.

3. The specialty store you announced in the Exercises in Chapters Two and Three needs a data base for its inventory. Create a new data base, and using the flyer you created in Chapter Three, Exercise 13 as a guide, create an inventory form for your store following the steps given below.

a) On a piece of paper create a list of data categories that describes the items in the inventory of your store. For example, categories for a store could include item names, departments, costs, price, stock number etc.

b) Be sure to include an item number, a brand name, quantity on hand, amount ordered, and a price for each item in your inventory. If you have not included these categories, add them to your list created in part (a).

c) Using your categories, create a list of field names, showing types and widths for each.

d) Design several thumbnail sketches of the form experimenting with order, groupings, and spacing. Be sure to include a title and labels for any fields that need clarification.

e) Pick the best form from part (d). Using Works, create the form in a new data base on the computer. Next to each field on the thumbnail sketch, indicate the field's X,Y coordinate.

f) Save the data base using the name STORE.WDB.

g) The width of the stock number field should be at least six. Change the field width at this time if you need to.

h) Insert three blank lines at the top of the form and add the following information at the X,Y coordinates given:

X3.80" Y1.00"	Store's Name
X2.80" Y1.17"	Store's Address
X3.80" Y1.33"	Store's Phone Number

i) Save the modified STORE data base.

j) Preview the form and make any changes required. When the form is complete, print a copy.

4. In the previous exercise you created a data base file for the inventory of your store. Using the STORE.WDB data base as a guide, you will create a data base to record the store's sales activity for one day.

a) On a piece of paper create a list of data categories for the store's daily sales log.

b) Be sure there is also a category for each of the following: item number, brand name, price, quantity sold, method of payment, sales tax, and total amount of purchases.

c) Using your categories, create a list of field names, showing types and widths for each.

d) Design several thumbnail sketches of the form experimenting with order, groupings, and spacing. Be sure to include a title and labels for any fields that need clarification.

e) Pick the best form from part (d). Using Works, create the form in a new data base on the computer. Next to each field on the thumbnail sketch, indicate the field's X,Y coordinate.

f) Create a label for the method of payment field that lists the types of payment you accept at your store. Use the following list and add at least four more types of payment a customer may use:

Payment Method	Code
Cash	CA
Diners Club	DC
Traveler's check	TC

g) Save the data base as STORELOG.

h) Preview the form and make any changes required. When the form is complete, print a copy.

5. A comic book company has hired you as a data base consultant. They would like a data base created that contains a list of their characters' names, any special advantages or powers they have, and the role of the characters (i.e., hero, villain, assistant, love interest, etc.).

a) On a piece of paper create a list of data categories for the comic data base from the specifications given above.

b) Most comic book characters have promotional items available for sale such as T-shirts, dolls, and coffee mugs. The company would like to add a category that contains the best-selling promotional item for each character. Add this category to the list you created in part (a).

c) Using your categories, create a list of field names, showing types and widths for each.

d) Design several thumbnail sketches of the layout of the form experimenting with order, groupings, and spacing. Add labels for any fields that need clarification, such as the character role and promotional item fields.

e) Pick the best form from part (d). Using Works, create the form in a new data base on the computer. Next to each field on the thumbnail sketch, indicate the field's X,Y coordinate.

f) Insert two blank lines at the top of the form. At X4.50" Y1.00" add the following bold and italicized title:

Comic Characters Data Base

g) Save the data base as COMIC. Preview the form and make any changes required. When the form is complete, print a copy.

5

6. Your insurance agent wants you to create a data base of all the important items in your room. The list should include the item brand name, amount paid, and model number. Examples might include: Sony 201X stereo with CD player, $398.99; Faberge 1 oz. lead crystal perfume bottle, $125.00; etc.

    a) On a piece of paper create a list of categories that describes the items in your room. Examples of categories could include electronics, art, clothing, jewelry, and equipment.

    b) Using your categories, create a list of field names, showing types and widths for each.

    c) Design several thumbnail sketches of the form experimenting with order, groupings, and spacing. Be sure to include a title and labels for any fields that need clarification.

    d) Pick the best form from part (c). Using Works, create the form in a new data base on the computer. Next to each field on the thumbnail sketch, indicate the field's X,Y coordinate.

    e) The insurance agent forgot to tell you to include a field with the age of the item. Add a field which shows the date of purchase.

    f) Create a label for the date of purchase field showing which date format to use, MM/DD/YY.

    g) Insert four blank lines at the top of the form. Starting at location X1.30" Y1.00" enter your full name, address, and phone number.

    h) Save the file as INSURE.WDB.

    i) Preview the form and make any changes required. When the form is complete, print a copy.

7. CityZoo needs your help to create a computerized data base of animals in the zoo. Using the listing shown in Chapter Three, Exercise 14 as a guide you will create a data base form for the zoo.

    a) On a piece of paper create a list of categories for the zoo data base as requested by the zoo. The form should include the name of the staff member who cares for the animal, the animal's name (American Black Bear, Asian Green Boa Constrictor, etc.), number of female animals, animal type (mammal, reptile, bird, etc.), location of animal (aquarium, rain forest, etc.), and number of male animals.

    b) Using your categories, create a list of field names, showing types and widths for each.

    c) The zoo has specified the order of the fields to be as follows: type of animal, animal name, location in the zoo, number of males, number of females, and the staff member who cares for it. Sketch two different forms that reflect this order. Be sure to include a title and labels for any fields that need clarification.

    d) Using the best form developed in part (c), create the data base form using Works and save it as ZOO.WDB. Next to each field on the sketch, indicate the field's X,Y coordinate.

    e) The zoo has decided it does not like the order and wants the animal name to come first. Move the animal name field to the top of the form, inserting and deleting blank lines as necessary.

f) Insert 5 blank lines at the top of the data base and enter the following information at the given X,Y coordinates:

Location	Information to be Entered
X4.5" Y1.0"	CityZoo
X4.0" Y1.17"	2323 Big Cat Bend
X3.8" Y1.33"	Longboat Key, FL 33548
X3.6" Y1.50"	(555) CITY-ZOO or 248-9066

g) Save the modified ZOO data base.

h) Preview the form and make any changes required. When the form is complete, print a copy.

8. The research scientists have received the grant for the research proposal you helped write in Chapter Three, Exercise 12. They are living on the tropical island of Bashibashi and need a computerized data base to keep track of the movements of the island's gibbon population.

a) On a piece of paper create a list of categories for the scientist's gibbon data base. Include the field names, types, and widths for each category. The data base should include a field for each of the following:

time of sighting
individual gibbon's name
gender: male or female
approximate age
the island's weather: sun, clouds, rain, wind, storm
temperature
location of the sighting
gibbon's activity: eating, sleeping, grooming, playing, aggression

b) To save space and reduce errors, the form should use abbreviations for the following fields: the island's weather, the gibbon's activity, and gender. Change the width for these fields.

c) Design several thumbnail sketches of the form experimenting with order, groupings, and spacing. Be sure to include a title and labels for any fields that need clarification, especially the abbreviated fields discussed in step (b).

d) Using the best form developed in part (c), create the data base form using Works and save it as MYGIB.WDB. Next to each field on the thumbnail sketch, indicate the field's X,Y coordinate.

e) Preview the form and make any changes required. When the form is complete, print a copy.

9. You would like to create a data base of all the major colleges and universities in the United States.

a) On a piece of paper create a list of data categories for the college data base. Be sure to include the full name, complete mailing address, and phone number for each entry, as well as the school's enrollment, tuition, and room and board fees.

b) It will be important to know if the school is public or private. Add a field to your list of categories which indicates this.

c) Using your categories, create a list of field names, showing types and widths for each.

d) Design several thumbnail sketches of the form experimenting with order, groupings, and spacing. Be sure to include a title.

e) Pick the best form from part (d). Using Works, create the form in a new data base on the computer. Next to each field on the thumbnail sketch, indicate the field's X,Y coordinate.

f) Save the data base using the name MYCOLLEG.WDB.

g) Preview the form and make any changes required. When the form is complete, print a copy.

10. Fantasy Wheels, Inc. is an automobile dealership that sells exotic used cars and wants to store their inventory of cars in a data base. Below is an example of the type of information that they wish to store:

1969 Maserati, blue exterior, black interior. Options: radio, 4 speed, and air. Originally paid $9,800 on May 9, 1991, now asking $21,600.

a) Using the record above as a guide, create a list of categories for the car inventory data base on a piece of paper. Pay special attention to the options.

b) Using your categories, create a list of field names, showing types and widths for each.

c) Fantasy has decided to use the following abbreviations for the exterior and interior color fields:

R Red	**Y** Yellow
W White	**A** Gray
B Blue	**O** Orange
K Black	**N** Brown
G Green	**P** Purple

Design several thumbnail sketches of the form experimenting with order, groupings, and spacing. Be sure to include labels for any fields that need clarification, especially the color fields.

d) Pick the best form from part (c). Using Works, create the form in a new data base named WHEELS.WDB. Next to each field on the thumbnail sketch, indicate the field's X,Y coordinate.

e) Insert two lines at the top of the form and add the following italicized title at X3.90" Y1.00:

Fantasy Wheels Inventory

f) Save the modified WHEELS data base.

g) Preview the form and make any changes required. When the form is complete, print a copy.

11. You are to produce a questionnaire to survey a group of students in your school.

   a) On a piece of paper create a list of categories for the questionnaire. Include categories concerning personal statistics, favorite course in school, favorite movie or band, etc., and anything else you would like to know.

   b) Using your categories, create a list of field names, showing types and widths for each.

   c) Design several thumbnail sketches of the form experimenting with order, groupings, and spacing. Be sure to include a title and labels for any fields that need clarification.

   d) Pick the best form from part (d). Using Works, create the form in a new data base on the computer. Next to each field on the thumbnail sketch, indicate the field's X,Y coordinate.

   e) Save the data base form using the name STUQUEST.WDB.

   f) Preview the form and make any changes required. When the form is complete, print a copy.

12. Holiday Airlines has weekly flights to the Bahamas and has decided to computerize its reservation system. Holiday owns one airplane which has 20 seats numbered as shown below:

W	1A	1B	A	1C	1D	W
i	2A	2B	i	2C	2D	i
n	3A	3B	s	3C	3D	n
d	4A	4B	l	4C	4D	d
o	5A	5B	e	5C	5D	o
w						w
s						s

   a) On a piece of paper create a list of data categories for the reservations data base. Be sure to include a seat number, location (aisle or window), whether the seat is in the first class section (Rows 1 and 2) or not, and the name and phone number of each passenger on its plane.

   b) Using your categories, create a list of field names, showing types and widths for each.

   c) Design several thumbnail sketches of the form experimenting with order, groupings, and spacing. Be sure to include a title and labels for any fields that need clarification.

   d) Pick the best form from part (c). Using Works, create the form in a new data base on the computer. Next to each field on the thumbnail sketch, indicate the field's X,Y coordinate.

   e) Save the data base form using the name HOLIDAY.WDB.

   f) Preview the form and make any changes required. When the form is complete, print a copy.

5

13. Some scientific experiments require that data be recorded over a period of weeks, months, or even years. The data base is very useful for recording the data in such experiments. Weather observation experiments require periodic data collection over a long period of time to establish trends and help meteorologists make predictions based on these trends, and are a good scientific use of the data base.

a) On a piece of paper create a list of data categories for a weather experiment data base. Each record should contain categories which store the date, time, temperature, amount of rain fall, and sky conditions for a single observation. Use the following observation as a guide:

Date	Time	Temp.F.	Rain	Sky
1/8/60	3:00 PM	79	0.0	Partly Cloudy

b) Using your categories, create a list of field names, showing types and widths for each. Use an abbreviation for the sky conditions field:

S Sunny   **P** Partly Cloudy
C Clear   **H** Hazy
L Cloudy   **W** Windy

c) Design several thumbnail sketches of the form experimenting with order, groupings, and spacing. Be sure to include a title and labels for any fields that need clarification, especially the sky conditions.

d) Pick the best form from part (c), and use Works to create a new data base on the computer. Next to each field on the thumbnail sketch, indicate the field's X,Y coordinate.

e) Save the data base form using the name WEATHER.WDB.

f) Preview the form and make any changes required. When the form is complete, print a copy.

Chapter Six

Manipulating Data with the Data Base

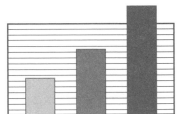

Format - Fixed

Select - Search

View - List

Format - Field Width

Print - Preview

View - Query

Select - Show All Records

File - WorksWizard

Edit - Insert Record/Field

Select - Sort Records

Objectives

After completing this chapter you will be able to:

1. Enter data into a new data base, record by record.

2. Use the Search command to locate text in a data base.

3. Display the data in both Form view and List view.

4. Query the data base for specific information.

5. Print the contents of a data base on a printer.

6. Change the data stored in a record or field.

7. Add records to and delete records from a data base.

8. Use WorksWizard to query a data base.

9. Rearrange records in a data base by sorting.

6

This chapter describes the steps necessary to create a computerized data base using Works and perform some common operations with it: search, query, update, and sort. Records will be entered into the data base created in the previous chapter. The data base will then be saved, searched for text, and printed. Commands which update and save the information stored in the data base are introduced. Queries will be defined and applied so that only records which meet certain criteria are displayed. The records in the data base will then be rearranged, or sorted, to make it easier to use.

6.1 Entering Records in a New Data Base

After the form of a data base has been completed, data can be entered into record 1. Each field name is displayed with space to enter data for that field. To enter data into a field, the cursor is first placed in the field (the dotted line) to the right of the desired field name by pressing Tab or clicking in the field with the mouse. Data can then be entered in either of two ways. One way is to type the data and then press Tab. The data is entered into the field, and the cursor is advanced to the next field. Data can also be entered into a field by typing the data and then pressing Enter. If you make a mistake before pressing Tab or Enter, press Escape to erase the current entry and start typing from the beginning of that field. To move to a previous field, keyboard users can press `Shift-Tab`.

When all of the fields in a record have been entered, pressing Tab advances Works to the next record where a new, empty form is displayed. Works keeps track of how many records have been entered, which field the cursor is on, and which record is currently displayed. This information is shown on the Status line.

Works can store up to 255 characters of data in a single field, but the number of characters actually *displayed* depends on the width set for that field. Any characters beyond the field's width are still stored, just not displayed. When the cursor is placed on a field, the actual contents of the field are shown on the Formula line located at the top of the screen.

Fields may be selected using the mouse. Pointing to the field and clicking where data will be entered moves the cursor to that field. After the data has been typed, it is entered into the field by clicking once anywhere on the screen with the mouse. When a record is complete, clicking on the down scroll-arrow at the side of the screen brings the next record into view. Because selecting fields with the mouse and then typing data on the keyboard require you to keep moving your hands between the mouse and the keyboard, many people prefer to use keystrokes to move the cursor rather than the mouse when entering data into a data base.

• •

Practice 1

In this Practice you will enter data into three student records and save the data base in a file on disk.

1) START WORKS AND OPEN STUDENT.WDB

a. Boot DOS and start Works as described in Chapter Two. The Quick Start dialog box is displayed.

b. From the Quick Start dialog box, select the **Open an Existing File** option. The Open Existing File dialog box is displayed. Select STUDENT.WDB to open the data base file.

2) TYPE A STUDENT'S FIRST NAME

a. Move the cursor to the First Name field. Be sure to select the field (the dotted lines) and not the field name.

b. Type Matilda. If you make a mistake, simply press Escape and retype the data.

c. Press Enter. Notice that the data is entered, but the cursor remains in the field.

d. Press Tab to advance the cursor to the next field, Last Name.

3) ENTER THE STUDENT'S LAST NAME

Type the last name Rose and press the Tab key. Notice that the data is entered into the field and the cursor is advanced to the next field, Address.

4) COMPLETE THE STUDENT RECORD

Enter the following data for the remaining fields, pressing Tab after each:

        Address: 435 Frelinghuysen Rd
        City: Leafville
        State: NJ
        Zip: 18049
        Admit Date: 2/14/91
        GPA: 3.4
        Paid: Y

Pressing Tab after typing the data in the Paid field enters the record into the computer's memory. The screen is cleared and a new, empty form is shown into which another record may be typed.

5) ADD THE FOLLOWING TWO STUDENT RECORDS

Follow the steps given above to enter the next two records into the file:

6

First Name: Sam
Last Name: Adams
Address: 121 Carey Quadrangle
City: Leaftown
State: PA
Zip: 19717
Admit Date: 3/12/92
GPA: 1.5
Paid: N

First Name: Roberta
Last Name: Poisson
Address: 8P Corwin Place
City: Five Points
State: FL
Zip: 33434
Admit Date: 6/27/93
GPA: 4
Paid: N (Press Enter, not Tab, after this field.)

Check - The final record entered should be similar to:

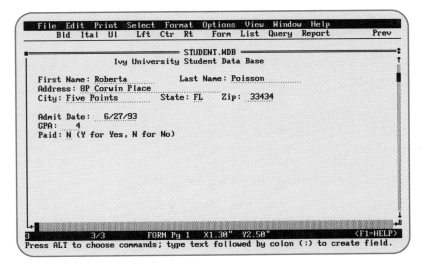

6) SAVE THE DATA BASE FILE

From the File menu, select the Save command to save the file on disk.

6.2 Changing the Data Stored in a Field

It is possible to change the data stored in a field. Changes to the entry in a field are made by moving the cursor to the desired field (the dotted line), typing the new data, and pressing Enter. The new data then replaces the old in that record.

You may also edit the contents of the current field by pressing F2 which displays the entry on the Formula line followed by a blinking cursor. Left-arrow, right-arrow, and Delete can then be used to edit the entry, and new characters may be inserted. When Enter is pressed, the new data is copied from the Formula line and placed in the field. If you choose not to make the update, pressing Escape instead of Enter erases the changes and restores the former entry. When using F2 to edit an entry, Works displays EDIT on the Status line and most commands may not be chosen from the menus.

Before the data in a record may be changed, it must be displayed on the screen. It is possible to scroll through the data base using the Tab key to move the cursor from field to field. The current record number and field name are shown on the Status line. Pressing Ctrl-PgUp moves the cursor to the previous record in the file, and Ctrl-PgDn to the next. Ctrl-Home moves the cursor to the first record in the file, and Ctrl-End to the last.

Using the mouse, the contents of a field may be edited by first clicking on the field to select it. The place where the edit is to be made is pointed to on the Formula line, and the mouse clicked. The blinking cursor appears at this point, and changes may be typed. Clicking back on the field enters the corrected entry, while pressing Escape erases the changes.

To scroll through the data base using the mouse, point to either the up or down scroll arrows at the right side of the screen. Clicking once moves one record, holding down the mouse scrolls through the records.

• •

Practice 2

In this Practice you will modify data in the STUDENT data base. Mouse users can skip this practice and do the special Mouse Practice below — you do not need to do both. Start Works and open STUDENT if you have not already done so.

1)   SCROLL THE CURSOR TO THE BEGINNING OF THE FILE

Press Shift-Tab until the cursor is on the First Name field in record 1. Note the 1 on the Status line showing the record number.

2)   JUMP FROM RECORD TO RECORD

a.   Press Ctrl-PgDn. Record 2 is displayed as indicated by the 2 on the Status line.
b.   Press Ctrl-PgDn. The cursor moves to the third record and a 3 is shown on the Status line.
c.   Press Ctrl-PgUp. Record 2 is again displayed.

3)   EDIT THE LAST NAME IN RECORD 3

A mistake has been made entering the last name of the student in record 3. Roberta Poisson's last name should be "Poston."

a.   Press Ctrl-PgDn to display record 3.
b.   With record 3 displayed, move the cursor to the Last Name field. Note that the contents of the field, Poisson, are shown on the Formula line.
c.   Press F2 to move the cursor to the Formula line. EDIT is displayed on the Status line.
d.   Move the cursor under the second "s".
e.   Press Delete to remove the "s".
f.   Type the new character, t. The "t" is inserted at the current cursor position.
g.   Move the cursor under the "i".

h. Press Delete to remove the "i". The proper last name, Poston, is shown on the Formula line.
i. Enter the corrected last name.

4) REPLACE THE CITY IN RECORD 3

a. Data in a field does not have to be edited; it may be replaced as a whole. With the cursor still on record 3, place the cursor on the City field.
b. Enter the new city data, Orlando. The previous city is replaced.

5) SAVE THE MODIFIED DATA BASE FILE ON DISK

From the File menu, select the Save command. The modified data base is saved on disk.

Mouse Practice

In this Practice you will modify data in the STUDENT data base by using the mouse. Start Works and open STUDENT if you have not already done so.

1) PLACE THE CURSOR ON RECORD 1

a. Click the mouse on the up scroll-arrow until record 1 is displayed. Notice that with every click, a new record is displayed.
b. Click the mouse on the First Name field. Note the 1 on the Status line showing the record number.

2) PLACE THE CURSOR IN RECORD 2

Click the mouse on the down scroll-arrow. Record 2 is displayed. Notice that the cursor remains in the same field, First Name, even when different records are displayed.

3) JUMP FROM RECORD TO RECORD

a. Click on the scroll box and drag it halfway down the bar. Release the mouse button.
b. The blank form for record 9 or 11 should be displayed, as indicated on the Status line.
c. Drag the scroll box back to the top of the scroll bar to display record 1 again.

4) EDIT THE LAST NAME IN RECORD 3

A mistake has been made entering the last name of the student in record 3. Roberta Poisson's last name should be "Poston."

a. Display record 3.
b. With record 3 displayed, move the cursor to the Last Name field. Note that the contents of the field, Poisson, are shown on the Formula line.
c. Click the mouse on the second "s" in the word Poisson on the Formula line. The cursor appears under the "s".
d. Press Delete to remove the "s".
e. Type the new character, t. The "t" is inserted at the current cursor position.
f. Click the mouse on the "i".
g. Press Delete to remove the "i". The proper last name, Poston, is shown on the Formula line.
h. Enter the corrected last name by pressing Enter or clicking the mouse anywhere in the form.

5) REPLACE THE CITY IN RECORD 3

a. Data in a field does not have to be edited; it may be replaced as a whole. With the cursor still on record 3, click on the City field.
b. Enter the new city data, Orlando. The old city is replaced.

6) SAVE THE MODIFIED DATA BASE FILE ON DISK

From the File menu, select the Save command. The modified data base is saved on disk.

6.3 *Formatting Fields*

Format

| General |
| Fixed... |
| Currency... |
| Comma... |
| Percent... |
| Exponential... |
| Leading Zeros... |
| Fraction... |
| True/False |
| Time/Date... |
| Font... |
| Style... |
| Field Width... |

If a field is to contain numbers with a fixed amount of decimal places, it should be formatted using the Fixed command from the Format menu. This command rounds the number to a specified decimal place. The number of decimal places is specified in the Fixed dialog box:

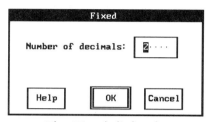

The Fixed dialog box

The default value of 2 can be changed by entering the desired number. Any number entered into a field formatted with Fixed is displayed with that specified number of decimal places. For example, we would like all GPA values to be displayed with 1 decimal place. By placing the cursor on the GPA field and executing the Fixed command, we can specify the value 1 in the dialog box. Now all GPA values will be displayed with 1 decimal place (e.g., 3 will be displayed as 3.0, etc.). It is important to note that applying a formatting option to a field affects that field in all of the records, not just the one currently displayed.

Another useful formatting option is the Currency command from the Format menu. A field formatted with the Currency command displays values as dollar amounts, such as $1,000.00. This command also allows the number of decimal places to be specified. When formatting dollar values, the default of 2 decimal places is usually used.

Works provides a number of shortcut keys to quickly perform many of these formatting functions. After highlighting the field, label, etc., pressing Ctrl and the appropriate key executes the command. Below are some of Works' most common shortcuts:

Bold	Ctrl-B	Center	Ctrl-C
Italic	Ctrl-I	Left align	Ctrl-L
Underline	Ctrl-U	Right align	Ctrl-R
Currency	Ctrl-4	Percent	Ctrl-5
Comma	Ctrl-, (comma)		

6

Practice 3

In this Practice you will modify the Ivy University student data base by formatting the GPA field. Start Works and open STUDENT if you have not already done so.

1) FORMAT THE GPA FIELD FOR 1 DECIMAL PLACE

  a. Move the cursor to the GPA field. Be sure to select the field and not the field name.
  b. From the Format menu, select the Fixed command. The dialog box is shown with the default value of 2.
  c. Type 1 and select OK. Any values now entered into the GPA field in any record will be displayed with 1 decimal place. For example, 3 is formatted to 3.0.

2) SAVE AND CLOSE THE MODIFIED FILE

  a. Save the modified file. When next retrieved, the STUDENT data base will have GPAs formatted to one decimal place.
  b. Because we are not going to use it again, close STUDENT to remove it from the computer's memory.

6.4 Searching for Text in a Record

Works can be used to locate records in a data base that contain a certain word or phrase. This operation is called "searching" and is performed using the Search command from the Select menu. Text to be found is entered in the Search dialog box:

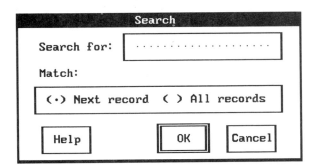

The Data Base Search dialog box

Once entered, the text is compared to the data stored in each field in the file. The first record which contains a matching **Search for** text is then displayed on the screen. Selecting the Search command again repeats the search using the same **Search for** text as before, and the next record containing that text is located and displayed. A new **Search for** text may also be entered at this time. After the last record in the file is checked, Works starts the Search over again at the top of the data base. Pressing F7 is a shortcut which tells Works to search again using the same **Search for** text.

Search cannot be used to search for text in a specific field because a match is considered found if the **Search for** text is contained anywhere in a record. For example, searching for "et" would locate a record which had "Jan<u>et</u>" in the First Name field, as well as a record which had the word "Str<u>et</u>" in the Address field. Works' Search command is not affected by uppercase and lowercase letters, so that entering "et" finds any combination of uppercase and lowercase letters as long as "e" is followed by "t" as in <u>Et</u>onic, be<u>et</u>s, STR<u>EET</u>, etc. When Works does not find any matching text, the message "No match found" is displayed.

• •

Practice 4

In this Practice you will use the Search command to find specific text in a large data base, IVYSTU.WDB. Start Works if you have not already done so.

1)   OPEN THE IVYSTU DATA BASE

2)   SEARCH FOR "STREET"

    a.   Place the cursor at the top of record 1.
    b.   From the Select menu, execute the Search command to display the Search dialog box.
    c.   Type `street` at the prompt and select OK. Works searches for the first occurrence of the text "street" and displays that record, Francis Ford's.

3)   REPEAT THE SEARCH SEVERAL TIMES

    a.   Select the Search command again. Note that the previous **Search for** text, street, is displayed. Select OK. Works searches for the next occurrence of street and displays that record.
    b.   Press F7. Works repeats the search for street and displays the next record.
    c.   Continue to press F7 until the cursor returns to Francis Ford's record. Note that the streets found may appear in any field, including Address and Last Name.

4)   ENTER A NEW SEARCH FOR TEXT

    a.   From the Select menu, execute the Search command. The previous Search for text, street, is shown.
    b.   Replace the previous text by entering: `zzz`
    Select OK. Because no records are found that contain "zzz", Works displays the dialog box:

    c.   Select OK and then press `Ctrl-Home` to return to the first record in the file.

An Introduction to Computing Using Microsoft Works

6.5 *List View and Form View*

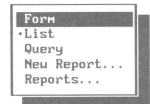

Selecting the List command from the View menu displays the contents of the data base file in List view:

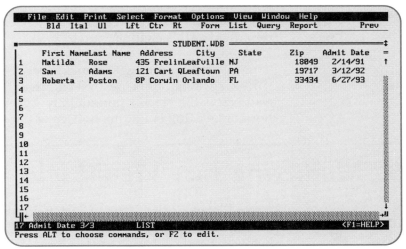

List view screen

In List view, the first few fields for up to 17 records are displayed. List view is useful because it allows records to be compared to one another. Note that until the width is changed only the first ten characters of the data stored in a field are displayed (e.g., the Address field shown above). The rest of the data is still stored in the entry, only not displayed. In the next section we will learn how to increase the size of a field in List view to show all of the data stored in it.

In List view, pressing the up- and down-arrows moves the cursor from record to record. Pressing the left- and right-arrow keys moves the cursor from field to field. The screen can be scrolled to view fields which are not currently visible. Home moves the cursor to the first field in a record, End to the last field. Ctrl-Home moves the cursor directly to the first record in the file, and Ctrl-End to the last.

One of the difficulties with List view is that all of the fields for a single record may not be displayed on the screen. For example, it is no longer possible to determine if Sam Adams has paid his tuition simply by looking at the screen because the Paid field is no longer displayed on the screen. Form view displays all of the fields for a single record and may be selected by executing the Form command from the View menu. Works enables you to switch between List view and Form view by pressing the F9 key.

When switching between List and Form views, the cursor remains on the same record in the same field. For example, if the cursor is on the Paid field in record 3 in List view when F9 is pressed, record 3 is displayed in Form view with the cursor on Paid. If the cursor is then moved to First Name in record 1 and F9 pressed again, the screen switches to List view and the cursor remains on First Name in record 1.

Most of the commands which may be executed in Form view may also be executed in List view. For example, the Search command may be used in either view. It is also possible to change the contents of a record while in List view by moving the cursor to the desired entry and entering the new data. Because it shows all of the fields, most data base operations are normally performed in Form view to ensure that the proper record is used. List view is used for those operations which involve determining the relationships between records, such as the Query command later described in this chapter.

Mouse users can switch quickly between List view and Form view by simply clicking on the desired choice in the Tool bar. Mouse users can also scroll the screen horizontally by clicking on the arrows in the horizontal scroll bar at the bottom of the screen.

6.6 Modifying List View Field Widths

In List view, the width of each field (the amount of space it takes up on the screen) may be changed from the default of 10 characters to between 1 and 79 characters. The Field Width command from the Format menu enables you to specify the number of characters to display in the current field. It is important to note that changing a field width has no effect on the data stored in the field, only its appearance on the screen. Also, changing a field width in List view has no effect on the Form view, and vice versa.

Works saves the List view screen layout of a data base along with the data it stores. If a data base file is saved after a field width has been changed, the next time the file is opened it will have the new width.

• •

Practice 5

This Practice demonstrates the differences between Form and List view. Field widths will be changed and a Search executed in List view. Start Works and open IVYSTU if you have not already done so.

1) SWITCH BETWEEN FORM VIEW AND LIST VIEW

    a. Make sure that the cursor is on record 1.

    b. Select List from the View menu or the Tool bar to display the data base in List view. Because of small field widths, several fields are shown truncated.

    c. Move the cursor to the Paid field in record 1. Note how the screen scrolls to reveal the other fields.

    d. Press F9 to display the data base in Form view. Note that the cursor remains on the Paid field in record 1.

    e. Move the cursor to the State field.

    f. Press F9. The file is displayed in List view with the cursor on the State field in record 1.

    g. Press Home to return the cursor to the First Name field.

2) CHANGE LIST VIEW FIELD WIDTHS

a. From the Format menu, select the Field Width command. The default width 10 is displayed.
b. Enter the new value, 1 2. The First Name field can now display up to 12 characters of data.
c. Move the cursor to the next field. Repeat parts (a) and (b) above using the following field widths:

Field Name	Width
Last Name:	14
Address:	25
City:	17
State:	5
Zip:	6
Admit Date:	11
Paid:	6
GPA:	5

d. Return the cursor to the First Name field.

Check - When complete, the List view screen should be similar to:

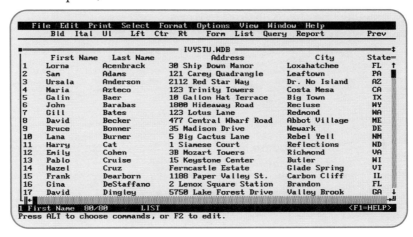

3) SEARCH IN LIST VIEW

a. Select the Search command from the Select menu. Works displays the dialog box.
b. Type street at the prompt and select OK. Works searches for the first occurrence of the text "street" and moves the cursor to it. The cursor should be on Francis Ford's record.

4) REPEAT THE SEARCH SEVERAL TIMES

a. Press the F 7 key. Works repeats the search and moves the cursor to the next field which contains "street".
b. Continue to press F 7 until the cursor returns to Francis Ford's record.

5) SAVE THE MODIFIED FILE ON DISK

Save the modified file on disk. The next time it is opened, IVYSTU will have the modified List view screen.

6.7 Printing a Data Base

```
 Print

 Print...
 Page Setup & Margins...
 Preview...

 Insert Page Break
 Delete Page Break
 Headers & Footers...

 Printer Setup...
```

After a data base has been created, it is often necessary to produce a printout of the contents. Before actually printing however, it is a good idea to preview the data base by selecting Preview from the Print menu or Tool bar (**Prev**). Preview displays a smaller version of the entire page, enabling its entire layout to be seen. By previewing a data base, printed mistakes and wasted paper are avoided because the data base is printed only after all mistakes have been corrected.

Selecting the Print command from the Print menu will print the data base. If the data base is currently displayed in List View, the Print command produces a listing of the data stored in each record in a format similar to List view:

```
Lorna Acenbrack   30 Ship Down Manor      Loxahatchee
Sam Adams         121 Carey Quadrangle    Leaftown
Ursala Anderson   2112 Red Star Way       Dr. No Island
Maria Azteco      123 Trinity Towers      Costa Mesa
Galin Baer        10 Gallon Hat Terrace   Big Town
                        . . .
```

Ivy Student printout, page 1

If the number of fields exceeds the width of the paper, an additional page is printed showing those fields:

```
        FL    33470    3/2/95      Y    3.8
        PA    19717    3/12/92     N    1.5
        AZ    86039    7/27/94     Y    1.5
        CA    92627    11/26/92    N    3.1
        TX    75149    9/25/92     Y    2.6
                       . . .
```

Works prints a second page when the number of fields
exceeds the width of page one

Note that no additional information is printed, only the contents of the records. The printouts produced by the Print command can be made easier to read by using the **Print record and field labels** option in the Print dialog box. When selected, this option includes the field name and record number in the printout:

```
     First Name      Last Name       Address
   1 Lorna           Acenbrack       30 Ship Down Manor
   2 Sam             Adams           121 Carey Quadrangle
   3 Ursala          Anderson        2112 Red Star Way
   4 Maria           Azteco          123 Trinity Towers
   5 Galin           Baer            10 Gallon Hat Terrace
                               . . .
```

Record and field labels help make a printed data base
easier to read and use

If the data base is displayed in Form view when the Print command is executed, only the current record will be printed. Selecting the **All records** option will print all of the records, one record to a page, each in Form view:

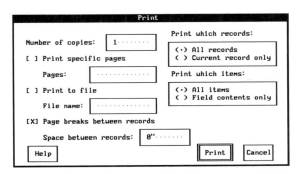

*All of the records can be printed in form view if **All records** is*
selected from the Print dialog box

The printed data base is not as well formatted as we might want, but it can be used to verify the contents of the records. Better formatted printouts called reports are described in Chapter Seven.

Practice 6

In this Practice you will preview and then print the contents of the IVYSTU data base in List view using the **Print record and field labels** option. You will then print a single record in Form view. Make sure that the computer is connected to a printer and that the printer is turned on. Start Works and open IVYSTU if you have not already done so.

1) PREVIEW THE DATA BASE

    a. If it is not already, display the data base in List view. Note that LIST is displayed on the Status line.

    b. Select the Preview command from the Print menu. The Preview dialog box is displayed.

    c. Select **Preview** to display a smaller printed version of the data base. Notice that there are no record or field labels.

    d. Press Escape. The data base is displayed.

2) PREVIEW WITH RECORD AND FIELD LABELS

a. Display the Preview dialog box again.
b. Select the **Print record and field labels** option. An X is displayed next to it.
c. Select **Preview**. Notice how Works includes the record and field labels on the page. When printed, this data base will be easier to read and use.
d. Press Escape to return to List view.

3) PRINT CONTENTS OF THE DATA BASE IN LIST VIEW

a. From the Print menu, select the Print command to display the Print dialog box.
b. Select **Print**. Works prints the contents of the data base on the printer. Because of the number of fields, four pages are needed. Note that the field names and record numbers are printed because the **Print record and field labels** option is selected.

4) PRINT RECORD 10 IN FORM VIEW

a. Move the cursor to record 10.
b. Switch to Form view.
c. From the Print menu, select the Print command and print the record.

Check - Printouts will differ depending on the printer used, but the first printed page should be similar to the examples in Section 6.7.

6.8 Using Queries

The Search command is limited because it cannot be restricted to a specific field. Specifying a **Search for** text of "Adams" would not only locate Sam Adams' record, but also anyone who lives on Adams Street or comes from Adamsville, etc. Also, Search does not have the important capability of searching for more than one piece of text at a time. That is, we cannot Search for the records of students who come from Maine or Vermont in a single command.

Works can be made to display only those records which contain specific data by applying "queries." A query is a description of the data that the displayed record must contain. Unlike the Search command, a query refers to a specific field and may contain more than one **Search for** text. A query can also locate and display more than one record at a time. For example, a query can locate and display all of the records in a data base where the last name is "Adams".

To apply a query, the Query command is selected from the View menu, or clicked on in the Tool bar if using a mouse. A blank form appears with all of the fields listed, and the word QUERY is displayed on the Status line indicating that a query can now be entered. The cursor is placed on the desired field and "criteria" which describe the needed records is entered. Pressing F10 or clicking on **List** in the Tool bar applies the query. Only those records which meet the criteria are then displayed; the other records are still in the file, only not displayed at this time. Those records which do not meet the query's criteria are therefore said to be "hidden." If no records meet the criteria, Works displays the message "No match found." Because they show a relationship between records, queries are normally applied on the List view screen, but can also be used in Form view.

The following query displays the records of all students with the last name "Adams":

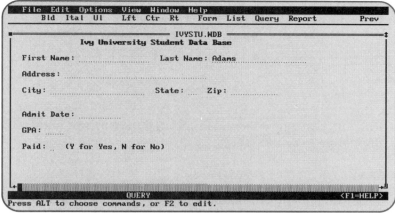

This query finds all records with Adams in the Last Name field

Students who live on Adams Street or who are from Adamsville, etc. would not be displayed. Like the Search command, queries ignore uppercase and lowercase differences. When a query is applied, the record indicator on the Status line changes to show the number of records found by the query and the total number of records in the file. For example, the Status line

Works found 3 records out of 80 that met the Query criteria

indicates that 3 records out of the 80 total records in the file meet the query's criteria. The other 77 are hidden at this time.

To cancel a query, the Show All Records command is executed from the Select menu. Works then removes the query and displays all of the records. When no query is applied, the record indicator on the Status line shows the same number, 80/80 for example, meaning that all 80 records in the file are displayed. Selecting the Query command again displays the QUERY screen, allowing a new query to be created.

After a query has been applied, Works suggests that the queried database be saved before it may be closed, even if no changes were made to the data. Note that all of the records in the data base will be saved, not just the records that were displayed by the query. Also note that if the Print command is issued while a query is applied, only the records displayed by the query are printed.

Mouse users can click on **Query** in the Tool bar to display the QUERY screen. After entering the desired criteria, clicking on **List** in the Tool bar applies the query, displaying any matching records in List view.

6.9 Text and Numeric Queries

Two of the most basic queries involve text and numeric criteria. A text query is used on fields that contain text. This type of query lists all records that meet the criteria of, for example, Name: Adams, State: NY, Zip: 20145-3560, and Part No: ZF-3699J.

Numeric queries are used on fields which contain numeric data such as GPAs, items in stock, and customer account numbers. For example, to create a list of all students in the Student database with a perfect GPA, GPA: 4.0 would be queried.

Practice 7

In this Practice you will query the IVYSTU data base for students who have not paid their tuition. You will also query the data base to find students with a 3.5 GPA. Open IVYSTU.WDB if you have not already done so.

1) **DISPLAY THE QUERY SCREEN**

Select the Query command from the View menu or Tool bar. The QUERY screen is displayed with a list of field names similar to Form view. Notice QUERY displayed on the Status line.

2) **ENTER THE CRITERIA INFORMATION**

a. Move the cursor to the Paid field.
b. Type N and press Enter. An N is shown on the query form. When applied, the query will display all records with an N in the Paid field.

3) **APPLY THE QUERY TO THE DATA BASE**

a. Select List from the View menu or click on **List** in the Tool bar to apply the query to the data base. Only those records which have an N stored in the Paid field are now displayed. Note that the record indicator on the Status line shows 38/80, meaning that 38 students out of the total 80 have not paid their tuition.
b. Scroll the Paid field. Verify that only records with an "N" in the Paid field are displayed.

4) **PREVIEW THE QUERIED DATA BASE**

a. From the Print menu, select the Preview command to preview the queried data base. Notice that only the records of the students who have not paid their tuition are displayed.
b. Press Escape to return to the data base.

5) **CREATE AND APPLY A NUMERIC QUERY**

a. Select Query from the View menu or Tool bar to display the QUERY screen. Note that the previous criteria is still displayed in the Paid field.
b. Move the cursor to the GPA field.
c. Enter 3.5 as the criteria.
d. The previous criteria must be removed. Move the cursor to the Paid field.
e. Press Delete, and then press Enter. The previous criteria is deleted.
f. Press F10 or click on **List** in the Tool bar to apply the new query. Only those students who have a 3.5 GPA are displayed. Who are they? 39, 40, 48, 52, 77

6) **CREATE AND APPLY A NEW QUERY**

a. Display the QUERY screen and delete the previous criteria.
b. Move the cursor to the Last Name field.
c. Enter Francouer as the new criteria.
d. Apply the new query. Works displays the message "No match found" because there is no person with the last name Francouer in the student data base.
e. Select OK to return to List view.

An Introduction to Computing Using Microsoft Works

7) DISPLAY ALL RECORDS AND THEN SAVE THE FILE

   a. From the Select menu, select the Show All Records command to remove the query. All records are again displayed.

   b. From the File menu, select the Save command to save the file.

6.10 *Time and Date Queries*

Queries can also be used to find information that is stored in time/date format. For example, Ivy University may want to know which students were admitted before a certain date, or the library's circulation office may want to know who has books that are overdue. Queries are used to find this type of information.

Time/date queries can be entered in either long (January 13, 1995) or short (1/13/95) form. Works displays each entry, however, to match the way the field is formatted. For example, if the Admit date field in the IVYSTU data base is formatted in long form, Works will display June 14, 1994 even if 6/14/94 is entered. On the other hand, if the field is formatted for short form, 6/14/94 is displayed even if the long form is entered. The same holds true for time queries. If a field is formatted in 24 hour format (14:00) and a 12 hour format is entered (2:00 PM), Works displays the time in 24 hour format, and vice versa.

• •

Practice 8

In this Practice you will query the IVYSTU data base for students who were admitted on April 7, 1992. Open IVYSTU if you have not already done so.

1) DISPLAY THE QUERY SCREEN

   a. Select Query from the View menu or Tool bar.

   b. Delete any previous criteria that may be displayed from a previous query.

2) CREATE AND APPLY THE DATE QUERY

   a. Move the cursor to the Admit Date field.

   b. Enter April 7, 1992 as the criteria. Notice that Works changes the date to short form because that is how the field was originally formatted. Remember, dates can be entered in either long or short form and will be interpreted correctly.

   c. Apply the new query by pressing F10 or by clicking on **List** in the Tool bar. Only those students who were admitted on April 7, 1992 are displayed. Who are they?

                                               50, 55, 63

3) SAVE THE DATA BASE FILE

6.11 Querying for More Than One Field at a Time

It is possible to include criteria for more than one field in a query. For example, applying the query

```
 File  Edit  Options  View  Window  Help
       Bld  Ital  Ul      Lft  Ctr  Rt     Form  List  Query  Report              Prev
 ══════════════════════════ IVYSTU.WDB ══════════════════════════
                    Ivy University Student Data Base

    First Name: ...............      Last Name: Adams.................

    Address: .....................................................

    City: ...................      State: PA  Zip: .................


    Admit Date: .............

    GPA: ......

    Paid: .   (Y for Yes, N for No)



 1                              QUERY                           <F1=HELP>
 Press ALT to choose commands, or F2 to edit.
```

This data base is being queried for two fields, Last Name and State

displays records for only those students with the last name of Adams who live in Pennsylvania. Queries are not limited to only one or two fields. In fact, any number of fields can include criteria, but in order for records to be displayed, all criteria must be met.

• •

Practice 9

In this Practice you will query the data base to list the students from North Carolina that have a 3.9 GPA. Start Works and open IVYSTU.WDB if you have not already done so.

1) DISPLAY THE QUERY SCREEN

   a. Select the Query command from the View menu or Tool bar.
   b. Delete any criteria from the previous queries.

2) ENTER THE FIRST CRITERIA INFORMATION

   a. Move the cursor to the State field.
   b. Enter NC. When applied, all records displayed will have an NC (North Carolina) in the State field.

3) ENTER THE SECOND CRITERIA INFORMATION

   a. Move the cursor to the GPA field.
   b. Enter 3 . 9. In order to be displayed by this query, a record must have both an NC in the State field *and* a GPA equal to 3.9.

4) APPLY THE QUERY TO THE DATA BASE

Apply the query to the data base. Only the records of the students from North Carolina who have a 3.9 are now displayed. Note that the record indicator in the Status line shows 2/80, meaning that 2 students out of the total 80 are from North Carolina and have a 3.9 GPA.

6.12 Using Ranges to Create Complex Queries

Previous queries displayed records when the value stored in a field was *equal* to the value specified as the criteria. Other comparisons may be performed in a query by including the desired operator from the following list:

Operator	Meaning
=	Equals (default)
>	Greater than
<	Less than
<>	Not equal to
>=	Greater than or equal to
<=	Less than or equal to

For example, it is possible to enter the following criteria in the GPA field on the QUERY screen:

```
>3.5
```

When applied, this query displays only those records that store a GPA value greater than 3.5. Queries like this are said to contain "ranges" because there are multiple values of GPA which meet this criteria. That is, a single range can be used to take the place of several separate queries. Using the range query GPA: >3.5 instead of separate queries of GPA=3.6, GPA=3.7, GPA=3.8, etc., finds all the records greater than 3.5 in one easy step.

Text can also be used in ranges. Works recognizes that certain letters follow others in the alphabet, therefore enabling ranges to be used in queries. For example, Works knows that the last name Schlager comes after Gurbuz in alphabetical order. Any text included in a range must be enclosed in double quotes ("). For example, to display those students whose last names come after "Jones" alphabetically, the criteria

```
>"Jones"
```

is entered in the Last Name field on the QUERY screen. If >Jones were typed without the quotes, Works would display an error message. Works ignores case and applies queries entered in all capital letters, all lowercase letters, or a combination of the two. The same results are produced.

Note that equals is the default operator and does not require the quotes when used in a "rangeless" query. When Adams is entered in the Last Name field on the QUERY screen, Works assumes that you mean ="Adams" and processes the query properly.

Refer to the following table for example numeric and text range queries:

The query:	**Will display all records with:**
GPA: 3.5	a GPA of 3.5.
GPA: <3.5	GPAs less than 3.5.
GPA: >3.5	GPAs greater than 3.5.
GPA: <>3.5	GPAs not equal to 3.5.
GPA: <=3.5	GPAs less than or equal to 3.5.
GPA: >=3.5	GPAs greater than or equal to 3.5.
Name: Jones	the name of Jones.
Name: <"Jones"	names that come before Jones in the alphabet.
Name: >"Jones"	names that come after Jones in the alphabet.
Name: <>"Jones"	names that are not Jones.
Name: <="Jones"	names that come before Jones in the alphabet, including Jones.
Name: >="Jones"	names that come after Jones in the alphabet, including Jones.

Practice 10

In this Practice you will query the IVYSTU data base for students whose last name comes before McDonough. You will also query for last names that begin with a letter in the latter half of the alphabet. You will then query the data base for students with a GPA higher than 3.5. Open IVYSTU if you have not already done so.

1) DISPLAY THE QUERY SCREEN

Select the Query command and delete any criteria from previous queries.

2) CREATE AND APPLY A TEXT QUERY

a. Move the cursor to the Last Name field.
b. Enter the criteria <"McDonough" to find all students whose last name precedes McDonough alphabetically. Notice that when an operator is used, double quotes must enclose the text, or an error will result.
c. Press F10 or click on **List** in the Tool bar to apply the query. How many records were found? ᐧ43

3) CREATE AND APPLY ANOTHER TEXT QUERY

a. Return to the QUERY screen and place the cursor on the Last Name field.
b. Enter the criteria >="n" to find all students whose last name begins with N or follows N alphabetically.
c. Apply the query. Note that Works ignores case and displays all last names that meet the criteria.

4) **_DEFINE AND APPLY A NUMERIC QUERY_**

    a.   Return to the QUERY screen and delete the previous criteria.
    b.   Move the cursor to the GPA field.
    c.   Enter the criteria >3.5 and then apply the query. How many records are displayed?   17

6.13 Using Conjunctions to Create Complex Queries

It is possible to put limits on both ends of a range by using "conjunctions." Conjunctions are operators which join two or more ranges together to form one large criteria. Available conjunctions include "and" specified by #AND# and "or" specified by #OR#.

#AND#

The #AND# conjunction enables you to include multiple comparisons in a single query criteria. For example, it is possible to specify the following query in the GPA field:

>1 #AND# <2

When this query is applied, only records with a GPA entry which is greater than 1 *and* less than 2 (GPAs between 1 and 2) are displayed. Note that a student with a GPA of 1.0 or 2.0 would *not* be found by this query.

#OR#

Criteria may also be joined with the "or" conjunction to produce a query that has different parts. When a query is joined with #OR#, records are displayed if any of the criteria conditions are met. For example, applying the GPA query

>2.7 #OR# =2.5

displays the records for all students with either a GPA greater than 2.7 or equal to 2.5.

The "or" conjunction is not always evaluated properly by Works when it is used with the equals operator. To avoid errors, parentheses and equal signs should be used. For example, to display all students who are from Maine or New Hampshire, the proper State query is:

=(="ME" #OR# ="NH")

Similarly, to list all students with a GPA of 3.3 or 3.9, the proper query is:

=(=3.3 #OR# =3.9)

Specifying =3.3 #OR# =3.9 will <u>not</u> produce the desired results.

Practice 11

In this Practice you will apply two complex queries to the IVYSTU data base and note their effects. Start Works and open IVYSTU if you have not already done so.

1) DEFINE A COMPLEX QUERY

    a. Select the Query command and delete any previous criteria.
    b. Move the cursor to the GPA field.
    c. Enter the criteria: `>=2.0 #AND# <=2.9`
       This query will display all students with a GPA between 2.0 and 2.9, inclusive.

2) APPLY THE QUERY AND VIEW THE RECORDS

Apply the query. Only students with a GPA within that range are displayed. How many records are displayed? 2 5

3) DEFINE AND APPLY A NEW QUERY

    a. A query which displays all students from Maine or Vermont will be created. Select the Query command. The QUERY screen is displayed.
    b. Delete the previous criteria and move the cursor to the State field.
    c. Enter the criteria: `=(="ME" #OR# ="VT")`
       Because of the width of the State field, only the first few characters of the criteria are shown on the form. The entire criteria is displayed on the Formula line. Note the parentheses which must be used when using #OR# and equals in a complex query.
    d. Apply the query. Only records for students from Maine or Vermont are displayed.

4) SAVE THE FILE

6.14 Complex Date and Time Queries

Dates and times may be included in complex queries to find specific ranges of values. Date queries using operators or conjunctions must be entered in short form (7/29/95) and enclosed by single quotes. If long form is used in a complex date query, Works displays an error message.

In complex time queries, a time can be entered in either short or long form. When entered onto the QUERY screen however, it is displayed in 24 hour format, no matter how the field is formatted. For example, the entered time 3:20:35 PM is displayed as 15:20:35 on the QUERY screen. This differs from a simple time query where the time is converted to reflect the current formatting in the field.

Some important differences should be noted at this time concerning fields that are formatted as time/date fields, and fields that are formatted as regular numeric fields but store part of a date. For example, the entry April 23, 1993 should be formatted as a date field because 1, it is a complete date, and 2, it can only be queried for a date value. On the other hand, a straight numeric entry like the year 1994, even though it is referring to a year (or date), is a numeric field and can therefore only be queried for numeric values. Whenever a piece of a complete date is included as an entry in a field, it is simply a numeric entry. Refer to the example below.

Year: 1995 ⎤
Month: March ⎬————————— Date: March 7, 1995
Day: 7 ⎦

These three fields are separate numeric entries.   *This is one field storing a single value, a date entry.*

Enclose time/date query criteria with single quotes when using the #AND# and #OR# conjunctions. The following examples illustrate complex time/date queries using conjunctions:

- To find all the students who were admitted to Ivy University after November 27, 1992 *and* before May 17, 1993, the following query would be typed in the Admit date field in IVYSTU:

  >'11/27/92' #AND# <'5/17/93'

- To find all the students who were admitted after February 27, 1995 *or* on May 19, 1994, the following query should be used:

  >'2/27/95' #OR# ='5/19/94'

- If a store manager wants to find out which employees are scheduled to begin work between 9AM *and* 2PM, the following query should be is used:

  >='9:00 AM' #AND# <='2:00 PM'

- If a store manager wants to find out which employees are scheduled to begin work at 11AM *or* at 6PM, the following query should be used:

  =(='11:00 AM' #OR# ='6:00 PM')

Remember, complex time/date queries need to be enclosed by single quotes to produce the correct information. Also, any #OR# criteria using the equals operator needs to be enclosed in parenthesis, as in the last example above.

Refer to the table on the next page for examples of complex time and date queries.

The query:	Will display all records with:
5/1/94	the date May 1, 1994.
<'5/1/94'	dates that come before May 1, 1994.
>'5/1/94'	dates that come after May 1, 1994.
<>'5/1/94'	dates that are not May 1, 1994.
<='5/1/94'	dates that come before May 1, 1994, including May 1, 1994.
>='5/1/94'	dates that come after May 1, 1994, including May 1, 1994.
>'4/1/95' #AND# <'10/1/95'	dates between April 1, 1995 and October 1, 1995.
<'4/1/95' #OR# >'10/1/95'	dates before April 1, 1995 or after October 1, 1995.
>'4/1/95' #OR# ='10/1/95'	dates after April 1, 1995, or the date October 1, 1995.
=(='4/1/95' #OR# ='10/1/95')	dates of April 1, 1995 and October 1, 1995.
<>'4/1/95' #AND# <>'10/1/95'	dates that are not April 1, 1995 and October 1, 1995.
>'4/1/95' #AND# <>'10/1/95'	dates after April 1, 1995, not including October 1, 1995.
9:30	the time 9:30 AM. (AM is the default)
9:30 PM	the time 9:30 PM.
21:30	the time 9:30 PM.
<'9:30'	times before 9:30 AM.
>'9:30'	times later than 9:30 AM
<>'9:30'	times that are not 9:30 AM.
<='9:30'	times before, and including, 9:30 AM.
>='9:30'	times after, and including, 9:30 AM.
>'11:00 AM' #AND# <'2:00 PM'	times between 11 AM and 2 PM.
<'11:00' #OR# >'2:00 PM'	times before 11 AM or after 2 PM. (AM is the default)
<'11:00' #OR# ='2:00 PM'	times before 11 AM, or the time 2 PM.
=(='11:00' #OR# ='2:00 PM')	the time 11 AM or 2 PM.

(handwritten above the date rows: *1997* ... *1990*)

• •

Practice 12

In this Practice you will perform complex date queries on the IVYSTU data base. Open IVYSTU if you have not already done so.

1)   PERFORM A COMPLEX DATE QUERY

   a.   Select the Query command from the View menu or Tool bar.

   b.   Delete any previous criteria and then move the cursor to the Admit date field.

   c.   Enter the criteria <='10/17/92' and apply the query. How many students were admitted on or before October 17, 1992?   *43*

2)   PERFORM A COMPLEX DATE QUERY USING CONJUNCTIONS

   a.   Return to the QUERY screen and delete the last criteria.

   b.   Enter the criteria >='1/1/93' #AND# <='3/30/94' in the Admit Date field. This query shows the records of all the students who were admitted between January 1, 1993 and March 30, 1994. Notice that the dates are enclosed in single quotes so Works will recognize the entry as a date query.

   c.   Apply the query. How many students were admitted between these two dates?   *14*

Check - The screen should be similar to:

```
   File  Edit  Print  Select  Format  Options  View  Window  Help
      Bld  Ital  Ul      Lft  Ctr  Rt      Form  List  Query  Report           Prev
  7/8/93
  ■══════════════════════ IVYSTU.WDB ════════════════════════╪
          City         State Zip  Admit Date  Paid  GPA                         =
  7     Redmond          WA  99134     7/8/93    Y   1.7                         ↑
  9     Newark           DE  19312     1/3/94    Y   3.7                         ▓
  12    Richmond         VA  23467    11/5/93    Y   3.1
  32    Jamaica          NY  11947    3/21/93    Y   3.8
  37    Stans Valley     VI  99999    9/20/93    Y   2.0
  39    Philadelphia     PA  17123     3/3/93    N   3.1
  48    Monticello       AR  71655    3/19/93    N   3.5
  51    Five Points      FL  33434    6/28/93    N   4.0
  59    Waumpum          IL  62920     2/2/94    Y   3.6
  60    Wallace          IL  60616    3/28/94    Y   3.3
  62    Boyton           OK  74107    6/17/93    N   1.1
  66    Saint Gabirel    LA  70776     2/5/93    Y   2.8
  70    Fostex           IN  47840    6/15/93    N   2.9
  78    New Philadelphia SD  57492    3/28/94    Y   3.4
  81
  82
  83                                                                            ↓
  └─┼─────────────────────────────────────────────────────────────────→┘
  7 Admit Date  14/80        LIST                                  <F1=HELP>
  Press ALT to choose commands, or F2 to edit.
```

3) PERFORM ANOTHER QUERY

a. Return to the QUERY screen and delete the previous criteria.

b. Enter the criteria >='8/22/94' #OR# ='2/12/92' into the Admit Date field. This query will show the records of all students who where admitted on or after August 22, 1994 or on February 12, 1992.

c. Apply the query. How many records were found? /2

4) SAVE THE DATA BASE

Remember that when a data base is saved, all of the records are saved, not just the ones displayed on the screen.

6.15 Querying Using WorksWizard

```
File
┌─────────────────────────┐
│ Create New File...      │
│ Open Existing File...   │
│ WorksWizards...         │
│ Save                    │
│ Save As...              │
│ Close                   │
├─────────────────────────┤
│ File Management...      │
│ Run Other Programs...   │
├─────────────────────────┤
│ Exit Works              │
└─────────────────────────┘
```

It is possible to perform a query on a data base using the WorksWizard. WorksWizard uses a menu driven, user-friendly approach to develop queries and automatically inserts the criteria onto the QUERY screen. WorksWizard asks questions concerning the needed information and then quickly formulates the query, in turn, helping to reduce errors.

To build and apply a query using the WorksWizard, WorksWizard is chosen from the File menu. **Data Finder** is then selected from the WorksWizards dialog box and Enter pressed to start building the query.

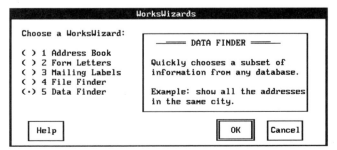

WorksWizard can automatically create and apply a query

Works displays a number of screens asking for information about the query and shows the results of each step in sentence form. Each screen explains what is needed while also giving examples of different formats. If a mistake is made, pressing PgUp displays the previous screen. To return to the data base and cancel the WorksWizard query, Escape is pressed.

After the final step is completed, WorksWizard compiles the supplied information and performs the query, displaying the results on the screen. If you are satisfied with the results, pressing Enter returns you to the data base. If another query needs to be applied, selecting **No, show all records. I'd like to start over** in the Data Finder dialog box enables another query to be built.

• •

Practice 13

Using WorksWizard, you will build and perform a query that lists the students who live in either Hawaii or Alaska. Start Works and open IVYSTU if you have not already done so.

1) START WORKSWIZARD

a.   Select WorksWizard from the File menu and choose **Data Finder**.
b.   Select **PgDn** to display the screen which lists the available fields.

2)   CHOOSE THE FIELD THAT IS TO BE QUERIED

Select State, and then **PgDn**.

3)   CHOOSE THE CRITERIA

a.   Using the arrow keys, move the highlight up and down the list of criteria choices. Notice that example query sentences are given in the right part of the screen.
b.   Because we want to find the students who live in Hawaii or Alaska, select **#5 Is either ... or ...** and select **PgDn**.

4)   ENTER THE VALUES

a.   Notice the query starts to grow in sentence form in the upper-right corner of the dialog box: State is either
b.   So Works will know what values to look for, type the abbreviation for Hawaii (HI) on the first blank line, and the abbreviation for Alaska (AK) on the second blank line. Choose **PgDn** to move on to the next step.
c.   Because we do not have to include any further information to the query, select **#2 No, this is all that I'm looking for** and then **PgDn** to continue to the next screen.

5)   PERFORM THE QUERY

a.   Look in the upper-right corner of the Data Finder dialog box. Your query should read: State is either HI or AK.
b.   If the query is correct, select **PgDn** to apply the query. Works performs the query. If the query needs to be changed, choose **PgUp** to go back to the screen where you can correct the mistake.

6)   RETURN TO THE DATA BASE

Select **Yes, this is it!** and then **PgDn** to return to the queried data base.

7)   SAVE THE DATA BASE

6

Check - Your screen should be similar to the following:

```
 ┌──────────────────────────────────────────────────────────────┐
 │  File  Edit  Print  Select  Format  Options  View  Window  Help│
 │     Bld  Ital  Ul    Lft  Ctr  Rt    Form  List  Query  Report        Prev│
 │ "Gerri                                                         │
 │ ■────────────────────── IVYSTU.WDB ──────────────────────────┤│
 │       First Name   Last Name        Address         City     State═│
 │  29  Gerri       Gurbuz      15 Beach Resort Blvd.  Mountainview  HI ↑│
 │  36  Derek       Kearley     13 Big Tree Circle     West Lafeet   AK ▓│
 │  50  Walter      Parrot      7 Bonner Lane          Volcano       HI ▓│
 │  58  Peter       Rodriguez   100 Aroura Borealis    Pedro Bay     AK ▓│
 │  81                                                           │
 │  82                                                           │
 │  83                                                           │
 │  84                                                           │
 │  85                                                           │
 │  86                                                           │
 │  87                                                           │
 │  88                                                           │
 │  89                                                           │
 │  90                                                           │
 │  91                                                           │
 │  92                                                          ↓│
 │  93                                                          ↓│
 │ ╙──┼─────────────────────────────────────────────────────→╢│
 │ 29 First Name 4/80        LIST                    <F1=HELP>│
 │ Press ALT to choose commands, or F2 to edit.                  │
 └──────────────────────────────────────────────────────────────┘
```

6.16 Updating Data in a Record

Any time a data base is displayed in either Form view or List view, it is possible to change the contents of a field. This is called "updating a record" and is accomplished by moving the cursor to the desired record and field and then typing the new data. If the file is then saved on disk, the new data stored in that field is retained.

The ability to update records is important because the data stored in a data base often changes; a person may move and have a new address, the price of an inventory item may go up or down, a student receives a new GPA at the end of a semester, etc. For example, suppose Ivy University's registrar receives a check from student Bruce Bonner to pay his tuition bill. Ivy's student data base can be accessed and a Y stored in the Paid field of Bruce Bonner's record, replacing the N. Should a query such as "show all records where Paid equals N" then be applied, Bruce's record would no longer be listed. It is important to realize that simply changing the value on the screen does not mean that it is changed in the file. The file must be saved on disk after the change is made. Should there be a power failure before you save the file, the change would not appear the next time the file was opened. Therefore, as a precaution you should frequently save a data base file when updating records.

Because an update usually involves a specific record, a Search or Query is often used to locate the record to be updated. In the example above, the Search command could be used to move the cursor to each record containing the text "Bonner". The correct record would then be easy to locate and the update made.

As we have stated before, List view is limited because it only displays the first few fields in a record. It is possible that an update may require changing the data in a field not currently displayed on the screen. When this occurs, the desired record is first located in the file (using a Search or Query if necessary). The display is then switched to Form view which displays all of the fields for that record, and the update then made. Switching to Form view makes it easy to insure that Bruce Bonner's record is updated, and not another.

Practice 14

In this Practice you will update two records in the IVYSTU data base to reflect new information. Start Works and open IVYSTU.WDB if you have not already done so.

1) LOCATE THE DESIRED RECORD IN THE FILE

<u>Update</u>: *Student Jenny Lee has moved to 129 Amostown Road.*

    a.   Display the data base in List view if it is not already.
    b.   From the View menu or Tool bar, select the Query command.
    c.   Delete any previous criteria.
    d.   In the Last Name field, enter the criteria `Lee`.
    e.   Apply the query.
    f.   If it is not already, place the cursor on Jenny Lee's record.

2) ENTER THE NEW DATA FOR THE ADDRESS FIELD

    a.   Move the cursor to the Address field.
    b.   Enter `129 Amostown Road`. Her new address is now stored in the field, replacing the old data.
    c.   From the Select menu, choose the Show All Records command to display the entire data base.

3) LOCATE THE DESIRED RECORD IN THE FILE

<u>Update</u>: *Student Bruce Bonner has paid his tuition bill.*

    a.   From the Select menu, select the Search command.
    b.   Enter `Bonner` and then select OK.
    c.   Press `F7` until the cursor is on Bruce Bonner's record.

4) SWITCH TO FORM VIEW AND ENTER THE NEW DATA

    a.   The Paid field is not displayed on the screen in List view. Switch to Form view.
    b.   Move the cursor to the Paid field.
    c.   Enter a capital Y. A "Y" is now stored in the Paid field in Bruce's record.

5) SAVE THE FILE TO RETAIN THE UPDATES

6.17 Adding Records

It is often necessary to add new records to a data base; new students enroll in a school, a store adds a new item to its inventory, etc. New record can be added to a data base in two ways: appended at the end of the file, or inserted into the file. In both cases it is usually easiest to add a new record using Form view because it displays all of the fields for the new record.

Appending a record is a simple process. In Form view, pressing `Ctrl-End` displays an empty record located at the end of the file. The data for the new record is then typed onto that form. When the file is saved the new record is stored on disk. In List view, a record may be appended by moving the cursor to the first empty record at the end of the file and typing the new data there.

Works allows a new record to be inserted in a data base using the Insert Record command from the Edit menu. Any new records inserted are placed in the file above the current cursor position. Executing the Insert Record command from Form view displays a new, empty record. The new data is then entered on that form. After inserting the data for any new records the file must be saved on disk to retain them.

6.18 Deleting Records

Just as it is necessary to add new records to a data base, records must often be deleted; a student graduates or drops out of school, a store decides to no longer carry an item, etc. In Works, the Delete Record command from the Edit Menu deletes the current record that the cursor is on. Records may be deleted from either Form or List view. Because of the possibility of damaging the data base by removing the wrong record, you must be certain you are deleting the correct record before executing the Delete Record command. A record deleted by mistake cannot be recovered, and must be re-entered. When the file is then saved on disk, the deleted record is no longer stored. As when updating a record, there is often a need to first locate the record to be deleted using a Search or Query.

●●●

Practice 15

In this Practice you will add Steve Rohrman's record to the IVYSTU data base and delete Ian Morrison's. Start Works and open the IVYSTU data base if you have not already done so.

1) **PERFORM A SEARCH**

    a. Display the data base in Form view if it is not already.
    b. From the Select menu, select Search to display the Search dialog box.
    c. Type Rolls in the **Search for** box and select OK. Harold Rolls' record is displayed. The new record should be inserted directly above this one.

2) **INSERT A NEW RECORD AND ENTER THE DATA**

    a. From the Edit menu, select the Insert Record command. A new, empty record is shown.
    b. Enter the following data for each field:

               First Name: Steve
               Last Name: Rohrman
               Address: 212 Phillips Ave.
               City: Magnolia
               State: NJ
               Zip: 08724
               Admit Date: 1 0/16/92
               GPA: <u>leave blank</u>
               Paid: Y

    c. Switch to List view. Note that the new student's record has been inserted above Harold Rolls'.

3) LOCATE THE RECORD TO BE DELETED

a. Switch to Form view.
b. Use the Search command to locate the record for Morrison.

4) DELETE THE RECORD

With the cursor on Ian Morrison's record, select the Delete Record command from the Edit menu. The entire record is removed from the screen.

5) SAVE THE MODIFIED FILE

Save the updated file containing Steve Rohrman's record, but without Ian Morrison's.

6.19 *Sorting Records in a Data Base*

Data stored in a data base can be made easier to use if the records are in order based on the data stored in a certain field called the "key field," listed as **1st**, **2nd**, and **3rd Field** respectively by Works. For example, it is easy to locate students in the IVYSTU data base because the records are in alphabetical order by Last Name. Placing a data base in order is called "sorting" and is accomplished by selecting the Sort Records command from the Select menu. To sort a data base, the desired key field (the field that contains the values on which to base the ordering) must be entered in the **1st Field** option in the Sort Records dialog box:

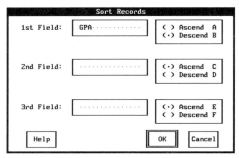

All records in the data base will be sorted in descending order according to GPA

Executing Sort with the example dialog box above would sort the file based on the values stored in the GPA field. Works automatically supplies a default key field, but this may be changed. Up to three key fields may be selected, and sorting may be done in Ascending (low to high) or Descending (high to low) order. Should the key field be a date or time field, chronological order is used. Ascending chronological order means earliest to latest (Jan, Feb, Mar, ... Dec, or 1:00 AM, 2:00 AM, etc.). Descending chronological order is latest to earliest (Dec, Nov, ... Jan, etc.). Ascend is the default.

An Introduction to Computing Using Microsoft Works

6

Once a key field and sorting order have been specified, Works changes the order in which the records are displayed based on the values stored in the key field. If sorted using the example shown in the dialog box above, a student record with a GPA of 4.0 would be moved before any records with a GPA of 3.9, and so on. If the data base is then saved on disk, the records are stored in the newly sorted order, so that the next time the file is opened, it will be sorted. Because sorting changes the order in which the records are placed in the file, a data base should be saved after executing the Sort Records command if the new record order is desired. Note that the sort ignores case if the key field is text.

• •

Practice 16

In this Practice you will sort the IVYSTU data base and print a copy of the sorted version. Start Works and open IVYSTU.WDB if you have not done so already.

1) SORT THE RECORDS ON THE GPA FIELD

a. If not already, display the data base in List view. Note that IVYSTU is in order by Last Name.
b. From the Select menu, select Sort Records. The Sort Records dialog box is displayed. Works automatically places the cursor in the **1st Field** box and selects **Ascend** for the order.
c. Type GPA for the **1st Field** name.
d. Select **Descend** and then OK to sort the records in descending order (high to low) based on the value stored in the GPA field. After a slight pause the records are rearranged and displayed in the new order on the screen.
e. Scroll to display the GPA field. Verify that the records are now in descending order by GPA by scrolling through the data base.

2) PRINT THE SORTED DATA BASE

a. From the Print menu, select the Print command.
b. Select the **Print record and field labels** option. An X appears in the box.
c. Print the data base. Compare the order of the records in this printout with the one produced in Section 6.7.

3) SORT THE DATA BASE ON THE LAST NAME FIELD

a. From the Select menu, select Sort Records.
b. Type Last Name as the key field, replacing the old value, GPA.
c. Select **Ascend** and then OK. The records are sorted and displayed in their new order.
d. Display the Last Name field to verify that the records are sorted by Last Name.

4) SAVE THE MODIFIED FILE

After a data base form has been completed, data can be entered into the fields. Works can store up to 255 characters in a single field, but the number displayed depends on the width set for the field.

Changes to the entry in a field are made by moving the cursor to the entry, typing the new data, and pressing Enter. The new data is then replaced by the old. Pressing F2 allows an entry to be edited on the Formula line.

Fields containing numbers can be formatted using the Fixed command from the Format menu by rounding the number to a specified decimal place. Fields containing dollar amounts can be formatted using the Currency command.

Once created, there are two ways to view a Works data base: Form view or List view. Form view shows all of the fields for one record, while List view shows only the first few fields for up to 17 records while Form view is useful for making changes to a record. List view makes it easy to see the relationships between the data stored in many records. It is possible to change the number of characters displayed for each field in List view by executing the Field Width command from the Format menu. Pressing the F9 key switches from one view to the other.

If a data base is currently displayed in List View, executing the Print command from the Print menu produces a listing of the data stored in each record. If a data base is in Form View, the Print command prints only the record currently displayed.

Works has two ways of locating specific data within a data base file. The first is by using the Search command from the Select menu. Search performs a general search for the entered text and moves the cursor to the first record which has that text stored in any of its fields. Subsequent searches for the same text are performed by pressing F7, locating a single record each time.

More specific than Search is the Query command found in the View menu. With this command, only the records which fit certain criteria are displayed. For example, using a query it is possible to display the records in a data base for each student from Maine, or all students with a GPA greater than 3. The criteria for a query is entered on the QUERY screen, and the F10 key is pressed to perform the query. Only those records which meet the criteria are then displayed. A Query is canceled by executing the Show All Records command from the Select menu. If the Print command is issued while a query is applied, only the records displayed by the query are printed. However, if the Save command is executed, all of the records will be saved even if not currently displayed.

It is possible to include criteria for more than one field in a query. For example, a data base could be queried for students with the name Jones who live in Florida. Complex queries using ranges may be created with the operators =, >, <, <>, >=, and <=. To display only the records of students with names that precede Smith alphabetically, the criteria <"Smith" would be entered in the Name field. Any text included in a range must be enclosed in double quotes.

Conjunctions like #AND# and #OR# are operators which join two or more ranges together to form one criteria. For example, to find the students with a GPA between 3.5 and 4.0 inclusive, the criteria >=3.5 #AND# <=4.0 would be entered in the GPA field.

Complex date queries must be entered in short form (7/15/95) and enclosed by single quotes. Complex time queries can be entered in either short or long form, but will be displayed in 24 hour format (13:07).

The WorksWizard uses a menu driven, user-friendly approach to develop queries, and automatically inserts the criteria onto the QUERY screen.

Because the data stored in a data base changes, Works can insert new records into a file with the Insert Record command, or delete existing records from a file with the Delete Record command. Both commands are located in the Edit menu. When a change has been made to a data base, the data base file must again be saved on disk to ensure that the change will be present the next time the file is used. The Save command saves the current file on disk and should be executed after every major change.

Placing a data base in a particular order is called "sorting" and is accomplished by choosing the Sort Records command from the Select menu. The records are re-ordered, or sorted, based on a desired field stored in a "key field."

Vocabulary

Ascending order - Placing in order from low to high.

Complex query - Criteria that includes more than one comparison.

Conjunction operator - Operator used to join criteria in a query: #AND# for "and", #OR# for "or".

Criteria - Description of the data that records must meet to be displayed. Refers to the contents of specific fields.

Delete Record command - Removes the current record from the data base.

Descending order - Placing in order from high to low.

Form view - All of the fields for a single record displayed on the screen at one time. Useful when updating a record or adding new records.

Hidden records - Records which do not meet the currently applied query's criteria. Hidden records are not displayed, but remain in the file.

Insert Record command - Adds a new, empty record to the data base above the current cursor position.

Key field - Field which stores the data used when determining the order during a sort.

List view - Displays the first few fields for up to 17 records. Useful when comparing records to one another or determining the results of a Query.

Query - Limiting the number of records in a data base that are displayed by defining criteria that they must meet.

Range - Criteria that includes an operator such as less than (<) or greater than (>).

Search command - Moves the cursor to the next record containing a specified Search for text in any field.

Search for text - Text entered by the user during a Search which records are compared to.

Show All Records command - Cancels a query and displays all records.

Sort - To place in order.

Sort Records command - Places records in order based on data stored in a "key field."

Update a record - Changing the contents of an entry or entries in a record.

•••

Reviews

Sections 6.1 - 6.7

1. A data base form has been created which contains three fields — Name, Age, and Street. Explain how data is entered into the first record of the data base.

2. a) If the name Joseph Josiah Kropeudopolis is entered into the data base of review 1, only part of it is displayed. What happens to the undisplayed part of the name?
   b) How can Works be instructed to display the complete name?

3. If a mistake is detected after a name has been entered into a data base, what two methods can be used to correct it?

4. List the steps required to format a field containing numeric data so that it will display:
   a) three decimal places.
   b) dollars to two decimal places.

5. a) How can a data base be searched for the name Kropeudopolis?
   b) What will happen if there are 3 people in the data base with that name?
   c) How can Works be instructed to find the second Kropeudopolis after finding the first?
   d) What will happen if a member lives at 35 Kropeudopolis Boulevard?
   e) How does Works respond if a search is performed and there is no Kropeudopolis in the data base?

6. a) Describe what is displayed in List view of a data base which contains many fields. How much of each field is displayed?
   b) How is it possible to display all of the fields in only the fifth record of a data base?

7. a) List the steps required to increase the widths in List view of the Last Name, Admit Date and Paid fields in the IVYSTU data base.
   b) If a file is saved after the List view has been changed, what format is displayed when the file is next accessed; the original format or the changed format?

8. Explain what is printed when the Print command is executed and a data base is in:
   a) List view.
   b) Form view.

6

9. a) List the steps required to display all records in the IVYSTU data base which contain the name Harold in their First Name fields.
   b) Which records containing the following entries would be displayed?

   > John Harold
   > Harold Smarold
   > 35 Harold Street
   > H. Arold Smythe
   > C. Tharold Jones
   > Heidi Smythe-Harold
   > Harold T. Harold

10. What is meant by the term criteria? Give 2 examples.

11. a) List the steps required to display all records in the IVYSTU data base for students who have not paid their tuition.
    b) If the Print command is issued while the query in part (a) is applied, what will be printed?

12. How does querying differ from searching a data base?

13. a) What happens to records that are "hidden" when a query is applied?
    b) How may hidden records be displayed?

14. Give an example of a date written in short form and long form.

15. Give an example of a time written in short form and long form.

16. Can a query be performed on more than one field? If yes, give an example using the IVYSTU data base.

17. What is meant by a range in a query? Give 2 examples.

18. Write queries for each of the following when applied to the IVYSTU data base:

    a) Students with GPA's greater than 2.5.
    b) Students from NY.
    c) Students with zip codes of 33432.
    d) Students named Zoler.
    e) Students who have GPA's greater than 3.0 and who have not paid their tuition.

19. Write queries which display the following when applied to the IVYSTU data base:

    a) Students with GPA's less than 1 or greater than 3.
    b) Students from CA or WA.
    c) Students with zip codes between 10016 and 11514.
    d) Students whose last names less than Brown or greater than Rose.
    e) Students who have GPA's greater than 3.5 or less than 2.0.
    f) Students with zip codes of 10016 or 10018.

20. Write queries which display the following when applied to a data base which contains dates and times:

a) dates between January 1, 1991 and September 30, 1994.
b) dates before January 10, 1950 or after December 20, 1980.
c) times equal to 10:00AM or 4:00 PM.
d) times after 10:15 AM or before 1:00 PM.

21. Briefly explain what is different between using the Query command and the WorksWizard to perform a query.

Sections 6.16 - 6.19

22. a) What does it mean to "update" a record?
    b) Why would records be updated?

23. Sam Adams has moved to 35 Cleve Street in Lawrenceville, NJ, 08618.

    a) List the steps required to change his address in the IVYSTU data base.
    b) Would it probably be better to make the corrections in List or Form view? Why?

24. A new student, Xin Tzeng, has enrolled at Ivy University. Explain the steps required to add his data to the IVYSTU data base. Because you are not sure where he fits alphabetically in the file, start by locating the position in the file where Xin's record should be added.

25. The Ivy University administration is discussing how to upgrade its standards by not allowing students with GPA's below 1.5 to enroll next year. Explain the steps that would be required to delete those students from the IVYSTU data base.

26. Ivy University is planning a mailing to its students and wants its data base IVYSTU ordered in ascending order by zip code. List the steps needed to do this.

An Introduction to Computing Using Microsoft Works

6 | Exercises

1. Print 10 copies of the questionnaire you designed in Chapter Five, Exercise 11 and distribute them to your friends at school. The data from your surveys will then be entered into the STUQUEST data base.

    a) After collecting your data, open STUQUEST.WDB and display the data base in Form view if not already.

    b) Enter the data from each questionnaire into the appropriate field in each record. Each questionnaire should correspond to a separate record.

    c) After entering data for all records, print one record in Form view.

    d) Switch to List view and sort the data base alphabetically by the person's last name.

    e) Print the data base in List view with the **Print record and field labels** option chosen, and then save the file.

2. In Chapter Five, Exercise 2 you created an author catalog data base form called CATALOG. In this Exercise you will enter 15 records into that data base form by following the steps below:

    a) Open CATALOG.WDB and display the data base in Form view if not already.

    b) Enter records for 15 books that your friends might write. Be sure to use a wide variety of names, states, etc., and include at least two books for each subject area.

    c) Print the seventh record in Form view.

    d) Perform a query that will display all authors of non-fiction books. Print out the results in List view.

    e) Print the entire data base in List view, sorted alphabetically by the author's last name. Be sure to select the **Print record and field labels** option.

    f) Save the modified data base.

3. Fantasy Wheels has decided it is going to use the data base form you created in Chapter Five, Exercise 10.

    a) Using the WHEELS data base form produced in that Exercise, enter the records below:

1984 Ferrari	1972 Corvette
exterior: gray	exterior: red
interior: black	interior: green
accessories: 4 speed, convertible	accessories: radio, automatic, air
paid: $22,000	paid: $8,500
asking price: $38,500	asking price: $25,800
date acquired: 7/12/92	date acquired: 10/12/93

1975 Aston Martin
exterior: red
interior: black
accessories: radio, air
paid: $56,700
asking: $120,000
date acquired: 10/6/94

1987 Porsche
exterior: black
interior: white
accessories: 4 speed, air
paid: $22,300
asking: $46,000
date acquired: 5/27/92

1988 Ferrari
exterior: red
interior: black
accessories: radio, air, 4 speed
paid: $72,300
asking price: $102,000
date acquired: 2/17/91

1985 Porsche
exterior: red
interior: blue
accessories: radio, 4 speed
paid: $31,000
asking price: $62,000
date acquired: 10/11/94

1978 Triumph
exterior: green
interior: white
accessories: 4 speed, air
paid: $4,560
asking price: $7,200
date acquired: 5/18/91

1958 Thunderbird
exterior: white
interior: red
accessories: radio, air
paid: $14,500
asking price: $31,000
date acquired: 2/14/93

1969 Maserati
exterior: blue
interior: black
accessories: radio, 4 speed, air
paid: $9,800
asking price: $21,600
date acquired: 5/9/91

1978 Nova
exterior: yellow
interior: orange
accessories: air
paid: $4,200
asking price: $6,600
date acquired: 8/19/92

b) Fantasy Wheels has had a great day and sold the 1985 Porsche. Delete this record from the data base.

c) A customer has come into Fantasy's show room and wants to buy her husband a red sports car as a Valentine's day present. Print a listing of only red cars.

d) Fantasy has had the 1969 Maserati painted purple, replaced the radio with a CD player, and raised the asking price to $29,000. Modify the record for the Maserati accordingly.

e) Apply a query which displays all cars with black interiors that originally cost under $25,000. Which cars meet this criteria?

f) Save the modified WHEELS data base.

4. Open IVYBOOKS.WDB and answer the following questions:

a) Apply queries to answer the questions below and write the answers on a separate piece of paper:

1. Which items have fewer than 10 in stock? less than 100? more than 250?
2. Which departments have items costing less than $1.00? more than $15.00?

b) Sort the data base by the Price field. What is the most expensive item in the inventory? What is the least expensive item?

c) Save and print the modified inventory.

5. Using the form you created in Chapter Five, Exercise 12, enter the following information into the HOLIDAY data base. Open HOLIDAY.WDB and display the data base in Form view if not already. It may be helpful to refer to the seating chart in the Chapter 5 exercise.

a) Add an empty record for each of the 20 seats on the plane. Enter the word "Empty" into the passenger name field of each record. Make all seats in rows 1 and 2 the first class section.

b) Make the following reservations by updating the proper records in the data base. Use queries to locate seats for passengers with preferences.

Mr. & Mrs. A. Irplane
Phone Number: (407) 555-6321
Mrs. Irplane: window seat, first class
Mr. Irplane: aisle seat (next to wife)

Mr. and Mrs. C. Brown
Phone Number: (407) 555-2475
Mrs. Brown: window seat, first class
Mr. Brown: aisle seat (next to wife)

Mr. Bruce Presley
Phone Number: (305) 555-7847
Mr. Presley: aisle seat, first class

Ms. Kerrin McGuire
Phone Number: (617) 555-5217
No preference

Ms. Heidi Crane
Phone Number: (609) 555-9165
Ms. Crane: window seat, first class

Mr. and Mrs. S. Morawski
Phone Number: (508) 555-3197
Mrs. Morawski: window seat
Mr. Morawski: aisle (next to wife)

Mr. John Borelli
Phone Number: (413) 555-8857
Mr. Borelli: window seat

Mrs. Ruth Wagy
Phone Number: (217) 555-3500
No preference

c) The reservation desk at Holiday needs to know the seat numbers of all empty seats. Apply a query which locates these seats, and then write down the empty seat numbers on a separate piece of paper.

d) Holiday Airlines has held a promotional contest and you have won 5 free trips to the Bahamas. Make 5 reservations using the names and phone numbers of friends.

e) The Holiday flight is about to take off for the Bahamas and the cabin staff needs to know the seat numbers and names of each passenger. Create and apply a query showing only the occupied seats.

f) Print the data base in List view with the query created in part (e) applied.

g) Ms. McGuire has changed her mind and would now like a seat in first class. Create and apply a query which lists all empty seats in first class. If such a seat is available, change Ms. McGuire's record.

6. In Chapter Five, Exercise 13 you created a data base form for a weather experiment. Open WEATHER.WDB and display the data base in Form view if not already. Complete this data base by following the steps below:

a) Enter the following records:

Date	Time	Temp. F.	Rain	Sky
1/8/60	3:00 PM	79	0	Partly Cloudy
11/5/61	5:46 AM	67	0	Sunny
4/20/62	6:19 PM	57	1.1	Cloudy
6/5/65	5:26 PM	29	.43	Cloudy
12/21/67	10:59 PM	46	0	Clear
10/15/69	7:15 AM	81	.2	Windy
3/16/70	4:00 PM	49	0	Partly Cloudy
7/12/72	1:00 PM	78	0	Sunny
12/11/73	12:59 AM	47	0	Hazy
7/19/74	6:49 AM	56	0	Sunny
10/31/75	9:15 AM	49	.3	Windy
11/16/77	11:50 PM	74	0	Clear
1/1/80	3:43 PM	32	0	Partly Cloudy
2/6/81	6:55 PM	21	.1	Cloudy
2/27/82	8:20 PM	90	1.2	Partly Cloudy
7/19/83	5:01 AM	72	0	Hazy
5/19/84	7:46 PM	62	0	Sunny
6/27/85	2:28 PM	68	.3	Cloudy
12/23/86	12:59 PM	36	0	Clear
5/19/87	2:49 PM	55	.75	Cloudy
8/24/87	5:33 AM	76	.5	Hazy
11/5/88	6:45 AM	44	.1	Windy
3/2/89	2:33 PM	66	.7	Cloudy
10/22/90	10:15 AM	83	.2	Windy
2/24/91	7:32 AM	78	0	Sunny
3/22/91	2:45 PM	72	.5	Windy
5/24/92	5:03 AM	69	1.5	Cloudy
8/22/92	9:30 PM	81	.3	Windy

b) Add a record to the file describing today's weather.

c) Center the Temp. F. column and left align the Rain column.

d) Use queries to answer the questions below. Write your answers on a separate piece of paper.

1. On which days was it sunny?
2. On what days were recordings taken between 1987 and 1990?
3. On which days was the temperature exactly 29 degrees, or above 80 degrees?
4. On which days was it windy and colder than 60 degrees?
5. What days were not sunny or clear and had temperatures lower than 50?

e) Apply a query that finds all days where the recording was taken after 2 PM.

f) Print the data base with the query created in part (e) applied.

An Introduction to Computing Using Microsoft Works

6

7. On your disk is a data base named CARPRICE which contains information about the price of new cars. Open CARPRICE.WDB.

   a) Format each price field for currency with 0 decimal places.

   b) Sort the data base alphabetically by the Make field. What is the first and last car on the list?

   c) The price for a Porsche 944S with sunroof has gone up $200. Search for this car and then modify the record to reflect this change.

   d) Use queries to answer the questions below. Write your answers on a separate piece of paper:

      1. How many cars have a base price under $12,000?
      2. How many cars have air conditioning for under $11,250?
      3. Your friend Anton needs a new car but does not have much money. How many cars with a stereo cost under $9,000?
      4. Which cars with sunroofs cost between $25,000 and $40,000 inclusive, but are not BMWs?

   e) Apply a query that will display all cars (makes) that begin with the letter "C".

   f) Print the data base with the query created in part (e) applied.

8. On your disk is a data base named COUNTRY which contains information about the countries of the world. Open COUNTRY.WDB and display the data base in List view if it is not already.

   a) Format both the Area and Population fields for commas with 0 decimal places.

   b) What country is the fifth most populated?

   c) Use queries to answer the questions below. Write your answers on a separate piece of paper:

      1. How many countries use the ruble as their currency?
      2. Which countries with areas over 3 million use the dollar as their currency?
      3. Which countries using the franc have capital cities beginning with the letter B?
      4. Which countries have populations under 100,000?

   d) Create and apply a query that will display all countries that begin with the letter M.

   e) Print the data base with the query created in part (d) applied.

9. CityZoo has decided to computerize its animal inventory. Using the ZOO data base form you created in Chapter Five, Exercise 7, enter the following records:

Animal Name	Males	Females	Type	Location	Staff
American Black Bear	0	1	M	American West	K. Morris
Asian Green Boa	1	2	R	Reptile Garden	T. Quay
Bison	2	3	M	American West	K. Morris
Blue-faced Angelfish	1	1	F	Aquarium	L. Wrighte
Bobcat	1	1	M	Eastern Forest	P. Sewell
Clown Anemonefish	7	8	F	Aquarium	L. Wrighte

Common Iguana	1	2	R	Reptile Garden	T. Quay
Eastern Indigo	2	0	R	Reptile Garden	T. Quay
Eastern Swallowtail	12	25	I	Insect Room	W. Carr
Egyptian Scarab Beetle	4	0	I	Insect Room	W. Carr
Gray Squirrel	6	9	M	Eastern Forest	P. Sewell
Great Horned Owl	0	1	B	Aviary	M. Rolls
Greater Mastiff Bat	2	5	M	Aviary	M. Rolls
Moray Eel	1	0	F	Aquarium	L. Wrighte
Mountain Lion	1	2	M	American West	K. Morris
Nurse Shark	0	1	F	Aquarium	L. Wrighte
Praying Mantis	3	7	I	Insect Room	W. Carr
Red Fox	1	2	M	American West	K. Morris
Ring-necked Pheasant	4	1	B	Eastern Forest	P. Sewell
Texas Horned Lizard	2	1	R	Reptile Garden	T. Quay
Toco Toucan	1	1	B	Aviary	M. Rolls
White Tail Deer	4	3	M	Eastern Forest	P. Sewell
Zebra Finch	6	14	B	Aviary	M. Rolls

a) Use queries to answer the questions below. Write your answers on a separate piece of paper:

    1. How many mammals are at the zoo?
    2. What is total number of animals in the Aviary and American West?
    3. Which animals have more than 5 females and more than 5 males?
    4. How many animals are cared for by P. Sewell and W. Carr?

b) A female Red Shoulder Hawk has been added to the Eastern Forest display. Add its record to the data base.

c) Sort the modified data base by the animal's type and then print a copy.

10. On your disk is a file named COLLEGE which contains information about colleges and universities in the United States. Open COLLEGE.WDB and complete the following steps:

a) Format the Enrollment field for commas with 0 decimals. Format the Tuition and Rm/Bd fields for currency with 0 decimal places.

b) Which college or university is located in Kalamazoo?

c) Based on tuition only, what are the three most expensive and inexpensive schools in the data base?

d) Use queries to answer the questions below. Write your answers on a separate piece of paper:

    1. How many schools are in Massachusetts?
    2. How many public schools enroll more than 10,000 students?
    3. Which public schools in California and Illinois enroll less than 20,000 students?

e) Print the data base with the last query created in part (d) applied.

6

11. Use the INVENTOR data base to answer the questions below.

   a) Which French inventors produced their inventions between the years 1900 and 1930?

   b) What things did Galileo invent?

   c) Which inventions were produced in Russia after 1960?

   d) How many things were invented in England and Italy between 1600 and 1830?

   e) Last week your friend Molly McVention invented a Peanut Butter and Tuna fish sandwich. Add a new record to INVENTOR file which chronicles this event.

   f) Create a query which displays all inventors from the United States.

   g) Sort the results of the query applied in part (f) in ascending order by year. Print the data base with the query still applied.

12. Open the ADDRESS data base form you created in Chapter Five, Exercise 1.

   a) Enter data into the file for a minimum of 10 friends.

   b) Apply a query which displays only the people born between 1975 and 1980. Who are they?

   c) You've made a new friend, Amy Eppelman. Add her data to ADDRESS:

   > Amy Eppelman
   > 713 Graisbury Avenue
   > Haddonfield, NJ 08033
   > (213) 555-1324
   > Born 7/5/75

   d) Amy Eppelman has moved. Change her address and phone number to:

   > 343 Nenue Street
   > Honolulu, HI 96810
   > (767) 555-5937

   e) You have decided that the first person in the file is no longer your friend. Delete that record from ADDRESS.

   f) Sort the data base alphabetically by the person's last name and then print it.

13. In Chapter Five you created a form for a gibbon observation data base. Open GIBBON.WBD which already contains a number of observations of the gibbons.

   a) Sort the data base by the age of the animal. Switch to form view and print the record of the oldest gibbon in the data base.

   b) How many gibbons are female?

   c) Find the record of the animal who was in Base Camp. What was the name of this animal, and what was it doing when it was being observed?

d) Use queries to answer the questions below. Write your answers on a separate piece of paper:

1. Which gibbons are under 5 years old?
2. Which gibbons older than 7 years old have male companions?
3. Which gibbons were observed either playing or eating when the temperature was above 80 degrees?
4. How many observations were made between 6 AM and 9AM? 3 PM and 6 PM?
5. What is the most common activity of the animals when it is raining?

e) Sort the data base alphabetically by name and print in List view.

14. On your disk is a data base named ACADEMY which contains information about the Academy Award winners since the Awards started in 1927. Each record contains the winners in each category for each year. Open ACADEMY.WDB and apply queries to answer the following questions:

a) How many winning films has United Artists produced?

b) Which winning movies did Columbia produce between the years 1960 and 1990?

c) How many times did Katherine Hepburn win the Academy Award for Best Actress?

d) What movies won in the 1940s?

e) Print the data base with the query created in part (d) applied.

Chapter Seven

Advanced Data Base Techniques

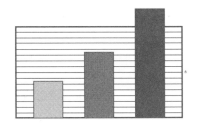

Objectives

After completing this chapter you will be able to:

1. Plan and produce printed reports containing specific information from a data base.

2. Load and modify previously created report formats.

3. Include totals and other calculations in a report.

4. Add a calculated field to a data base.

7

The previous two chapters described the commands and processes necessary to create and manipulate a data base using Works. It is only after a data base has been created that one of its most powerful features can be employed: the ability to produce printed reports detailing the information stored in its records. In this chapter the commands necessary to produce such reports will be discussed. A powerful Works feature which allows a field in a data base to be calculated based on the data stored in other fields will be introduced.

7.1 Report Sections

Once a computerized data base has been created, its versatility becomes apparent as people access its information in different ways. One of the most common ways to use the information in a data base is in the printed report. Reports organize and summarize information from a data base, displaying the desired data in a variety of formats. For example, it is possible to produce a report which lists only the names and GPAs of each student in the IVYSTU data base, while a different report can be produced to show the students' names, addresses, and if they have paid their tuition.

In Works, a report is organized into a number of sections, each identified by a different name. Each of the sections is optional, so that a report may contain as few as one or two sections. A sample printed report is shown below, along with the names that are used to identify the different sections:

```
Title                         Student List

Headings        First Name    Last Name    GPA

                Amy           Freitas      4.0
                Nancy         Rorhman      3.8
                Thom          Steves       3.9     Data from 1 record
Record                                             in the data base file
                Jack          O'Leary      3.7
                John          Parker       3.9
                Barri         Attis        3.6
                Luke          Burke        3.6

Summary                       Average:     3.78    Value calculated by
                                                   Works
```

Different sections of a printed report

Title:	The report may include a title which can be used to show the report's purpose, the date the report was printed, the name of the preparer, etc. This title is printed only once at the top of the first page of the report.
Headings:	Because reports may be several pages long, Works enables headings to be placed at the top of each page above each column of data. These headings help the reader of a report keep track of the data from page to page.
Record:	In a report, the actual data from the data base is listed like a table, one record per row. The data from each field is listed in a separate column. It is possible to exclude fields from a report, so that only part of the data base is listed. For example, the report above includes only three fields from the IVYSTU data base (First Name, Last Name, and GPA) even though there are more fields in the data base.
Summary:	Works can keep track of certain values and print a summary at the end of a report. In the summary Works can print totals, averages, and other calculations based on the values included in the report. The average GPA shown in the report above is an example of a report summary calculated by Works.

7.2 Planning a Report

A report should be planned carefully before creating its report format. This is done by applying some of the same rules used when first creating a data base:

1. What information should be included?
2. How should that information appear on the page?

The information to be included in a report is determined by analyzing the needs of the person that will use the report. Including unnecessary information in a report makes it harder to find desired information. It is important to consider how the different fields should appear when printed. For example, in what order should the information be presented, and how much space should be given to each. Thought must also be given to the titles and summary calculations that are to be included as part of the report. All of these options are specified when creating the report format.

7.3 Creating a Report Format

Before a report may be printed, a "report format" or definition must be created. The report format describes the contents of the report to Works. A report format can be created by selecting the New Report command from the View menu. Executing this command displays the New Report dialog box:

An Introduction to Computing Using Microsoft Works

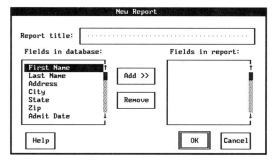

The New Report dialog box: The first step in creating a report

From here, a report title is entered into the **Report title** box. Next, the fields to be included in the report are selected. Highlighting a field name from the **Fields in database** list and then selecting **Add** enters the field into the report format. For example, to create a report listing the names and addresses of all the students, each field name would be highlighted and added to the **Fields in report** list.

After choosing the desired fields, selecting OK displays the Report Statistics dialog box:

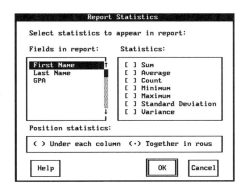

*Calculations on specific fields can be assigned in the
Report Statistics dialog box*

Here Works can be told to perform specific calculations such as adding, averaging, or finding the maximum value on any number of fields. Works includes the results of these calculations in the report summary.

Selecting a calculation while a field is highlighted performs the calculation in the report summary (We will discuss Report summaries in more detail later). If no calculations need to be performed, clicking on OK displays the requested information in the report preview:

```
                        Student GPA

    First Name      Last Name      GPA

    Lorna           Acenbrack      3.8
    Sam             Adams          1.5
    Ursala          Anderson       1.5
    Maria           Azteco         3.1
    Galin           Baer           2.6
    John            Barabas        2.7
    Gill            Bates          1.7
    David           Becker         1.9
    Bruce           Bonner         3.7
    Lana            Burner         2.1
    Harry           Cat            2.7
    Emily           Cohen          3.1
    Pablo           Cruise         2.5
    Page 1                    REPORT
    Press ENTER to continue, ESC to cancel.
```

Because the entire report cannot be displayed on the screen, Enter must be pressed to view each part of the report, page by page, or Escape pressed to cancel viewing.

7.4 *The Report Screen*

After the report preview, the REPORT screen is displayed, showing the report's format:

Report sections
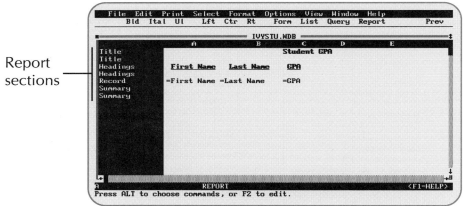

A report format with three fields (First Name, Last Name, GPA) on the REPORT screen

Like List view, the REPORT screen is divided into a series of rows and columns. Each column is identified with a letter shown at the top of the column (A, B, C, etc.). Columns have an initial width equal to the width set in List view, but this may be changed. Each row is identified by the section name showing how the information in that row will be printed in the report (Title row, Record row, etc.).

The left side of the REPORT screen shows the names used by Works to identify the different rows in the report. For example, any text that appears on a Title row is printed as the report's title. A Record row prints data taken from the data base for the fields listed in that row. The right side of the screen is the work area. The text, field names, etc. that make up the report are displayed here. For example, the =First Name shown in the Record row above is replaced by the actual first names from the

An Introduction to Computing Using Microsoft Works

7

data base when the report is printed. A marker such as =First Name is called a "field reference." A report format may contain one field reference, or many. Field references always begin with an equal sign (=).

The intersection of a row and column is called a "cell." Each cell may store one piece of information, either a field reference or some text. Text, such as a title, is printed as typed into the report format. In the example report format above, First Name is text and =First Name is a field reference.

Selecting Form or List from either the View menu or Tool bar, or pressing the F10 key exits the REPORT screen and displays the data base.

• •

Practice 1

In this Practice you will create a report format for the IVYSTU data base and then preview the report on the screen.

1) START WORKS AND OPEN IVYSTU.WDB

    a. Boot DOS and start Works as described in Chapter Two. The Quick Start dialog box is displayed.

    b. From the Quick Start dialog box, select **Open an Existing File**. The Open Existing File dialog box is displayed. Select IVYSTU.WDB to open the data base file.

2) CREATE A NEW REPORT FORMAT

From the View menu, select the New Report command to create a new report format. The New Report dialog box is displayed.

3) ADD A TITLE AND A FIELD TO THE REPORT FORMAT

    a. With the cursor in the **Report title** box, type the title of the data base: Student GPAs

    b. We want to include first and last names of each student, as well as their GPAs in this report. Move the cursor to the **Fields in database** list and highlight the First Name field if not already. Select **Add** to add this field to the report format. Notice that the First Name field appears in the **Fields in report** list.

4) ADD THE OTHER FIELDS

    a. Highlight Last Name in the **Fields in database** list and select **Add**.

    b. Scroll through the list of fields in the **Fields in database** list. Add the GPA field to the **Fields in report** box, and select OK. The Report Statistics dialog box is displayed.

5) PREVIEW THE REPORT

    a. Because no calculations are needed on these fields, select OK to see a view of the report. The requested fields are displayed on the screen in report form.

    b. Press Enter to scroll through the report. Notice that only the fields selected in steps (3) and (4) are included in the report.

6) DISPLAY THE REPORT SCREEN WITH THE REPORT FORMAT

    a. Continue to press Enter until the REPORT screen is displayed. Note the different rows, columns, and section titles. What data is in each section?

    b. Exit the REPORT screen by pressing F10 or clicking on **List** in the Tool bar.

7.5 Viewing Reports on the Screen

View

- Form
- List
- Query
- New Report...
- Reports...
- •1 Report1

In addition to being printed, reports may also be viewed on screen. Selecting the report's name from the View menu displays a preview of the current report on the screen. Pressing Enter continues the report, displaying the next screenful. Escape may be pressed to terminate the display and return to the REPORT screen. It is a good idea to preview a report on screen before printing in order to save time and paper.

Also remember that the Preview command from the Print menu can display a smaller version of the report, one complete page at a time. This command is helpful when the report needs to be seen in pages, instead of in separate screenfuls as described above using the View menu.

Do not confuse the preview produced by selecting the report's name from the View menu with the preview produced using the Preview command from the Print menu. In the preview produced from the View menu, the report is displayed in sections and text is shown in its formatted form (bold, italic, etc.). In the preview produced with the Preview command, however, the report is displayed one entire page at a time, and no formatting is shown.

In the remaining Practices, when we say to "preview the report," you should select the report's name from the View menu to display the report on the screen.

7.6 Printing a Report

Print

- Print...
- Page Setup & Margins...
- Preview...
- Insert Page Break
- Delete Page Break
- Headers & Footers...
- Printer Setup...

Once the report format has been created, executing the Print command while on the REPORT screen prints the report. Before printing, check that your computer is connected to a printer, and that the printer is turned on.

It is important to note that a report format is saved when the data base file is saved. For this reason the data base should be saved after a report format is created. A report format may then be modified to produce a new report. Note that the report is named the default Report1, but that this may be changed. This is discussed in more detail in the next section.

• •

Practice 2

In this Practice you will print the report created in Practice 1. You will then save the data base and retain the report for future use. Start Works and open IVYSTU.WDB if you have not already done so.

1) DISPLAY REPORT1

a.   From the View menu, select Report1 to see a preview of the report.
b.   Press Enter until the REPORT screen is displayed.

2) PRINT THE REPORT AND RETURN TO LIST VIEW

a. From the Print menu, select the Print command to print the report.
b. Return to List view by selecting the List command from the View menu, or clicking on **List** in the Tool bar.

3) SAVE REPORT1 WITH THE DATA BASE

From the File menu, select the Save command to save the data base file. Both the data base file and the Report1 format are saved on disk. When the IVYSTU data base is next opened, it will be possible to access the report created in this Practice, print it again, or modify it.

<u>Check</u> - Reports differ depending on the printer used, but your printed report should be similar to the example shown in Section 7.3.

7.7 Naming a Report

Because up to eight different report formats can be saved with a single data base file, names are needed to distinguish one format from another. Works uses the default names Report1, Report2, etc. to name each report format as it is created. After a report has been created, it should be renamed to reflect the specialized information it holds. For example, in the report created in Practice 1, the default name Report1 does not tell the user of the data base anything about what the report is about. A more useful name would be Student GPAs or GPAs. It is important to realize that a report's name is not the title that is printed on the top of the report. The title of a report is simply any text entered on the Title row of a report format. The report's name appears in the View menu, and after a number of reports has been created, each one can be viewed by selecting its name from the View menu. Pressing the corresponding number previews that report, which may then be modified, printed, etc.

To rename a report, the Reports command is selected from the View menu. The Reports box dialog is displayed, listing the current reports stored with the data base:

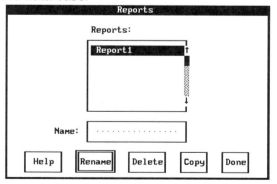

The Reports dialog box

The report that is to be renamed is highlighted in the Reports list. The cursor is then moved to the **Name** box, and the new name (up to 15 characters) is entered. Selecting **Rename** renames the report, and the change is reflected in the Reports list. **Done** is selected to complete the process.

Practice 3

In this Practice you will rename the report you created in Practice 1 with a more meaningful name. Start Works and open IVYSTU.WDB if you have not already done so.

1) RENAME THE REPORT

   a. From the View menu, select the Reports command to display the Reports dialog box.

   b. Highlight the report named Report1 in the **Reports** list if it is not already.

   c. Move the cursor to the **Name** box and enter Student GPAs. Select the **Rename** button and notice that the old name, Report1, is replaced with the new name, Student GPAs, in the **Reports** list.

   d. Select **Done** to return to the data base.

2) SAVE THE DATA BASE

7.8 Inserting and Deleting Rows and Columns in a Report Format

The REPORT screen enables a previously created report format to be modified. A new row can be inserted into the format by selecting the Insert Row/Column command from the Edit menu, and then selecting **Row** from the dialog box. A list of row types are displayed:

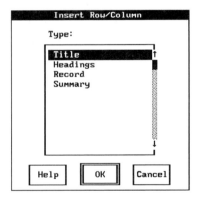

Any type of row may be inserted into a report format

Works automatically inserts the row into the correct position on the report format. For example, if **Heading** were selected, Works would insert a Heading row in the proper position, moving all sections below it down one line.

To insert a column in a report, the cursor is placed in the desired location in the report format, and the Insert Row/Column command is chosen from the Edit menu. **Column** is then chosen from the dialog box, and OK selected to insert a new column into the report format. All data to the right of the cursor is moved to the right when the new column is inserted.

7

Deleting unnecessary rows and columns can be done by first placing the cursor in the unwanted row or column and then selecting the Delete Row/Column command from the Edit menu. **Row** or **Column** is chosen depending on what needs to be deleted, and OK selected. Remember, everything in the row or column will be deleted from the report, but not the data base.

7.9 Improving the Appearance of a Report

After viewing your report, you may want to change its appearance and make it easier to read. For example, a column may have to be made wider to fit the data, a title moved, or important data made bold to draw more attention to it.

Columns are originally set to the same width as in List view. This may be changed using the Column Width command from the Format menu. When the columns are wide, or many columns are used, Works splits the report over several pages. Like the Word Processor, Works can adjust the margins using the Page Setup & Margins command from the Print menu. Decreasing the margins allows more of the report to be displayed on each page.

In a report, text is automatically left aligned while numeric, time, and date data are right aligned. Headings are automatically made bold, centered, and underlined. It is possible, however, to change the justification and formatting of the fields, headers, and any other part of the report by first placing the cursor on the desired item and then selecting the Style command from the Format menu. Here, alignment and styles of text can be chosen. Mouse users can simply highlight the desired items and select the formatting option in the Tool bar (**Bld, Ital, Ul, Lft, Ctr, Rt**).

Items on the REPORT screen may be moved to other parts of a report format by using the Move command from the Edit menu. For example, to move the title of the Student GPAs report closer to the left margin, the cursor is first placed on the Title, and Move selected from the Edit menu. MOVE is displayed on the Status line along with some brief instructions. The cursor is then moved to the new location and Enter pressed to complete the task.

●●

Practice 4

In this Practice you will modify the appearance of the Student GPAs report which was saved with the IVYSTU data base. You will widen a column, italicize the title, left align the name headings, and move the report title. You will also insert a column in preparation for the next Practice. Start Works and open IVYSTU.WDB if you have not already done so.

1)   DISPLAY THE STUDENT GPAs REPORT SCREEN

   a.   From the View menu, select the Student GPAs report. A preview of the report is displayed.
   b.   Press Escape to cancel the preview and display the REPORT screen.

2) LEFT ALIGN THE NAME HEADINGS

a. Place the cursor on the heading First Name.
b. From the Format menu, select the Style command to display the Style dialog box.
c. Select **Left** from the **Alignment** box, and then select OK.
d. To left align the heading Last Name, place the cursor on Last Name and repeat steps (b) and (c).

3) INSERT A COLUMN

a. Place the cursor in column C and select the Insert Row/Column command from the Edit menu.
b. Select **Column** and then OK. A new column is inserted between the Last Name and GPA columns.

4) ITALICIZE THE REPORT'S TITLE

a. Place the cursor on the report's title, Student GPAs. From the Format menu, select the Style command to display the Style dialog box.
b. Select **Italic** from the Styles box. An X is displayed next to **Italic**, meaning that this style has been selected. Select OK to format the title.

5) MOVE THE REPORT TITLE

a. With the cursor still on the report title, select the Move command from the Edit menu. Notice MOVE displayed on the Status line along with some brief instructions on the Message line.
b Move the cursor one column to the left to column C. Be sure the cursor is still in the first Title row.
c. Press Enter to move the title to its new position.

6) VIEW THE REPORT

a. From the View menu, select Student GPAs to see a preview of the report, or click on **Report** in the Tool bar. Notice the changes that have been made: the left justified name headings, the italicized title in its new position, and the blank column:

```
                       Student GPA

First Name  Last Name                  GPA

Lorna       Acenbrack                  3.8
Sam         Adams                      1.5
Ursala      Anderson                   1.5
Maria       Azteco                     3.1
Galin       Baer                       2.6
John        Barabas                    2.7
Gill        Bates                      1.7
David       Becker                     1.9
Bruce       Bonner                     3.7
Lana        Burner                     2.1
Harry       Cat                        2.7
Emily       Cohen                      3.1
Pablo       Cruise                     2.5
Page 1                    REPORT
Press ENTER to continue, ESC to cancel.
```

b. Press Escape to display the REPORT screen.

7) SAVE THE DATA BASE

7.10 Adding New Fields to a Report

The report format created in the previous Practices does not print all of the fields in an IVYSTU record, and it is likely that different users will require reports showing the missing fields, or want the fields printed in a different order. For this reason it is possible to create up to eight different report formats for each data base and store them on disk with the file. Report formats have some of the characteristics of Works files; they have a specific name, may be opened, modified, and saved. The difference is that a report format is not a separate file, but part of a specific data base and may only be used when that data base is open.

As mentioned above, it is sometimes necessary to add other fields to a report to give more information. This is a two step process. First, the field name must be inserted in the Headings row in the report format, and second, the field contents, or field reference, must be inserted in the Records row. Both sections are needed to provide the requested information.

To insert the field name into the Headings row in the report format, the cursor must be placed on the Headings row in a blank cell above the column where the field contents reference will be placed. Insert Field Name is selected from the Edit menu, displaying the Insert Field Name dialog box which lists all the fields in the data base:

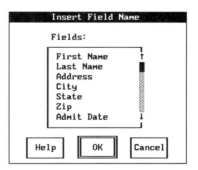

Fields can be inserted into a report by using the Insert Field command.

The desired field name is then selected, and OK chosen to insert the field name in the Headings row. Note that the field name may need to be formatted to match the other field names in the Heading row using Style from the Format menu.

To insert the field contents reference into the report format, the cursor must next be placed directly below the field name in the Record row. From the Edit menu, Insert Field Contents is selected, displaying the Insert Field Contents dialog box listing all the fields in the data base. Highlighting the desired field (which should match the Field Name heading) and selecting OK inserts the field contents reference, indicated by the field name preceded by an equal sign (=).

Practice 5

In this Practice you will further modify the Student GPAs report format to include the student's address. Column widths will be changed and headings formatted. Open the IVYSTU.WDB data base if you have not already done so and display the Student GPA report format.

1) INSERT THE ADDRESS FIELD HEADING

a. Place the cursor in the first Headings row in column C.
b. From the Edit menu, select the Insert Field Name command. The Insert Field Name dialog box is displayed.
c. Highlight Address in the **Fields** list and then select OK. The field name "Address" will now be printed as text in column C.

2) FORMAT THE ADDRESS FIELD NAME HEADING

a. Place the cursor on the Address field name in the heading row.
b. Format the field name by selecting **Underline**, **Bold**, and **Left** from either the Style command in the Format menu or the Tool bar.

3) INSERT THE ADDRESS FIELD CONTENTS REFERENCE

a. Place the cursor in the Record row in column C.
b. From the Edit menu, select the Insert Field Contents command. The Insert Field Contents dialog box is displayed.
c. Select Address from the **Fields** list and then select OK. The field reference "=Address" is inserted, and will be replaced by the actual addresses when the report is viewed or printed.

4) INCREASE COLUMN WIDTH

Place the cursor in the Address field. From the Format menu, select Column Width. Enter 25.

5) VIEW THE REPORT

a. From the View menu, select Student GPAs to see a preview of the report. Mouse users can click on **Report** in the Tool bar to preview the report. All headings should be bold, underlined, and left aligned, addresses should be displayed in column C, and the report title should be bold and italicized:

```
                          Student GPA

First Name   Last Name   Address                GPA

Lorna        Acenbrack   30 Ship Down Manor      3.8
Sam          Adams       121 Carey Quadrangle    1.5
Ursala       Anderson    2112 Red Star Way       1.5
Maria        Azteco      123 Trinity Towers      3.1
Galin        Baer        10 Gallon Hat Terrace   2.6
John         Barabas     1800 Hideaway Road      2.7
Gill         Bates       123 Lotus Lane          1.7
David        Becker      477 Central Wharf Road  1.9
Bruce        Bonner      35 Madison Drive        3.7
Lana         Burner      5 Big Cactus Lane       2.1
Harry        Cat         1 Siamese Court         2.7
Emily        Cohen       3B Mozart Towers        3.1
Pablo        Cruise      15 Keystone Center      2.5
Page 1                   REPORT
Press ENTER to continue, ESC to cancel.
```

b. Press Escape to display the REPORT screen.

6) SAVE THE DATA BASE

7) PRINT THE REPORT

7.11 Sorting Records

Select

Cells
Row
Column
All

Sort Records...

Sorting a data base file affects not only the order in which the records are displayed on the screen, but also the order in which they appear when printed. This makes it possible to have one report printed in order by Last Name and another by GPA, and so on. In addition, it is possible to specify the key field and sorting order from the REPORT screen, making it easy to generate different versions of the same report. It is important to note that the sorting options defined from the REPORT screen are saved with the report format. Should a report format specifying sorting by GPA be saved and the data base then sorted by Last Name, the next time the report format is printed or viewed it will re-sort the data base and display the records in order by GPA.

• •

Practice 6

In this Practice you will sort the Student GPAs report by GPA. Open IVYSTU.WDB if you have not already done so and display the Student GPAs report format.

1) SORT THE DATA BASE

  a. From the Select menu, select the Sort Records command.
  b. Type GPA as the **1st Field**.
  c. Select **Descend** which will sort the records in descending order (high to low) based on the GPA field.
  d. Select OK. The data base is now sorted in order by GPA.

2) VIEW THE REPORT

  View the report by selecting Student GPAs from the View menu or by clicking on **Report** in the Tool bar. Note that the order of the records is by descending GPA. Return to the REPORT screen by pressing Escape.

3) RETURN TO LIST VIEW AND SORT THE RECORDS

  a. Select List from the View menu or Tool bar. Scroll to view the GPAs. The data base is sorted by GPA.
  b. From the Select menu, select the Sort records command.
  c. Type State in the **1st Field** box and select **Ascend**.
  d. Select OK. The data base is sorted by state in ascending order. Note the order of the records.

4) DISPLAY THE STUDENT GPAs REPORT

  a. From the View menu, select the Student GPAs report. The report preview is displayed.
  b. Note the order of the records. The report is still sorted by GPA because Works allows sorts to be saved with report formats.
  c. Press Escape to display the REPORT screen.

5) SAVE THE DATA BASE

7.12 Using Queries with Reports

Queries were employed in the last chapter to limit the number of records displayed to only those which met certain criteria. When a query is applied, the records printed in a report are also limited. This allows special reports to be printed which display, for example, only students with GPA's greater than 3.5, or only students from Maine or Vermont.

Queries may be applied either from the data base screen or the REPORT screen. In either case, the query remains in effect until it is removed or changed. Note that the query is not saved with the report format and must be reentered if another query was defined for that data base.

7.13 Copying and Deleting Report Formats

Many printed reports have similar features. For this reason, Works allows a previously created report format to be copied under a new name and then modified and saved.

To copy a report format, the Reports command is selected from the View menu, displaying the Reports dialog box. The report needed to be copied is then highlighted and **Copy** is selected. The highlighted report format is copied using the next available default name (Report1, Report2, etc.). The **Rename** option can then be used to change the name of the copied report format. The copied format will have all of the characteristics of the old one, and may then be modified, printed, and saved like any other report format.

Because Works allows only 8 report formats to be saved with a data base, it is sometimes necessary to delete old, unwanted reports. Attempting to create a ninth report displays the error:

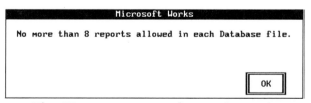

The "Too many report formats" Error box

A report can be deleted by selecting the **Delete** option from the Reports dialog box. The Delete option removes the highlighted report format, allowing a new one to be created or an existing format to be copied.

7

•••

Practice 7

In this Practice you will create a new report format named Honors by copying the current Student GPA report format. Honors will use a query to print only students with a GPA greater than 3.5. Start Works and open the IVYSTU.WDB data base if you have not already done so.

1) COPY THE STUDENT GPA REPORT FORMAT UNDER THE NAME HONORS

a. Select the Reports command from the View menu. A dialog box is displayed. Highlight Student GPA if it is not already, and then select **Copy**. The copy is given the default name Report1 and is shown in the Reports list.
b. Highlight Report1.
c. Move the cursor to the **Name** option.
d. Type Honors and select **Rename**. Both the Student GPA and Honors report formats are now listed.
e. Select **Done** to return to the data base.

2) APPLY A QUERY TO HONORS

a. From the View menu, select the Honors report.
b. Press Escape to display the REPORT screen.
c. Define a new query by selecting the Query command from the View menu. The QUERY screen is displayed.
d. Delete any old criteria that may exist. Move the cursor to the GPA field.
e. Enter the criteria > 3.5 in the GPA field.
f. Press Enter and then F10 to apply the query. Only those records with GPAs greater than 3.5 will be included in the report.

3) CHANGE THE REPORT TITLE

a. Move the cursor to column C of the first Title row.
b. Enter the new title Students with Honors GPAs to replace the old report title.

4) VIEW AND PRINT THE NEW REPORT

a. View the report on screen by selecting Honors from the View menu. Only those students with a GPA greater than 3.5 are listed in the report.
b. Press Escape to return to the REPORT screen.
c. From the Print menu, select Print to print the Honors report.

5) RETURN TO LIST VIEW AND SAVE THE DATA BASE

a. Display the data base in List view.
b. Remove the query and display all records by selecting the Show All Records command from the Select menu.
c. From the File menu, select the Save command to save the new Honors report format with the data base. IVYSTU now has two report formats saved with it, Student GPA and Honors.

7.14 Adding Summaries to Reports

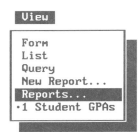

Reports can do more than just list the information stored in a data base in an organized manner. In addition to printing the contents of fields, Works data base reports can also calculate the total or average of all of the values printed in a field and count the number of records printed. These values can then be printed at the end of the report as part of the report's summary in a Summary row.

A summary can be added when a new report is first created. After the fields to be included in the report have been selected, the Report Statistics dialog box is displayed:

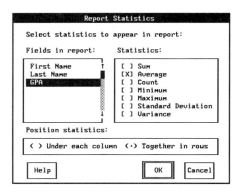

When creating a new report, calculations can be selected from the Report Statistics dialog box

The field to be calculated is selected from the **Fields in report** list. Then the calculation to be performed is chosen from the **Statistics** box, and OK selected. A summary reference is inserted in the report format where Works will display the results. For instance, in the example above, Works would display the average of only the values printed in the GPA column of that report, not the average of all the GPAs in the data base. Formatting options may then be applied to the summary reference using the commands from the Format menu. When the report is viewed or printed, the value is calculated and displayed.

• •

Practice 8

In this Practice you will create a new report which calculates the average GPA for the IVYSTU data base. Start Works and open IVYSTU.WDB if you have not already.

1) CREATE A NEW REPORT

From the View menu, select New Report to create a new report. The New Report dialog box is displayed.

2) ADD THE FIELDS TO THE REPORT

a. Enter `Student GPA Average` in the **Title** box.
b. Add the following fields to the **Fields in report** list: First Name, Last Name, and GPA.
c. When finished, select OK. The Report Statistics dialog box is displayed.

An Introduction to Computing Using Microsoft Works

3) SELECT THE FIELD AND CALCULATION

a. Because we want to have Works calculate the average GPA, highlight GPA in the **Fields in report** list.

b. Select Average in the **Statistics** box. An X is displayed next to Average.

4) VIEW THE REPORT

a. Select OK. The report preview is shown.

b. Press Enter four times to scroll through the report. Notice that Works has inserted the label **AVERAGE GPA:** and displays the numeric average at the bottom of the report.

c. Press Escape to view the REPORT screen. Notice that Works has inserted the label and summary reference in the Summary row.

5) RENAME REPORT1

a. From the View menu, select Reports. A dialog box is displayed.

b. Highlight Report1. Move the cursor to the **Name** box and type: Average of GPAs

c. Select **Rename** and then **Done**. Report1 is now named Average of GPAs.

d. Return to List view.

6) SAVE THE DATA BASE

7.15 Adding Summaries to Existing Reports

Summary calculations can be inserted into existing report formats just as additional titles and headings can. To include a summary, the cursor is placed in a Summary row in the desired column of the report format. Insert Field Summary is then selected from the Edit menu, displaying the Insert Field Summary dialog box:

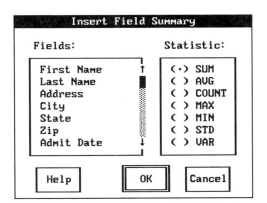

Field summaries are chosen from the Insert Field Summary dialog box

The field to be calculated is selected from the **Fields** list. Then the calculation to be performed is chosen from the **Statistic** box, and OK selected. A function is inserted in the report format where Works will display the results.

Practice 9

In this Practice you will add a summary to the Honors report format which counts the number of students who have made Honors. Open IVYSTU.WDB if you have not already done so and display the Honors report format screen.

1) RE-APPLY THE QUERY

a. Because queries are not saved with reports, you must re-apply the query used to create the Honors report. Select Query from the View menu to display the QUERY screen.

b. Delete any previous criteria.

c. Place the cursor in the GPA field and enter the criteria: > 3 . 5

d. Select Honors from the View menu to apply the query to the report. Honors will now display only those records with GPAs higher than 3.5. Press Escape to display the REPORT screen.

2) ADD THE COUNT STATISTIC TO THE HONORS REPORT FORMAT

a. Place the cursor in the second Summary row in column D. From the Edit menu, select Insert Field Summary. A dialog box is displayed.

b. Highlight GPA in the **Fields** list and select **COUNT** from the **Statistics** box.

c. Select OK to enter the summary into the report format. Notice that Works places a function into the report format. Due to the width of the column, the formula is truncated.

3) ADD A LABEL

Place the cursor in the second Summary row in column C and enter the label: No . of Honors Students:

4) VIEW THE MODIFIED REPORT

a. From the View menu, select Honors to see a preview of the report on the screen. Press Enter until the summary label is shown. How many records were counted?

b. Return to the REPORT screen.

Check - Your report format should be similar to:

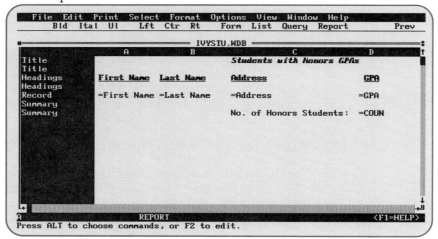

5) SAVE AND PRINT THE MODIFIED DATA BASE

6) CLOSE THE FILE

An Introduction to Computing Using Microsoft Works

7.16 Calculated Fields in a Data Base

Data base fields can store more than just information entered from the keyboard. It is possible for a field to be added to a record that performs a calculation using the data contained within other fields. These "calculated fields" contain a formula which performs a calculation. In other words, a field in a Works data base can be told to perform a calculation based on the numeric values stored in other fields in the data base.

Formulas can be entered into a field in either Form or List view and must always begin with an equal sign (=), using the following mathematical operators:

Operator	Action
+	Add
–	Subtract
*	Multiply
/	Divide
^	Raise to a power (exponentiation)

The usefulness of a calculated field can be illustrated by examining the partial data base below. This data base lists all items sold at the Ivy Bookstore, how many of each are in stock, and the price of each item:

```
   Item Name        Dept.      In Stock   Price
1  School Jacket    Clothing        100   $34.95
2  School Tie       Clothing         15   $17.50
                      . . .
```

The Bookstore manager knows how many of each item are in stock, but needs to know their total cash value. To find this, she would multiply the number in stock by its price, giving the total value. For example, there are 100 jackets in stock and each one costs $34.95. To find the total value of all the jackets combined, 100 would be multiplied by $34.95, producing $3495.

This would be a very time-consuming process if the total value of each and every item (record) in the data base needed to be found, or if quantities and prices changed frequently due to sales or price increases. Instead, the formula =In Stock * Price could be entered once into a new field, Value, to perform this calculation for all the records. Works performs the calculation by multiplying the numeric value in the In Stock field (100) by the numeric value in the Price field ($34.95). The product ($3495.00) is then displayed in the Value field where the formula was originally entered (100 * $34.95 = $3495.00). The formula =In Stock * Price is displayed on the formula line, but the result of the formula is displayed in the field itself.

Works automatically copies the formula into the same field in every other record in the data base and displays the product. For example, the number displayed in the Value field for record 2 above would be $262.50 (15 * $17.50).

While the formula in a calculated field remains constant and does not change, the data in the field changes if any value in any of the other fields in the formula changes. For example, if five school ties were sold one day, therefore reducing the In Stock value to 10, the Value field would automatically reflect this change. Works would now multiply 10 * 17.50 to get the new cash value of the ties, $175.00.

It is also possible to include numeric constants in a formula. For example, to quickly figure a 5% tax on each item, a new field called Tax could be added to the data base and the formula =Price * 0.05 entered. Works multiplies each item's price by 0.05 and displays the product in the Tax field. The tax on ties, for example, would be 17.50 * 0.05, or $0.88.

Remember, the value stored in a calculated field is determined when the other values are entered into that record, not when the formula is created. This allows the calculated field to store the correct value when changes are made to the data base after the field has been created. Note also that a calculated field is stored as part of the data base record, just like any other field. The difference is that a calculated field stores a formula which is evaluated by Works, and is not a single value.

Practice 10

In this Practice you will modify the bookstore's data base, named IVYBOOKS, to include a calculated field which displays the value of the inventory. First a new field will be added to the form, then the formula entered into that field in Form view. Start Works and open IVYBOOKS.

1) INSERT A NEW FIELD ON THE FORM

   a.   Display the data base in Form view if it is not already. Place the cursor below the Price field at X1.30" Y2.67", leaving one blank line between Price and the cursor.
   b.   Enter the name of the new field: Value:
        The width dialog box is displayed.
   c.   Enter 10 for the width.

2) ENTER THE CALCULATION FORMULA AND VIEW THE DATA

   a.   Move the cursor to the Value field (the dotted line) and enter the formula: =In Stock * Price
        The value is calculated and displayed on the screen. Notice that the formula is displayed on the Formula line, but the actual value is displayed on the form.
   b.   Switch to List view. Note that a Value field is calculated for each record.

4) FORMAT THE VALUE FIELD FOR CURRENCY AMOUNTS

   a.   Place the cursor in the Value field if it is not already there.
   b.   From the Format menu, select the Currency command to format the Value field for dollars. Accept the default value of 2 decimals. Each record is now displayed using currency format. Note the dollar sign and two decimal places.

   Check - Your List view should be similar to:

```
   File  Edit  Print  Select  Format  Options  View  Window  Help
        Bld  Ital  Ul      Lft  Ctr  Rt      Form  List  Query  Report              Prev
=In Stock*Price
▪━━━━━━━━━━━━━━━━━━━━━━━━ IVYBOOKS.WDB ━━━━━━━━━━━━━━━━━━━━━━━━▪
         Item Name         Department   In Stock   Price     Value
  1   Dictionary           Books              22   $12.95     $284.90
  2   Thesaurus            Books              12   $15.00     $180.00
  3   Class Ring           Clothing           50  $198.95   $9,947.50
  4   School Bookbag        Clothing          125   $15.99   $1,998.75
  5   School Jacket        Clothing          100   $34.95   $3,495.00
  6   School Logo T-Shirt  Clothing          250    $9.99   $2,497.50
  7   School Tie           Clothing           15   $17.50     $262.50
  8   School Umbrella      Clothing           26   $10.99     $285.74
  9   Calculator           Electronics       136   $17.88   $2,431.68
 10   Cheetos              Food              280    $0.97     $271.60
 11   Chips                Food               77    $0.65      $50.05
 12   Doritos              Food              145    $2.49     $361.05
 13   Heath Bars           Food              167    $0.97     $161.99
 14   Pepsi                Food              444    $0.65     $288.60
 15   Ball Point Pen       Pens/Pencils      150    $0.89     $133.50
 16   Felt-tip pen         Pens/Pencils       76    $0.98      $74.48
 17   Highlite Markers     Pens/Pencils      158    $1.49     $235.42
1 Value       25/25         LIST                              <F1=HELP>
Press ALT to choose commands, or F2 to edit.
```

5) MODIFY AN ENTRY

   a.   Move the cursor to the In Stock field in record 1.
   b.   Enter 105. Works automatically calculates and displays the new Value.

6) SAVE THE MODIFIED DATA BASE

7.17 Where can you go from here?

The last three chapters introduced the concepts of data bases; their design, creation and use. The Works data base has a number of other options not discussed in this text which you may want to explore on your own. One of the best ways to begin is by reading the data base sections of the Works manual supplied by Microsoft. A powerful feature of Works is its ability to integrate the information stored in a data base file with a word processed document to produce personalized form letters. This process is called "mail merge" and is described in Chapter Eleven.

Larger, more powerful data base programs have even more options for generating reports and performing various operations with the data. Several of the most widely used packages for microcomputers are dBASE, Paradox, and R:Base. Because you have learned how to use the Works data base, it will be easier to learn a new package such as one of the ones listed above.

As the use of computerized data bases becomes more widespread, the knowledge of what a data base is and what it can be used for will be an increasingly important skill. There are many job opportunities for people to work with computer data bases. Information about careers involving computers and data bases is given in Chapter Thirteen.

This chapter covered one of the most important aspects of the computerized database: its ability to produce printed reports. Works reports have several different parts and may include a title, column headings, records, and report summaries. Works can print calculations based on the values included in the report in the Summary line. A report should be planned carefully so that it will include the desired information in an appropriate format.

Before a report may be printed, a "report format" must be created which describes the contents of the report to Works. Report formats are created by selecting the New Report command from the View menu. From here, a report title is entered and the fields to be included are selected. Next, the Report Statistics dialog box is displayed and calculations chosen based on the data in specified fields. When the report is complete, a preview of the report is displayed, followed by the REPORT screen where the report format is displayed. If the data base is then saved, any report formats created are saved with it, and may be modified or printed later.

The REPORT screen is divided into rows and columns. Each column has a letter (A, B, C, etc.) and an initial width equal to the width set in List view. Each row is identified by the section name indicating how information will be printed in that row. A Title row prints a title, while a Record row prints data from the data base. A marker such as =GPA is called a "field reference" and indicates that data from the GPA field will be printed at the field reference location. The intersection of a row and column is called a "cell." A cell may store either a field reference or label. Up to eight report formats can be saved with a single data base. with Works naming each newly created report Report1, Report2, etc. In order to distinguish between different reports, each report should be renamed with a meaningful name.

From the REPORT screen, new rows or columns can be inserted into a report by using the Insert Row/Column command from the Edit menu. Similarly, rows and columns can be deleted using the Delete Row/Column command from the Edit menu.

The appearance, or format, of a report can be changed by using the commands in the Format menu, the Page Setup & Margins command from the Print menu, or the Move command from the Edit menu. To insert a field name into a report the Insert Field Name command from the Edit menu is executed. To insert the field contents, the Insert Field Contents command from the Edit menu is selected.

With longer reports it is often necessary to organize the data in the report so that the desired information is easy to find. This may be done by sorting the data or applying a query. When a data base file is sorted, its records are placed in order according to the data stored in a key field. When a report is then printed, the records are displayed in order according to that field.

To copy a report format, the Reports command from the View menu is selected. The **Rename** option can then be used to change the name. Selecting the **Delete** option will delete a report.

Summary calculations which perform calculations based on the data stored in a specific field can be added to a report when it is first created, or later using the Insert Field Summary command from the Edit menu.

A calculated field stores a value based on the data stored in other fields. This calculation is performed based on the numeric values stored in other fields in the data base. For example, the formula `=In Stock * Price` would multiply the data in the In Stock field by the data in the Price field, displaying the product in the calculated field. When entered, the formula is displayed on the Formula line, while the product is displayed in the field itself. Also remember that when the formula is first entered into the field, Works copies it into the same field in every other record.

Vocabulary

Calculated field - Numeric field which is calculated based on the value(s) stored in other fields using a formula.

Cell - Intersection of a row and column in a report format.

Column - Vertical line in a report identified by a letter.

Field reference - Field name placed in a report format which is replaced by the actual data from the data base when the report is printed.

Formula - Mathematical statement which describes how the value stored in a calculated field is determined.

Function - Used in formulas to perform a calculation. AVG, COUNT, and SUM are examples.

Key field - Field which stores the data used when determining the order during a sort.

Report - Printed description of the information stored in a data base.

Report format - Description of the order and placement of fields in a report. May include titles, column headings, records, and summaries.

REPORT screen - Displays the report format.

Row - Horizontal line in a report identified by a section name.

Sort - To place a data base's records in order based on the value stored in a specific field.

Summary - Part of a report where calculations are displayed.

Reviews

Sections 7.1 - 7.6

1. Briefly explain what each of the four sections of a report contains.

2. In planning a report, what factors should be considered?

3. a) What is a report format?
   b) What happens to a report format when a data base is saved?

4. List the steps needed to produce a report format similar to the following using data stored in IVYSTU:

Students and Where They are From

Last Name	City	State
Freitas	Boca Raton	FL
Presley	Lawrenceville	NJ
Herskovitz	San Diego	CA
Weekley	Pensecola	FL

. . .

5. What is a cell and what might it store?

6. a) What is a field reference and what is it used for?
   b) List the field references needed to produce the report in Review 4.
   c) What is the difference between text and a field reference in a report format?

Sections 7.7 - 7.13

7. a) How many separate report formats may be stored with a single data base?
   b) What distinguishes one report format from another?

8. List the steps required to rename a report named Jones to Smith.

9. a) List the steps required to delete a row from a report.
   b) List the steps required to insert a column in a report.

10. List the steps required to perform each of the following format changes to the report displayed in Review 4:

    a) bold and underline the title.
    b) decrease the width of the Last Name column.
    c) right align the state names.

11. Explain how the First Name field could be added to the report displayed in Review 4.

12. If a report format is printed, the data base then sorted, and the report format printed again, will the two printed reports be different? Explain.

13. Explain how 3 different queries might be used to produce reports from the IVYSTU data base.

14. Why might you want to copy a report format?

Sections 7.14 - 7.16

15. A report is created which lists only those students in IVYSTU who have not paid their tuition. Explain how to add a summary to the report which will print the number of students listed.

16. On your data disk is a file named CARPRICE which lists different makes of automobiles and their prices. Explain the steps required to produce a report that lists the prices of only Chevrolets and includes a summary that prints both the number of cars listed in the report and the average price of the cars.

An Introduction to Computing Using Microsoft Works

17. A data base named GRADES stores each student's grades in fields named GR1, GR2, GR3, GR4, and GR5. The grades are numeric values from 0 to 100. Explain how a calculated field named Average can be added to the data base which calculates and stores the grade average for each student.

18. A data base named SAVINGS contains the following fields:

```
First Name:
Last Name:
Acct Number:
Deposit Date:
Withdrawal Date:
Acct Balance:
```

a) List the steps required to produce a report named Bank Balance from this data base. Bank Balance should display only the Last Name, Acct Number, and Acct Balance for each depositor.
b) What additional steps are required to add a summary to the report that gives the sum and average of all of the account balances.
c) What formula should be entered into a calculated field named Interest which calculates the interest in each account by multiplying the account balance by 5%?
d) What steps are necessary to print a copy of the Balance report for only those customers having more than $10,000 in their account?

Exercises

1. CARPRICE.WDB lists prices for a number of foreign and domestic cars. Open the CARPRICE data base.

    a) Create a new report format with the title: `Cars Costing Less Than $9,000`

    b) Include the make, model, and base price fields in the report format.

    c) Include a summary that displays the average price of these cars.

    d) Apply a query that will display only those cars which cost under $9,000, and display a preview of the report.

    e) Rename the report Inexpensive. Save the data base and then print the report.

    f) Create a new report format with the title: `Cars w/Stereos Costing Less Than $10,000`

    g) Include the make, model, and price with stereo fields in the report format.

    h) Add a summary that displays the average price of these cars.

    i) Apply a query that will display only those cars which have stereos and cost less than $10,000.

    j) Rename the report Inexp. w/Stereo. Save the data base and then print a copy of the Inexpensive with Stereo report.

2. Open the ADDRESS data base you created in Chapter Six, Exercise 12.

    a) Create a new report format with the title: `Birthdays in Town`

    b) Include the name, birth date, and city fields in the report format.

    c) Include a summary that displays the number of people in this group.

    d) Apply a query that will display only the people from your town.

    e) Sort the data base alphabetically by last name.

    f) Rename the report Presents. Save the data base and then print a copy of the Presents report.

    g) Create a new report format with the title: `Birthdays in 1975 - 1985`

    h) Include the name, address, city, state, zip code, and birth date field in the report format.

i) Apply a query that will display only those people in the data base who were born between 1975 and 1985.

j) Rename the report Birthdays. Save the data base and then print a copy of the Birthday report.

3. INVENTOR.WDB contains a list of inventors and their inventions. Open INVENTOR and display the data base in List view if not already.

a) Create a new report format titled: `Famous French Inventors`

b) Include the date, invention, and inventor fields in the report format.

c) Apply a query that displays only French inventors.

d) Sort the data base chronologically by date.

e) Rename the report French Inventors. Save the data base and then print a copy of the French Inventors report.

f) Copy the French Inventors report format and rename it New French.

g) Modify the New French report to list the names of French inventions and inventors from the 20th century only. Add a summary that prints the number of inventors in this group and then modify the title to: `Famous French Inventors of the 20th Century`

h) Save the data base and print a copy of the New French report.

4. Open the WHEELS data base you created in Chapter Six, Exercise 3.

a) Create a calculated field named Profit which displays the profit on each sale (asking price minus the price paid). Format the field for currency with zero decimal places.

b) Create a new report format with the title: `Profit`

c) Include the make, price paid, asking price, and profit fields in the report format.

d) Include a summary that displays the asking price for the most expensive car in the inventory. Include another summary that displays the asking price of the least expensive car.

e) Sort the report in descending order by asking price.

f) Insert two more summaries which display two separate totals for the asking price and profit fields.

g) Rename the report Car Profit. Save the data base and then print a copy of the Car Profit report.

h) Create a new report format with the title: `Fantasy Car Sticker Price`

i) Include the year, make, exterior, accessories, and asking price fields in the report.

j) Sort the report in descending order by year.

k) Move the title to the first Title row in Column B.

l) Rename the report Sticker. Save the data base and then print a copy of the Sticker report.

5. Open the WEATHER data base you created in Chapter Six, Exercise 6.

a) Create a calculated field that converts degrees Fahrenheit (F) to degrees Celsius (C), using the conversion formula: C = 5 / 9 * (F - 32). Format the field to zero decimal places.

b) Create a new report format with the title: Good Days in Our Town

c) Include the date, time, temperatures, and sky fields in the report format.

d) Insert a summary for both Fahrenheit and Celsius that displays the average temperature for this group of observations.

e) Apply a query that will display only those days where it was warmer than 65 F. and did not rain.

f) Add a label to the report that describes the criteria for being a good day.

g) Sort the report in ascending order by date.

h) Rename the report Good Days. Save the data base and then print a copy of the Good Days report.

i) Copy the Good Days report format and rename it Bad Days. Modify Bad Days so that it prints the records of only cloudy days with a temperature below 40 F. Be sure to change the report title and the descriptive label.

j) Save the data base and then print a copy of the Bad Days report.

6. Open the ACADEMY data base which contains information about Academy Award winners since 1927 and create the following reports.

a) Create a new report format with the title : UA Best Films

b) Include the year and picture fields in the report format.

c) Include a summary that displays the total number of winning films.

d) Apply a query that will display only those films produced by United Artists.

e) Sort the report chronologically by year.

f) Rename the report UA Winners. Save the data base and then print the UA Winners report.

An Introduction to Computing Using Microsoft Works

g) Create a new report format with the title: `Winners from 1960 - 1992` and include the year, picture, actor, actress, supporting actor, and supporting actress fields in the report format.

h) Apply a query that will display only those records between 1960 and 1992.

i) Insert the Director field between the Picture and Actor fields. Make the Director field heading bold and underlined.

j) Left align all column headings and move the title of the report to the first Title row in column B.

k) Sort the report in ascending order by year. Save the data base and then print the Recent Winners report.

7. Open the COLLEGE data base which contains information about colleges and universities in the United States and create the following reports.

a) Create a calculated field that calculates the total cost of attending each school (tuition plus room and board). Format the field for currency with zero decimal places.

b) Create a new report format with the title `Expensive Schools with Low Enrollments` and include the school, enrollment, and total cost fields in the report format.

c) Include summaries that display the average total cost, the least expensive total cost, and the most expensive total cost of these selected schools.

d) Apply a query that will display only those schools with less than 8,000 students and whose total cost is more than $15,000.

e) Move the title to the first Title row of column A.

f) Display a preview of the report. Notice that two pages are needed to display all the information. Change the left and right margins to .75" to keep all the information on one page.

g) Left align the Name heading and center the Enrollment and Total Cost field contents. Increase the width of the Total Cost field to 12.

h) Sort the report alphabetically by name and then rename the report Small Expensive.

i) Save the data base and then print the Small Expensive report.

j) Create a new report format with the title `Schools in CA and MA` and include the school, state, and private/public fields in the report format.

k) Add a summary that prints the total number of schools listed.

l) Apply a query that limits the report to only schools in California or Massachusetts.

m) Move the title to the first Title row of column A.

n) Display a preview of the report. Notice that two pages are needed to display all the information. Change the left and right margins to .75" to keep all the information on one page.

o) Sort the report by state and then rename the report CA/MA Schools.

p) Save the data base and then print the CA/MA Schools report.

8. Open the COUNTRY data base which contains information about the countries of the world, and create the following reports.

a) Create a new report format with the title `Countries Using the Peso or Pound` and include the country, capital, population, and currency fields in the report format.

b) Apply a query that will display all counties that use either the peso or pound as their currency.

c) Sort the report in ascending order by currency and then rename the report Peso and Pound.

d) Insert the Area field between the Population field and the Currency field. Make the field heading bold and underlined, and center the field contents.

e) Right align the field contents of the Currency field and the Population heading, and left align the headings for Country and Capital.

f) Include two summaries that display the average area and average population of these countries. Format the averages for commas and zero decimal places.

g) Save the data base and then print a copy of the Peso and Pound report.

h) Create a new report with the title: `Small Countries Using the Dollar` and include the country and population fields in the report format.

i) Include a summary that displays the average population of these countries. Format the average for commas and zero decimal places.

j) Apply a query that will display only those countries who have a population less than one million and who use the dollar as currency.

k) Left align the Country heading and right align the Population heading.

l) Include a label under the title describing the criteria for a small country.

m) Rename the report Dollar and sort the report alphabetically by country.

n) Save the data base and then print the Dollar report.

9. Open GIBBON.WDB which contains a number of observations of gibbons, and create the following reports.

   a) Create a new report format with the title `Male Gibbons on Bashibashi Island` and include the name, age, companion, and location fields in the report format.

   b) Include two summaries which will display the total number of males and the average age. Format the average to zero decimal places.

   c) Apply a query that will display only male gibbons.

   d) Left align the Name and Companion headings.

   e) Sort the report in descending order by age.

   f) Rename the report Males. Save the data base and then print the Males report.

   g) Copy the Males report and rename it Females. Modify the report to show the females in the data base.

   h) Sort the report in descending order by age.

   i) Save the data base and then print a copy of the Females report.

Chapter Eight

Introducing the Spreadsheet

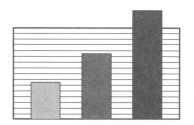

File - Create New File

File - Save

Print - Print

Print - Preview

Format - Column Width

Format - Fixed

Format - Currency

Format - Style

Objectives

After completing this chapter you will be able to:

1. Understand what a spreadsheet is and define its vocabulary.

2. Plan a spreadsheet.

3. Create a simple spreadsheet on the computer and enter data into it.

4. Perform and display the value of calculations using formulas and functions.

5. Use formatting commands to change the layout of a spreadsheet.

6. Save and open spreadsheets from the disk.

7. Print a spreadsheet.

8

The third Works application is the spreadsheet. This chapter explains what a spreadsheet is and how to use one. We will first concentrate on the spreadsheet vocabulary and then with the specific commands needed to produce a simple spreadsheet on the computer. The next chapter explains how Works is used to create larger and more powerful spreadsheets.

8.1   What is a Spreadsheet?

A spreadsheet is simply rows and columns of data. The term comes from the field of accounting where accountants keep track of business activities on large sheets of paper that spread out to form a "spreadsheet." Accounting spreadsheets contain rows and columns of figures with totals and other calculations that relate to the flow of money in a business, but spreadsheets can be used to organize any type of numeric data.

Spreadsheets are record keeping tools that work primarily with numbers. An example of a simple non-computerized spreadsheet is the grade book used by Ivy University's chemistry professor, Dr. Sulfuric. In her grade book the names of her students run down the left side of the page, while labels running across the top of the page indicate each test and the date on which it was given:

Name	Test 1 9/9/94	Test 2 10/20/94	Test 3 11/15/94	Test 4 12/12/94
J. Borelli	50	83	68	64
W. Freitas	86	89	78	88
M. Porter	78	100	90	89
B. Presley	45	78	66	78
H. Crane	66	76	78	55
M. Lui	85	74	83	66

Dr. Sulfuric's grade book

The grade book is organized into rows and columns. A row runs horizontally and stores both the name and grades for one student. The name J. Borelli and the grades 50, 83, 68, and 64, which run across the page form a row. A column runs vertically and stores a title and all of the grades for a single test. The title Test 1, the date, and the grades from 50 to 85 run vertically forming a column.

Computerized spreadsheets appear similar to manual ones but have the added capability of using the computer to perform calculations on the data stored in the spreadsheet. If instead of storing her grades in a gradebook, Dr. Sulfuric were to use a computerized spreadsheet she would be able to have the computer calculate averages on her grades. Then if she were to change one of the grades the computer would automatically redo the calculations. This is the primary advantage of a computerized spreadsheet; the ability of the computer to perform calculations on the data stored in it and to redo the calculations when any changes are made to the data.

8.2 Cells, Labels, and Values

Computerized spreadsheets store data in a grid of columns and rows. Columns are identified by letters which run along the top of the spreadsheet. In Works these letters run from A to Z, and then AA to AZ, BA to BZ, and so on to column IV, allowing for a maximum of 256 columns. Rows are numbered on the left side of the spreadsheet from row 1 to row 16,384. In most instances a much smaller number of rows and columns are actually used to store data. Due to memory limitations, some computers are not able to store a spreadsheet as large as the maximum allows.

The Works spreadsheet screen is shown below. Note the column letters running horizontally across and the row numbers running down the left side of the screen:

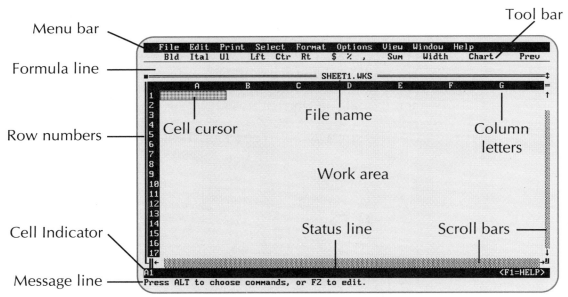

The Works spreadsheet screen

Data is entered into a spreadsheet on this screen. The intersection of a row and column is called a "cell." A single cell is identified by its column letter followed by its row number. Therefore, the third cell from the top in column C is named C3. Each cell can store a single item of data. This system is similar to mailboxes at the post office where each box (or cell) has a name and can store information. Be careful not to confuse the name of a cell with the data it stores. The rectangle shown at cell A1 is called the "cell cursor." Data can be entered from the keyboard into the cell where the cell cursor is located. The "cell indicator" at the bottom of the screen shows the current location of the cell cursor, in this case A1.

The Works spreadsheet screen has seven main areas: the Menu bar, Tool bar, Formula line, Title bar, Work area, Status line, and Message line. The top line of the spreadsheet screen is the Menu bar which gives you access to nine menus. Beneath the Menu bar is the Tool bar containing several formatting options. The third line is the Formula line which displays the contents of the current cell. Under the Formula line is the Title bar which displays the name of the file being worked on. The bottom line on the screen is the Message line where Works displays various prompts and error messages. The current message "Press ALT to choose commands." means that pressing the Alt key will allow you to select a menu from the Menu bar. Above the Message line is the Status line. Here Works shows the cell indicator and other information.

Between the Title bar and the Status line is the Work area. Data entered into the cells of the spreadsheet is displayed here.

Note that the screen currently displays only columns A to G and rows 1 to 17. The other columns and rows can be displayed by "scrolling" the screen, similar to the Word Processor. When this is done columns and rows move off the screen and new ones appear. The old columns and rows are not lost, just not displayed.

Spreadsheets can store three types of data in cells: labels, values, and times/dates. Labels are entries that include words or letters and cannot be used in calculations. Values are entries that have numeric values and can be used in calculations. In the gradebook spreadsheet, student names and titles (e.g., J. Borelli and Test 1) are labels, while a grade such as 50 is a value. Time/date is the third type of entry that can be stored in a cell. A date is a calendar date such as 9/9/94. 12:10 PM is an example of a time. A time/date entry may be used in some kinds of calculations. When planning a computerized spreadsheet it is important to first determine what data will be stored as labels, values, or times/dates.

8.3 Creating and Opening a Spreadsheet

Works provides two ways to create a new spreadsheet. From the Quick Start dialog box **Create a New File** can be selected. If Works is already running, the Create New File command can be selected from the File menu. In either case, the Create New File dialog box is displayed. Selecting the **Spreadsheet** option and then OK creates a new spreadsheet.

The procedure to transfer a previously saved spreadsheet file from disk to the computer's memory is the same as that used for word processor or data base files. If Works has just started, select **Open an Existing File** from the Quick Start dialog box. From the File menu select the Open Existing File command if Works has been running. All Works files will then be listed. Scroll through the **Files** list until the desired file is highlighted. Selecting OK transfers a copy of the highlighted spreadsheet from the disk into the computer's memory. All spreadsheet files end with the extension .WKS (for WorKSheet).

8.4 Moving Through the Spreadsheet

There are several ways to move the cell cursor through the spreadsheet. Besides moving the cursor one cell at a time, several rows or columns may be bypassed by scrolling. In both cases, the keyboard and the mouse can be used.

The arrow keys can be used to move the cursor from cell to cell. Pressing the right-arrow key moves the cell cursor one cell to the right into the next column. Pressing the left-arrow key moves it one cell to the left. The up- and down-arrows move the cell cursor one cell up or down, into the adjacent row. Because spreadsheets can get large, there are several keys that move the cell cursor more than one row or column at a time. Ctrl-Home moves the cell cursor directly to cell A1 while Ctrl-End directly to the last cell in the spreadsheet that contains data. Pressing the PgUp key scrolls the screen up 17 lines while pressing PgDn scrolls it down 17 lines.

Moving the mouse pointer to a cell and clicking once selects the cell for data entry. The selected cell is highlighted, and the cell indicator in the bottom of the screen displays the column letter and row number of the cell. After data is typed on the keyboard, clicking the mouse enters the data into the cell.

The mouse may be used to scroll through the spreadsheet by clicking on one of the scroll arrows. Clicking the mouse once moves the screen one row or column in the direction of the arrow. Holding the mouse down continues the scroll in the direction of the arrow. Dragging the scroll box within the scroll bar moves the cursor over a greater distance faster. For example, dragging the box to the middle of the scroll bar causes Works to display the middle of the spreadsheet.

◆ ● ◆

Practice 1

In this Practice you will create a new spreadsheet and use the keyboard to move the cell cursor around it and scroll through the empty spreadsheet. Mouse users should also complete the *Mouse Practice* immediately following this one.

1) BOOT DOS AND START WORKS

Following the steps given in Chapter Two, boot DOS and start Works.

2) CREATE A NEW SPREADSHEET

From the Quick Start dialog box, select **Create a New File**. Select **Spreadsheet** in the Create New File dialog box. Press Enter to select OK. A new empty spreadsheet is displayed.

3) MOVE THE CELL CURSOR TO CELL D8

Move the cell cursor to cell D8 by pressing the right-arrow key 3 times and then the down-arrow key 7 times. The Status line should indicate that cell D8 is currently selected.

4) SCROLL THE SCREEN BY USING THE ARROW KEYS

a. Move the cell cursor to cell Z8 by holding the right-arrow key down until the cursor is on cell Z8. Note how the columns on the left scroll off the screen.
b. Move the cell cursor to cell Z50 by holding the down-arrow key until the cursor is on cell Z50. Note how the rows on the top scroll off the screen.

5) SCROLL THE SCREEN BY USING THE PAGE UP AND PAGE DOWN KEYS

a. Press PgUp once. The cell cursor is now on cell Z33 as indicated on the Status line.
b. Press PgUp two more times. Cell Z1 is selected.
c. Press PgDn several times. Note how 17 lines at once scroll off the screen each time the key is pressed.

6) RETURN THE CELL CURSOR TO CELL A1

Press Ctrl-Home.

• •

Mouse Practice

In this Practice you will use the mouse to select cells and scroll through the empty spreadsheet.

1) MOVE THE CELL CURSOR TO CELL D8 BY MOVING THE MOUSE POINTER

Move the cell cursor to cell D8 by moving the mouse pointer to cell D8 and clicking once. Note that the Status bar indicates that cell D8 is selected.

2) SCROLL THE SCREEN USING THE SCROLL BARS

a. Click once on the right-arrow of the horizontal scroll bar. Note how the column on the left moves off the screen. Click and hold the mouse on the right-arrow of the horizontal scroll bar until cell Z8 becomes visible. When scrolling with the mouse, the cell cursor does not move requiring the cell to be selected. Click on cell Z8 to select it.
b. Click once on the down-arrow of the vertical scroll bar. Note how the top row moves off the screen. Click and hold the mouse on the down-arrow of the vertical scroll bar until cell Z50 becomes visible. Click on cell Z50 to select it.

3) RETURN THE CELL CURSOR TO CELL A1 USING THE SCROLL BOXES

a. Drag the scroll box to the far left of the horizontal scroll bar. Column A should be visible.
b. Drag the scroll box in the vertical scroll bar to the top. Row 1 should be visible. Click on cell A1.

8.5 Entering Data into the Spreadsheet

Entering data into a cell in a spreadsheet requires that the cell cursor be moved to that cell and the data entered from the keyboard. As the data is typed, it appears both on the Formula line above the Title bar and in the cell. When the data entry is complete, pressing the Enter key or clicking the mouse enters the data into the cell. For example, if the cell cursor is moved to cell C3 and the value 60 typed, the 60 appears on the

Formula line and in the cell. When Enter is pressed or the mouse clicked, the 60 is entered into cell C3. If the label *Hello* is entered, a quotation mark (") is shown on the Formula line in front of the label ("Hello). This makes it easy to distinguish values from labels. An entry made up of both numbers and letters, such as *35XYZ*, is considered a label and a quotation mark is displayed in front of it on the Formula line when entered ("35XYZ).

If a mistake is made in entering data into a cell, it may be corrected by returning the cell cursor to the cell and entering the correct data. The new data will then replace the incorrect data in the cell. If the mistake is noticed before Enter is pressed, the Backspace key may be used to erase data from the Formula line, and the correction typed. Pressing Enter replaces the contents of the cell with the new data. Pressing Escape before the data has been entered leaves the contents of the cell unchanged.

Works automatically displays values up to 10 digits long in a single cell. In order to display the contents of cells containing values with more than 10 digits, formatting commands which are explained later must be used. Labels are displayed in their entirety until they encounter another cell containing data.

8.6 *Saving a Spreadsheet on Disk*

Selecting the Save command from the File menu transfers a copy of the spreadsheet from the computer's memory to the disk. The first time a spreadsheet is saved, the Save As dialog box is shown:

The Save As dialog box

A default name, SHEET1.WKS, appears on the **Save file as** line. Rather than using this name, a file name that describes the contents of your spreadsheet is entered. For example, a spreadsheet containing Dr. Sulfuric's grades might be named GRADES. After the name is typed (up to 8 characters) select OK. Works automatically adds the .WKS extension to the file name.

An Introduction to Computing Using Microsoft Works

Each time the Save command is executed, the latest version of the spreadsheet is placed on disk, replacing any earlier version. To maintain the most recent version on disk, it is necessary to use the Save command after making changes to a previously stored spreadsheet.

Practice 2

In this Practice you will enter the data from Dr. Sulfuric's grade book into the spreadsheet created in the last Practice. If the spreadsheet is not open, create a new one following the steps given in Practice 1.

1) ENTER THE COLUMN TITLES IN ROW 1

a. Move the cell cursor to cell A1. Type `Name` and then press the Enter key or click the mouse to enter the data. Cell A1 now contains the label Name. On the Formula line at the top of the screen, Name is displayed preceded by a quotation mark indicating that it is a label.

b. Move the cell cursor to cell B1 and enter `Test 1`. Note the contents of the cell shown on the Formula line.

c. Move the cell cursor to cell C1 and enter `Test 2`.

d. Continue this procedure to place the headings `Test 3` in cell D1 and `Test 4` in cell E1.

2) ENTER THE TEST DATES

a. Move the cell cursor to cell B2 and enter the date `9/9/94`. Works right aligns a date when entered into a cell. As with other values, a quotation mark does not precede the entered date as shown on the Formula line.

b. Move the cell cursor to cell C2 and enter the date `10/20/94`.

c. Continue this procedure to place the date `11/15/94` in cell D2 and `12/12/94` in cell E2.

4) ENTER THE STUDENT NAMES

a. Move the cell cursor to cell A4. Row 3 is skipped to make the spreadsheet more readable. Enter the name: `J. Borelli`

b. Move the cell cursor to cell A5. Enter the name: `W. Freitas`

c. Continue this process to place the names:

`M. Porter`	into cell A6
`B. Presley`	into cell A7
`H. Crane`	into cell A8
`M. Lui`	into cell A9

5) ENTER THE GRADES

Move the cell cursor to cell B4 to enter the first grade for J. Borelli, a 50. Continue entering the grades from Dr. Sulfuric's grade book. If a mistake is noticed before a cell's data has been entered, the Backspace key may be used to erase data from the Formula line, and the correction typed. Incorrect data that has already been entered may be corrected by moving the cell cursor to the cell and entering the data to replace the incorrect data. When complete your spreadsheet should look like the one on the next page:

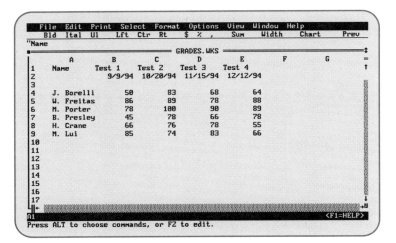

6) **SAVE THE SPREADSHEET ON DISK AND CLOSE THE FILE**

   a. From the File menu, select the Save command.
   b. Type GRADES to replace the default file name on the **Save file as** line and select OK. Your spreadsheet is now saved using the name GRADES.WKS.
   c. From the File menu, select the Close command to remove the file from the screen.

8.7 *Using Formulas to Perform Calculations*

We have stated that the primary benefit of a computerized spreadsheet is its ability to perform calculations. To perform these calculations, "formulas" are used. Formulas are mathematical statements used to calculate values. For example, entering the formula =25 * 38 will show the value 950 in the cell. Note that every formula in Works must begin with an equal sign (=).

The following mathematical operators may be used in writing a formula:

Addition	+
Subtraction	-
Multiplication	*
Division	/
Exponentiation	^

Exponentiation means to raise to a power and is represented by the caret ($\wedge$) symbol. For example, $2 \wedge 2 = 4$ and $5 \wedge 3 = 125$.

When Works evaluates a formula, it follows the rules of order of operations. These rules indicate the priority of operators. For example, what value is displayed when the formula

   =9 + 12 / 3

is evaluated? Does Works add 9 and 12 and then divide by 3? If it does, the answer is 7. Or does it first divide 12 by 3 and then add 9 resulting in an answer of 13? Entering the formula we discover that Works produces

An Introduction to Computing Using Microsoft Works

an answer of 13. Works divided first and then added 9 to the result because a specific order of operations is followed.

Works reads a formula from left to right; therefore, if a formula contains two operators of equal priority, the leftmost operator is used first in the evaluation. The following order of operations is used when a formula is evaluated:

FIRST:

<u>Exponents</u>: Any number raised to a power (e.g., 2^2) is calculated first.

$$=4 + 3\wedge2 \qquad \text{produces the value } 13$$

SECOND:

<u>Multiplication and Division</u>: Calculations involving multiplication and division, which are of equal priority, are performed next.

$$=3 + 5 * 6 / 2 \qquad \text{produces the value } 18$$

First, Works multiplies 5 and 6 to get 30, then it divides by 2 to produce 15. Finally it adds 3 resulting in the value 18. When there is more than one operation of the same priority in a formula, they are performed in order from left to right.

THIRD:

<u>Addition and Subtraction</u>: Third in the order of operations is addition and subtraction which are of equal priority.

$$=7 + 4 * 2 \qquad \text{produces the value } 15$$

Since multiplication and division are done before addition, the computer first calculates the product of 4 and 2, which is 8. To produce the final result, 7 is added to 8, which is 15.

When parentheses are used the computer performs whatever operations are within the parentheses first. By using parentheses you can tell the computer to change the order of operations. For example, to add 7 and 4 and then multiply the result by 2, parentheses must be used:

$$=(7 + 4) * 2 \qquad \text{produces the value } 22$$

Here are a number of example formulas and the results they yield:

```
=2 * 2 + 3 * 2          = 10
=25 * 8 / 4             = 50
=35 + 12 / 3            = 39
=3 + 5 * 8 + 7          = 50
=(3 + 5) * (8 + 7)      = 120
=3^2 * 8 + 4            = 76
=6 + 2^2                = 10
=(6 + 2)^2              = 64
```

Entering an improper formula in a cell causes Works to display ERR in that cell. For example, it is illegal to divide a number by zero because this result is undefined in mathematics. Therefore, entering =10 / 0 in a cell causes Works to display ERR in that cell.

Practice 3

In this Practice you will enter formulas into the cells of a new spreadsheet to perform calculations. Boot DOS and start Works if you have not already done so.

1) CREATE A NEW SPREADSHEET

a. If the Quick Start dialog box is displayed, select the **Create a New File** option. Otherwise, from the File menu, select the Create New File command.
b. Select **Spreadsheet** in the Create New File dialog box. Select OK to create a new spreadsheet.

2) ENTER A FORMULA INTO CELL A1 OF THE SPREADSHEET

a. Move the cell cursor to cell A1.
b. Enter =35 * 12 / 3. The result 140 is displayed in cell A1. Note that the formula itself is shown on the Formula line, but the results of the formula are shown in the cell.

3) ENTER FORMULAS

a. Move the cell cursor to cell B1.
b. Enter each of the following formulas into cell B1, replacing any existing formula, and note the resulting values:

Formula	Resulting value
=20 / 50	0.4
=20 * 50	1000
=20 - 50	-30
=2 + 20 * 5 + 50	152
=(2 + 20) * (5 + 50)	1210
=20 / 0	ERR
20 + 50	20 + 50

In the last example, the result is a <u>label</u> because it is not preceded by an equal sign.

4) SAVE THE SPREADSHEET

From the File menu, select the Save command and enter the name TEST. A copy of the TEST.WKS spreadsheet is saved on disk.

8.8 Using Cell Names in Formulas

Works allows cell names to be used in formulas. A cell name in a formula tells Works to use the value stored in that cell. When Works evaluates a formula, it uses the cell name as the address, or location of where the value to use in the calculation is stored. If the cell is empty or contains a label, Works uses 0 for the cell value. For example, if cell B3 stores the value 20 and cell C2 the value 50, the formulas below would produce the following:

Formula	Result
=B3 / C2	= .4
=B3 * C2	= 1000
=B3 - C2	= -30
=2 * B3 + 5 * C2	= 290
=B3 + 5 * C2 + 8	= 278
=B3 + 5 * (C2 + 8)	= 310
=(B3 + 5) * (C2 + 8)	= 1450

To store the product of the values stored in cells B3 and C2 in a cell, enter the formula =B3 * C2 in any cell other than B3 or C2. Works then automatically calculates the product of the two stored numbers and places it in the cell. Below are some examples of formulas that could be stored in cells:

```
=3 * H5 + Y15
=25 + (L19 / 22)
=B10 * 2
=A3^3
```

If cells C1 to C6 store values, the sum of those values can be calculated with the formula:

```
=C1 + C2 + C3 + C4 + C5 + C6
```

The average of the values in cells C1 to C6 can be calculated with the formula:

```
=(C1 + C2 + C3 + C4 + C5 + C6) / 6
```

8.9 Editing Entries

When there is a mistake in a formula or a change is desired, the complete formula can be retyped and entered, but this is unnecessary. Works allows a cell's entry to be edited by placing the cell cursor on the cell and pressing the F2 key. In edit mode EDIT is displayed in the Status line, the Message line displays "Press ENTER, or ESC to cancel.", and the cell contents appears on the Formula line with a blinking cursor located at its rightmost character. The cursor can then be moved to the position where an insertion is to be made and the insertion typed. A character may be deleted by moving the cursor to it and pressing the Delete key. When the formula is correct, Enter is pressed or the mouse clicked.

If there is an error in a formula, a dialog box will be displayed with a message describing the error. Selecting OK will remove the box. Removing the dialog box automatically switches Works to edit mode and places the blinking cursor near the error. The error can then be corrected and Enter pressed or the mouse clicked.

The mouse may also be used to edit entries. After placing the cell cursor on the cell to be modified, the mouse is used to place the blinking cursor at the location of the error. To do this, point to the the error on the Formula line and click the mouse. The Message line will display "Press ENTER, or ESC to cancel." When the error has been corrected clicking again enters the correct formula into the cell.

8.10 Clearing Cells

To erase the contents of a cell, whether it is a value, label, or formula, the cell cursor is first placed on the cell whose contents are to be erased. The Delete key is pressed, clearing the Formula line. Pressing the Enter key or clicking the mouse will then erase the contents of the cell.

Practice 4

In this Practice you will enter values and formulas into the cells of a new spreadsheet and perform calculations. Start Works and open the TEST spreadsheet created in Practice 3 if you have not already done so.

1) ENTER VALUES INTO THE SPREADSHEET

a. Move the cell cursor to cell B3 and enter the value 20.
b. Move the cell cursor to cell C2 and enter the value 50.

2) ENTER FORMULAS

a. Move the cell cursor to cell D5.
b. Enter each of the following formulas into cell D5 and note the resulting values:

Formula	Resulting value
=B3 / C2	0.4
=B3 * C2	1000
=B3 - C2	-30
=2 + B3 * 5 + C2	152
=(2 + B3) * (5 + C2)	1210
=B3^2 + C2^2	2900
=(B3 + C2)^2	4900
=B3 / 0	ERR
B3 + C2	B3 + C2

In the last example, the result is a <u>label</u> because it was not preceded by an equal sign.

3) BLANK EACH CELL

Move the cell cursor to each cell displaying a value. Press the Delete key. Note that the Formula line is now cleared. Press Enter or click the mouse to erase the values from the cell. The spreadsheet Work area should now be blank.

4) ENTER NEW VALUES

a. Move the cell cursor to cell C1 and enter the value 50.
b. Move the cell cursor to cell C2 and enter the value 85.
c. Continue entering the values:

   75 in cell C3
   83 in cell C4
   34 in cell C5
   55 in cell C6

5) CALCULATE THE SUM OF THE VALUES IN COLUMN C

a. Move the cell cursor to cell C8.
b. Enter the formula:

      =C1 + C2 + C3 + C4 + C5 + C6

Cell C8 displays the sum of the values stored in cells C1 through C6, 382.

6) CALCULATE THE AVERAGE OF THE VALUES IN COLUMN C

a. Move the cell cursor to cell C10.

b. Enter the formula:

$$=(C1 + C2 + C3 + C4 + C5 + C6) / 6$$

The average of the values, 63.666667, is shown in cell C10.

7) EDIT THE FORMULA TO AVERAGE THE FIRST 3 CELLS ONLY

a. Make sure the cell cursor is still on cell C10.
b. Press the F2 key to edit the formula stored in cell C10. Note the blinking cursor in the formula shown on the Formula line. EDIT should be displayed on the Status line.
c. Move the cursor to the divisor 6 and press Delete. Type a 3.
d. Move the cursor to the left until it reaches the + sign in front of C4.
e. Press Delete 9 times. The formula should now read:

$$=(C1 + C2 + C3) / 3$$

Press Enter. The average of the first three cells only is shown in cell C10. What is it? *70*

8) SAVE THE TEST SPREADSHEET

<u>Check</u> - Your spreadsheet should be similar to:

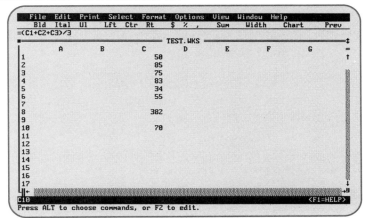

9) ENTER A NEW VALUE IN CELL C1

a. Move the cell cursor to cell C1.
b. Enter 20 to replace the current value. Cell C8 displays the sum 352. The average in cell C10 is now 60. Every formula in the spreadsheet referencing cell C1 is automatically recalculated. This is one advantage of using a computerized spreadsheet.
c. Enter 50 in cell C1. Note how the values are again automatically recalculated.

8.11 Using Functions to Perform Calculations

To perform common calculations Works contains built-in "functions" that may be used as part of a formula. A function performs a set of calculations on an argument and then returns a single value that is the result of those calculations. To better understand this, consider the formula $=C1 + C2 + C3 + C4 + C5 + C6$ used in Practice 4 to add the values of a column of numbers stored in cells C1 to C6. We could also have used a formula that contained Works' built-in SUM function:

=SUM(C1:C6)

The SUM function requires that the first and last cell names in the sum be entered as the argument. The argument is the value used by the function to perform its calculation. A colon (:) is used to indicate a "range" of cells. For example, C1:C6 refers to cells C1, C2, C3, C4, C5, and C6. Works automatically calculates the value of C1 + C2 + C3 + C4 + C5 + C6 resulting in the sum of the values of the cells.

Values stored in a row of cells may also be added together. For example, the formula

=SUM(B2:E2)

sums the values in cells B2, C2, D2, and E2. It is important to realize that only a section of adjacent cells can be used to define a range.

In Practice 4, we could replace the formula in cell C10 used to average the column of grades with

=SUM(C1:C6) / 6

and obtain the same result. Note that we must still divide the sum by 6 to obtain the average.

An easier method for averaging is the AVG function. To average the values for cells C1 through C6 we can use a formula with the AVG function:

=AVG(C1:C6)

● ●

Practice 5

In this Practice functions will be used to sum and average rows and columns of values. Start Works and open the TEST spreadsheet created in Practice 3 if you have not already done so.

1) USE A FUNCTION TO SUM COLUMN C

a. Move the cell cursor to cell C8.
b. Enter the following to replace the current formula:

=SUM(C1:C6)

The sum 382 is displayed.

2) USE A FUNCTION TO AVERAGE COLUMN C

a. Move the cell cursor to cell C10.
b. Enter the formula:

=AVG(C1:C6)

The previous formula has been replaced and the average 63.666667 is displayed.

3) ENTER VALUES IN ROW 2

a. Move the cell cursor to cell A2.

b. Enter the following values into the cells in row 2 (note that C2 already has the value 85):

$$97.8 \quad \text{into cell A2}$$
$$109.4 \quad \text{into cell B2}$$
$$105.8 \quad \text{into cell D2}$$

4) USE A FUNCTION TO SUM ROW 2

a. Move the cell cursor to cell F2.
b. Enter the formula:

`=SUM(A2:D2)`

The sum of the values, 398, is displayed.

5) USE A FUNCTION TO AVERAGE ROW B

a. Move the cell cursor to cell G2.
b. Enter the formula:

`=AVG(A2:D2)`

The average of the values, 99.5, is displayed.

6) CHANGE THE VALUE IN CELL C2

a. Move the cell cursor to cell C2.
b. Enter the new value 30. Note how four values at once are recalculated. The values in cells C8, C10, F2, and G2 have all been recalculated to reflect the new data in cell C2.

Check - The modified spreadsheet should be similar to:

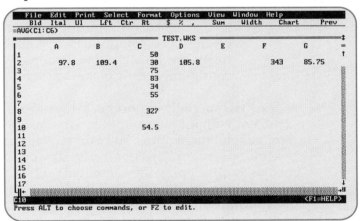

7) SAVE AND CLOSE THE TEST SPREADSHEET

a. From the File menu, select the Save command. The modified TEST spreadsheet is saved on disk.
b. From the File menu, select the Close command to close TEST.

8.12 Planning a Spreadsheet

It is important to first plan a spreadsheet carefully before using Works. This can best be done by answering the following questions:

1. What new information should the spreadsheet produce?

2. What data must the spreadsheet store to produce the new information?

3. How would the new information be produced without using a computer?

4. How should the spreadsheet be organized and displayed on the computer?

We will use Dr. Sulfuric's grade book, shown in Section 8.1, to answer these questions:

1. Dr. Sulfuric wants to calculate each student's term average and the class average on each of her tests.

2. The data to be stored is the student names and their grades.

3. Without using a computer Dr. Sulfuric could produce the class average on each test by adding all the grades for that test and dividing by the number of students (6). Each student's term average could be calculated by adding the four grades and dividing by 4.

4. The spreadsheet format is easy to determine since we want it to resemble Dr. Sulfuric's grade book. Later when we create more complicated spreadsheets, especially those involving financial calculations, we will have to spend considerable time planning them.

Step 3 is especially important. In the process of planning how to solve a problem without the computer, we must determine the sequence of steps the solution requires. Since the computer solution usually requires the same or very similar steps, we can use our non-computer solution to assist us in developing the computer version.

Working out the details, as we have above, is very important before proceeding to the computer. In the next chapter we will expand our discussion of spreadsheet planning.

●●●

Practice 6

In this Practice you will enter formulas to calculate the average grade on each test and the term averages for each of Dr. Sulfuric's students in the GRADES.WKS spreadsheet. Start Works if you have not already done so.

1)   OPEN THE GRADES SPREADSHEET

2) ENTER THE FORMULA TO AVERAGE THE GRADES FOR TEST 1

a. Move the cell cursor to cell B11.
b. Enter the formula:

$$=AVG(B4:B9)$$

The average grade on Test 1, 68.333333, is displayed in cell B11.

3) ENTER FORMULAS TO CALCULATE THE OTHER TEST AVERAGES

=AVG(C4:C9)	into cell C11
=AVG(D4:D9)	into cell D11
=AVG(E4:E9)	into cell E11

4) CALCULATE EACH STUDENT'S TERM AVERAGE

a. Move the cell cursor to cell F4.
b. Enter the formula:

$$=AVG(B4:E4)$$

The average for J. Borelli, 66.25, is displayed in cell F4.
c. Repeat this process by entering the formulas:

=AVG(B5:E5)	into cell F5
=AVG(B6:E6)	into cell F6
=AVG(B7:E7)	into cell F7
=AVG(B8:E8)	into cell F8
=AVG(B9:E9)	into cell F9

5) ADD TITLES FOR THE NEW INFORMATION

a. Move the cell cursor to cell F1 and enter the label: Student Average
b. Move the cursor to cell A11 and enter the label: Average:

6) SAVE THE MODIFIED GRADES SPREADSHEET

<u>Check</u> - The averages for Dr. Sulfuric's class should now appear in the spreadsheet as shown below:

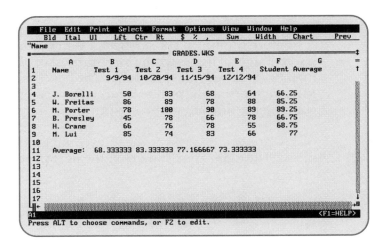

8.13 The ROUND Function

Works includes a number of other functions which are listed in Appendix A. We have already discussed SUM and AVG and will now explain ROUND which rounds a number to a specific number of decimal places. In the spreadsheet containing Dr. Sulfuric's grades, the test averages are printed to 6 decimal places, but only 1 place is desired. For example, the class average on Test 1 appears as 68.333333, but Dr. Sulfuric wants it computed as 68.3.

To round the number of decimal places of a stored value, the cell name is entered into the ROUND function followed by the number of decimal places the result is to be rounded to. For example, to round the value stored in cell C16 to 2 places the formula is written:

=ROUND(C16, 2)

If the value stored in C16 is 42.865 the rounded result is 42.87.

To round the result of a formula, the formula followed by the number of decimal places the result is to be rounded to is entered into the ROUND function. For example, J. Borelli's average can be rounded to 1 place with the formula:

=ROUND(AVG(C4:F4), 1)

To round the average to the nearest integer, a 0 is used to indicate no decimal places:

=ROUND(AVG(C4:F4), 0)

It should be noted that rounding changes the actual value stored in the cell, not just the way the original value is displayed. Therefore, the result of a calculation involving a rounded value may be different from the same calculation using the value before rounding.

8.14 Printing a Spreadsheet

Before printing a spreadsheet it is important to first save it on disk. If something then goes wrong in the process of printing and the computer's memory is erased, the spreadsheet can be retrieved from disk. Also check to make sure that the printer is turned on and properly connected to your computer before attempting to print.

To print a spreadsheet, the Print command is executed from the Print menu. The dialog box shown on the next page then displayed:

An Introduction to Computing Using Microsoft Works

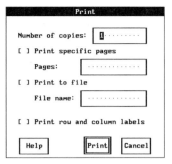

The Print dialog box

This dialog box enables you to enter the number of copies to print. It also makes it possible to include the row numbers and column letters in the printout by selecting the **Print row and column labels** option.

Often a spreadsheet is too wide to print on a single standard sheet of paper. When this is true, the spreadsheet will be printed on consecutive sheets starting from the leftmost columns and proceeding to the right. It is then possible to tape the separate sheets together to form a printout of the complete spreadsheet.

8.15 *Previewing a Spreadsheet*

Works supplies the Preview command so that the overall layout of a spreadsheet may be viewed without actually having to print it. Executing this command shows a smaller version of the spreadsheet as it would appear on a printed page. In addition, it is also possible to see how many pages are required to print the entire spreadsheet.

To preview a spreadsheet, select the Preview command from the Print menu to display the following dialog box:

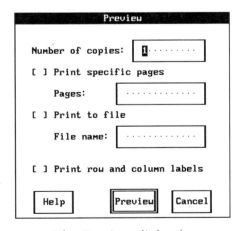

The Preview dialog box

Since it is possible to execute the Print command directly from the Preview screen, the printing options are available from the Preview dialog box.

When previewing a spreadsheet, only the keyboard can be used to execute commands; the mouse is no longer active. PgUp and PgDn may be used to move through the spreadsheet. Pressing P prints the spreadsheet. Pressing Escape exits the Preview screen and returns to the spreadsheet.

8

• •

Practice 7

In this Practice you will round the averages in the GRADES spreadsheet by editing the existing formulas. The modified spreadsheet will then be previewed and printed. Start Works if you have not already done so and open the GRADES spreadsheet.

1) ROUND THE FORMULA FOR TEST 1 TO 2 DECIMAL PLACES

a. Move the cell cursor to cell B11.
b. Press the F2 key to enter edit mode. The formula is shown on the Formula line with a blinking cursor.
c. Place the cursor on the A in AVG and type: ROUND (
d. Place the cursor one space beyond the end of the formula and type , 2) so that the formula on the Formula line appears:

=ROUND(AVG(B4:B9),2)

Press Enter or click the mouse and note that the average is now rounded to 2 decimal places, 68.33.

2) ROUND ALL TEST AVERAGES TO 2 DECIMAL PLACES

Repeat step 1 for cells C11, D11, and E11.

3) ROUND J. BORELLI'S AVERAGE TO 1 DECIMAL PLACE

a. Move the cell cursor to cell F4.
b. Press the F2 key to enter edit mode. The formula is shown on the Formula line.
c. Place the cursor to the A in AVG and type: ROUND (
d. Place the cursor one space beyond the end of the formula and type , 1) :

=ROUND(AVG(B4:E4),1)

Press Enter or click the mouse and note that the average is rounded to one decimal place, 66.3.

4) ROUND ALL STUDENT AVERAGES TO 1 DECIMAL PLACE

Repeat step 3 for cells F5, F6, F7, F8, and F9.

5) SAVE THE SPREADSHEET ON DISK

Your spreadsheet should be similar to:

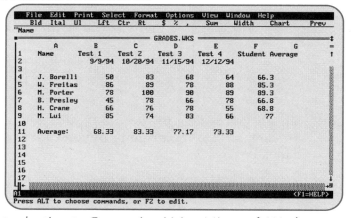

An Introduction to Computing Using Microsoft Works

6) PREVIEW AND THEN PRINT THE SPREADSHEET

    a. From the Print menu, select the Preview command.

    b. In the Preview dialog box, select **Preview** to accept the default settings.

    c. After viewing the spreadsheet, press P to print the spreadsheet.

8.16 *Formatting a Spreadsheet*

How a spreadsheet is displayed on the computer screen is called its layout. Determining the layout of a spreadsheet is an important step. If we choose a proper layout, the spreadsheet will not only be easy to use, but easy to expand so that it can perform additional tasks. Formatting commands are used to change the layout of a spreadsheet. This Section will introduce three formatting options: column width, value formats, and label formats. Chapter Nine will introduce and discuss planning the spreadsheet layout and other formatting commands and techniques.

The default column width is 10 characters. Often this is insufficient to hold a column's data, requiring the column width to be increased. This is done by executing the Column Width command from the Format menu which displays the dialog box:

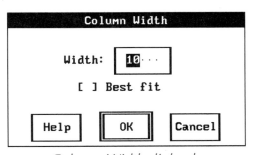

Column Width dialog box

Note the default width of 10 characters. This number can be changed to either increase or decrease a column's width.

It is important to realize that the width of single cells cannot be changed, only whole columns. If a cell is not wide enough to display its value, Works switches to scientific notation. For example, the value 15588770000 is displayed as 1.559E+10. Pound signs (#) are displayed if a cell is not wide enough to display a formatted value.

Except for the Column Width command which changes the width of a whole column, the other Format menu commands require that the cell to be formatted first be highlighted and then the command executed.

To format cells to a specific number of decimal places, the Fixed command from the Format menu is selected. When executed, Fixed displays a dialog box containing a default value of 2:

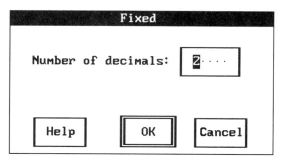

Fixed dialog box

This number can be changed and OK selected or the 2 accepted by selecting OK. The highlighted cell then displays a number rounded to the selected number of decimal places. Unlike the ROUND function, the Fixed command only changes how a value is displayed not the value itself. For example, a cell containing 27.8 fixed to 0 decimal places displays the value 28. Adding 10 to the value in this cell produces 37.8, not 38.

The Currency command formats cells for dollar values. When executed, dollar signs are displayed in front of the values and commas are used. An option is given by the Currency dialog box as to how many decimal places (cents) are to be displayed. The default value of 2 is usually accepted.

The Style command from the Format menu allows labels or values to be displayed as left aligned, right aligned, or centered. By default, cells containing labels are automatically left aligned while values are right aligned. For this reason labels and values displayed in the same column do not line up. The Test labels and dates in the GRADES spreadsheet demonstrate this. To line up label headings over columns of values, the labels can be right aligned by highlighting them and then selecting the Style command which displays the dialog box:

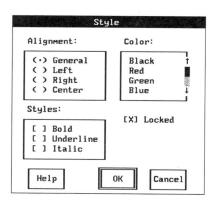

Style dialog box

Selecting the **General** option causes Works to use the default: left aligned for labels, right aligned for values and times/dates. Also in the Style dialog box are **Styles** options. Selecting these options will format a cell for bold, italic, or underline. More than one style may be applied to a cell at a time. For example, a cell can be formatted as bold and italic.

It is important to realize that formatting options only affect the way that the data in a spreadsheet is displayed, and have no effect on the actual contents of the cells. For example, giving a Currency format to a cell that stores the value 5 will display $5.00 in that cell. However, the contents of the cell can be seen to be only a 5 by checking the Formula line.

8.17 Formatting Shortcuts

Works provides shortcuts for commonly used formatting commands. Many of the Word Processor formatting shortcuts described in Chapter Three may also be used for the Spreadsheet. Shortcuts for the style and alignment options are examples:

Left aligned	Ctrl-L		Bold	Ctrl-B
Right aligned	Ctrl-R		Italic	Ctrl-I
Centered	Ctrl-C		Underline	Ctrl-U

The currency format can be applied to the current cell by pressing `Ctrl-4`; the same shortcut used to apply the currency format to a field in the Data Base. Commands that are alike for different applications are one advantage of using an integrated package like Works.

Mouse users may use the Tool bar located directly below the Menu bar to apply formatting to selected cells:

Bld Ital Ul   Lft Ctr Rt $ % ,   Sum   Width   Chart   Prev

The Spreadsheet Tool bar

Tool bar options used to format a selected cell are displayed in highlighted text. Bold, italic, and underline may be applied to selected cells by clicking on **Bld**, **Ital**, or **Ul** in the Tool bar. A cell's alignment can be changed by clicking on **Lft**, **Ctr**, or **Rt** which formats a highlighted area as left aligned, centered, or right aligned respectively. Clicking on **$** in the Tool bar automatically formats the cell for dollar values displayed to 2 decimal places. Selecting **Width** in the Tool bar will display the Column Width dialog box.

Also in the Tool bar is the **Prev** command. Clicking on this command displays the Preview dialog box. Other Tool bar options will be discussed in Chapter Nine. In the Practices that follow, Mouse users may apply formatting using the Tool bar where directions are given for using commands from the Format menu.

Practice 8

In this Practice you will format GRADES. Start Works and open the GRADES spreadsheet if you have not already done so.

1)   CHANGE THE AVERAGE: LABEL

   a.   Move the cell cursor to cell A11.
   b.   Enter the label `Test Average:` replacing the current label. Notice how the label appears truncated in the cell, but is shown in its entirety in the Formula bar.

2) FORMAT COLUMN A TO 15 CHARACTERS WIDE

a. Place the cell cursor in column A.
b. From the Format menu, select the Column Width command. The Width dialog box displays the default value of 10.
c. Enter 15 for the new width. Notice the label in cell A11 is now shown in its entirety.

3) RIGHT ALIGN AND BOLD THE TEST AVERAGE LABEL

a. From the Format menu, select the Style command.
b. From the **Alignment** box, select **Right**.
c. Form the **Styles** box, select **Bold**.
d. Select OK to apply the formatting. The Test Average: label should appear bolded and right aligned in cell A11.

4) FORMAT COLUMN F TO 15 CHARACTERS WIDE

Notice that as a result of widening column A, column G is no longer displayed and therefore the label in column F has been truncated.

a. Place the cell cursor in column F.
b. Repeat parts (b) and (c) in step 2 to format column F for a width of 15. The Student Average label is now shown in its entirety.

5) RIGHT ALIGN AND BOLD THE TEST 1 TITLE

a. Move the cell cursor to cell B1.
b. From the Format menu, select the Stlye command.
c. From the **Alignment** box, select **Right**. From the **Styles** box, select **Bold**.
d. Select OK to apply the formatting. The Test 1 label in cell B1 should appear bolded and right aligned.

6) RIGHT ALIGN AND BOLD THE TITLES IN C1, D1, E1, AND F1

7) FORMAT AVERAGES TO DISPLAY 1 DECIMAL PLACE

a. Place the cell cursor on cell F4.
b. From the Format menu, select the Fixed command which displays the dialog box.
c. Enter a 1. The average is now displayed to 1 decimal place.
d. Follow parts (b) and (c) to format cells F5 through F9 for 1 decimal place. Notice how the value in cell F9 is displayed with a trailing zero in order to display it to 1 decimal place. When the ROUND function was applied to the value in this cell in Practice 7, there was no change in the display because the value remained the same. Applying the Fixed command changes the display, the ROUND function changes the value.

8) SAVE GRADES ON DISK

Your spreadsheet should be similar to:

```
 File  Edit  Print  Select  Format  Options  View  Window  Help
  Bld  Ital  Ul    Lft  Ctr  Rt   $  %  ,      Sum    Width    Chart      Prev
"Name
                              GRADES.WKS
              A              B         C         D         E          F
 1   Name              Test 1    Test 2    Test 3    Test 4  Student Average
 2                      9/9/94   10/28/94  11/15/94  12/12/94
 3
 4   J. Borelli            50        83        68        64        66.3
 5   W. Freitas            86        89        78        88        85.3
 6   M. Porter             78       100        90        89        89.3
 7   B. Presley            45        78        66        78        66.8
 8   H. Crane              66        76        78        55        68.8
 9   M. Lui                85        74        83        66        77.0
10
11   Test Average:      68.33     83.33     77.17     73.33
12
13
14
15
16
17
                                                              <F1=HELP>
Press ALT to choose commands, or F2 to edit.
```

9) PREVIEW AND THEN PRINT THE FINAL VERSION OF THE GRADES SPREADSHEET

From the Preview screen, press PgDn to view the second page of the spreadsheet. Two pages will be used to print the spreadsheet. Press P to print the spreadsheet.

• •

Chapter Summary

This chapter covered the basics of planning and creating a computerized spreadsheet. A spreadsheet is simply rows and columns of data with rows running horizontally and columns vertically. The primary advantage of a computerized spreadsheet is that it has the ability to perform calculations on the data it stores with the calculations automatically changing to reflect any changes in the data.

In a Works spreadsheet the rows are numbered on the left side and the columns identified by letters which run along the top of the spreadsheet. Where a row and column intersect is called a cell. A single cell is identified by its column letter and row number. For example, C3 is the name of the cell located in column C at row 3.

Spreadsheet cells can store three types of data; labels, values, and times/dates. Labels can be words or characters and cannot be used in calculations. Values are numeric and can be used in calculations. Time/Date entries are either times (12:30 AM) or calendar dates (9/21/95) and both can be used in certain types of calculations.

A new spreadsheet is created by selecting the Spreadsheet option from the Create New File dialog box. Data is entered into a spreadsheet by moving the cell cursor to a cell, typing the data and pressing Enter or clicking the mouse. The cell indicator at the bottom of the screen shows the current location of the cell cursor. The Formula line shows the contents of the cell. To move through a spreadsheet (scroll) either the PgUp and PgDn keys or the mouse and scroll arrows are used.

Formulas are mathematical statements used to calculate values which can be stored in cells. All formulas must begin with an equal (=) sign and may contain cell names. For example, if cell B5 stores the value 12 and cell C8 stores 10, the formula =B5 * C8 would produce 120.

The computer uses an order of operations in evaluating a formula. First it performs exponentiation, second multiplication and division, and third addition and subtraction. Operations of the same priority are performed from left to right. The order of operations may be changed by using parentheses. For example:

```
=3 + 5 * 8 + 7          = 50
=(3 + 5) * (8 + 7)      = 120
```

Functions are predefined formulas that are used by the computer to perform common calculations. The formula =SUM(B3:B8) includes the SUM function. B3:B8 is called a range which may define a portion of a row or column. This chapter covered the following three functions:

SUM

=SUM(B3:B8)

sums the values in the column of cells B3, B4, B5, B6, B7, and B8.

=SUM(A5:E5)

sums the values in the row of cells A5, B5, C5, D5, and E5.

AVG

=AVG(C3:C8)

averages the values in the column of cells C3, C4, C5, C6, C7, and C8.

=AVG(B7:F7)

averages the values in the row of cells B7, C7, D7, E7, and F7.

ROUND

=ROUND(C5, 2)

rounds the value stored in cell C5 to 2 decimal places.

=ROUND(AVG(B7:F7), 1)

rounds the average of the values in the range B7:F7 to 1 decimal place.

It is important to carefully plan a spreadsheet before using Works. This is best done by first deciding what new information the spreadsheet will produce, what data it will store, how that data could be produced without a computer, and what the spreadsheet should look like when displayed on the computer.

A spreadsheet is saved on disk by selecting the Save command from the File menu. It is printed by selecting the Print command from the Print menu.

Commands from the Format menu are used to change the layout of a spreadsheet. The width of a column can be changed using the Column Width command while cells can be formatted to a specific number of decimal places or to dollars by selecting the Fixed or Currency commands. The Style command allows labels or values to be displayed as left aligned, right aligned, or centered.

• •

Vocabulary

Argument - Value used by a function to perform its operations.

Cell - Where a row and column intersect. A cell is identified by its column letter and row number, for example C3.

Cell cursor - Rectangle on the screen which is used to indicate the current cell. It can be moved from cell to cell using the arrow keys or mouse. Data may be entered into a cell when the cell cursor is located on it.

Cell indicator - Location at the bottom of the screen that displays the current location of the cell cursor.

Cell name - The column letter and row number used to identify a cell (i.e., B3).

Column - Vertical line of data identified by a letter.

Date - Entry in the form of a date (i.e., 9/5/96).

Formula line - Line at the top of the screen where data entered from the keyboard is displayed before it is entered into a cell.

Formulas - Mathematical statements used to calculate values which are stored in cells. The statement =C5 + D7 + E8 is a formula.

Functions - Used in formulas to perform common calculations. =SUM(B3:B8) is a function.

Label - Words or characters stored in a cell that cannot be used in calculations.

Order of operations - The rules the computer uses to evaluate a formula.

Range - Partial row or column of adjacent cells. B3:B8 is a range.

Row - Horizontal line of data identified by a number.

Scroll - Moving the cell cursor to view different parts of a spreadsheet.

Spreadsheet - Rows and columns of data on which calculations can be performed.

Time - Entry in the form of a time (i.e., 12:30 PM).

Values - Numeric data that can be stored in cells and used in calculations.

● ●

Reviews

Sections 8.1 - 8.5

1. What is the primary advantage of using a computerized spreadsheet rather than a spreadsheet produced using paper and pencil?

2. a) What is a cell in a spreadsheet?
   b) What is the difference between a row and a column?
   c) What is the difference between the cell cursor and cell indicator?

3. a) What is the difference between a label and a value entry?
   b) What is a date entry? Give an example.
   c) What is a time entry? Give an example.

4. What information is displayed on the screen by the:

   a) Formula line
   b) Status line
   c) Message line
   d) Title bar

5. a) How can spreadsheet columns that are off of the screen be moved on to the screen?
   b) What is this action called?

6. How many of each of the following types of entries are stored in the GRADES spreadsheet shown in Practice 2?

a) labels
b) values
c) dates
d) times

7. How can the cursor be moved directly to:

   a) cell A1?
   b) the last cell in a spreadsheet that contains data?

8. a) What is the difference between a cell name and the data stored in a cell? Give an example.
   b) Can the name of a cell be changed? If so, how?
   c) Can the data stored in the cell be changed? If so, how?

9. Draw a diagram that shows all of the cells in the first three columns and five rows of a spreadsheet. Show the name of each cell and store the value 27 in cell B3.

10. What is the maximum number of digits that may be displayed in a single cell without using special commands?

11. How does Works distinguish between numeric and label entries when they appear on the Formula line?

12. If a mistake has been made entering data into a cell, how may it be corrected?

13. What steps would you take to enter the value 65 into cell C4 of the spreadsheet produced in Practice 2.

Sections 8.6 - 8.10

14. How do you transfer a copy of a spreadsheet from the computer's memory to disk?

15. Briefly explain what a formula is and give two examples.

16. a) What is meant by order of operations?
    b) Which operation is performed first?
    c) Which operation is performed last?
    d) How may the order of operations be changed?

17. If a formula contains 3 operations all of the same order which will be performed first?

18. If 10/20 is entered into a cell, Works considers it a date. How must the entry be changed so that 10 will be divided by 20?

19. Write formulas for each of the following calculations:

    a) The product of the values stored in cells A1, B3, and C4.
    b) The sum of the values stored in cells A3, A4, A5, A6, A7, and A8.
    c) The average of the values stored in cells B5, B6, and B7.
    d) The average of the values stored in cells A1, B3, and C4.

An Introduction to Computing Using Microsoft Works

20. What value would be calculated by Works for each of the following formulas?

    a) =2 + 7 * 5 + 4
    b) =(2 + 7) * (5 + 4)
    c) =5 + 10 / 5
    d) =(5 + 10) / 5
    e) =2^3 + 4
    f) =15 + (12 / 4)

21. What value would be calculated by Works for each of the following formulas if cell C15 stores a value of 16 and cell D8 a value of 4?

    a) =C15 * D8
    b) =C15 + 5 + D8
    c) =C15 * 5 + D8
    d) =C15 * (5 + D8)
    e) =C15 / D8
    f) =C15 + 4 / D8
    g) =C15 + (4 / D8)

22. If a mistake has been made in a formula what are two ways it may be corrected?

23. How can the value stored in a cell be erased?

24. a) What is meant by a range of cells?
    b) Give an example of a range of cells contained in a row.
    c) Give an example of a range of cells contained in a column.

25. Write a formula which calculates the average of the values stored in cells B3, B4, B5, C5, D5, and E5.

Sections 8.11 - 8.13

26. What is the difference between a formula and a function?

27. Write formulas using functions that will calculate each of the following:

    a) The sum of the values stored in cells B4, B5, B6 and B7.
    b) The sum of the values stored in cells B4, C4, D4, and E4.
    c) The average of the values stored in the column of cells D7 to D35.
    d) The average of the values stored in the row of cells F3 to J3.

28. Answer the four questions presented in Section 8.11 to plan a spreadsheet that will list the name of each member of your class, his or her height in inches, and calculate the average height of your classmates. Produce a sketch of the spreadsheet on paper.

29. Using functions, write formulas to calculate each of the following:

    a) The sum of the values in cells C5, C6, C7, C8,and C9 rounded to 2 decimal places.
    b) The sum of the values in cells B5, C5, D5, and E5 rounded to the nearest integer.
    c) The average of the values in cells A1, A2, A3, B1, B2, B3 rounded to 1 decimal place.

30. a) What happens when you print a spreadsheet that is too large to fit on a single piece of paper?
    b) How can you determine what a spreadsheet will look like when printed without actually printing it?

31. Is it possible to change the width of only a single cell?

32. Explain the difference between using the ROUND function or the Fixed command to display a value to 2 decimal places.

33. List the steps required to perform the following operations:
    a) Change the width of a column to 20 characters.
    b) Format a cell to display a value to 3 decimal places.
    c) Bold and right align the contents of a cell.
    d) Format a cell to display a value in dollars to 2 decimal places.

Exercises

1. Create a spreadsheet that converts a Fahrenheit temperature to the equivalent temperature in Celsius. When a Fahrenheit temperature is entered into cell C3, the corresponding Celsius temperature is displayed in cell G3:

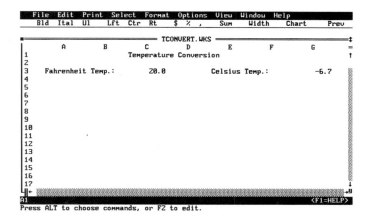

a) The formula for converting Fahrenheit (F) to Celsius (C) is $C = 5/9(F - 32)$. Enter the appropriate formula and labels into the spreadsheet to produce output as shown above. Format the cells displaying temperature values as Fixed to 1 decimal place. Save the spreadsheet as TCONVERT.

b) In row 5 have the spreadsheet convert a Celsius temperature to the equivalent temperature in Fahrenheit. That is, a Celsius temperature entered into cell C5 would be shown converted to Fahrenheit in cell G5. Be sure to use the correct formula.

c) Save the modified spreadsheet and then print a copy of it.

2. The Ivy University Sports Car Club is testing different sports cars and storing the results in a spreadsheet.

a) Create a new spreadsheet and enter the following data exactly as shown below. Change the column width of column A to 13 so that all the labels are shown in their entirety. Save the spreadsheet naming it TRACKTST. Your spreadsheet should be similar to the one shown on the next page:

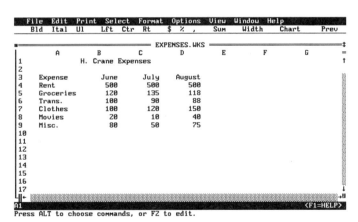

```
 File  Edit  Print  Select  Format  Options  View  Window  Help
   Bld   Ital  Ul      Lft  Ctr  Rt    $  %  ,    Sum    Width    Chart      Prev

                              ============= TRACKTST.WKS =============
          A            B         C         D         E         F         G
  1                 Track Test
  2
  3     Car        Distance  Time
  4                (feet)    (seconds)
  5     Porsche      123.45      6.78
  6     Ferrari      145.67      7.77
  7     Lotus        123.66      5.99
  8     Aston-Martin 148.99      7.89
  9     Corvette     156.34      6.68
 10     Jaguar       123.87      5.34
 11     Supra        136.98      7.11
 12
 13
 14
 15
 16
 17
 A1                                                              <F1=HELP>
 Press ALT to choose commands, or F2 to edit.
```

b) In column D, enter the title `Velocity`. Velocity is calculated by dividing distance travelled by time. Use a formula to calculate the velocity for each trial. Make sure that any change made to a distance or time will automatically change the corresponding velocity.

c) In cell D13 have the spreadsheet calculate the average velocity for the trials. Be sure to include a label for the average.

d) Edit the formulas for velocity and average velocity to round the results to 2 decimal places. Save the modified spreadsheet on disk and print a copy.

3. Heidi Crane has recently graduated from Ivy University and has decided to keep track of her personal finances using a spreadsheet.

   a) Create a new spreadsheet and enter H. Crane's expenses for the months of June, July, and August. Save the spreadsheet naming it EXPENSES:

```
 File  Edit  Print  Select  Format  Options  View  Window  Help
   Bld   Ital  Ul      Lft  Ctr  Rt    $  %  ,    Sum    Width    Chart      Prev

                              ============= EXPENSES.WKS =============
          A            B         C         D         E         F         G
  1                 H. Crane Expenses
  2
  3     Expense      June      July    August
  4     Rent          500       500       500
  5     Groceries     120       135       118
  6     Trans.        100        90        88
  7     Clothes       100       120       150
  8     Movies         20        10        40
  9     Misc.          80        50        75
 10
 11
 12
 13
 14
 15
 16
 17
 A1                                                              <F1=HELP>
 Press ALT to choose commands, or F2 to edit.
```

b) At the bottom of column A, enter the label `Total`. At the bottom of column B, enter a formula to total the expenses for June. Add similar formulas to total the expenses for July and August.

c) In column E, add the titles and formulas to display the average for each of the expenses over the three months and the total average expenses.

d) Format the values in columns B, C, D, and E to display currency. Format all the titles to be bold. Right align the average title.

e) Save the modified spreadsheet on disk. Preview and then print a copy of the spreadsheet.

When complete your spreadsheet should be similar to:

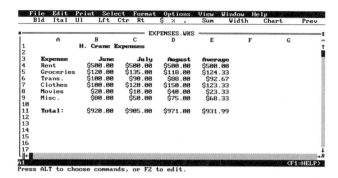

4. Create a spreadsheet that displays a multiplication table. When a number is entered into cell D3, it is displayed multiplied by 1 through 10. Save the spreadsheet naming it MULTIPLY.

Your spreadsheet should be similar to the following:

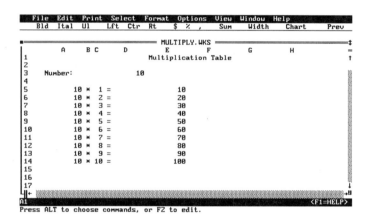

Change the column widths where appropriate. The formulas created to compute the product should use cell references for both the multiplier and the multiplicand.

5. Mr. Hernandez, owner of the Aztec Café has decided to use a spreadsheet to keep track of the number of hours his employees work.

a) Create a new spreadsheet and enter the employee data as shown on the next page. Save the spreadsheet naming it ACEMP.

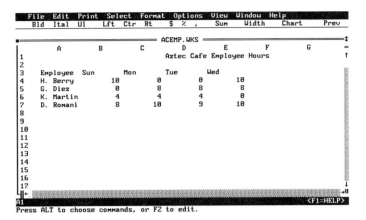

b) Add the following data for the remaining part of the week:

Employee	Thu	Fri	Sat
H. Berry	8	8	4
G. Diez	8	10	0
K. Martin	4	0	4
D. Romani	0	10	0

c) In column I, enter formulas to display the total number of hours worked by each employee. Title the column.

d) Format the day and total titles to be right aligned and bold. Format the columns storing the hours worked per day and total hours worked to a width of 6.

e) Save the modified spreadsheet and print a copy of it.

6. Mr. Horatio von Money, Ivy University's major benefactor, keeps track of his stock portfolio in a spreadsheet named STOCKS. Open the STOCKS spreadsheet. Note that the spreadsheet displays the price of each stock and the number of shares Mr. von Money owns.

a) You are to assist Mr. von Money by adding a column to his spreadsheet that calculates the value of each stock he owns. Title the column Value. The value is calculated by multiplying the price of the stock by the number of shares owned. Add formulas to compute the value of each stock.

b) Mr. von Money has decided that he will donate one fourth of his portfolio to Ivy University. Add formulas to total the value of all of his stocks and to compute the amount of his donation. Be sure to label both figures.

c) Format the Value label to be right aligned and bold. Change the width of column E to 15. Format the values in column E for currency displayed to 2 decimal places.

d) Save the spreadsheet and then print a copy of it.

An Introduction to Computing Using Microsoft Works

7. Varsity baseball coach Slugger Ryan needs a spreadsheet to store the statistics on each of his players. Below are listed the names, times at bat, and number of hits for the players:

Player	At bats	Hits
Attis	10	3
Baker	11	3
Connelly	9	5
Doucette	12	4
Enders	15	2
Fritz	10	6
Gold	14	4
Hernandez	12	6
Li	11	5

a) Enter the above statistics into a new spreadsheet. Be sure to include proper titles. Save the spreadsheet naming it BASEBALL.

b) Batting averages are calculated by dividing the number of hits by the number of times at bat. Add a column to BASEBALL that calculates and displays each player's batting average rounded to 3 decimal places. Be sure to title the column.

c) Coach Ryan would like to know the overall team batting average. Use the average function to produce the calculation for him. Be sure to include rounding and a proper label.

d) Bold all the labels and right align the labels describing the At Bats, Hits, and Average columns. Save the modified spreadsheet on disk and print a copy.

8. Spreadsheets can be used to keep track of any type of numerical data. You are to produce a spreadsheet to help determine your caloric intake for a week.

a) Create a spreadsheet which keeps a record of the calories you consume each day for a week. Save the spreadsheet naming it DIET. Your spreadsheet should be similar to the following:

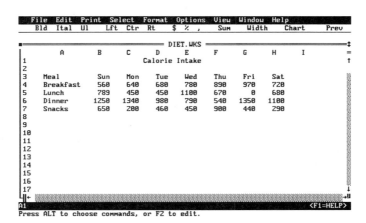

b) Have the spreadsheet calculate the total number of calories consumed each day, the total for the week, and the average number of calories consumed per day. Be sure to include rounding and appropriate labels.

c) It has been determined that aerobic exercise burns 360 calories per hour. Have the spreadsheet calculate the number of hours for a workout to burn off half of the total calories consumed for each day. Include an appropriate label. Save the modified spreadsheet on disk and print a copy.

9. Spreadsheets can be helpful in personal time management.

a) Create a spreadsheet which stores the number of hours you spend each day of the week at each of the following activities:

    school classes
    athletics
    extra-curricular groups and clubs
    studying and doing homework
    eating
    sleeping
    watching television or listening to music
    talking on the phone
    doing chores at home
    working at a part-time job

Save the spreadsheet on disk naming it ACTIVITY.

b) For each activity have the spreadsheet calculate the total hours spent for the week on the activity. Also calculate the average number of hours spent per day on each activity for the week.

c) Most people's schedules do not exactly account for all 24 hours in a day. Add a row which calculates and displays the amount of unaccounted time in your schedule for each day. Save the modified spreadsheet on disk and print a copy.

Manipulating Data with the Spreadsheet

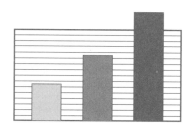

Objectives

After completing this chapter you will be able to:

1. Plan a large spreadsheet including its layout.

2. Copy labels, values, and formulas.

3. Search for a particular cell or label.

4. Use the MAX and MIN functions.

5. Use the IF function to make decisions.

6. Insert and delete rows and columns.

7. Create charts and graphs of spreadsheet data.

9

This chapter discusses how to plan and produce a large spreadsheet on the computer. You will be taught how to format and manipulate data so that your spreadsheets are easy to read and use. Commands will be introduced which enable you to copy formulas from one set of cells to other cells. The chapter ends by teaching you how to produce graphs and charts of the data stored in a spreadsheet.

9.1 Planning a Large Spreadsheet

The spreadsheets produced in Chapter Eight required little planning because they were small and easy to understand. In this chapter, planning will be more important as we develop large spreadsheets which can be continually modified and expanded.

As an example of the need for planning, we will produce a spreadsheet for Ivy University's accounting department to assist it in calculating its payroll. To do this we will follow the four steps for planning a spreadsheet discussed in Chapter Eight.

The first step in developing such a plan is to determine what new data the spreadsheet is to generate. This will be each employee's gross pay for the week. Gross pay is the pay earned before any deductions (such as taxes) are made.

The second step is to decide what data to include in the spreadsheet. This is:

- Employee name
- Pay rate per hour
- Hours worked per day for each of 5 days

The third step is to decide what calculations must be performed to produce the desired new data. The employees of Ivy University work by the hour for an hourly pay rate which differs from employee to employee. Multiplying the total number of hours worked for the week by the pay rate produces the gross pay.

The fourth step in planning is to determine how the spreadsheet is to appear on the computer screen — its layout. We begin planning the layout by determining what type of data is to be placed in each column. The order of the columns is important because we want related data grouped by columns. Next we will decide how wide each column should be to display its longest entry. The 10 character default width may be

either too small or too large, so we can use Works to change column widths.

Before using the computer, a sketch of the spreadsheet showing each column heading, the width of the column, and the type of data it will store should be drawn using paper and pencil. Here is a sketch of our plan for Ivy's payroll spreadsheet:

Name	Rate/Hr	Mon	Tue	Wed	Thu	Fri	Gross Pay
15	9	9	9	9	9	9	12
(label)	(dollars)		(1 decimal place)				(dollars)

Note that each column width is shown along with the type of data it will store. Later we will add columns to the spreadsheet that contain other calculations.

9.2 Highlighting

In the Spreadsheet, several cells can be selected together by highlighting. An entire row, column, or a block consisting of cells from both rows and columns may be highlighted. Many of the formatting, editing, and printing commands can be applied to a highlighted area so that several cells of the Works spreadsheet can be modified at once.

Placing the cell cursor in a cell in the row to be highlighted and pressing Ctrl-F8 will highlight all the cells in the row. A column may be selected by moving the cell cursor into a cell in the desired column and pressing Shift-F8. To highlight a block, the cell cursor is moved to the first cell in the block and the F8 key pressed. EXT will be displayed on the Status line. Next, pressing the arrow key that denotes the direction of the highlight will extend the selected area. The entire spreadsheet may be highlighted by pressing Ctrl-Shift-F8. Highlighting commands may also be selected from the Edit menu.

The mouse can also be used to highlight portions of the spreadsheet. An entire row is selected by clicking on the row number. Clicking on a column letter will highlight a column. A block is highlighted by dragging the mouse from the cell in the upper-left of the block to the cell in the lower-right of the block. Clicking in the area above row 1 and to the left of column A will select the entire spreadsheet.

9.3 Margins

```
Print
Print...
Page Setup & Margins...
Preview...

Set Print Area
Insert Page Break
Delete Page Break
Headers & Footers...

Printer Setup...
```

In the Word Processor, decreasing the margins created a longer line length. Similarly, decreasing the spreadsheet margins can increase the number of columns printed on a page. To change the spreadsheet margins, the Page Setup & Margins command from the Print menu is selected. The following dialog box is displayed:

An Introduction to Computing Using Microsoft Works

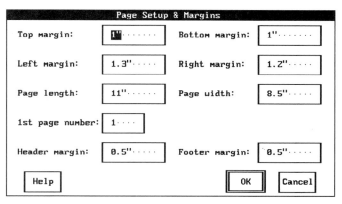

Page Setup & Margins			
Top margin:	1"	Bottom margin:	1"
Left margin:	1.3"	Right margin:	1.2"
Page length:	11"	Page width:	8.5"
1st page number:	1		
Header margin:	0.5"	Footer margin:	0.5"
Help		OK	Cancel

Margins may be changed from the Page Setup & Margins dialog box

As you learned in Chapter Three, other page format options such as headers and footers may be defined using commands from the Print menu. Dates, times, and other information included in a header or footer can be printed with each page of the spreadsheet.

● ●

Practice 1

In this Practice you will create a new spreadsheet named PAYROLL which stores the names, hourly wages, and hours worked each day for three of the employees at Ivy University.

1) BOOT DOS AND START WORKS

2) CREATE A NEW SPREADSHEET

From the Quick Start dialog box, select **Create a New File**. Select **Spreadsheet** in the Create New File dialog box. Select OK to create a new spreadsheet.

3) FORMAT COLUMN A TO 15 CHARACTERS WIDE

a. Place the cursor in column A. This column will store the employee names.
b. From the Format menu, select the Column Width command. The Width dialog box displays the default value of 10.
c. Enter the new width, 15.

4) FORMAT CELLS B3 TO B5 TO DISPLAY DOLLAR AMOUNTS WITH 2 DECIMAL PLACES

a. Move the cursor to cell B3.
b. Press the F8 key to start highlighting. Mouse users: clicking and holding the mouse button may also be used to start highlighting.
c. Use the arrow keys to move the cell cursor to cell B5. Mouse users should drag from cell B3 to cell B5. Cells B3, B4, and B5 are now highlighted.
d. From the Format menu or the Tool bar, select the Currency ($) command.
e. The Currency dialog box appears if the Currency command is executed from the Format menu. Select OK to accept the default value of 2 decimal places.

5) FORMAT BLOCK TO DISPLAY 1 DECIMAL PLACE

a. Place the cell cursor on cell C3.
b. Start highlighting.
c. Move the cursor to cell G5. A block of 15 cells is now highlighted.

d. From the Format menu, select the Fixed command which displays the dialog box.
e. Enter a 1. All five columns are now formatted to display 1 decimal place each.

6) RIGHT ALIGN THE COLUMN HEADINGS

The column headings in your spreadsheet need to be right aligned to line up with the numbers in the columns.

a. Place the cursor on cell B1.
b. Highlight the block of cells from B1 to G1.
c. From the Format menu, select the Style command which displays the dialog box.
d. From the **Alignment** box, select **Right**. Any headings entered in columns B through G will be now right aligned.

7) CHANGE THE MARGINS

Reducing the margins will enable Works to print the entire spreadsheet on one page. This not only saves paper, but makes the spreadsheet easier to read.

a. From the Print menu, select the Page Setup & Margins command. The dialog box is displayed.
b. Move the cursor to the **Left margin** box. Type 0.5.
c. Move the cursor to the **Right margin** box. Type 0.5. Select OK to apply the margin changes.

8) ENTER DATA

Enter data into the spreadsheet so that it appears like the one shown below. Be sure to include names and column headings.

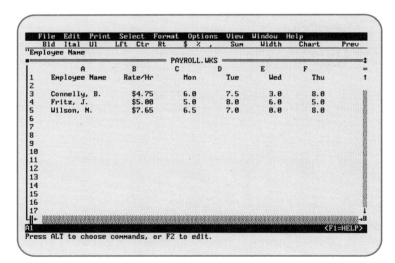

In column G, add the following data for Friday:

```
Fri
7.0
7.5
8.0
```

9) SAVE PAYROLL ON DISK

From the File menu, select the Save command. Name the spreadsheet PAYROLL.

An Introduction to Computing Using Microsoft Works

9.4 Entering Formulas — Pointing

A useful technique to employ when entering a formula which contains cell names is to have Works enter the cell names in a process called "pointing." This is accomplished by typing the formula up to the point where the first cell name appears and then moving the cell cursor to that cell. The cell name appears highlighted in the formula. Typing the next character, an operator for example, places the cell name into the formula. This process is continued until the formula is complete.

This technique can be used to calculate the Gross Pay column for PAYROLL. This calculation is performed by multiplying the pay rate by the total number of hours worked for the week. To calculate B. Connelly's gross pay we will enter the formula

$$=B3 * SUM(C3:G3)$$

into cell H3.

After the cell cursor is placed into cell H3, the equal sign is typed. The cell cursor is then moved to cell B3 using the arrow keys and the next character in the formula, an asterisk (*), typed. Works automatically enters the cell name B3 into the formula. SUM(is then typed and the cursor moved to the first cell in the range, C3. After typing a colon (:), the cell cursor is moved to the last cell in the range, in this case G3. This causes all of the cells contained in the range to be highlighted. A right parenthesis is then typed and the entire formula entered by pressing the Enter key.

The advantage of using pointing is that in a large spreadsheet it helps to avoid the possibility of making a mistake by including the wrong cells in the formula. This is especially useful when the cells you wish to include in the formula are not currently shown on the screen. Whenever pointing is being used to enter cell names in a formula, Works displays POINT on the Status line.

The mouse may also be used for pointing. For example, the Gross Pay column is calculated by first clicking on cell H3. An equal sign (=) is typed. Cell B3 is then selected by clicking on it, and an asterisk (*) typed. SUM(is then typed. Selecting cell C3 and dragging the mouse to cell G3 highlights the range of cells to be summed. The colon is automatically inserted. A right parenthesis is then typed and the mouse clicked to enter the completed formula.

9.5 Printing a Selected Spreadsheet Area

Selected portions of a spreadsheet may be printed using the Set Print Area command from the Print menu. First, the block to be printed is highlighted. The Set Print Area command from the Print menu is then chosen. The message "Set print area to current selection?" is displayed in a dialog box. Selecting OK makes the highlighted area in the spreadsheet the current print area. Only the highlighted block will be printed when the Print command is next selected. Previewing the spreadsheet displays only the selected print area as well.

It is important to note that Works saves the print area setting with the spreadsheet, so only that area will be printed the next time the spreadsheet is opened and the Print command executed. To remove a selected print area, the entire spreadsheet is highlighted and the Set Print Area command selected.

Practice 2

In this Practice you will add a Gross Pay column to PAYROLL and calculate B. Connelly's gross pay for the week. Start Works and open the PAYROLL.WKS spreadsheet if you have not already done so.

1)   FORMAT COLUMN H TO 12 CHARACTERS WIDE

   a.   Move the cell cursor to cell H1.
   b.   From the Format menu or the Tool bar, select the Column Width command.
   c.   Enter 1 2 into the dialog box.

2)   ENTER THE GROSS PAY HEADING AND RIGHT ALIGN IT

   a.   Enter the label Gross Pay in cell H1.
   b.   The cell cursor should still be located on cell H1. From the Format menu, select the Style command. The dialog box is displayed.
   c.   From the **Alignment** box, select **Right**. The heading is now right aligned in the cell.

3)   FORMAT CELLS H3, H4, AND H5 TO DISPLAY DOLLARS

   a.   Place the cell cursor on cell H3.
   b.   Highlight the block of cells from cell H3 to H5.
   c.   From the Format menu, select the Currency command. The Currency dialog box is displayed.
   d.   Select OK to accept the default value of 2 decimal places.

4)   ENTER GROSS PAY FORMULA IN CELL H3

   a.   Place the cell cursor on cell H3.
   b.   Type an equal sign (=).
   c.   Move the cursor to point to cell B3. Note how the Formula line displays the formula with cell name B3 highlighted.
   d.   Type an asterisk (*). B3 is now entered into the formula, and the cell cursor has moved back to cell H3.
   e.   Type: SUM (
   f.   Move the cursor to point to cell C3 and type a colon (:). Mouse users need only select cell C3 to start highlighting.
   g.   Move the cursor to point to cell G3. Mouse users should drag from cell C3 to cell G3. Type a right parenthesis:)
   h.   Press Enter or click the mouse to end the formula. The Formula line displays =B3 * SUM(C3:G3). The calculated gross pay for B. Connelly, $149.63, is shown in cell H3.

9

5) SAVE PAYROLL AND PREVIEW THE DATA IN ROW 3

a. From the File menu, select the Save command.

b. Highlight row 3 containing the gross pay for B. Connelly by moving the cell cursor to a cell in row 3 and pressing `Ctrl-F8` or by clicking on the row number.

c. From the Print menu, select the Set Print Area command. From the dialog box, select OK to make the highlighted area the current print area.

d. From the Print menu, select the Preview command. Select **Preview** to view the spreadsheet. After viewing, press Escape to return to the spreadsheet.

e. From the Select menu, highlight the All command to select the entire spreadsheet.

f. From the Print menu, select the Set Print Area command. From the dialog box, select OK.

g. Save the spreadsheet once again so that the correct print area will be selected the next time the spreadsheet is opened.

<u>Check</u> - Your spreadsheet should be similar to:

```
 File  Edit  Print  Select  Format  Options  View  Window  Help
  Bld  Ital  Ul      Lft  Ctr  Rt    $  %  ,    Sum    Width    Chart      Prev
=B3*SUM(C3:G3)
                              PAYROLL.WKS
        B           C          D         E         F         G          H
 1    Rate/Hr      Mon        Tue       Wed       Thu       Fri      Gross Pay
 2
 3    $4.75        6.0        7.5       3.0       8.0       7.0       $149.63
 4    $5.00        5.0        8.0       6.0       5.0       7.5
 5    $7.65        6.5        7.0       0.0       8.0       8.0
 6
 7
 8
 9
10
11
12
13
14
15
16
17
H3                                                                <F1=HELP>
Press ALT to choose commands, or F2 to edit.
```

9.6 Copy, Fill Right, and Fill Down

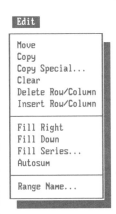

Edit

Move
Copy
Copy Special...
Clear
Delete Row/Column
Insert Row/Column

Fill Right
Fill Down
Fill Series...
Autosum

Range Name...

Often the same label, value, or formula should be stored in a number of different cells. We can of course type it over and over again, but Works makes such copying easy with the Copy command from the Edit menu. To copy the contents of a single cell, the cursor is placed on the cell and the Copy command executed. The message "Select new location and press ENTER. Press ESC to cancel" appears on the Message line at the bottom of the screen and COPY is shown on the Status line. When the cursor is moved to the destination cell and Enter pressed, Works copies the contents of the source cell into the destination. The format of the source is also retained. When COPY is displayed on the Status line only a limited number of commands may be chosen from the menus - the rest are shown in dimmed text.

The Fill Right and Fill Down commands from the Edit menu are used when a cell's contents are to be copied to an adjacent row or column of cells. This is useful when placing a line of dashes across or down a spreadsheet to separate rows or columns. For example, to place dashes across a spreadsheet, dashes are typed in the leftmost cell in the row. Because the dash (-) is also used as a minus sign, it is necessary to first enter a quotation mark (") to inform Works that a label rather than a value is to be entered. Next, a highlight is extended from the current cell to the end of the desired row and the Fill Right command executed. Fill Down is used to copy the source cell's contents into a highlighted range of cells in the same column.

•••

Practice 3

In this Practice you will place a line of dashes across row 2 of the PAYROLL spreadsheet using the Fill Right command. Start Works and open the PAYROLL.WKS spreadsheet if you have not already done so.

1)   ENTER DASHES

    a.   Move the cell cursor to cell A2.
    b.   Enter a quotation mark (**"**) followed by 15 dashes.
    c.   In cell B2, enter a quotation mark and 7 dashes.
    d.   In cell C2, enter a quotation mark and 3 dashes.
    e.   In cell H2, enter a quotation mark and 9 dashes.

2)   RIGHT ALIGN THE DASHES

    a.   Place the cell cursor in cell B2.
    b.   Highlight cells B2 through H2 as a block.
    c.   From the Format menu, select the Style command. The Style dialog box is displayed.
    d.   From the **Alignment** box, select **Right** to right align the dashes.

3)   USE FILL RIGHT TO COPY THE DASHES

    a.   Place the cell cursor on cell C2.
    b.   Highlight cells C2 through G2 as a block.
    c.   From the Edit menu, select the Fill Right command. The dashes are copied into cells D2 through G2.

4)   SAVE PAYROLL ON DISK

    From the File menu, select the Save command.

Check - The spreadsheet should contain a line of dashes in row 2:

```
 File  Edit  Print  Select  Format  Options  View  Window  Help
   Bld  Ital  Ul    Lft  Ctr  Rt    $  %  ,    Sum    Width    Chart    Prev
"Employee Name
■━━━━━━━━━━━━━━━━━━━━━━━━ PAYROLL.WKS ━━━━━━━━━━━━━━━━━━━━━━↕
        A            B          C        D        E        F        =
 1   Employee Name  Rate/Hr     Mon      Tue      Wed      Thu      ↑
 2   -------------  -------     ---      ---      ---      ---
 3   Connelly, B.   $4.75      6.0      7.5      3.0      8.0
 4   Fritz, J.      $5.00      5.0      8.0      6.0      5.0
 5   Wilson, N.     $7.65      6.5      7.0      0.0      8.0
 6
 7
 8
 9
10
11
12
13
14
15
16
17
╢←                                                            →↲
A1                                                       <F1=HELP>
Press ALT to choose commands, or F2 to edit.
```

An Introduction to Computing Using Microsoft Works

9.7 Relative Copying

Another useful application of the Fill Down and Fill Right commands is for copying formulas. In the PAYROLL spreadsheet the formula to calculate B. Connelly's gross pay, =B3 * SUM(C3:G3) is stored in cell H3. To calculate J. Fritz's and N. Wilson's gross pay the formula has to be entered into rows 4 and 5 with the cell names adjusted for the new row numbers. For example, because J. Fritz's data is stored in row 4, the gross pay formula must be changed to refer to the values stored in row 4 instead of row 3: =B4 * SUM(C4:G4)

When copying a formula, Works automatically changes the cell references to apply to the new row or column. This is called "relative" copying. To produce relative copies in a column of cells the formula is entered into a cell called the "source" cell. A highlight is then created from the source cell to the last cell in the column into which relative copies will be made. When the Fill Down command is executed, formulas are automatically copied into the cells with their cell references changed to reflect their location in the spreadsheet. The Fill Right command can be used to make relative copies in the same row.

If we copy the formula that calculates B. Connelly's wage from cell H3

        =B3 * SUM(C3:G3)

into cells H4 and H5, the formula copied into H4 will automatically be changed to

        =B4 * SUM(C4:G4)

and in H5 to:

        =B5 * SUM(C5:G5)

Although this technique of copying formulas is useful for making copies into only two cells, think how much time it would save if the spreadsheet contained a larger number of employees. Another important advantage of this approach is that it avoids the possible errors that would be made if each formula were required to be typed separately, changing the cell names for each one.

9.8 Displaying Formulas

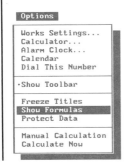

When a spreadsheet becomes large it is helpful to view the many formulas it may contain at their cell locations. This can be accomplished by executing the Show Formulas command from the Options menu. When this is done Works displays the formula stored in each cell, rather than its value. Printing when Show Formulas is selected prints the spreadsheet using the formulas stored in the cells rather than the values. To return to the regular screen the Show Formulas command is selected again.

Practice 4

In this Practice you will create copies of the wage formula in cell H3 for cells H4 and H5 in the PAYROLL spreadsheet. Start Works and open PAYROLL if you have not done so already.

1) COPY THE FORMULAS USING FILL DOWN

   a.   Place the cell cursor on cell H3.
   b.   Highlight cells H3 to H5 as a block.
   c.   From the Edit menu, select the Fill Down command.
   d.   Move the cell cursor to cell H4. The formula displayed on the Formula line shows how the cell names have been changed because Works used relative copying when the formula was copied.

2) VIEW THE FORMULAS ON SCREEN

From the Options menu, select the Show Formulas command. Scroll to the right, if necessary, to view the formulas in column H. Note how the cell references were changed during the copy.

3) RETURN TO THE REGULAR DISPLAY

From the Options menu, select the Show Formulas command. The formulas are replaced on screen by the values they calculate.

Check - The gross pay for J. Fritz and N. Wilson now appear in cells H4 and H5:

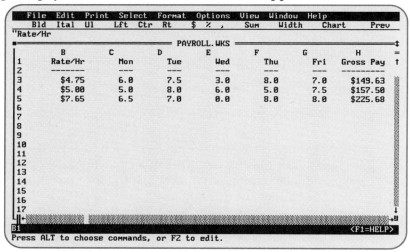

4) CHANGE THE PAY RATE OF N. WILSON

   a.   Move the cell cursor to cell B5.
   b.   Enter 7 . 5, replacing the current value. $7.50 is displayed in the cell. Note how Works automatically recalculates the gross pay. The new gross pay is $221.25.

5) SAVE PAYROLL ON DISK AND CLOSE THE FILE

   a.   From the File menu, select the Save command.
   b.   From the Print menu, select the Print command. Print a copy of the spreadsheet with the **Print row and column labels** option selected.
   c.   From the File menu, select the Close command.

9.9 The Search and Go To Commands

When working with a large spreadsheet it is sometimes cumbersome to locate the cell or cells which contain a particular value or label. To assist in such a search, Works contains the Search command in the Select menu. When executed, the Search command displays a dialog box with a **Search for** option. The value or label to be searched for can be typed here, and Works can be told to search by rows (from left to right) or by columns (top to bottom):

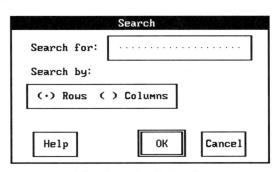

The Search dialog box

Selecting OK initiates the search from the current cursor position. Works then places the cell cursor in the first cell displaying the label or value being searched for. To search from the beginning of the spreadsheet, the cursor must be moved to cell A1 (Ctrl-Home) before the search is initiated. Executing the Search command again finds the next occurrence of the same **Search for** text, and so on until all occurrences have been found. A subsequent search would then return to the first occurrence. Pressing the F7 key is a shortcut for repeating the same search. If the label or value cannot be found anywhere in the spreadsheet, Works displays the message:

Works displays "No match found" when a search is unsuccessful

Only displayed values can be searched; therefore, to search for a formula that is used to compute a value, the Show Formulas command must first be executed. Searches are not case sensitive, which means that it does not matter if letters are typed in uppercase or lowercase. Also, the search will stop if Works finds the **Search for** text in any part of a value or label. That is, specifying a search text of "P" will find both "Presley" and "Roper".

To move the cursor directly to a particular cell, the Go To command from the Select menu is chosen. When executed the following dialog box is displayed:

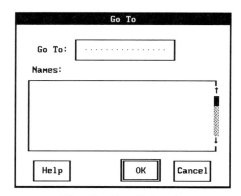

The Go To dialog box

Entering a cell name moves the cell cursor directly to that cell. This can be faster than scrolling when moving long distances in a spreadsheet.

9.10   The MAX and MIN Functions

Works includes two functions which determine either the maximum or minimum value stored in a range of cells. These functions are useful to the Ivy University accounting department in determining the highest and lowest salaries earned by its employees. The MAX function takes the form:

=MAX(<range of cells>)

For example,

=MAX(C3:C10)

displays the maximum value stored in the range of cells C3 to C10. The MIN function takes the form:

=MIN(<range of cells>)

For example,

=MIN(C3:F3)

displays the minimum value stored in the range of cells C3 to F3.

• •

Practice 5

In this Practice you will search a large spreadsheet using commands from the Select menu. The maximum and minimum gross pay will also be computed.

1)   OPEN THE IVYPAY SPREADSHEET

Open IVYPAY.WKS which calculates the payroll for 25 Ivy University employees.

2)   GO TO CELL F34

a.   From the Select menu, execute the Go To command. The Go To dialog box is displayed.
b.   Type F34 and select OK. The cell cursor is placed directly on cell F34.

9

3) DETERMINE THE MAXIMUM GROSS PAY

a. Enter the label: `Max pay:`
b. From the Format menu, select the Style command. Format the label as bold.
c. Place the cursor on cell H34. From the Format menu, Use the Currency command to format the cell for currency to 2 decimal places.
d. Enter the formula:

      `=MAX(H7:H31)`

The gross pay of J. Sowers, $348.25 has been computed as the maximum value in the cell range used in the function.

4) DETERMINE THE MINIMUM GROSS PAY

a. From the Select menu, select the Go To command. The Go To dialog box is displayed.
b. Enter `F35`. The cell cursor is placed in cell F35.
c. Enter the label: `Min pay:`
d. From the Format menu, select the Style command. Format the label as bold.
e. Place the cursor on cell H35. Use the Currency command to format the cell for currency to 2 decimal places.
f. Enter the formula:

      `=MIN(H7:H31)`

S. Munger's gross pay of $75.00 has been calculated as the minimum value in the cell range used in the function.

5) SEARCH FOR THE TEXT "PRESLEY"

a. From the Select menu, select the Search command. The Search dialog box is displayed.
b. Type `Presley` and select OK. The cell cursor is placed in cell A23 which contains the name Presley, B.

6) SEARCH FOR ALL OCCURRENCES OF THE LETTER P

a. Return the cell cursor to cell A1.
b. From the Select menu, select the Search command. The Search dialog box is displayed with the previous **Search for** text displayed.
c. Enter a P to replace the old **Search for** text. The cell cursor moves to the label "Ivy University Payroll" which is the first cell after cell A1 to contain a P.
d. From the Select menu, select the Search command and select OK to repeat the search. The cursor moves to the label "Employee Name", which is the next cell to contain a P.
e. Press F7. The search for P is repeated and the cell cursor moves to the label "Gross Pay", which is the next cell to contain a P.
f. Continue pressing F7 until the cell cursor returns to the "Ivy University Payroll" label.
g. From the Select menu, select the Search command to display the Search dialog box.
h. Enter XYZ replacing the old text. Works displays a dialog box with the message "No match found." Select OK to remove the box.

7) SAVE THE SPREADSHEET

9.11 Expanding a Spreadsheet

Data can be added to a spreadsheet by simply making entries into unused rows and columns, but this should be done with care. If data is added without thought to the overall plan, the spreadsheet will quickly become a jumble of unrelated data.

Expanding a spreadsheet requires the same planning as the initial spreadsheet. The four steps for planning a spreadsheet should again be used so that the modified spreadsheet will easily support further modification and expansion if desired.

The Ivy University accounting department has determined that the IVYPAY spreadsheet would be more useful if it could calculate and deduct taxes and social security from each employee's gross pay. The four steps for planning are used to determine how the spreadsheet should be modified to incorporate these changes. The new data generated is the taxes, the social security, and the net pay which is the actual pay an employee receives after deductions have been made. The modified spreadsheet will need to include the tax rate which will be 15% and the social security rate which will be 6.0%. The calculations that must be performed to generate the new data are the deductions and net pay. Multiplying the tax and social security rates by the gross pay generates the deductions. Net pay is computed by subtracting the deductions from the gross pay. The spreadsheet format is very important — careful planning not only makes the spreadsheet easy to use, but also easy to modify. To display this data on the spreadsheet we add three columns titled Taxes, Soc. Sec., and Net Pay. For ease of modification, the social security rate is stored in a cell that may be referenced in a formula. By doing this, it will only be necessary to change the value in one cell whenever a rate changes rather than the formulas for each employee.

9.12 Absolute Copying

Relative copying enables formulas to be copied to other cells with Works changing any cell references automatically. In some situations we will want to copy formulas in which certain cell references do not change. For example, if all the employees of Ivy University were to receive a bonus amount which is stored in cell A3 in addition to their gross pay, the following formula could be entered into cell I7:

```
=H7 + A3
```

If we were to make copies of this formula into cells I8 and I9, A3 would become A4 and A5. To avoid this problem Works enables cell references to be kept constant if a dollar sign is placed in front of both the column letter and row number ($A$3). This is called "absolute" copying. When copies are now made, the cell reference A3 does not change.

9.13 Other Formatting Options

In addition to the formatting options introduced in Chapter Eight, the Format menu contains the Percent and Comma commands. Both the Comma and Percent commands alter how a cell's value is displayed, but not the value itself.

Selecting the Percent command from the Format menu displays the Percent dialog box. From here, the number of decimal places to be displayed can be typed and OK selected to apply the format. Works automatically converts the cell value to a percentage by multiplying it by 100 and displaying the value. It should be noted that the cell contents are not changed, just displayed differently. For example, if a cell containing the value 0.15 was formatted using the Percent command and 0 entered for the number of decimal places, 15% would be displayed, but the cell value would still be 0.15. Works has the added feature of automatically converting a percentage value into the equivalent decimal value. For example, entering 15% into a cell formats the cell for percent, displaying the percentage value (15%) in the cell. The actual value, 0.15 is displayed on the Formula line.

Executing the Comma command displays the Comma dialog box. The number of decimal places to display may be chosen from here. Applying the comma format causes a cell's value to be displayed using commas. For example, a cell containing the value 30450 displays 30,450 after the comma format is applied.

As with the other formatting commands, there are shortcuts for applying the ones introduced here. Pressing Ctrl-5 formats a cell for percent. The comma format can be applied by pressing Ctrl-, (comma). Both of these shortcuts automatically display values to 2 decimal places.

Mouse users may use the Tool bar to apply the percent and comma formats. Clicking on % in the Tool bar formats a cell as percent displayed to two decimal places. To format a cell for comma displayed to two decimal place, the , (comma) is clicked.

• •

Practice 6

In this Practice you will add columns to IVYPAY which calculate taxes, social security, and net pay for each of the 25 Ivy University employees. Start Works and open the IVYPAY spreadsheet if you have not already done so.

1) **WIDEN COLUMNS I, J, K, AND ADD HEADINGS**

a. Move the cell cursor to cell I1.
b. Highlight cells I1 through K1 as a block.
c. From the Format menu, select the Column Width command to display the Width dialog box.
d. Enter 12. Each of the three columns is now 12 characters wide.
e. With the cell cursor on cell I5, enter the label: Taxes
f. Move the cell cursor to cell J5 and enter the label: Soc. Sec.
g. Move the cell cursor to cell K5 and enter the label: Net Pay

2) RIGHT ALIGN THE HEADINGS

a. Move the cell cursor to cell I5.
b. Highlight cells I5 through K5 as a block.
c. From the Format menu, select the Style command which displays the dialog box.
d. From the **Alignment** box, select **Right**. The three headings are now right aligned.

3) ENTER DASHES AND RIGHT ALIGN THEM

a. Move the cell cursor to cell I6.
b. In cell I6, enter a quotation mark and 5 dashes.
c. From the Format menu, select the Style command. Select **Right**.
d. In cell K6, enter a quotation mark and 7 dashes.
e. From the Format menu, select the Style command. Select **Right**.

4) COPY A LINE OF DASHES

a. Move the cell cursor to cell H6.
b. From the Edit menu, select the Copy command. COPY is displayed in the Status line.
c. Move the cell cursor to cell J6 and press Enter. A row of dashes is displayed in the cell below the Soc. Sec. label. Notice how the dashes are right aligned because the cell format was copied as well.

5) FORMAT COLUMNS TO DISPLAY DOLLAR VALUES

a. Place the cell cursor on cell I7.
b. Start highlighting by pressing the F8 key.
c. Move the cell cursor to cell K31 by selecting the Go To command from the Select menu. The Go To dialog box is displayed. Enter K31. A highlighted block now runs from cell I7 to cell K31.
d. From the Format menu, select the Currency command. Accept 2 decimal places. All cells from I7 to K31 are formatted to display dollar amounts with 2 decimal places.

6) ADD SOCIAL SECURITY RATE LABEL

a. Move the cell cursor to cell A3.
b. Enter the label: Soc. Sec. rate:

7) ENTER SOCIAL SECURITY RATE

a. Move the cell cursor to cell B3.
b. Enter 6.0% for the Social Security rate. Notice how the cell is automatically formatted for percent with 2 decimal places, and the Formula line shows the actual value, 0.06.

8) ENTER FORMULAS FOR TAXES COLUMN

a. Move the cell cursor to cell I7.
b. Enter the formula

```
=H7 * 15%
```

to calculate the taxes as 15%. $28.80 is displayed in cell I7.
c. With the cell cursor on cell I7, highlight a block from cell I7 through I31.
d. From the Edit menu, select the Fill Down command to copy the formulas into cells I8 through I31. A 15% tax is now calculated for each employee.

9) ENTER FORMULAS FOR SOCIAL SECURITY COLUMN

a. Place the cell cursor on cell J7.

b. Enter the formula

```
=H7 * $B$3
```

to calculate the social security deduction as 6% of the gross pay. The social security deduction displayed in cell J7 is $11.52.

c. With the cell cursor on cell J7, highlight a block from cell J7 through J31.

d. From the Edit menu, select the Fill Down command to copy the formulas into cells J8 through J31. A 6% social security deduction is now calculated for each employee.

e. Move the cell cursor to cell J8. Note how Works used relative copying for the cell reference that does not use the dollar signs and absolute copying for the cell reference using the dollar signs.

10) ENTER FORMULAS TO CALCULATE NET PAY

a. Place the cell cursor on cell K7.

b. Enter the formula

```
=H7 - I7 - J7
```

to calculate the net pay by taking the gross pay minus the taxes and social security deductions. $151.68 is displayed in cell K7.

c. Repeat parts (c) and (d) from step 9 to copy the formula, being careful to highlight the proper cells in column K.

11) CHANGE THE SOCIAL SECURITY RATE

a. Move the cell cursor to cell B3.

b. Enter 0.065 to replace the current value. 6.50% is displayed in the cell. Scroll so that columns J and K are visible. Note how Works automatically recalculates all the values in the columns.

Check - The IVYPAY should look like the following:

```
 File  Edit  Print  Select  Format  Options  View  Window  Help
   Bld  Ital  Ul    Lft  Ctr  Rt    $  %  ,    Sum    Width    Chart       Prev

                           IVYPAY.WKS
          A            B         C     D      E     F     G        H
1                            Ivy University Payroll
2
3     Soc. Sec. rate:     6.50%
4
5     Employee Name    Rate/Hr    Mon   Tue    Wed   Thu   Fri   Gross Pay
6     -------------    -------    ---   ---    ---   ---   ---   ---------
7     Attis, B.         $8.00     6.0   4.0    4.0   3.0   7.0    $192.00
8     Ball, R.          $4.00     9.5  12.0    9.0   5.5   3.0    $156.00
9     Bickle, R.        $6.00     5.0   7.0    0.5   7.0   6.0    $153.00
10    Cambell, M.       $4.50     5.0   6.0    7.0   5.0   6.0    $130.50
11    Connelly, B.      $4.75     6.0   7.5    3.0   8.0   7.0    $149.63
12    Crane, H.         $5.90     7.5   6.0    7.5   6.0   7.5    $203.55
13    Fritz, J.         $5.50     5.0   8.0    6.0   5.0   7.5    $173.25
14    Gilman, J.        $7.00     8.0   7.8    8.0   8.0   3.5    $247.10
15    Graham, T.        $4.45     8.0   7.0    6.0   7.0   7.5    $157.98
16    Jefferson, T.     $3.75     7.0   6.0    4.5   8.0   8.0    $125.63
17    Jimenez, W.       $6.60     8.0   7.0    9.0   6.0   7.3    $246.18

A1                                                        <F1=HELP>
Press ALT to choose commands, or F2 to edit.
```

12) SAVE IVYPAY ON DISK

a. From the File menu, select the Save command.

b. Print a copy of the spreadsheet with the **Print row and column labels** option selected.

9.14 *Insert, Delete, and Clear*

```
 Edit 
Move
Copy
Copy Special...
Clear
Delete Row/Column
Insert Row/Column

Fill Right
Fill Down
Fill Series...
Autosum

Range Name...
```

It is possible to insert or delete whole rows or columns in a spreadsheet. This is especially helpful to Ivy University when a new employee has been hired and a row must be inserted, or an old employee leaves and a row must be deleted. It is also useful when columns must be inserted between existing columns. For example, a new column to deduct pension plan contributions can be inserted between the Soc. Sec. and Net Pay columns in IVYPAY.

Inserting a new row is accomplished by moving the cell cursor to the position where the row is to be inserted and then executing the Insert Row/Column command from the Edit menu. The following dialog box appears asking you to select Row or Column:

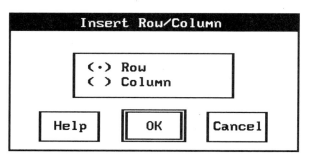

Insert Row/Column dialog box

When Row is selected a new row is inserted at the cell cursor and all rows below move down.

To insert a new column, the cell cursor is moved to the position where the column is to be inserted and the Insert Row/Column command executed. Selecting Column from the dialog box inserts the column and moves all columns to the right of the insertion over.

To delete a row, the cell cursor is moved into the row to be deleted and the Delete Row/Column command from the Edit menu executed. When Row is selected from the dialog box, the row containing the cell cursor is deleted and all rows below move up to fill the space. A column is deleted by placing the cell cursor in it and executing the Delete Row/Column command. Column is then selected from the dialog box. The columns to the right of the deleted column then move to the left to fill the space. Once a row or column has been deleted it cannot be recovered, so use caution when deleting.

When a column or row is inserted or deleted, Works automatically changes the range of any formulas that are involved. For example, if row 3 is deleted, the formula =SUM(C1:C10) changes to =SUM(C1:C9). If instead a row is inserted between rows 1 and 10, the formula becomes =SUM(C1:C11). Care must be taken when deleting the first or last cell reference in a range because this will cause an error. For example, if row 1 is deleted, the formula =SUM(C1:C10) changes to =SUM(ERR) and ERR is displayed in the cell. Any affected formulas must then be edited to enter the proper range.

The Clear command is similar to Delete except that it only removes the <u>contents</u> of cells, not the cells themselves. Clear also works on a highlighted block of cells, while Delete Row/Column affects an entire row or column. Clear leaves any formatting intact, so that new entries into Cleared cells have the same format as the previous ones.

Practice 7

In this Practice, rows will be deleted and inserted into the IVYPAY spreadsheet. Employee H. Crane, who has quit, will be deleted and a new employee, A. Nitrate, added. Start Works and open IVYPAY.WKS if you have not already done so.

1) DELETE ROW CONTAINING EMPLOYEE CRANE, H.

a. Move the cell cursor to the row containing H. Crane's data.
b. From the Edit menu, select the Delete Row/Column command which displays the dialog box.
c. Select OK to accept the **Row** option. The row is deleted and all rows below move up to fill the space.

2) INSERT ROW AND DATA FOR NEW EMPLOYEE

a. Move the cell cursor to row 22.
b. From the Edit menu, select the Insert Row/Column command. The Insert dialog box is shown.
c. Select OK to accept the **Row** option. A new row is inserted at row 22 and the rows below moved down to make room.
d. Enter the following data in the inserted row:

```
Nitrate, A.    5.5    6.5    7    8    2    1.5
```

3) TRANSFER FORMULAS TO THE NEW ROW

Note that the formulas that are needed to calculate A. Nitrate's salary and deductions do not appear in the newly inserted row. The new row will require the copying of the four formulas into columns H through K. We can copy all of the formulas at once by highlighting them together as the source.

a. Move the cell cursor to cell H21.
b. Highlight the block of cells from H21 through K22.
c. From the Edit menu, select the Fill Down command. The new formulas are copied into A. Nitrate's row and the values automatically calculated.

4) SAVE IVYPAY ON DISK

Check - A. Nitrate's salary and deductions should be shown in row 22:

Gross Pay	Taxes	Soc. Sec.	Net Pay
$137.50	$20.63	$8.94	$107.94

9.15 Using the IF Function

It is sometimes desirable to have simple decisions made based upon the data stored in a spreadsheet. In Works such a decision is made using the IF function. The decision is based on a comparison entered into the function. If the comparison is true one value is placed in the cell; if not, a second value is used. The IF function has the form:

=IF(<comparison>, <true value>, <false value>)

For example,

=IF(C5 < E7, 10, 20)

stores a 10 in the cell containing the IF statement if the value in cell C5 is less than the value in cell E7, and a 20 if it is not.

The comparison part of the IF function can contain one of the following relational operators:

=	equals
<	less than
>	greater than
<=	less than or equal to
>=	greater than or equal to
<>	not equal to

The following are examples of valid IFs:

```
=IF(N1 <= 25, 50, 100)
=IF(B2 < K25, 0, B2 * .15)
=IF(C10 > MIN(C3:C8), C12, C14)
=IF(D22 <> F25, 0, SUM(E1:E10))
```

The IF function can be used by Ivy University's accounting department to calculate two tax brackets rather than one in the IVYPAY spreadsheet. For example, if an employee's gross pay exceeds $250, 25% should be deducted for taxes. If the gross pay is less than or equal to $250, 15% should be deducted. Calculating all of the salaries by hand for the two tax brackets would be quite a job. The IF function can be used to automatically determine which tax bracket the employee's gross pay falls into and then calculate the correct amount of taxes. Another advantage of our computerized spreadsheet is that when the taxes are recalculated the net pay will also be recalculated automatically.

To calculate B. Attis' taxes to take into account the two tax brackets, we could replace the formula in cell I7 with:

=IF(H7 > 250, H7 * 25%, H7 * 15%)

This formula states that if the gross pay stored in cell H7 is greater than 250, multiply it by 25%. If the value stored in H7 is less than or equal to 250, multiply it by 15%.

Practice 8

In this Practice you will further expand the IVYPAY spreadsheet to allow for two tax brackets. Start Works and open IVYPAY if you have not already done so.

1) ENTER NEW TAX FORMULA

a. Move the cell cursor to cell I7.
b. Enter the formula:

```
=IF(H7 > 250, H7 * 25%, H7 * 15%)
```

2) COPY THE NEW FORMULA TO CELLS I8 THROUGH I31

a. Make sure the cell cursor is on cell I7.
b. Highlight the block of cells from I7 through I31.
c. From the Edit menu, select the Fill Down command to copy the new tax calculation. Notice how the cells in column I have automatically been recalculated and the new values displayed.

3) SAVE THE MODIFIED SPREADSHEET AND CLOSE THE FILE

a. From the File menu, select the Save command. The IVYPAY spreadsheet should look like the one below:

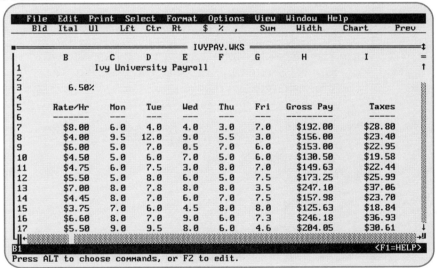

b. From the File menu, select Close to remove the spreadsheet from the screen.

9.16 Charts and Graphs

Numeric data can be difficult to interpret when it is presented in rows and columns in a spreadsheet. For this reason data is often better displayed in the form of a chart or graph. Studies have shown that people remember more about information that is presented graphically. Also, charts show the relationships between the different pieces of data better than columns of figures. Works can produce several different types of charts that display the data stored in a spreadsheet.

Bar Chart:

One of the most common charts is the bar chart in which each piece of data is represented by a bar:

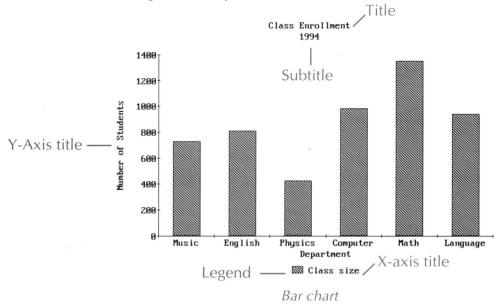

Bar chart

Taller bars are used to represent larger numbers. Bar charts are useful when comparing the differences between many values and may include titles and legends as shown above.

Line Chart:

Line charts, or "graphs", are normally used to show changes in a value over time. For example, this chart shows a city's average temperature for each month over the period of a year:

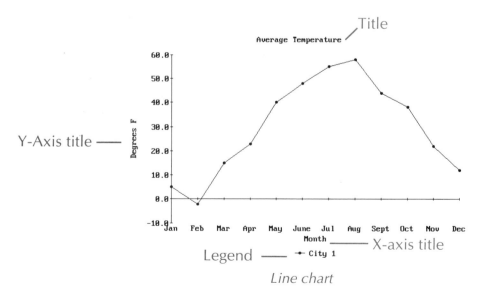

Line chart

Note that a line chart may also include titles and legends.

An Introduction to Computing Using Microsoft Works

Pie charts are used to show the relation between the fractional parts that make up a whole amount:

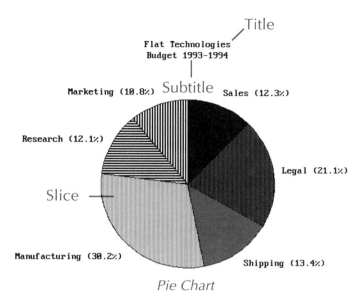

Pie Chart

Each "slice" in the pie represents one fractional part of the whole. The size of the slice varies with the percentage of the total.

The data shown in the first two charts above has two separate parts: the "X-Series" and the "Y-Series." The X-Series runs from left to right on the chart. For example, the months in the line chart above is the X-Series. The Y-Series is the actual values being charted. In the line chart, the temperatures are the Y-Series. For a pie chart the Y-Series determines the size of each slice of the pie while the X-series, if defined, identifies each slice. Bar and line charts may have several Y-Series:

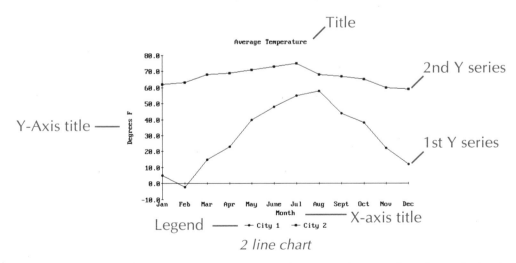

2 line chart

City 1 is the first Y-Series and City 2 the second. Note that the X-Series is the same for both lines.

Just as with spreadsheets, a chart should be carefully planned. You must first decide what information the chart is to contain, and in what order. Next, consider what type of chart to use. Finally, thought should be given to the titles and legends that make the chart easier to read and understand.

9.17 Creating Charts

Works can create charts of the data stored in a spreadsheet. Up to 8 different charts can be created and stored with each spreadsheet. Once created, a chart is automatically linked to the spreadsheet from which its data is taken, so that if a number is changed in the spreadsheet, the chart also changes. After the chart has been created, titles and legends may be added, and the chart printed.

To create a chart, the cells that contain the values to be used in the chart must first be highlighted. Next, the New Chart command is selected from the View menu. If a range of cells has not been selected when the New Chart command is executed, the following dialog box is displayed:

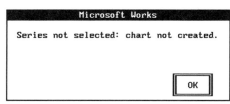

A range of cells must be selected before executing the New Chart command

Works then displays a default bar chart using the values from the highlighted cells. Pressing Escape exits to the CHART screen where modifications, including chart type, can be made to the chart.

New Menu bar and Tool bar

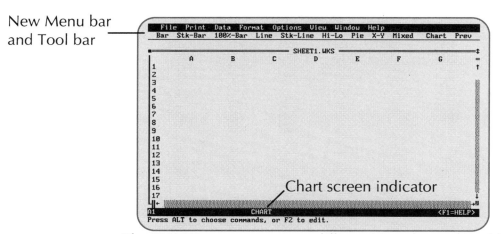

The CHART screen contains a different Menu bar and Tool bar

The commands in the CHART screen's menu bar are used to create, modify, and print charts. Selecting the Spreadsheet command from the View menu will return to the spreadsheet screen. Pressing the F10 key from this screen also returns to the standard spreadsheet screen.

From the CHART screen, there are three main modifications that can be made to a chart:

An Introduction to Computing Using Microsoft Works

1. Redefine the X-Series.
2. Redefine the Y-Series.
3. Choose a chart style other than Bar (Line, Pie, etc.)

Both the X-Series and Y-Series are defined from the Data menu while the style of the chart is chosen from the Format menu. To define a data series, the values to be included are highlighted in the spreadsheet and the desired command executed. Up to 6 different Y-Series may be included in a single chart, which means that up to 6 separate lines or sets of bars can be shown on the same chart.

Only one X-Series may be defined, which can be either values or labels. When creating bar or pie charts it is often useful to use labels in the spreadsheet to define the X-Series so that each bar or portion of the pie is labeled.

Once created, a chart may be displayed on the screen by selecting the chart from the View menu, previewed using the Preview command, or printed using the Print command.

9.18 Saving Charts

Like the report formats in a data base, charts are saved when the spreadsheet file is. Therefore it is important to save a spreadsheet each time a chart is created or modified. When a chart is first created, Works refers to it using the default name Chart1. The next new chart defined is named Chart2, etc. Previously created charts may be renamed, copied, and deleted by selecting the Charts command from the View menu.

Works allows up to 8 charts to be created and stored with a spreadsheet, each of which must have a unique name. Works assigns a default name (such as Chart1) to a chart when created, but this may be changed by selecting the Charts command from the View menu. This command displays the Charts dialog box:

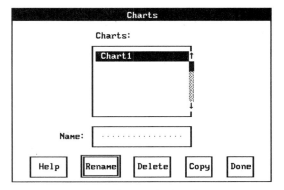

The Charts dialog box

From this dialog box, an existing chart can be renamed, deleted, or copied. When a spreadsheet has more than one chart it is a good practice to change the default name to something more meaningful using the **Rename** option, e.g., Enrollment rather than Chart1.

9.19 The Chart Tool Bar

The CHART screen Tool bar enables mouse users to change the chart type by clicking on an option:

Bar Stk-Bar 100%-Bar Line Stk-Line Hi-Lo Pie X-Y Mixed Chart Prev

The CHART screen Tool bar

Clicking on **Prev** in the Tool bar shows how the chart will look printed. Chart is clicked to display the current chart.

• •

Practice 9

In this Practice you will create a chart using the data stored in the IVYENROL.WKS spreadsheet. Start Works if you have not already done so.

1) OPEN THE IVYENROL SPREADSHEET

IVYENROL contains data on the Freshman course enrollment for Ivy University over a period of years.

2) HIGHLIGHT CELL RANGE TO BE USED IN A CHART

a. Move the cell cursor to cell A5.
b. Highlight cells A5 to B12.
c. Select the New Chart command from the View menu. A bar chart is displayed. Works automatically used the highlighted data in the first column as the X-Series. The second column is the Y-Series.
d. Press Escape to return to the CHART screen.

3) CHANGE THE CHART TYPE

a. From the Format menu, select the Pie command.
b. From the View menu, select Chart1.
c. Using the same data, a pie chart is displayed. This chart displays the data as a fractional part of the total. The labels include the percentage amount its corresponding slice represents.
d. After viewing press Escape to return to the CHART screen.

4) CHANGE A VALUE IN THE SPREADSHEET

a. Move the cursor to the first 1989 enrollment value, 1248 in cell B5.
b. Enter a new value of 1380.
c. From the View menu, select Chart1 to view the chart. The chart should be similar to the one shown below. Note how the change in the data is automatically reflected in the chart.

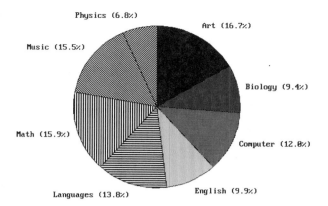

Physics (6.8%)   Art (16.7%)
Music (15.5%)
Biology (9.4%)
Math (15.9%)
Computer (12.0%)
Languages (13.8%)   English (9.9%)

d. Press Escape to return to the CHART screen.

5) *EXIT THE CHART SCREEN AND SAVE THE SPREADSHEET*

a. Press F10 to exit the CHART screen and return to the spreadsheet screen.
b. From the File menu, select the Save command. The defined chart is saved with IVYENROL.WKS under the name Chart1.

9.20 *Adding Titles and Legends to Charts*

Data

1st Y-Series
2nd Y-Series
3rd Y-Series
4th Y-Series
5th Y-Series
6th Y-Series
X-Series

Series...

Titles...
Legends...
Data Labels...

A chart is easier to read and understand if it has a title that describes its data and legends which describe the X-Series and the Y-Series. Each of these is created from the Data menu.

Titles are created using the Title command from the Data menu:

```
                    Titles
    Chart title:   [....................]

    Subtitle:      [....................]

    X-axis:        [....................]

    Y-axis:        [....................]

    Right Y-axis:  [....................]

    [ Help ]         [ OK ]  [ Cancel ]
```

Chart Titles dialog box

You may enter a two line title which is centered above the chart. The first line is entered in the **Title** box and the second in the **Subtitle** box. Each title may be up to 39 characters long. It is also possible to create labels for each axis using the **X-axis** and **Y-axis** options. These should indicate what values are presented in the chart and the units used.

Legends indicate the shading or line style used to represent each Y-Series. By creating a table at the bottom of the chart, legends help the reader keep track of the different values displayed. This is done using the Legends command from the Data menu.

9.21 *Working with Multiple Charts*

9

Works may only work with one chart at a time, the "active" chart. All charting commands (Print, Titles, etc.) affect only the active chart. When multiple charts have been created, the active chart is chosen from the View menu either by typing the corresponding number or by clicking on the chart title:

```
┌─────────┐
│ View    │
├──────────────────┐
│ Spreadsheet      │
│ New Chart        │
│ Charts...        │
│•1 Enrollment     │
│ 2 Class size     │
│ 3 Dept growth    │
│ 4 Avg 1989-1994  │
└──────────────────┘
```

View menu with multiple charts

The active chart will be bulleted. For example, Enrollment is the active chart as shown in the menu above.

• •

Practice 10

In this Practice you will create a line chart which graphs the changing enrollment in three of Ivy's academic departments. A title will be included. Start Works and open IVYENROL.WKS if you have not already done so. Make sure that a printer is connected to your computer and that it is ready to print.

1)   CREATE A NEW CHART

    a.   Move the cell cursor to cell A5.
    b.   Highlight cells A5 to G5.
    c.   From the View menu, select the New Chart command. A bar chart similar to what was created in Practice 9 is displayed. This chart is automatically named Chart2 by Works.
    d.   Press Escape to return to the CHART screen.

2)   CHANGE THE CHART TYPE

    a.   From the Format menu, select the Line command.
    b.   From the View menu, select Chart2. After viewing the line chart, press Escape to return to the CHART screen.

3)   REDEFINE THE X-SERIES

    a.   Move the cell cursor to cell B3.
    b.   Highlight cells B3 to G3.
    c.   From the Data menu, select the X-Series command.

4)   VIEW THE Y-SERIES

    a.   From the Data menu, select the Series command.

b. The Series dialog box is displayed. Works has automatically chosen the range B5:G5 as the 1st Y-Series from the cells highlighted prior to selecting the New Chart command.

c. Select **Done** to exit the dialog box.

5) ADD TWO ADDITIONAL Y-SERIES

a. Place the cell cursor on cell B6.

b. Highlight cells B6 to G6 to include the 6 years of Biology enrollments.

c. From the Data menu, select the 2nd Y-Series command, making the highlighted block the second Y-Series for the chart.

d. Repeat steps (a) through (c) for the Computer enrollments in row 7, being careful to select 3rd Y-series in step (c).

6) VIEW THE Y-SERIES

a. From the Data menu, select the Series command.

b. The Series dialog box is displayed. Note the ranges listed for the 2nd and 3rd Y-Series.

c. Select **Done** to exit the dialog box.

7) ADD LEGENDS TO THE CHART

a. From the Data menu, select the Legends command.

b. Move the cursor to the **Legend** box.

c. Because 1st Y is highlighted in the **Series** list, type `Art`. Select Create. "Art" is now the legend for the first Y-Series.

d. Highlight 2nd Y in the **Series** list by pressing the down-arrow key or by clicking on it using the mouse.

e. Move the cursor to the **Legend** option box.

f. Because 2nd Y is highlighted in the Series list, enter `Biology`. "Biology" is now the legend for the second Y-Series.

g. Highlight 3rd Y.

h. Move the cursor to the **Legend** option box.

i. Enter `Computer` to create a legend for the third Y-Series.

j. Select **Done** to return to the CHART screen.

k. From the View menu, select Chart2 to view the chart with its legends.

8) ADD TITLES AND VIEW THE CHART

a. Press Escape to return to the CHART screen.

b. From the Data menu, select the Titles command.

c. In the **Chart title** box, type `Freshmen Enrollment`.

d. Move the cursor to the **Subtitle** box.

e. Type `from 1989 - 1994` as the Subtitle.

f. Move the cursor to the **X-axis** box.

g. Type `Year`.

h. Move the cursor to the **Y-axis** box and type `Enrollment`.

i. Select OK to exit the dialog box.

j. From the View menu, select Chart2 to display the chart. Note the positions of the titles.

9) RENAME THE CHART

a. Press Escape to return to the CHART screen.

b. From the View menu, select the Charts command. Chart2 should be highlighted in the Charts list.

c. Move the cursor to the **Name** box.

d. Enter `Enrollment` and then select **Done**. Chart2 is now renamed as Enrollment as can be seen in the View menu.

10) SAVE THE FILE AND PRINT THE CHART

a. From the File menu, select the Save command. The Enrollment chart is saved with IVYENROL.WKS.

b. From the Print menu, select the Preview command to preview the chart. Press P to print the chart. Because charts are complex, some printers may require 10 to 20 minutes (or more) to print a single chart. During the printing, Works displays the percentage of the chart printed on the Status line.

c. Press F10 to exit the CHART screen and return to the spreadsheet screen.

<u>Check</u> - Printed charts vary depending on the printer used, but yours should be similar to:

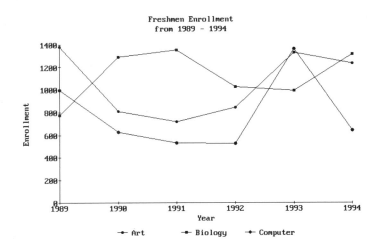

11) SAVE AND THEN CLOSE IVYENROL

a. From the File menu, select the Save command to save IVYENROL.

b. From the File menu, select the Close command.

• •

Chapter Summary

Before using a computer, a sketch of a spreadsheet should be done which shows column headings, widths, and the type of data each column will store. Many formatting, editing, and printing commands can be applied to a highlighted area. A row is highlighted by placing the cell cursor in the row and pressing Ctrl-F8, while a column is highlighted by placing the cell cursor in the column and pressing Shift-F8. A block is highlighted by pressing the F8 key and then using the arrow keys. Using the mouse, a row is selected by clicking on the row number, a column by clicking on the column letter, and a block by dragging the mouse.

The Page Setup & Margins command from the Print menu is used to change a spreadsheet's margins. Decreasing the margins increases the number of columns printed on a page.

The cell names needed to define a formula's range may be entered into the formula by "pointing" to the cells using either the arrow keys or the mouse. A selected portion of a spreadsheet is printed by highlighting it and then executing the Set Page Area command from the Print menu.

The Copy command from the Edit menu is used to copy a cell's contents into another cell. To copy a cell's contents into a row or column of cells, the cells are highlighted and the Fill Right command used in a row or the Fill Down command in a column. Both commands are in the Edit menu. One of their most useful applications is in copying formulas. When this is done Works automatically changes the cell names in the copies to reflect the new rows or columns they are in. To view the formulas in a spreadsheet the Show Formulas command from the Options menu is executed.

Searches for a label or value are performed using the Search command from the Select menu. The Go To command from the Select menu moves the cursor to a particular cell by specifying its cell name.

The MAX and MIN functions display the maximum or minimum value stored in a range of cells.

To keep Works from changing cell references when cells are copied, a dollar sign ($) is placed in front of both the column letter and row number (i.e., $A$3). This is called "absolute copying."

Executing the Percent command from the Format menu formats a cell to display percents (30%). Executing the Comma command from the Format menu formats a cell to display a number with commas (45,321,000).

Rows or columns can be inserted into a spreadsheet using the Insert Row/Column command or deleted using the Delete Row/Column command from the Edit menu. Works automatically changes the ranges of any involved formulas when a column or row is deleted or inserted.

Decisions can be performed based on data in a spreadsheet using the IF function. If a comparison is true the first value in the function is displayed in the current cell, if false the second value is shown. For example, when the formula

```
=IF(A5 > B5, 30, 15)
```

is evaluated, 30 is displayed if the value in A5 is greater than the value in B5 and 15 is displayed if the value in A5 is less than or equal to the value in B5.

Works can use the data stored in a spreadsheet to produce bar, line, or pie charts. Generally, a bar chart is used to compare different items, a line chart to track values over time, and a pie chart to show the relationship in percent between different parts of a whole quantity. A new chart is created using the New Chart command from the View menu. Titles and legends may be added to a chart using the Titles and Legends commands from the Data menu. Up to 8 different charts can be created and stored with each spreadsheet.

Vocabulary

Absolute copying - Copying formulas without allowing cell references to change (i. e., $A$5).

Bar chart - Data graphed as a series of bars.

Chart - A graphical representation of numeric data.

Destination - Cell or cells where copied data is placed.

Fill Down command - Copies a cell's contents to an adjacent column of cells.

Fill Right command - Copies a cell's contents to an adjacent row of cells.

Format - The way that data is displayed in a cell, such as cell width. Formatting options include Fixed and Currency and are selected from the Format menu.

Go To command - Moves the cursor directly to a specified cell.

Highlight - To select a group of cells so that they may be formatted or edited.

Layout - The design of a spreadsheet including the placement of data in its rows and columns, column widths, and the use of formatting options.

Legend - Identifies the shading or line style used in a chart.

Line chart - Data graphed using a continuous line.

Pie chart - Data graphed as segments of a circular pie.

Pointing - Moving the cell cursor to specify cell names in formulas.

Relative copy - Formulas copied in a spreadsheet so that the cell names reflect the new rows and columns they are in. The Copy, Fill Right, and Fill Down commands are used to make relative copies.

Search command - Works moves the cursor to the next cell containing a specified **Search for** text.

Source - Cell or cells where data to be copied is taken from.

X-Series - Data used for the X (horizontal) values in a chart.

Y-Series - Data used for the Y (vertical) values in a chart.

Reviews

Sections 9.1 - 9.5

1. What factors should be considered when planning the layout of a large spreadsheet?

2. Sketch a layout for a spreadsheet that will contain the inventory for an automobile dealership. The spreadsheet should include the names of the different automobile models, the number of each model in stock, and the price of each model. Show the width of each column and tell what type of data it stores.

3. List the steps required to highlight cells B5 to F10.

4. How may a column be formatted to contain dollar values with 2 decimal places.

5. a) Why should the label headings over columns of values be right aligned?
   b) Explain how all of the column headings in a spreadsheet may be right aligned at one time.

An Introduction to Computing Using Microsoft Works

9

6. a) What is usually the best method to use when entering field references in a formula in a large spreadsheet?
   b) What is the primary advantage of using this method?

7. List the steps required to print only the block of spreadsheet cells B5 to F10.

Sections 9.6 - 9.13

8. List the steps required to place a line of dashes from cell B1 to cell J1.
9. What is meant by the term "relative" copying? Give an example.

10. What steps must be taken to copy the formula

   =AVG(C6:C20)

   stored in cell C22, into the range of cells D22 to G22 so that the formula correctly calculates the average for each column?

11. How can Works be instructed to display the formulas stored in the cells of a spreadsheet rather than the values they calculate?

12. What is the fastest way to move the cell cursor from cell A1 to cell Z14?

13. a) What steps must be taken to find each cell in a spreadsheet that contains the label Harry?
    b) What is displayed if a search is performed for a label that does not appear in a spreadsheet?

14. Which of the following labels would be found in a repeated search for the characters PO?

   pox
   Oprah
   hippo
   Porter
   opposite
   Hoppy

15. a) Write a formula that calculates the maximum value stored in the range of cells D5 to Y5.
    b) Write a formula that calculates the minimum value stored in the range of cells C2 to C20.

16. Why is it usually not a good practice to keep adding data to a spreadsheet without careful planning?

17. a) When copying formulas how is it possible to keep one cell reference constant while allowing others to change.
    b) Give two examples of when you would need to do this.

18. List the steps required to format cells B5 to F10 to display values in comma format (i.e., 4,372).

19. What steps must be taken to delete the Net Pay column from the IVYPAY spreadsheet?

20. What steps must be taken to insert a column titled Tue into IVYPAY that follows the column titled Mon and comes before the column titled Wed?

21. a) The formula =SUM(C3:C22) is used to sum the values in cells C3 to C22. If a row is inserted directly above row 20, what must be done to include the new cell in the sum?
    b) If a row is inserted directly above row 23, what must be done to include the new cell in the sum?

22. What will be displayed in the cell containing the following formulas if cell D5 stores a value of 30 and E7 a value of -12?

    a) =IF(D5 <= E7, 10, 20)
    b) =IF(E7 * D5 < -5, E7, D5)
    c) =IF(D5 - 42 = E7, D5 * 2, E7 * 3)

23. Write formulas that perform each of the following:

    a) Store 50 in the current cell if the value stored in D20 equals the value in C90, or 25 if they are not equal.
    b) Store the value contained in B50 in the current cell if the sum of the range of cells C30 to C40 exceeds 1000, otherwise store a 0.
    c) Store the value of X20 * 10 in the current cell if X20 is less than 30; otherwise store just X20's value.

Sections 9.16 - 9.21

24. Would a bar chart, line chart, or pie chart best be suited to display:

    a) a student's GPA over four years at college
    b) the percentages spent on different parts of Ivy University's budget
    c) the number of faculty members in each department at Ivy
    d) the number of books sold each day for a month at the college bookstore
    e) the percentage of Ivy's students from each state in the United States

25. For each of the charts described in Review 24, explain what the X-series and Y-series would be.

26. a) How many charts can be created and stored with a single spreadsheet?
    b) What happens to charts stored with a spreadsheet if the data in the spreadsheet is changed?

27. Explain the steps required to create a bar chart from the IVYPAY spreadsheet displaying each employee's net pay.

28. a) How many separate data lines can be included on a single line chart?
    b) Describe a chart you could produce containing 3 data lines. Explain what each line would display.
    c) Explain how to give the chart a title and subtitle.
    d) Explain how to produce legends for each of the 3 data lines.

29. List the steps required to add a title to a chart and label its X and Y axes.

30. If you are working with a chart and wish to switch to a second chart, what must be done?

Exercises

1. The Ivy University Alumni Association has decided to use a spreadsheet to determine how much it must charge each member attending its annual Homecoming Dinner Dance so that it will not lose money. Below are listed the costs of each item based upon 50 members attending:

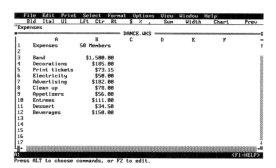

a) Create a new spreadsheet similar to the one above which calculates the cost per ticket when 50 members attend. All of the costs are summed and the total divided by the number of members attending to produce the cost per member. Format the spreadsheet appropriately. Save the spreadsheet naming it DANCE.

b) In columns C, D, and E calculate the cost per ticket when 100, 150, or 200 members attend. Consider the following when adding these columns:

(1) The expenses for Band through Clean up remain the same no matter how many members attend. Be careful to set up these values in the new columns so that if the value in column A is changed it will also change in the other columns. For example, if Band is changed to $785.50 in column A, it should also appear as $785.50 in the three new columns.

(2) The values for Appetizers through Beverages change depending on how many members attend. Therefore, the cost for Dessert for 50 members must be multiplied by 2 to calculate the cost for 100 members, by 3 to calculate the cost for 150 members, and so on. The values for Appetizers, Entrees, and Beverages are calculated similarly.

Your spreadsheet should be similar to the following:

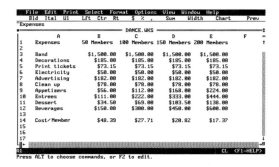

c) Produce the following charts using the data in DANCE:

(1) A pie chart which displays the percent amounts of each cost when 50 members attend. Name the chart Expense for 50. Title the chart Dance Expenses for 50 Members, as shown below:

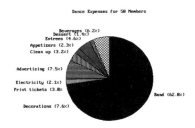

(2) Produce charts similar to that created in part (1) for 100, 150, and 200 members attending. Title and name the charts appropriately.

(3) A bar chart which displays the cost per member when 50, 100, 150, and 200 members attend as shown below:

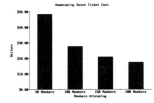

(4) A bar chart which displays the costs when 50, 100, 150, and 200 members attend. Name the chart Expense. Title the chart as shown:

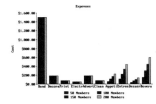

2. Mr. Hernandez, owner of the Aztec Café, would like to expand the spreadsheet created in Chapter Eight, Exercise 5 to compute the gross and net pays of his employees.

a) The spreadsheet expansion should first be planned. Determine what new data will be produced, what data should be included in the spreadsheet, and what calculations must be performed to produce the desired new data. Also, determine the spreadsheet layout.

b) Open the ACEMP spreadsheet. The planning done in part (a) should have included the pay rate per hour as the data that needs to be in the spreadsheet. In column J, enter an appropriate label and the following pay rates:

Employee	Pay Rate
H. Berry	$2.80
G. Diez	$3.60

An Introduction to Computing Using Microsoft Works

| K. Martin | $2.80 |
| D. Romani | $10.40 |

c) Gross pay is computed by multiplying the total number of hours worked by pay rate. In column K, enter an appropriate label and the formulas necessary to compute the gross pay for each employee.

d) Net pay is computed by making the necessary deductions from the gross pay. Taxes are 12% and social security is 6%. In column L, enter the appropriate label and formulas to compute 12% of each employee's gross pay. In column M, compute the social security deductions. Column N should display the label Net Pay and formulas should be entered to deduct the amounts computed in columns L and M from the gross pay.

e) Mr. Hernandez has hired two more employees. Insert the new employee data shown below so that the employee names remain in alphabetical order by last name. Add the necessary formulas to the spreadsheet.

| D. Roberts | 8 | 8 | 6 | 0 | 10 | 12 | 0 | $4.20 |
| P. Jorge | 0 | 0 | 8 | 8 | 8 | 8 | 8 | $3.60 |

f) Save ACEMP and print a copy of it. The expanded spreadsheet should look similar to the following:

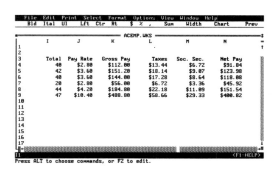

3. The STOCK2.WKS spreadsheet stores the names, purchase price, and number of shares of stocks owned by Grace van Ivy, a relative of Ivy University's founder. You are to assist her by expanding the spreadsheet to produce calculations.

a) Change the width of columns D and G to 15. Format the columns to display dollar values.

b) Add the title Original Value to column D. Enter formulas to compute the original value of each stock. The original value is calculated by multiplying the shares bought by the purchase price.

c) At the bottom of column D calculate the total paid for all of the stock.

d) Ms. van Ivy wants to know how much money she has made or lost on each stock. Listed on the next page is the current price per share for each stock:

Campbell's Soup	$41.38
Chrysler	$40.88
Coca Cola	$40.63
Digital	$43.38
Disney	$47.00
Eastman Kodak	$51.88
Federal Express	$58.88
Ford Motor Co.	$50.63
General Motors	$31.88
Heinz	$41.50
Hershey	$41.13
IBM	$51.13
McDonald's	$14.00
Microsoft	$85.25
Pepsi Co.	$40.63

Add the title `Current Price` to column E and display the current price per share.

e) Add the title `Current Value` to column F and calculate the current value of each stock. Current value is found by multiplying the number of shares by the current price. Sum column F to find the current total value of the stocks.

f) Ms. van Ivy wants to know what stocks have gained in value and which ones have lost in value. Add a column G titled `Gain or Loss` and calculate the gain or loss of each stock by subtracting the original value from the current value. Note that Works displays negative dollar amounts by enclosing them in parentheses.

g) Produce a bar chart to show Ms. Ivy how her stocks are performing. Make the first Y-Series the purchase price and the second Y-Series the current price. Name the chart Compare. It should look similar to the following:

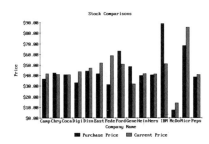

h) Save the modified spreadsheet and print a copy of it.

4. Fantasy Wheels Used Cars wants to use a spreadsheet to keep track of the value of its inventory. The spreadsheet should record the year and model of each car for sale, and the price Fantasy paid for it. In addition, Fantasy typically sells their cars at a 15% markup, and would like to include this information in the spreadsheet. Here is a partial list of Fantasy's inventory. Be imaginative and add three of your own cars to the list:

1972 Corvette   1989 Ferarri
price paid: $8,500   price paid: $22,340

An Introduction to Computing Using Microsoft Works

1990 Porsche price paid: $31,000	1955 Studebaker price paid: $950
1957 Bel Aire price paid: $1,250	1980 Aston-Martin price paid: $56,700
1978 Triumph price paid: $4,560	1958 Thunderbird price paid: $14,000
1983 Rolls Royce price paid: $34,460	1967 Mustang price paid: $11,230
1958 Cadillac price paid: $8,895	1948 Bentley price paid: $49,500
1993 Jaguar price paid: $24,650	1968 GTO price paid: $12,000
1985 DeLorean price paid: $28,999	1978 Bricklin price paid: $36,200

a) Carefully design your spreadsheet. Take into consideration all of the ways the spreadsheet might be used. In your plan, make a column for the selling price.

b) Using the design from part (a) create a new spreadsheet named CARS and enter the above data. Use proper formatting and labels. Calculate the following in your spreadsheet:

> Total of prices paid for inventory
> Average price paid per car
> The minimum price paid for a car
> The maximum price paid for a car
> Profit for each car when it sells at the 15% markup price
> Total profit if all of the cars were to sell at the 15% markup price

c) The 1972 Corvette has been sold. Delete its row from the data base. Be sure to modify any formulas that might need to be changed.

d) Fantasy has acquired two new cars. Add the following data to the spreadsheet, being sure to modify any formulas that might need to be changed:

> 1991 Honda
> price paid: $6,500
>
> 1989 Jeep
> price paid: $5,350

e) Fantasy is having a sale on all cars built before 1970. Create a properly formatted column titled Sale which displays only a 7.5% markup on the price paid if the car is on sale, and 0 if it is not.

f) Create a properly formatted column titled Sale Profit which displays the profit that Fantasy would earn if all of the pre-1970 cars sold at the 7.5% markup price described in part (e). Total this column.

g) Save the spreadsheet on your data disk naming it CARS and print a copy of it.

5. Your best friend, Mike Entrepreneurial, is opening a lawn mowing service and wants you to set up a spreadsheet named LAWNS for his business.

    a) Plan the spreadsheet so that Mike can enter his customers' names, and the lengths and widths of their lawns in feet. Have Works calculate lawn area and the price of cutting the lawn. Mike charges $0.002 per square foot. Be careful to properly format each column and to use meaningful labels.

    b) Using the design from part (a), create the spreadsheet on the computer. Include data for a minimum of 15 customers. Display the total income Mike receives from mowing all his customer's lawns and the average income per lawn.

    c) Mike wants to include his expenses in the spreadsheet so that he can determine his profits. Add a column with the title Expense. Change the column width to 12. He has determined that his fuel and maintenance costs are $.20 per 500 square feet of lawn area. Create a formula to compute the expense for each lawn. Display the total and average expenses as well.

    d) Profit is computed by deducting the expense from the price. Add a column titled Profit. Change the column width to 12. Use formulas to compute the profit made on each lawn and the total and average profit.

    e) Create a bar chart titled Mike's Lawn Service which displays the price, expense, and profit for each of the first five customers in the spreadsheet. Your chart should be similar to the following:

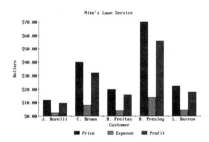

    f) Save the spreadsheet on disk using the name LAWNS and print a copy of it.

6. You have been given an assignment in science class to record the average yearly temperature for your city for a 50 year period. You can find this information in an almanac or at the town library or use the example data given below:

Year	Temp	Year	Temp	Year	Temp
1943	64	1960	49	1977	69
1944	73	1961	54	1978	74
1945	62	1962	65	1979	80
1946	51	1963	53	1980	76
1947	66	1964	55	1981	68
1948	55	1965	63	1982	59
1949	67	1966	75	1983	58
1950	78	1967	67	1984	67
1951	76	1968	76	1985	72
1952	65	1969	58	1986	65

1953	64	1970	69	1987	64
1954	53	1971	70	1988	58
1955	54	1972	65	1989	67
1956	65	1973	56	1990	68
1957	74	1974	57	1991	74
1958	73	1975	72	1992	73
1959	65	1976	70		

a) Create a spreadsheet named TEMP which shows the year and average temperature for a 50 year period. Use proper formatting and labels. To save typing include a formula to calculate and display the year.

b) Add formulas to the spreadsheet which calculate each of the following. Use proper formatting and labels:

   * The average temperature over the past 50 years.
   * The average of the first 25 years only.
   * The average of the last 25 years.
   * The minimum and maximum temperatures for the first 25 years.
   * The minimum and maximum temperatures for the last 25 years.

c) Create a chart named Temp Change which is a line graph of the temperature for years 1945 to 1960.

d) Modify Temp Change to chart all of the yearly data and print a copy.

7. Heidi Crane would like to modify the EXPENSES spreadsheet created in Chapter Eight, Exercise 3 to determine her monthly savings.

a) Add a row to the EXPENSES spreadsheet titled `Income` that stores Ms. Crane's monthly net income of $1,420.00. Savings is computed by subtracting total expenses from income. Add a row to compute the monthly savings. Compute the savings for June, July, and August. In column E, enter a formula to compute the average savings.

b) Create a pie chart named HC Expenses that displays the average expenses as percentages of the overall expenses. The chart should look like the following:

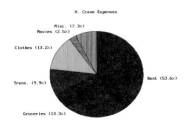

8. The following figures represent the data for the last 10 years for Flat Technologies, a one-product manufacturer:

Year	Expenses	Units Sold	Price/Unit
1	$50,000.00	6,000	$14.50
2	$60,000.00	7,500	$15.50
3	$65,000.00	8,000	$16.00
4	$75,000.00	10,000	$17.00
5	$77,500.00	15,000	$17.75
6	$70,000.00	14,000	$19.00
7	$65,000.00	11,500	$19.00
8	$63,500.00	10,250	$18.50
9	$60,000.00	10,750	$18.25
10	$62,500.00	11,000	$18.50

a) Create a new spreadsheet named FLAT and enter the above data into it. Be sure to use proper formatting.

b) Add a column titled `Profit` which calculates the profit (income minus expenses) for each year. Income is computed by multiplying Units Sold by Price/Unit.

c) Add rows to the bottom of the spreadsheet which calculate the average of the yearly expenses, unit sales, price, and profit columns. Be sure to include proper labels for these figures.

d) Produce and print a line chart named Growth which graphs both expenses and profits for years 1 to 10, similar to the following:

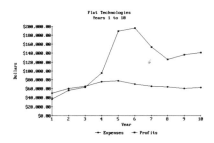

e) Produce and print a pie chart named Sales Pie which shows the units sold each year for years 1 to 10.

f) Save the spreadsheet and print a copy of it.

9. You have been asked to get price quotes from several printers to have a small newsletter printed for your club:

Printer A:	$.25 per copy up to 1000 copies $.23 per copy for every copy over 1000
Printer B:	$.27 per copy for up to 900 copies $.15 per copy for every copy over 900
Printer C:	$.28 per copy for up to 500 copies $.20 per copy for every copy over 500

An Introduction to Computing Using Microsoft Works

a) Create a new spreadsheet named PRINTER which shows the cost for printing 500, 1000, and 1500 copies of the newsletter for each of the three printers. Use the IF function in a formula to calculate the prices.

b) Add a column to the spreadsheet which shows the minimum cost for printing each of the three numbers of copies.

c) The club president would also like quotes for 750 and 1250 copies. Add two rows to the spreadsheet which calculate and display the costs for these numbers of copies. Be sure to copy the appropriate formulas. Save the spreadsheet when completed and print a copy.

d) Produce a bar chart that displays the cost that each printer charges for the different number of copies:

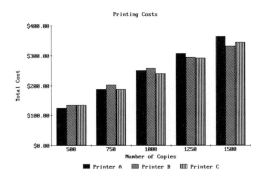

e) Printer C has heard about the other printer's prices and has decided to change his quote to the following:

$.27 per copy for up to 500 copies
$.21 per copy for every copy over 500

Change the formulas for Printer C to reflect this new price. Save the modified spreadsheet on disk and print a copy of it.

Chapter Ten

Advanced Spreadsheet Techniques

Options - Freeze Titles

CHOOSE

VLOOKUP

PMT

Objectives

After completing this chapter you will be able to:

1. Answer What If? questions using a spreadsheet.

2. Use text in functions.

3. Use the CHOOSE and VLOOKUP functions.

4. Create an Amortization table using the PMT function.

10

I n Chapter Nine, the four steps for planning a spreadsheet were used to create a large spreadsheet. Planning was emphasized to make the spreadsheet easy to modify and expand. Functions were used to compute values. In this chapter you will use these skills to ask and answer "What If?" questions so that predictions can be made based upon data that is stored in a spreadsheet. Advanced spreadsheets will be produced using functions that are introduced in the Sections following. The usefulness of text in functions will be demonstrated by including them in formulas.

10.1 Asking "What If?"

One of the most powerful features of a spreadsheet is its ability to answer "What If?" questions. By modifying a spreadsheet to include the factors relating to a particular situation, a simulation or model is produced. Financial predictions can be made based on a spreadsheet model. Many businesses use this technique to help make decisions. Because spreadsheets perform calculations rapidly, a number of different situations can easily be tested. For example, consider a tennis shoe manufacturer. Factors involved in producing a tennis shoe include the cost of leather, laces, rubber, and labor. A spreadsheet model would need to include these factors in order to make financial predictions. If the cost of leather were to go up, the new cost could be entered into the spreadsheet to see how the overall cost of production will be affected. A decision as to whether or not the price of the shoe should increase could then be made based on this model.

Another example is an automobile manufacturer who uses a spreadsheet to determine the cost of producing cars. The spreadsheet could be used to predict the cost under various price changes: What if the price of steel were to increase by 15%? What if the cost of labor were to increase by 6%? What if taxes were halved? The effects of such changes can be quickly calculated by entering the new information in the appropriate cell or cells. All formulas would then be automatically recalculated. It is in using a spreadsheet to produce such models that its calculation power is truly utilized.

The employees of Ivy University have not had a pay raise in five years and have decided to strike if their demand for wage increases is not met. Because the budget at Ivy is already very tight, this threat has the administration concerned about how much the raises will cost. The accounting department will modify the IVYPAY payroll spreadsheet to calculate various wage projections. The employees want an increase of 15% of their gross pay. Ivy plans to offer a 5% increase, but may have to compromise at 10% or may even be forced to accept the full 15%. To see how much each of these percentages will cost, three new columns are added to the spreadsheet which calculate the new gross pay for each of the raises and the total payroll for all employees.

• •

Practice 1

In this Practice you will answer the "What If?" question described in Section 10.1 by adding three columns to the IVYPAY spreadsheet which calculate raises of 5%, 10%, and 15% for the Ivy University employees.

1) START WORKS AND OPEN IVYPAY

Start Works and open IVYPAY.WKS.

2) FORMAT THE NEW COLUMNS

a. Move the cell cursor to cell L1.
b. Highlight cells L1 through N1. From the Format menu, select the Column Width command. Enter 12 to change the width of columns L, M, and N.
c. Highlight cells L5 through N6 as a block. From the Format menu, use the Style command to format the cells for **Right** alignment.
d. Move the cell cursor to cell L6. Enter a quotation mark and 9 dashes.
e. Highlight cells L6 to N6. From the Edit menu, use the Fill Right command to copy the dashes.
f. Highlight cells L7 through N31.
g. From the Format menu, use the Currency command to format the block of cells to display dollar amounts with 2 decimal places.

3) ENTER HEADINGS AND FORMULAS FOR THE RAISES

a. In cell L5, enter the heading: 5% Raise
b. In cell L7, enter the formula:

    =H7 * 105%

This formula calculates a new gross pay which is 5% higher than the original, $201.60.
c. In cell M5, enter the heading: 10% Raise
d. In cell M7, enter the formula =H7 * 110% to calculate a 10% raise.
e. In cell N5, enter the heading: 15% Raise
f. In cell N7, enter the formula =H7 * 115% to calculate a 15% raise.

4) COPY THE RAISE FORMULAS AS A BLOCK

a. Move the cursor to cell L7.
b. Highlight cells L7 through N31 as a block.
c. From the Edit menu, select the Fill Down command.
d. Move the cell cursor to cell L8. Note how relative copying was used to change the cell name in the formula in the Formula line. Note also how Works has converted 105% to 1.05, the actual value.

5) SUM THE NEW GROSS PAYS

a. In cell K33, enter the label: Pay Raise =

b. Move the cell cursor to cell L33. From the Format menu, select the Currency command. Accept 2 for the number of decimal places.

c. In cell L33, enter the formula:

```
=SUM(L7:L31)
```

d. Copy the formula in cell L33 into cells M33 and N33. The model now includes the sums of each of the pay increase columns. Works uses relative copying to change the cell references in the formula.

6) CALCULATE THE INCREASED COST OF RAISES

a. In cell K34, enter the label: `Raise Cost =`

b. Move the cell cursor to cell L34. From the Format menu, select the Currency command. Accept 2 for the number of decimal places.

c. In cell L34, enter the formula:

```
=L33 - $H$33
```

We want to make copies of this formula so that it will always subtract the value stored in H33. This requires the dollar signs in the cell name.

d. Use the Fill Right command to copy the formula in cell L34 into cells M34 and N34. Because of the dollar signs, the cell reference H33 does not change when copied.

Check - The last rows of the new columns should contain the values:

```
Pay Raise  =    $5,118.70    $5,362.45    $5,606.20
Raise Cost =      $243.75      $487.50      $731.24
```

7) SAVE THE MODIFIED SPREADSHEET AND CLOSE IT

a. From the File menu, select the Save command.

b. From the Print menu, select the Preview command. Use the `PgDn` and `PgUp` keys to view the entire spreadsheet. Press Escape to return to the spreadsheet.

c. From the File menu, select the Close command.

10.2 Using Text in Functions

In a Works spreadsheet, a cell label begins with a quotation mark and may contain letters and numbers. Text is similar to a label in that it may contain letters and numbers, but it must be enclosed in quotation marks ("). Text may be used in some functions in the same way values are used. Of the functions discussed so far, the IF function is the only one that can use text. For example, the following formula is valid in Works:

```
=IF(B3 >= 70, "Above average", "Below average")
```

The text Above average is displayed if the value in cell B3 is greater than or equal to 70. Otherwise, Below average is displayed. Text is displayed the same way labels are — the quotation marks are not displayed.

The cell name of a cell storing a label can also be used in the IF function. For example, suppose Above average were stored in cell C1, and Below average in cell C2. The following formula produces the same result as the above formula:

```
=IF(B3 >= 70, C1, C2)
```

Text can be compared using relational operators. Decisions in the comparison part of the IF function can therefore be made based upon the result of comparing text. The examples below are true comparisons:

"Bill" = "Bill"
"Bill" < "John"
"John" > "Bill"
"Beth" <= "John"
"Bruce" >= "Beth"
"John" <> "Bruce"

Comparisons may also be made using the cell names of cells storing a label. For example, if the label John were stored in cell B3, and the label Bill stored in cell B5, the formula =IF(B3 > B5, B3, B5) displays John.

Practice 2

In this Practice, the GRADES spreadsheet created in Chapter Eight will be modified to determine a student's status and display the appropriate label. Boot DOS and start Works if you have not already done so.

1) OPEN THE GRADES SPREADSHEET

2) ENTER STATUS LABEL AND FORMAT COLUMN

a. Move the cell cursor to cell G1.
b. Enter the label: Status
c. From the Format menu, select the Style command. From the Style dialog box, select **Bold** and **Right**.
d. Move the cell cursor to cell G4. Highlight cells G4 to G9 as a block.
e. From the Format menu, select the Style command. From the dialog box, select **Right** so that any text displayed in the cells will be right aligned.

3) ENTER FORMULA TO DETERMINE A STUDENT'S STATUS

a. Move the cell cursor to cell G4.
b. Enter the following formula:

```
=IF(F4 >= 70, "Passing", "Failing")
```

Since the value in cell F4 is less than 70, Failing is displayed in cell G4.

4) COPY THE FORMULA TO CELLS G5 THROUGH G9

a. Move the cell cursor to cell G4 if it is not already.
b. Highlight cells G4 to G9.
c. From the Edit menu, select the Fill Down command. The formula is copied to all the cells.

Check - Your spreadsheet should look like the following:

An Introduction to Computing Using Microsoft Works

```
   File  Edit  Print  Select  Format  Options  View  Window  Help
    Bld  Ital  Ul    Lft  Ctr  Rt    $  %  ,     Sum    Width    Chart      Prev
=IF(F4>70,"Passing","Failing")
=========================== GRADES.WKS ===========================
         B        C        D        E                F          G          =
 1     Test 1   Test 2   Test 3   Test 4 Student  Average    Status        ↑
 2     9/9/94  10/20/94 11/15/94 12/12/94
 3
 4       50       83       68       64              66.3     Failing
 5       86       89       78       88              85.3     Passing
 6       78      100       90       89              89.3     Passing
 7       45       78       66       78              66.8     Failing
 8       66       76       78       55              68.8     Failing
 9       85       74       83       66              77.0     Passing
10
11     68.33    83.33    77.17    73.33
12
13
14
15
16
17
G4                                                         <F1=HELP>
Press ALT to choose commands, or F2 to edit.
```

5) SAVE THE SPREADSHEET AND CLOSE THE FILE

a. From the File menu, select the Save command.

b. From the File menu, select the Close command.

10.3 CHOOSE

The IF function allows a formula to be created which displays one value if a comparison is true, and another value if the comparison is false. Because the comparison in the IF function evaluates to only one of two possibilities, only one of two values can be displayed. Sometimes it is necessary to select one value from a list of many. The CHOOSE function can be used to do this.

The CHOOSE function has the form

$$=\text{CHOOSE}(<position>, <option_0>, <option_1>, \ldots <option_N>)$$

where <position> is a numeric value between 0 and N. CHOOSE displays the value in the list which corresponds to <position>. If <position> is 0, CHOOSE displays <option_0>, if it is 1 then <option_1> is displayed, and so on. For example, given the formula

$$=\text{CHOOSE}(A1, 10, 15, 20, 25)$$

Works displays 10 if the value stored in cell A1 is 0, 15 if the value stored in A1 is 1, 20 if the value is 2, and 25 if it is 3. A formula may also be used to determine the value of <position>. If <position> is negative or greater than N (the number of possible values) ERR is displayed, meaning that a corresponding value is not available. Note that only the integer portion of <position> is used to determine which value to display. If A1 stores 2.6, 20 is displayed because the 2.6 is truncated to 2.

The options (<option_0>, <option_1>, etc.) in the CHOOSE function may be values, formulas, cell names, or text. (Options as text is discussed later in the chapter.)

Practice 3

In this Practice you will modify the IVYPAY spreadsheet to include a retirement deduction which allows employees to contribute different percentages of their salaries. This will be done using the CHOOSE function.

1) OPEN THE IVYPAY SPREADSHEET

a. Boot DOS and start Works if you have not already done so.
b. Open the IVYPAY spreadsheet modified in Practice 1.

2) INSERT COLUMNS TO CALCULATE RETIREMENT CONTRIBUTION

a. Move the cell cursor to column I.
b. From the Edit menu, select the Insert Row/Column command. Select **Column** and then OK to insert a new column.
c. Repeat part (b) to insert a second column. Taxes is now column K.

3) FORMAT THE COLUMNS

a. Move the cell cursor to cell I5.
b. Highlight cells I5 and J5. From the ~~Edit~~ menu, select the Column Width command. Enter 12 as the new width.
c. Highlight cells I5 to J6.
d. From the Format menu, select the Style command. From the **Alignment** box, select **Right**.
e. Highlight cells I7 through I31. From the Format menu, select the Fixed command. Format the block to display 0 decimal places.
f. Highlight cells J7 through J31. From the Format menu, select the Currency command. Format the block to display 2 decimal places.

4) ENTER TITLES

a. Move the cell cursor to cell I5.
b. Enter the title: Retire Code
c. In cell J5, enter the title: Retirement
d. In cell I6, enter a quotation mark (") and 11 dashes.
e. In cell J6, enter a quotation mark and 10 dashes.

5) ENTER THE RETIREMENT CODES

There are five retirement codes numbered 0 through 4 which determine the percentage of gross pay that will be deducted for each employee.

Enter the following numbers into column I as indicated:

Cell	Code	Cell	Code	Cell	Code
I7	1	I16	3	I24	1
I8	2	I17	1	I25	2
I9	0	I18	0	I26	0
I10	3	I19	2	I27	3
I11	1	I20	1	I28	2
I12	1	I21	0	I29	1
I13	4	I22	4	I30	1
I14	2	I23	1	I31	4
I15	2				

6) ENTER THE FORMULA TO CALCULATE RETIREMENTS

Each of the codes above corresponds to the following percentages which are used to calculate the retirement deduction:

Code	Percentage
0	0%
1	2%
2	5%
3	8%
4	10%

a. In cell J7, enter the following formula:

```
=CHOOSE(I7, 0, H7 * 2%, H7 * 5%, H7 * 8%, H7 * 10%)
```

The CHOOSE function first looked in cell I7 which contains the retirement code 1 to determine the value of position. Because the formula H7 * 2% corresponds to position in the CHOOSE function, Works multiplied the gross pay in cell H7, $192.00, by 0.02 to compute the retirement deduction. Cell J7 displays $3.84, the result of the calculation.

b. Highlight cells J7 through J31.

c. From the Edit menu, use the Fill Down command to copy the formula into cells J8 through J31.

7) RECALCULATE THE NET PAY

a. Move the cell cursor to cell M7.

b. Edit the existing formula so that the cell will store following formula:

```
=H7 - J7 - K7 - L7
```

$146.88 is displayed. Net pay is now computed by subtracting taxes, social security, and retirement from the gross pay.

c. Highlight cells M7 to M31. From the Edit menu, use the Fill Down command to copy the formula.

8) SAVE THE SPREADSHEET

<u>Check</u> - Your spreadsheet should look like the following:

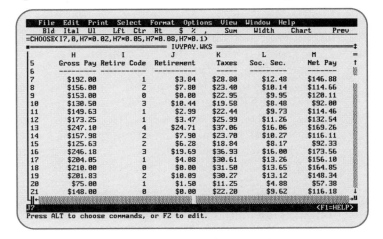

PRINT + SAVE

The example given in Chapter Nine used the IF function to calculate tax withholdings using two different rates based on gross pay: 25% for those employees earning over $250 and 15% for all others. Suppose, however, that there were 10 or 15 different tax rates. The IF function required to calculate the tax would be extremely long and complex, and might exceed the maximum length for formulas, 255 characters. To solve such a problem, Works includes the VLOOKUP function. The VLOOKUP function is similar to CHOOSE except that the values to be displayed are stored in cells in the spreadsheet, not listed in the function itself. This has the advantage of being able to print the values with the spreadsheet, showing the table used. VLOOKUP has the form

=VLOOKUP(<position>, <range>, <columns>)

where <position> is a numeric expression and <range> is the cell range where the values to be displayed are stored. When evaluated, Works finds the largest number in <range> which is less than or equal to <position>, and then displays the value which is stored in the cell <columns> adjacent to the right of that cell (usually 1). This is similar to the manual operation of looking up a value in a two column table: the first column is searched for the desired data, then the value read from the adjacent column. As an example, assume the following spreadsheet fragment:

	B	C
1	1	10
2	2	15
3	3	20
4	4	25
5	5	30

The formula

=VLOOKUP(A1, B1:C5, 1)

displays 10 if cell A1 stores the value 1. This is because cell B1 stores the largest value which is less than or equal to 1, so VLOOKUP displays the value stored in the cell that is 1 column adjacent to B1, the 10 in cell C1. If A1 stores 3.5, this function would display 20, because cell B3 stores the largest value in <range> which is less than or equal to 3.5. (If A1 stored the value 0, ERR would be displayed.)

Note that the values in <range> must be in ascending order for VLOOKUP to work correctly. If the <position> is less than the first value stored in <range> ERR is displayed. For this reason it is important to make the first value in <range> less than any value that will be looked up. If <position> is larger than the last value in <range>, the last value in the lookup table is displayed. For example, if A1 stores 100, the function above would display 30. VLOOKUP differs from CHOOSE in that the <position> may be negative or zero as long as it is greater than or equal to one of the values stored in <range>.

When using the VLOOKUP function, dollar signs should be used to define <range>. This guarantees that the cell references in the table will not change if Fill Down or Fill Right is used to copy the formula containing the VLOOKUP function to other cells.

Assume that a payroll spreadsheet is to calculate withholding using the tax rates shown below:

Gross Pay	Tax Rate
under $100	0%
$100-$149	8%
$150-$199	10%
$200-$249	12%
$250-$299	17%
$300-$599	28%
$600-up	33%

If gross pay were stored in cell H1, the formula

```
=H1 * VLOOKUP(H1, $Y$1:$Z$7, 1)
```

would properly calculate withholding if the tax lookup table was stored in the spreadsheet as:

	Y	Z
1	0	0
2	100	0.08
3	150	0.10
4	200	0.12
5	250	0.17
6	300	0.28
7	600	0.33

For example, if cell H1 stores the value 120, $9.60 is displayed because the VLOOKUP function returns the value 0.08 which is then multiplied by the value in cell H1.

10.5 Freezing Titles

A problem encountered when working with large spreadsheets is that as you scroll across or down the spreadsheet, rows and columns containing labels that describe the data scroll off the screen. This makes it difficult to determine what columns or rows the displayed cells are in. The Freeze Titles command from the Options menu is a solution to this kind of problem. When executed, Freeze Titles locks the columns on the screen to the left of the cursor so that they will always be displayed — scrolling to the right does not affect them. Freeze Titles also locks the rows above the cursor so that they are frozen at the top of the screen, and not affected by scrolling down.

It is important to realize that when the Freeze Titles command is executed, the columns and rows that you want to freeze must be visible on the screen. For example, suppose column A has been scrolled off the screen. If Freeze Titles was executed with the cell cursor in cell B1, it would not be possible to scroll over to column A. When a spreadsheet is printed, any rows or columns affected by the Freeze Titles command are printed on each page, similar to the way the **Print row and column labels** option causes column letters and row numbers to be printed on each page. To "unfreeze" any rows or columns, the Freeze Titles command is again selected from the Options menu.

Practice 4

The IVYPAY spreadsheet will be modified to allow for seven tax rates using the VLOOKUP function. Freeze Titles will be used to keep the employee names and column titles on the screen. Start Works and open IVYPAY if you have not already done so.

1) ADD A VLOOKUP TABLE TO THE SPREADSHEET

The following tax rates will be used in calculating taxes:

Salary	Tax Rate
under $100	0%
$100-$149	8%
$150-$199	10%
$200-$249	12%
$250-$299	17%
$300-$599	28%
$600-up	33%

a. The tax table will be stored in cells R7 through S13. Move the cell cursor to cell S5.
b. In cell S5, enter the title `Tax Table`.
c. In cell S6, enter a quotation mark and 9 dashes.
d. Enter the following values into the indicated cells to create the tax table:

Cell	Salary	Cell	Tax Value
R7	0	S7	0%
R8	100	S8	8%
R9	150	S9	10%
R10	200	S10	12%
R11	250	S11	17%
R12	300	S12	28%
R13	600	S13	33%

2) FREEZE EMPLOYEE NAMES

a. Press `Ctrl-Home` to move the cell cursor to cell A1.
b. Move the cursor to cell B7. From the Options menu, select the Freeze Titles command.
c. Scroll to column J. Note how column A does not scroll off the screen.
d. Scroll down to row 34 and note how the titles in rows 1 through 6 remain on the screen as the employee names are scrolled off the screen.

3) CALCULATE TAXES USING THE VLOOKUP FUNCTION

a. In cell K7, enter the formula:

```
=H7 * VLOOKUP(H7, $R$7:$S$13, 1)
```

The gross pay stored in H7, $192.00 is multiplied by 0.10 to compute the tax deduction of $19.20. Dollar signs ($) are needed in the function to keep the cell references for the lookup table from changing when Fill Down is used.

b. Highlight cells K7 to K31.

c. From the Edit menu, select the Fill Down command. The old formulas are replaced.

d. Move the cell cursor to cell K8. Note the formula in the Formula line. Both relative and absolute copying were used when the Fill Down command was executed.

Check - The modified file should look like the following:

```
 File  Edit  Print  Select  Format  Options  View  Window  Help
   Bld  Ital  Ul    Lft  Ctr  Rt     $  %  ,    Sum    Width    Chart      Prev
=H8×VLOOKUP(H8, $R$7: $S$13,1)
                                    IVYPAY.WKS
            A            H         I         J          K          L        =
  1                                                                          ↑
  2
  3    Soc. Sec. rate:
  4
  5    Employee Name  Gross Pay Retire Code  Retirement    Taxes    Soc. Sec.
  6    ------------   --------- -----------  ----------    -----    ---------
  7    Attis, B.      $192.00        1         $3.84     $19.20      $12.48
  8    Ball, R.       $156.00        2         $7.80     $15.60      $10.14
  9    Bickle, R.     $153.00        0         $0.00     $15.30       $9.95
 10    Cambell, M.    $130.50        3        $10.44     $10.44       $8.48
 11    Connelly, B.   $149.63        1         $2.99     $11.97       $9.73
 12    Fritz, J.      $173.25        1         $3.47     $17.33      $11.26
 13    Gilman, J.     $247.10        4        $24.71     $29.65      $16.06
 14    Graham, T.     $157.98        2         $7.90     $15.80      $10.27
 15    Jefferson, T.  $125.63        2         $6.28     $10.05       $8.17
 16    Jimenez, W.    $246.18        3        $19.69     $29.54      $16.00
 17    Johnson, T.    $204.05        1         $4.08     $24.49      $13.26  ↓
K8                                                                  <F1=HELP>
Press ALT to choose commands, or F2 to edit.
```

4) SAVE THE SPREADSHEET AND CLOSE THE FILE

a. From the Options menu, select the Freeze command.

b. From the File menu, select the Save command.

c. From the Print menu, select the Print command. Print a copy of the spreadsheet with the **Print row and column labels** option selected.

d. From the File menu, select the Close command.

10.6 Using Text in CHOOSE and VLOOKUP

As with the IF function, text may be used in the CHOOSE and VLOOKUP functions. In both functions, a label may correspond to <position>. The label may be the actual text enclosed in quotation marks or a cell name which stores a label. The following formula includes a CHOOSE function which uses text:

```
=CHOOSE(C3, "Freshman", "Sophomore", "Junior", "Senior")
```

In this function, Freshman is displayed if the value stored in cell C3 is 0. If the value stored in C3 is 1 then Sophomore is displayed, etc.

Text may be used in the VLOOKUP table. The lookup table referenced in the VLOOKUP function can store labels in the cells in the column adjacent to the column storing the range values. For example, assume the following spreadsheet fragment:

	I	K
1	1	Accounting
2	2	Marketing
3	3	Research
4	4	Sales
5	5	Distribution

The formula

```
=VLOOKUP(A1, $I$1:$K$5, 1)
```

displays Accounting if the value 1 is stored in cell A1. Research would be displayed if the value 3 is stored in cell A1.

• •

Practice 5

In this Practice, the GRADES spreadsheet will be modified to display each student's letter grade. Boot DOS and start Works if you have not already done so.

1) OPEN THE GRADES SPREADSHEET

Open the GRADES spreadsheet modified in Practice 2.

2) ENTER GRADE LABEL AND FORMAT THE COLUMNS

a. Move the cell cursor to cell H1.
b. From the Format menu, select the Column Width command. Enter 7 to change the current width.
c. In cell H1, enter the label: Grade
d. From the Format menu, select the Style command. From the Style dialog box, select **Bold** and **Right**.
e. Highlight cells H4 to H9. From the Format menu, select the Style command. From the **Alignment** box, select **Center**.

3) ADD A VLOOKUP TABLE

a. In cell J3, enter the label: Grade Table
b. Move the cell cursor to cell J4.
c. Enter the following data into the indicated cells to create the grade table:

Cell	Average	Cell	Grade
J4	0	K4	F
J5	60	K5	D
J6	70	K6	C
J7	80	K7	B
J8	90	K8	A

Note that the scores in the grade table must be in ascending order for VLOOKUP to work properly.

4) ENTER FORMULA TO DETERMINE A STUDENT'S GRADE

a. Move the cell cursor to cell H4.
b. Enter the following formula:

```
=VLOOKUP(F4, $J$4:$K$8, 1)
```

Since the value in cell F4 is less than 70, but greater than 60, the label D is displayed in cell H4.

5) COPY A FORMULA TO CELLS H5 THROUGH H9

a. Move the cell cursor to cell H4 if it is not already.
b. Highlight cells H4 to H9.
c. From the Edit menu, select the Fill Down command. The formula has been copied to all the cells.

Check - Your spreadsheet should look like the following:

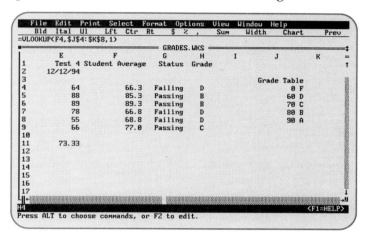

6) CHANGE J. BORELLI'S SCORE ON TEST 1

J. Borelli has taken a makeup test that replaces Test 1.

a. Move the cell cursor to cell B4.
b. Enter J. Borelli's new score: 90. Works automatically recalculates any formulas that refer to the cell containing the test score. Note how J. Borelli's average has been recalculated, status has changed to Passing, and grade is now a C. This example demonstrates the computing power of the spreadsheet, and its usefulness for answering What If? In this case, what if J. Borelli had scored a 90 on Test 1?

7) SAVE THE SPREADSHEET AND PRINT A COPY

a. From the File menu, select the Save command.
b. From the Print menu, select the Print command. Select **Print** to print a copy of the spreadsheet.
c. From the File menu, select the Close command.

10.7 Amortization Tables

One of the most useful applications of a spreadsheet is to produce an amortization table. Amortization is a method for computing equal periodic payments for a loan. Installment loans are loans paid back in a series of periodic payments and are often computed using this method. Each installment, or payment is the same and consists of two parts: a portion of the principle and the interest due on the principle for that period.

An amortization table displays how much interest and principal make up each payment of an installment loan. The principle is the amount of money borrowed. Interest is charged for borrowing the money and is computed as a percentage of the current principle. The principal portion of the payment goes toward reducing the amount owed. For example, the payment made each month on a 30 year loan of $100,000 borrowed at an interest rate of 12% is $1,028.61. On the first payment made, $1,000.00 goes toward the interest on the loan and $28.61 goes to reducing principal (i.e., the amount owed). On the 60th payment, $977.15 goes toward paying the interest and $51.47 to reducing the principal. The final payment pays $10.18 in interest and $1,018.43 in principle.

The PMT function is used to calculate the periodic payments for an installment loan. The amount of the loan (principal), interest rate, and the number of payments to be made are the arguments. A formula using the PMT function takes the form

=PMT(<principal>, <rate>, <term>)

where <principal> is the amount of the loan, <rate> is the interest rate per period, and <term> is the number of payments to be made. As an example, if you borrow $100,000 to purchase a house at an interest rate of 12% for 30 years, the formula would be:

=PMT(100000, 12% / 12, 360)

Since the payments are monthly, the interest rate must also be monthly. This is computed by dividing the annual rate of interest, 12%, by 12. The number of payments is 360, 30 years * 12 months. When entered into a cell, the formula displays a value of 1028.612597.

● ●

Practice 6

In this Practice you will complete an amortization table in a spreadsheet named LOAN which displays the interest and principal paid on the payments made on a loan. Start Works if you have not already done so and open LOAN.WKS.

1) ENTER THE LOAN'S INFORMATION

The loan information is stored in cells that can be referenced in formulas. By using cells to store the data, it is easy to answer What If? questions. For example, what if 10% were the interest rate at which the loan was obtained? To answer this, 10% is entered into the cell storing the interest rate. Works automatically recalculates any formulas referencing this cell and displays the new values, including the payment amount.

  a. In cell C3, enter the principal: 100000
  b. In cell C4, enter the yearly interest rate: 12%
  c. In cell C5, enter the number of payments: 360 (30 years * 12 monthly payments)

2) CALCULATE THE MONTHLY PAYMENT

In cell C7, enter the formula:

=PMT(C3, C4 / 12, C5)

The division by 12 is needed to convert the yearly interest rate in cell C4 to a monthly value. $1,028.61 is displayed.

3) CALCULATE TOTAL PAID AND TOTAL INTEREST

a. In cell C9, enter the formula: =ROUND(C5 * C7, 2). This formula computes the total paid for the loan, including principle and interest.
b. In cell C10, enter the formula: =C9-C3

4) ENTER THE FIRST PAYMENT DATA

a. In cell A14, enter the number 1.
b. In cell B14, enter: =C3
c. In cell C14, enter =B14 * ($C$4 / 12) to calculate one month's interest on the loan. The cell reference C4 contains dollar signs because the interest rate will be the same for each payment. $1,000.00, which is 1% (12% / 12) of the principle is displayed.
d. In cell D14, enter the formula =IF(C14 < 0.01, 0, $C$7 - C14) to calculate the amount of the payment which is applied to the principal, $28.61. If the value in cell C14 is less than 0.01 then 0 is the correct value. This comparison must be made because it is not possible to pay less than a penny.
e. In cell E14, enter the formula =B14 - D14 to calculate the principal owed.

5) ENTER FORMULAS FOR THE SECOND PAYMENT

a. In cell A15, enter the formula: =A14 + 1
b. To display the new principal, enter =E14 in cell B15.
c. Highlight cells C14 to E15.
d. From the Edit menu, use the Fill Down command to copy the formulas in cell C14 through E14 into cells C15 through E15. This completes the data for the second payment and the principal owed, $99,942.49 is displayed in cell E15.

6) COMPLETE THE TABLE USING FILL DOWN

a. Highlight cells A15 to E373.
b. From the Edit menu, select the Fill Down command to copy cells A15 through E15 into rows 16 through 373. Because of the large number of cells and formulas involved, it will take a moment for the computer to recalculate the spreadsheet.
c. From the Select menu, execute the Go To command. Enter E373. The cell cursor is placed on cell E373. The principle owed is $0.00 which indicates the loan has been paid off.

Check - Your spreadsheet should be similar to that shown below. Experiment by changing the principal and interest rate values in cells C3 and C4 to see the effects on the monthly payment and the total amount of interest paid.

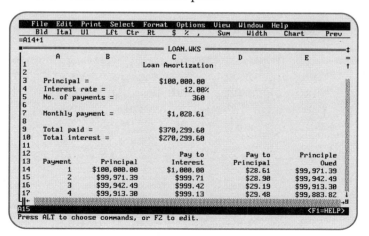

7) SAVE THE TABLE AND PRINT THE FIRST THREE YEARS

a. From the File menu, select the Save command to save the modified LOAN spreadsheet.
b. Highlight cells A1 to E49.
c. From the Print menu, select Set Print Area.
d. From the Print menu, execute the Print command. Select **Print** to print the selected area.
e. Highlight the entire spreadsheet. From the Print menu, select the Set Print Area command.

8) CREATE AN AUTO LOAN MODEL

The LOAN spreadsheet models an amortized loan. The present values represent a house loan. By changing the appropriate values, the spreadsheet could represent a car loan. A decision could then be made based on the model.

a. In cell C3, enter the new principle: 10000
b. In cell C4, enter the new yearly interest: 10%
c. In cell C5, enter the new number of payments: 60. The car loan is a 5 year loan; therefore, the number of monthly payments will be 5 * 12.
d. Note how the spreadsheet has been recalculated. Scroll down to row 73 which contains the last payment. The spreadsheet can easily model loans with less than 360 payments.
e. From the Format menu, select the Save command.
f. From the File menu, select the Close command.

10.8 Where can you go from here?

The last three chapters introduced you to the concepts of a spreadsheet: how one is designed, created on the computer, and used to produce calculations. There are other Works spreadsheet options we have not discussed which you may want to learn about. Reading the spreadsheet sections in the Works manual supplied by Microsoft is a good place to start.

Spreadsheets may be used to store laboratory data to produce scientific and statistical calculations as well as financial calculations. There are larger and more powerful spreadsheet programs available with names such as Lotus 1-2-3, Excel, and Quattro which include many advanced calculating features. Although more complicated to use, these spreadsheet programs are similar to the Works program and will look familiar to you in many ways. Having learned the Works spreadsheet, you will be able to easily learn and use other spreadsheet software.

With the advancements in computer science, computers have become accessible to many, making it easier to employ spreadsheets in almost every type of endeavor that involves numbers. The introduction you have had should be helpful when you encounter these other applications, either in school or on the job.

• •

Summary

A spreadsheet can be used to answer What If? questions. By including factors that relate to a particular situation, a spreadsheet model can be produced. The spreadsheet model may be used to help make financial decisions.

Text may be used in the IF function. For example,

```
=IF(A5 > 30, "Expensive", "Cheap")
```

displays `Expensive` if A5 is greater than 30 and `Cheap` if A5 is less than or equal to 30. The cell name of a cell storing a label can also be used in the IF function.

Relational operators may be used to compare text in the IF function. For example, if cell A5 contains `George` and B12 `Andrews` then the function

```
=IF(A5 < B12, "Yes", "No")
```

displays `No` since `George` is greater than `Andrews`.

The CHOOSE function can select one value from a list of many. When given a position 0 to N the CHOOSE function displays the appropriate option.

The VLOOKUP function uses a lookup table stored in another part of a spreadsheet from which to select values. When given a numeric expression, <position>, and the cell range where values are stored, <range>, VLOOKUP finds the largest number in <range> which is less than or equal to <position>. It then displays the value stored in the cell adjacent to the right of the cell. Text can be used in the CHOOSE function and the VLOOKUP table.

The Freeze Titles command from the Options menu locks the columns to the left of and the rows above the cursor so that they cannot be scrolled off the screen.

An amortization table displays how much interest and principal make up each payment of an installment loan. The PMT function is used to calculate the periodic payments of an installment loan.

Vocabulary

Amortization table - Displays the interest and principal paid on each payment of a loan.

Ascending values - Increasing in value from low to high.

Descending values - Decreasing in value from high to low.

Freeze Titles command - Locks the columns to the left and rows above the cursor so that they are frozen on the screen and will not be affected by scrolling.

What If? question - Performing calculations to make predictions based upon the data stored in a spreadsheet.

Reviews

1. a) Explain what is meant by a "What if?" question.
    b) How can a spreadsheet be used to answer "What if?" questions?

2. Make a list of 5 "What if?" questions that could be answered using the IVYPAY spreadsheet.

3. Write formulas using the IF function for each of the following:

    a) If B3 is less than or equal to C12 display *Low*, if greater than display *High*.
    b) If A5 is equal to Z47 display *Jonathan*, if not equal to display *Judith*.
    c) If C25 is greater than D19 display *Wonderful*, if less than or equal to display *Not so great!*
    d) If B19 is not equal to J37 display *Incompatible*, if equal display *Definitely compatible!*

4. Give three situations in which the CHOOSE function could be used.

5. Write a CHOOSE function which displays 100 if cell B20 contains a value of 0, 500 if a 1, 900 if a 2, and 1200 if a 3.

6. Give three situations in which a VLOOKUP table could be used.

7. The Lawrenceville Widget Company uses the following discount rates when large numbers of widgets are ordered:

Number of Widgets	Discount %
100 - 149	10%
1000 - 1999	30%
2000 or over	70%

    Write a VLOOKUP function that can be used to display the proper discount percent if cell C12 stores the number of widgets. In a diagram show the contents of the lookup table.

Section 10.5 - 10.8

8. Explain what will happen if the cell cursor is located on cell B4 and the Freeze Titles command executed.

9. Write a CHOOSE function which displays the word Red if cell C15 contains a value of 0, Blue if a 1, and White if a 2.

10. The following VLOOKUP table is stored in a spreadsheet:

	L	M
1	100	Poor
2	300	Fair
3	400	Good
4	700	Excellent

What will the formula

```
=VLOOKUP(A5, $L$1:$M$4, 1)
```

display when A5 contains each of the following values:

a) 50   d) 580
b) 390   e) 830
c) 212   f) 400

11. Briefly explain what an amortization table is and how it might be used.

12. a) How much interest is paid in the first month of a loan of $5,000 borrowed for 5 years at 12% per year interest?
    b) Show what PMT function is used to calculate the monthly payments on the above loan.

Exercises

1. The Ivy alumni are unhappy about most of the dance plans. Perform the following What If? questions using the DANCE spreadsheet created in Chapter Nine, Exercise 1.

    a) They hate the band, the Poison Ivy's. Many of the younger alumni want the Dreadful Greats instead, but they will cost $3,500. Calculate the cost per member with the new band.

    b) Many alumni want better desserts. Calculate the costs with Desserts doubled.

    c) A group of alumni do not want to hold the dance in Ivy Hall which the University will let them use if they pay for electricity and clean up. These members want to hold the dinner dance at the Newton Hilton which will cost $7,000. Add a row to your spreadsheet to include the new hotel cost and delete the rows for Electricity and Clean up because these costs are included in the Hilton's fee.

2. The STOCK2 spreadsheet modified in Chapter Nine, Exercise 3 contains Grace van Ivy's stock portfolio information. Open the spreadsheet so that it may be modified to help her evaluate the portfolio.

    a) Ms. van Ivy has decided that it would be best to sell those stocks which have lost more than 30% of their original value. In column H, add the title `Stock Status` and use the IF function in a formula to display `Sell` for stock that should be sold or `Retain` for stock that should be retained. Be careful in creating the IF statements. Use proper formatting so that labels are displayed in their entirety. Format the column so that text displayed by the IF function is right aligned.

    b) Grace van Ivy must pay a commission to her stock broker when she sells stock. The commission is based on the following scale:

Number of Shares	Commission
0 - 29	5%
30 - 69	4%
70 - 99	2%
100 - 149	1%
150 and over	0.5%

    The dollar amount of the commission is calculated by multiplying the current value of the stock by the appropriate commission percent. Title column I `Commission`. In this column, use the VLOOKUP function in a formula to calculate and display the sales commission on each of Ms. van Ivy's stock.

3. Fantasy Wheels Used Cars would like to have the CARS spreadsheet created in Chapter Nine, Exercise 4 modified to determine the markup of its cars based on each car's condition.

a) Open the CARS spreadsheet. A rating system of 0 to 4 will be used. The rating for each car is shown below:

Rating	Cars
0	Studebaker, Thunderbird, DeLorean, Bricklin
1	Mustang, Jaguar, Honda, Jeep
2	Ferarri, Aston-Martin, Triumph, GTO
3	Bel Aire, Rolls Royce, Cadillac
4	Porsche, Bentley

Title column H `Rating` and format the title as right aligned and bold. Enter each car's rating.

b) The percent (%) markup for each rating is listed below:

Rating	Markup
0	10%
1	20%
2	35%
3	50%
4	75%

In column I, enter the title `Rating Markup`. Format the title as right aligned and bold. Change the width of column I to 14. Create a formula that computes the price of each car after its markup. Use the CHOOSE function to compute the markup for each car.

4. Mike Entrepreneurial wants to ask What If? questions about raising his prices for his lawn service. Open the LAWN spreadsheet created in Chapter Nine, Exercise 5 so that modifications can be made to it.

a) Modify the LAWN spreadsheet so that only one entry needs to be changed to raise the price per square foot. Make any necessary changes to formulas that use this value. Determine what happens to his total profits when he doubles and triples his price per square foot.

b) Mike's customers who have large lawns are complaining bitterly about his prices. In response to the complaints he has decided that all customers with lawns of less than 20,000 square feet will pay $0.003 per square foot and those with larger lawns will pay $0.001 per square foot. Modify the spreadsheet so that there is one entry for lawns greater than 20,000 square feet and another entry for lawns with an area under 20,000 square feet. Use an IF statement in a formula to calculate the price each customer will pay.

c) Mike must pay taxes on the price he charges so he wants the following tax table built into the LAWN spreadsheet:

Price	Tax
$0 - $14	0%
$15 - $39	5%
$40 - $59	7%
$60 - $99	12%
$100 - $199	15%
$200 and above	30%

Add a column titled `Taxes` which displays the taxes Mike must pay for each of his customers. Use a lookup table to produce the calculations. Display the total and average tax amounts as well.

5. Mr. Hernandez, owner of the Aztec Café is planning to give his employees a bonus based on their position. He would like to use the ACEMP spreadsheet modified in Chapter Nine, Exercise 2 to compute the bonuses.

   a) Open the ACEMP spreadsheet. Insert a new column after column A which stores the employee names. Title the column `Position`. D. Romani and D. Roberts are managers. The other employees are servers. Enter the employee titles into the new column. Right align all the titles. Bold the column title.

   b) Title column P `Bonus`. Right align and bold the title. Managers are to receive 10% of their gross pay as a bonus, while servers should receive 5% of their gross pay. Use the IF function in a formula to compute the bonuses.

6. Heidi Crane needs to borrow $10,000 to purchase a car and would like to ask What If? about different car loans.

   a) Open the LOAN2 spreadsheet which contains the formulas to compute the monthly payment, total paid, and total interest of an amortized loan. Change the widths of columns D, E, and F to 14. Copy the formulas in column C into columns D, E, and F.

   b) Change the interest rate in column C to 8%, column D to 9%, column E to 10%, and column F to 11%.

   c) Create a bar chart that shows the monthly payment at different interest rates.

Chapter Eleven

Integrating the Word Processor, Data Base, and Spreadsheet

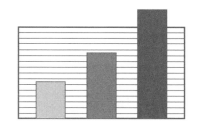

Window - #

File - Close

Edit - Copy

File - Create New File

Edit - Insert Chart

Edit - Insert Data Base Field

Print - Print Form Letters

Objectives

After completing this chapter you will be able to:

1. Open multiple files and switch between them.

2. Transfer text between word processor files.

3. Transfer data between data base files.

4. Transfer data between spreadsheet files.

5. Share data between the data base and spreadsheet.

6. Integrate spreadsheet data with a word processed document, including charts.

7. Use the word processor to create a mail merge document for use with the data base.

8. Print personalized form letters.

Works is an "integrated" software package. That is, it is possible to use the word processor, data base, and spreadsheet by running only one program. There are two important reasons for using integrated packages. The first is that, because the applications are integrated, it is possible to share data between them. The second is that it is easy to learn and use such a package because it has similar commands in each of the applications. For example, the Save command from the File menu always saves the current file whether you are using the word processor, data base, or spreadsheet. This chapter will discuss the different ways of sharing data between the applications areas and assumes that you have completed the previous chapters.

11.1 Windows

The operations used in Works mimic the work done in an actual office. For example, like Works, in an office a file is retrieved from storage and must be opened before it may be used. It is unlikely in a real office that only one file would be worked on at a time. For this reason Works allows up to eight files to be open at any one time. This can include any mix of word processor, data base, and spreadsheet files, but may be limited by the amount of memory your computer has available.

When opening files, Works displays a list of the different files available on your data disk. It is possible to open a single file by placing the cursor on its name and selecting OK, which places a copy of the file on disk in the computer's memory. It is then possible to use the Open command again to open a second file. Up to eight files can be opened in this manner. Each file is placed in its own "window." The term window refers to the portion of the screen displaying the file. Works displays a numbered list of the open files in the Window menu:

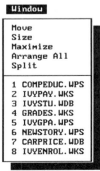

The Window menu shows the names of all currently open files

Typing a number (1 to 8) switches to the file in the corresponding window. When a file is selected, Works automatically switches to the proper application and displays that file. The three letters after the file's name indicate the type of the file: WPS for Word Processor, WDB for Data Base, and WKS for Spreadsheet.

There are many different reasons for switching between files. For example, you may be writing a letter in the word processor and wish to refer to some figures stored in a spreadsheet. With both files open, you could use the Window menu to switch to the spreadsheet file, view the figures, and then switch back to the word processed letter. Other reasons include integrating the data between applications as described later in this chapter.

Works maintains the current status of each open file, including any changes made, in that file's window. This includes the position of the cursor and any options set so that it is possible to work with one file, switch to another, and return to the first file, picking up exactly where you left off. An option set in one window has no effect on any other. For example, it is possible to have a database displayed in List view in one window, and another data base displayed in Form view in a different window.

An open file does not have to be saved until you have finished working with it. However, it is a good idea to save modified files from time to time as a precaution. Selecting the Save command from the File menu saves only the file in the window currently displayed on the screen.

• •

Practice 1

The Practices in this Chapter deal with problems that require several open files at one time. We will start by opening several Ivy University files in different windows and switching between them.

1) BOOT DOS AND START WORKS

2) OPEN THREE FILES

   a. Open IVYCONGR.WPS. The IVYCONGR word processing file is placed in the first window and displayed on the Word Processor screen.
   b. From the File menu, select the Open Existing File command and open IVYSTU.WDB. The IVYSTU data base is placed in the second window and displayed on the Data Base screen. IVYCONGR is still open in window one, only not displayed.
   c. Use the Open Existing File command to open IVYPAY.WKS. The IVYPAY spreadsheet is placed in the third window and displayed on the Spreadsheet screen.
   d. Move the cell cursor to cell A5.

   Check- Works has three open files in three different windows:

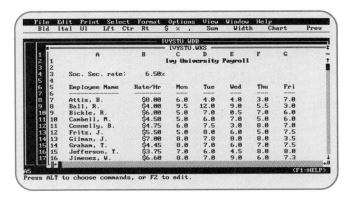

3) SWITCH TO THE IVYSTU DATA BASE

a. Display the Window menu. Note the three open files listed at the bottom of the menu.
b. From the Window menu, select IVYSTU.WDB. The application switches to data base and displays the IVYSTU file.

4) SWITCH TO THE IVYCONGR DOCUMENT AND BACK TO IVYPAY

a. From the Window menu, select IVYCONGR.WPS. The application switches to word processor and displays the IVYCONGR file.
b. From the Window menu, select IVYPAY.WKS. The application switches to the spreadsheet. Note that the cell cursor is still on cell A5, where it was placed in step 2 above.

<u>Check</u> - The IVYPAY spreadsheet file should again be displayed with IVYCONGR visible behind it.

11.2 Removing Files from Memory

When work on an open file is complete, it should be closed by selecting the Close command from the File menu to free memory for other files. Works performs certain operations faster when more memory is available. Also, should some accident occur that clears the computer's memory, limiting the number of open files to only those necessary means that less data from modified files would be lost.

It is not possible to close all of the open files at one time. Each file must first be displayed before it may be closed. When a file is closed its window is removed from the screen, and Works automatically switches to the next open window.

If changes have been made to a file, it should be saved on disk before it is closed. If you attempt to close a file which has been modified before saving it, or to exit Works, you are warned that changes will be lost unless the file is saved.

11.3 Copying Data Between Word Processor Documents

As you saw in Practice 1, Works can open several files at one time and switch easily between them. However, only one file at a time is considered the "active" file. It is possible, however, to transfer data between different open files and applications areas using the Copy command in a special way.

You have previously used the Copy command to copy data within the same file. To copy data between different open files, four steps are required:

1. The data to be copied is highlighted.
2. The Copy command is executed from the Edit menu.
3. The file to receive the copied data is displayed.
4. The cursor is placed at the position to copy the data and Enter pressed.

We will begin by copying data from one word processed document to another. This is a powerful tool, allowing blocks of text to be entered into the word processor once and then shared among different documents.

It is usually best that both the file providing the text to be copied and the file to receive the text already be open before the Copy command is executed. Copying the text simply transfers a copy of the highlighted block to the receiving document; the original file remains unchanged. Because the file receiving the block is modified, it should be saved before it is closed or Works exited.

• •

Practice 2

In this Practice you will copy a paragraph from one word processed document into another. The three files IVYCONGR, IVYSTU and IVYPAY should still be open from the last Practice. We will first close IVYSTU and IVYPAY, and then copy a paragraph from the IVYHAND document into the IVYCONGR letter.

1) REMOVE THE UNNEEDED FILES FROM MEMORY

a. From the File menu, select the Close command to close the currently displayed file, IVYPAY. Window 3 is closed.
b. From the Window menu, select IVYSTU.WDB and then close it. Window 1 containing IVYCONGR is again displayed.

2) OPEN THE IVYHAND FILE

IVYHAND contains a passage from the Ivy University student handbook that is to be copied into IVYCONGR. From the File menu, select the Open Existing File command and open IVYHAND.WPS. IVYHAND is opened and placed in the next available window, window 2. Two word processor files are currently open in memory.

3) HIGHLIGHT THE TEXT TO BE COPIED

a. Move the cursor to the first paragraph which begins "One of the most. . .".
b. Highlight the entire paragraph as a block.

4) COPY THE PARAGRAPH INTO THE IVYCONGR LETTER

a. From the Edit menu, select the Copy command. COPY is displayed on the Status line.
b. From the Window menu, select IVYCONGR.WPS. IVYCONGR is displayed. Note that COPY is still displayed on the Status line.
c. Move the cursor to the position where the text should be inserted, the second blank line after the sentence which reads "To quote the student handbook:".
d. Press Enter to complete the Copy command. The highlighted paragraph from IVYHAND is copied from the file and placed at the current cursor position.
e. Save the modified congratulations letter on disk.

Check - The paragraph should be inserted in the congratulations letter:

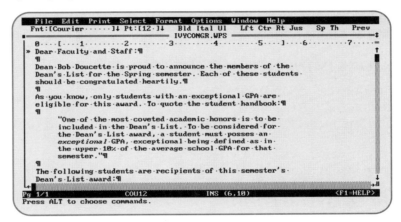

f. Close IVYCONGR. IVYHAND is again displayed.
g. Close IVYHAND.

11.4 Sharing Data between two Spreadsheets

It is possible to share data between two spreadsheets by opening both files and Copying the data between them. Just as when copying within a single spreadsheet, cells copied from one spreadsheet to another retain their formulas and formatting.

To transfer data between two open spreadsheets, the following steps are taken:

1. The desired spreadsheet cells are highlighted.
2. The Copy command is executed.
3. The Window menu is used to display the second spreadsheet.
4. The cursor is positioned where the copy is to be placed and Enter pressed to copy the cells.

You must make room for the new data before copying if you wish to insert the copied cells between already existing cells. For example, to copy a row from one spreadsheet into the center of another you must first insert a blank row in the receiving spreadsheet. The Copy command overwrites existing data if this is not done.

Practice 3

In this Practice you will copy a group of cells from one spreadsheet to another, adding the data for a group of new employees to the IVYPAY spreadsheet. Start Works if you have not already done so.

1) PREPARE THE WINDOWS

    a. Close all open files.
    b. Open IVYNEWEM.WKS in window 1. These are four new employees who need to be added to the IVYPAY spreadsheet.
    c. Open IVYPAY.WKS in window 2.

2) INSERT EMPTY ROWS IN THE RECEIVING SPREADSHEET

    a. Move the cursor to cell A8 in IVYPAY.
    b. Highlight cells A8, A9, A10, and A11.
    c. From the Edit menu, select the Insert Row/Column command to display the Insert dialog box.
    d. Select **Row**. Four new rows are inserted.
    e. Press an arrow key to remove the highlight.

3) HIGHLIGHT THE CELLS TO BE COPIED

    a. From the Window menu, select IVYNEWEM.WKS.
    b. Make sure that the cell cursor is on cell A1 and start highlighting.
    c. Press Ctrl-End to select all of the cells containing data.

4) COPY THE HIGHLIGHTED DATA TO THE PAYROLL SPREADSHEET

    a. From the Edit menu, select the Copy command.
    b. From the Window menu, select IVYPAY.WKS. Note that COPY is displayed on the Status line.
    c. Move the cursor to the position where the cells are to be inserted, the blank rows starting at cell A8.
    d. Press Enter to complete the Copy command. The highlighted cells are copied from IVYNEWEM and placed at the current cursor position.
    e. The formulas need to be copied for the new employees. Highlight cells H7 through H11. Extend the highlight to the last column containing data.
    f. Execute the Fill Down command. The formulas are copied into the new rows and recalculated.
    g. Save the modified spreadsheet on disk.

    Check - The new employees inserted into the spreadsheet automatically change the payroll totals displayed at the bottom of the spreadsheet:

Pay Raise =	$5,880.58	$6,160.61	$6,440.64
Raise Cost =	$280.03	$560.06	$840.08

11.5 Sharing Data between two Data Bases

It is possible to transfer data between two data bases by using the Copy command. After opening both files, the desired records from the first file are highlighted, and then copied into the second file. If the first data base is displayed in Form view, only the displayed record may be copied. If the file is displayed in List view, the highlighted block of records and fields is copied. Because of this, records are best copied when both files are displayed in List view.

The process of sharing records between data bases is made slightly more complex when the files contain different fields. When this occurs, the entries from the first field in the original file are copied to the first field in the second file, and so on, regardless of the field names. Therefore, care must be taken when transferring records from one data base to another to ensure that the entries are placed in the proper fields. Like the spreadsheet, if the copied records are to be inserted into the middle of a data base, empty records must first be created; otherwise existing records will be overwritten with the copied data.

● ●

Practice 4

In this Practice you will transfer records between two data base files. Start Works if you have not already done so.

1) PREPARE THE WINDOWS

   a.   Close any open files.
   b.   Open IVYSTU.WDB in window 1. If the file is displayed in Form view, switch to List view.
   c.   Open IVYSTU2.WDB in window 2. If the file is displayed in Form view, switch to List view.

2) HIGHLIGHT THE RECORDS TO BE COPIED

We want to copy all of the records in IVYSTU2. Highlight from the First Name field in record 1 to the GPA in record 3.

3) COPY THE HIGHLIGHTED RECORDS TO THE IVYSTU DATA BASE

   a.   From the Edit menu, select the Copy command.
   b.   From the Window menu, select IVYSTU.WDB. Note that COPY is still displayed on the Status line.
   c.   Move the cursor to the first field in the empty record at the end of the file. This is where the records are to be inserted.
   d.   Press Enter to complete the Copy command. The highlighted records from IVYSTU2 are copied from that file and placed at the current cursor position.

   Check - The new student records should be transferred into the IVYSTU data base.

   e.   Sort the data base on the Last Name field. The records are again in order by last name.
   f.   Save the modified data base on disk.

11.6 Merging Spreadsheets with the Word Processor

One of the options when copying spreadsheet data is to copy the data into a word processed document. Businesses and offices must often send memos or letters which contain the figures from a spreadsheet. Usually the files produced by a separate (non-integrated) spreadsheet are not compatible with a separate word processor, requiring the figures to be entered by hand. This is a time consuming and error prone process. The ability to copy a portion of a spreadsheet to a word processed document is one of the most powerful features of an integrated package like Works.

The steps required to copy cells from an open spreadsheet to an open word processed document are:

1. The desired spreadsheet cells are highlighted.
2. The Copy command from the Edit menu is executed.
3. The Window menu is used to display the word processor document.
4. The cursor is positioned and Enter pressed to copy the cells.

Cells copied into a document are automatically separated by tabs, forming a table like the ones created in Chapter Three. Works creates tab stops for the table which match the position and alignment of the original cells in the spreadsheet. You may wish to change the stops to better fit your document using the Tabs command from the Format menu.

• •

Practice 5

In this Practice, part of a spreadsheet will be copied into a word processed document. Start Works if you have not already done so.

1) PREPARE THE WINDOWS

a. Close any open files.
b. Open IVYCONGR.WPS in window 1.
c. Open GRADES.WKS in window 2. (You created GRADES in the Practices of Chapter Eight.)

2) HIGHLIGHT THE CELLS TO BE COPIED

a. In GRADES, move the cursor to cell A1 if it is not already.
b. Highlight from cell A1 to cell E9.

3) COPY THE CELLS TO THE DOCUMENT

a. From the Edit menu, select the Copy command.
b. From the Window menu, select IVYCONGR.WPS.
c. Move the cursor to the second blank line after the paragraph which begins "Dr. Sulfuric's Chemistry class. . .".

d. Press Enter to complete the Copy command. The highlighted cells from GRADES are copied from that file and placed at the current cursor position. Note how tabs are used to separate the different columns.

e. Save the modified letter on disk.

<u>Check</u> - A portion of the spreadsheet showing Dr. Sulfuric's grades should be inserted into the letter.

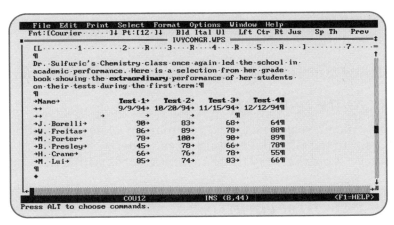

11.7 Merging Data Bases with the Word Processor

Data from a data base may also be copied into a word processed document. This is often done when a word processed report must contain information from the contents of a data base. The ability to copy records from a data base to a document is another powerful feature of Works.

The steps required to copy data from an open data base into an open word processed document are:

1. The desired data base records are highlighted.
2. The Copy command from the Edit menu is executed.
3. The Window menu is used to display the word processor document.
4. The cursor is positioned and Enter pressed to copy the data.

List view is useful when copying records because it allows more than one record to be highlighted. Also, only the highlighted fields are copied, so the entire record does not have to be selected. Queries can be used to limit the number of records copied. The fields copied into a document are automatically separated by tabs, with Works creating tab stops which match the position and alignment of the fields in the data base. You may change the stops to better fit the document using the Tabs command from the Format menu.

Practice 6

In this Practice selected fields from a data base will be copied into a word processed document. A query will be first applied to limit the number of records copied. Start Works if you have not already done so.

1) PREPARE THE WINDOWS

a. Close the GRADES spreadsheet by switching to window 2 and executing the Close command.
b. Open IVYSTU.WDB in window 2. If it is not already, display the data base in List view.

2) APPLY A QUERY TO THE DATA BASE

a. From the View menu, select the Query command. Delete any existing criteria.
b. Move the cursor to the GPA field and enter the criteria: `>3.7`
c. Apply the query. Note that only those student records with a GPA greater than 3.7 are displayed.

3) HIGHLIGHT THE DATA TO BE COPIED

a. Make sure the cursor is located on the first record by pressing `Ctrl-Home`.
b. Highlight the First Name and Last Name fields only in all of the records shown.

4) COPY THE HIGHLIGHTED DATA IN TO THE DOCUMENT

a. From the Edit menu, select the Copy command.
b. From the Window menu, select IVYCONGR.WPS.
c. Move the cursor to the second blank line after the paragraph which begins "The following students. . .".
d. Press Enter to complete the Copy command. Only the highlighted fields from IVYSTU are copied from that file and placed at the current cursor position. Note how tabs are used to separate the fields.
e. Save the modified letter on disk.
f. Print the letter.
g. Close IVYSTU and select No to ignore the changes caused by applying the query.

Check - The first and last names of all students in IVYSTU with a GPA greater than 3.7 should be inserted into the letter. You may wish to use the Tabs command to change the position of the tab stops.

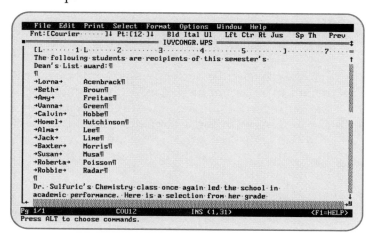

An Introduction to Computing Using Microsoft Works

11.8 Integrating the Data Base and Spreadsheet

It is often desirable to have the information stored in a data base available for use in a spreadsheet, and vice versa. This allows users to employ the power of the spreadsheet to ask "What If?" questions and perform calculations on numerical data base fields. For example, the Ivy University Bookstore data base could be transferred into a spreadsheet to determine the profit that would result from raising the cost of all items by 10 percent.

The steps for copying data between a spreadsheet and data base are the same as those described above: the data to be copied is highlighted, the Copy command executed, the receiving file displayed and Enter pressed. Remember that if the copied data is to be inserted between existing data, new rows or records must be created before copying.

So far, we have used the Copy command to copy data into a previously opened file. Copy can also be used to transfer data to a new file. When this is desired, the new file can be created by selecting the Create New File command from the File menu during the Copy process. For example, creating a new spreadsheet from a data base file is a four step process:

1. The desired entries are highlighted in the data base.
2. The Copy command from the Edit menu is executed.
3. The Create New File command is selected from the File menu and used to create a new, empty spreadsheet.
4. Enter is pressed to copy the fields into cells in the new spreadsheet.

A new data base could be created from a spreadsheet in a similar manner.

When records are copied into a spreadsheet, the data from the first field is placed in the first column, the second field in the second column, and so on. The new spreadsheet can then be used in the same ways as any other spreadsheet, including entering formulas to perform calculations, formatting, etc. To copy more than one record, the data base must be displayed in List view; if the data base is displayed in Form view, only the visible record may be copied. When the records are copied, the formats of the entries in the data base are retained in the spreadsheet cells.

When cells are copied from a spreadsheet to a data base, the first column is copied to the first field, the second column to the second field, and so on. Cell formats are retained, but formulas are not copied — only the result of the formula.

Practice 7

In this Practice you will create a new spreadsheet named BOOKS using the information from the IVYBOOKS data base file. Start Works if you have not already done so.

1) PREPARE THE WINDOWS

a. Close any open files.
b. Open IVYBOOKS.WDB.
c. If the data base is displayed in Form view switch to List view.

2) HIGHLIGHT THE RECORDS TO BE COPIED

We want to copy all of the records into the new spreadsheet, so from the Select menu, execute the All command.

3) COPY THE HIGHLIGHTED RECORDS INTO THE NEW SPREADSHEET

a. From the Edit menu, select the Copy command.
b. From the File menu, select the Create New File command.
c. Select Spreadsheet. A new, empty spreadsheet is shown on the screen.
d. Press Enter to complete the Copy command. The highlighted records from IVYBOOKS are copied from that file starting at the current cursor position, each field in a separate column. Note that formatting is retained, as shown by the Price field.
e. Change the width of column A to 20 and column B to 15.
f. Save the new spreadsheet naming it BOOKS and print a copy.

Check - Data from the Ivy Bookstore data base has been copied into a spreadsheet. Formatting commands can now be used to change the layout of the spreadsheet and formulas added to perform calculations.

11.9 Inserting a Chart in a Document

Works' ability to create different charts was described at the end of Chapter Nine. Once a chart has been created, Works can insert it into a word processed document so that when the document is printed, the chart will be included. This feature is especially important to businesses and other organizations which must produce reports that include charts.

To insert a chart into a document, the following steps are required:

1. The spreadsheet which contains the desired chart is opened.
2. The document is opened and the position where you wish the chart to be printed is indicated using the Insert Chart command from the Edit menu.

When the Print command is executed, Works prints a copy of the chart inside the document.

The position of the chart in the document is specified by inserting the chart's name into the document using the Insert Chart command from the Edit menu. Works then displays a list of the open spreadsheet files. For example:

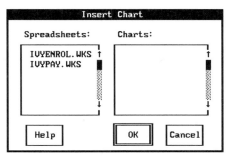

The Insert Chart dialog box - a spreadsheet must be selected

When you select the desired spreadsheet, a listing of the **Charts** saved with that file is displayed from which you may select:

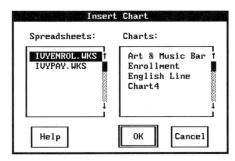

The dialog box shows the chart names for the selected spreadsheet

After a chart is selected, Works inserts a marker into the text showing the name of the spreadsheet and the chart. For example, selecting the Enrollment chart from the above menu would place the marker

```
*chart IVYENROL.WKS:Enrollment*
```

in the document at the current cursor position.

• •

Practice 8

In this Practice you will insert a chart into a word processed document and print a copy. Start Works if you have not already done so.

1) PREPARE THE WINDOWS

a. Close any open files.
b. Open the IVYENROL.WKS spreadsheet in window 1. Charts were created in IVYENROL in Chapter Nine.
c. Open the IVYREPOR.WPS document in window 2.

2) INSERT THE CHART INTO THE LETTER

a. Place the cursor on the second blank line after ". . .in this chart:".
b. From the Edit menu, select the Insert Chart command.
c. Highlight IVYENROL. A list of the charts stored with IVYENROL is shown in the **Charts** list.
d. Move the cursor into the **Charts** list.
e. Highlight Enrollment in the list.
f. Select OK to insert the chart. A marker is inserted into the report showing the spreadsheet and chart names.

3) PREVIEW AND PRINT THE REPORT WITH THE CHART

    a.   Save the modified document on disk.

    b.   Preview the document. Note how the marker is replaced by the actual chart.

    c.   Print the document. Because charts are complex, printing a document which contains a chart can take considerable time.

       <u>Check</u> - The marker has been replaced by the chart from the spreadsheet in the printed copy.

11.10 *Mail Merge and Form Letters*

One of the most powerful applications provided by an integrated package is the ability to use "mail merge" to create personalized form letters. You have undoubtedly received letters that begin "The next winner of 10 Million dollars could be" followed by your name. This is an example of a mail merged form letter.

Mail merge takes advantage of the computer's ability to integrate the information stored in a data base with a word processed letter, and print the result. To create such a letter, a data base which contains the names and addresses of the people you wish to write to must be opened. (Any other personalized data which is to appear in the letter must also be stored in the data base.) The letter is then typed into the word processor, indicating where to print the data from the data base fields. When completed, Works prints one copy of the letter for each record in the data base, substituting the data in that record into the printed version of the letter.

To mail merge a letter, the following steps are required:

1.   The desired data base file is created or opened.

2.   The letter is typed into the word processor and the Insert Database Field command from the Edit menu used to indicate where you wish the data from the different fields to be printed.

3.   The Print Form Letters command from the Print menu is executed.

When the Print Form Letters command is executed, Works generates and prints a personalized copy of the letter for each record in the data base. If there are 50 records in the data base, 50 personalized letters will be printed. Works merges data only from visible records, making it possible to use queries to limit the number of letters printed. For example, Ivy University could print mail merge letters for only those students with an honors GPA.

The position of the merged data in the letter is specified by inserting the name of a field into the document using the Insert Database Field command from the Edit menu. Works then displays a list of the open data base files. For example:

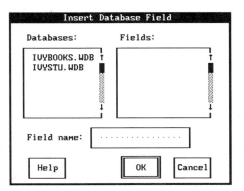

The Insert Database Field dialog box - a data base must be selected

When you select the desired data base file, a listing of the Fields in that data base is displayed from which you may select:

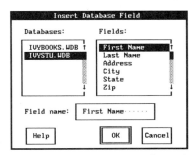

The dialog box shows the fields in the selected data base

Works then inserts a marker into the text showing the name of the selected field. For example, selecting First Name from the above menu would place the marker

《First Name》

in the document at the current cursor position. These markers can be positioned throughout the document until all the required fields have been specified, and may be moved, copied, and deleted like ordinary text. When the letter is printed you have the option of printing a plain or merged copy. To print a plain document which shows the markers, allowing you to review the placement of the fields, the Print command is selected from the Print menu. To print merged documents which display the actual information from the data base in place of the markers the Print Form Letters command is selected from the Print menu.

Practice 9

In this Practice you will modify and print a mail merged letter. Although this letter contains data from only two fields, it is possible to create a mail merged document which contains data from any field in the open data base. Start Works if you have not already done so.

1) PREPARE THE WINDOWS

a. Close any open files.
a. Open the STUDENT.WDB data base in window 1.
b. Open the IVYTUIT.WPS letter in window 2. Switch to Show All Characters mode if not already.

2) INSERT THE FIRST FIELD INTO THE LETTER

a. Place the cursor on the paragraph marker after "Dear" and type a space.
b. From the Edit menu, select the Insert Database Field command.
c. Select STUDENT from the **Databases** list if it is not already highlighted. A list of the fields in STUDENT is shown in the **Fields** list.
d. Move the cursor into the **Fields** list.
e. Highlight First Name and select OK. A marker is inserted into the letter.

3) INSERT THE NEXT FIELD INTO THE LETTER

a. Press the Space bar to insert a space after the First Name marker.
b. Repeat steps (b) through (d) in step 2 above and insert the Last Name field.
c. Type a colon (:).

Check - The First Name and Last Name markers should be inserted into the letter so that the line appears on the screen as:

```
Dear «First Name» «Last Name»:
```

4) PRINT PLAIN AND MERGED COPIES OF THE TUITION LETTER

a. Save the modified letter on disk.
b. Print a plain (non mail-merged) copy of the letter using the Print command. Note the position of the field markers in the text. Only one copy of the letter is printed and the word processor screen is again displayed.
c. From the Print menu, select the Print Form Letters command.
d. Select the STUDENT database.
e. Accept the default of printing 1 copy. A personalized copy of the letter will be printed for each record in the data base. Note how the markers have been replaced by the different names from the data base in the printed copies.

11.11 Expanding Mail Merge

In the previous Practice you created and printed a simple mail merge document. While this document contained the data from only two fields, it is important to realize that any field from the open data base may be included in a mail merge. In addition, it is possible to re-use fields. For example, the recipient's first name could appear in the mail merged letter twice; once in the address and once in the greeting. Also, data from fields may be printed inside other text. That is, a field marker may be placed inside a sentence and Works will adjust any text following the marker to make room for the merged data.

Another powerful mail merge technique involves using queries to limit the number of mail merged documents produced. It is not usually the case that a mail merge document will be printed for every record in a database. Normally a query will be first used to limit the number of records displayed. When the Print Form Letters command is then executed, documents are produced for only those selected records which meet the query's criteria.

An Introduction to Computing Using Microsoft Works

Practice 10

In this Practice you will modify and print a more complex mail merged letter. A query will be used to limit the number of letters printed.

1) PREPARE THE WINDOWS

   a. Close any open files.
   b. Open the IVYSTU.WDB data base.
   c. Open the IVYGPA.WPS letter in window 2. Switch to Show All Characters if not already. Note that several field markers have already been inserted into this letter.

2) INSERT A FIELD INTO THE LETTER

   a. Place the cursor on the paragraph marker on the line below «First Name» «Last Name».
   b. From the Edit menu, select the Insert Database Field command.
   c. Select IVYSTU from the **Database** list if it is not already.
   d. Move the cursor into the **Fields** list.
   e. Highlight Address and select OK. A marker is inserted into the letter.

3) INSERT THE NEXT FIELDS INTO THE LETTER

   a. Move the cursor to the paragraph marker below «Address».
   b. Following parts (b) through (d) above, insert the City field.
   c. Type a comma (,) followed by a space.
   d. Insert the State field.
   e. Type a space.
   f. Insert the Zip field.

   Check - Markers should be inserted into the letter so that the heading appears on the screen as:

       «First Name» «Last Name»
       «Address»
       «City», «State» «Zip»

       Dear «First Name»:

4) INSERT THE GPA INTO THE LETTER

   a. Move the cursor into the body of the letter, on the second space after "Your GPA of...".
   b. Insert the GPA field.

   Check - Your screen should be similar to:

```
 File  Edit  Print  Select  Format  Options  Window  Help
Fnt:[Courier······]↕ Pt:[12·]↕   Bld Ital Ul   Lft Ctr Rt Jus   Sp Th   Prev
════════════════════════════════ IVYGPA.WPS ════════════════════════════════
[·········1·········2·········3·········4·········5·········]·········7·····=
» ×date×¶                                                                    ↑
   ¶
   «First·Name» «Last·Name»¶
   «Address»¶
   «City», «State» «Zip»¶
   ¶
   ¶
   Dear··«First·Name»:¶
   ¶
   →     It·is·with·the·greatest·of·pleasure·that·I·inform·you·
   of·your·selection·as·an·Ivy·Scholar.··Your·GPA·of·«GPA»·makes·
   you·an·academic·winner·eligible·for·a·tuition·reduction·next·
   term.¶
   ¶
   →     Do·not·consider·transferring·to·another·college.·We·
   need·you·at·Ivy!¶
   ¶
   Yours·truly,¶
Pg 1/1              COU12              INS (55,11)              <F1=HELP>
Press ALT to choose commands.
```

5) APPLY THE QUERY GPA > 3.8 TO THE DATA BASE

a. From the Window menu, select the IVYSTU data base.
b. From the View menu, select the Query command. Delete any old criteria.
c. Move the cursor to the GPA field and enter the criteria: >3.8
d. Apply the query. Note that the number of student records displayed is limited to only those with a GPA greater than 3.8.

6) PRINT PLAIN AND MERGED COPIES OF THE TUITION LETTER

a. From the Window menu, select IVYGPA.WPS.
b. Print a plain (non mail-merged) copy of the letter using the Print command. Note the position and number of the field markers.
c. From the Print menu, select the Print Form Letters command.
d. Select the IVYSTU database from the dialog box.
e. Accept the default of printing 1 copy. A personalized copy of the letter is printed for only the records which meet the query's criteria (GPA greater than 3.8). You may press Escape and select Cancel to terminate the printing after two or three letters have been printed.
f. Save the modified of IVYGPA on disk.

•••

Chapter Summary

This chapter presented the commands necessary to share data between the applications areas and different files produced by the same application. The ability to share data between applications is the primary reason for using an integrated package such as Works.

Works is capable of opening up to 8 different files, each in its own window. This can include any mixture of word processor, data base and spreadsheet files. It is possible to switch between any open file using the Window menu. When work has been completed on a file, it may be saved using the Save command and then closed using the Close command to make room for other files.

To transfer data between different files the Copy command is used. The data to be transferred is first highlighted and the Copy command executed. After switching to the second file, the highlighted information is copied by pressing Enter.

The chapter explained how data may be transferred between:

- 2 word processor documents (Section 11.3)
- 2 spreadsheets (Section 11.4)
- 2 data bases (Section 11.5)
- a spreadsheet and word processor document (Section 11.6)
- a data base and word processor document (Section 11.7)
- a data base and spreadsheet (Section 11.8)
- a chart and word processor document (Section 11.9)
- mail merging a data base and word processor document (Sections 11.10 and 11.11)

One of the most powerful abilities of an integrated package is the ability to produce mail merge documents. In mail merge, a document is created in the word processor with markers showing where data should be inserted. When the document is printed, the markers are automatically replaced with information from a data base, creating a different copy of the document for each record. In this way, the computer can produce personalized form letters. Queries can be used to limit the number of records displayed, which has a corresponding effect on the number of mail merged documents printed.

Vocabulary

Active file - The file currently being worked on.

Integrated - A software package that contains different applications. Because Works is integrated, data may be shared between its three applications areas.

Mail merge - Using the contents of a data base file and a word processed document to have the computer produce personalized form letters.

Window - Location in the computer's memory and on screen used to store an open file. Works may have up to 8 files open at one time.

Window Menu - Listing of the files currently open which allows switching between files.

Reviews

Sections 11.1 - 11.5

1. a) What is meant by an integrated software package?
   b) What are two advantages of using such a package?

2. What is the purpose of having more than one file open at any one time?

3. a) What is a "window"?
   b) What is the maximum number of windows Works allows to be open at one time?
   c) What steps are required to switch from one window to another window?

4. Give 3 examples of when you might want to switch between windows. Explain what files would be stored in the different windows.

5. a) Why should files be closed after you are through working with them?
   b) What steps are required to close 3 currently open files?

6. The file IVYNEWS contains a paragraph which describes the inauguration of Ivy University's new president. Explain the steps required to copy this paragraph into a file named ALUMNI which contains a letter to be sent to all Ivy alumni.

7. What steps are required to copy two columns from a spreadsheet named OWED and insert them between two existing columns in a spreadsheet named ASSETS?

8. Fantasy cars has just bought out Luxury Autos and wants to merge the data bases which contain both dealership's inventories into a single file. Explain the steps required to do this.

9. What must be watched for when transferring records between two data bases?

Sections 11.6 - 11.11

10. Give 3 examples when you might want to merge part of a spreadsheet with a word processed document.

11. List the steps required to copy part of a spreadsheet to a word processed document.

12. List the steps required to copy part of a data base to a word processed document.

13. Give 3 examples where you might want to copy information from a data base into a spreadsheet. For each example explain what the spreadsheet would be used for.

14. What steps are required to copy a chart displaying Ivy University alumni donations into a word processor document being used to produce a publicity brochure?

15. What does "mail merge" mean?

16. a) Explain the steps required to mail merge the names and addresses of customers from Fantasy Cars customer data base into a letter to be sent each customer.
    b) What additional steps would be required to send the letters to only customers living in Boca Raton, Florida?

17. When printing a mail merge letter what is the difference between executing the Print command or the Print Form Letters command?

Exercises

1. Ivy University must raise next semester's tuition in order to cover its increasing labor costs.

   a) Create and save a letter named INCREASE using the Word Processor which notifies students of the upcoming tuition increase. INCREASE should be similar to:

   ```
   Dear Student:

   We are sorry to inform you that due to rising labor
   costs we are forced to raise your tuition by $1,000
   dollars. This increase is effective next semester.

   Sincerely,

   The Administration
   ```

   The administration has decided that students might take the news of a tuition increase better if it came in a personalized letter.

   b) Using the IVYSTU data base, modify the INCREASE letter to mail merge the students' first name in place of the word "Student". Save the modified version.

   c) Sort IVYSTU by Last Name. Print mail merged letters for all students from Texas.

   d) In order to keep its better students from transferring to less expensive schools, the Ivy administration has decided that the tuition increase should be on a sliding scale based on the student's GPA. Each student's tuition will increase by $500. An additional $100 will be charged for each tenth of a GPA point below 4.0, for example:

GPA	INCREASE
4.0	$500.00
3.9	$600.00
3.8	$700.00
. . .	
0.1	$4,400.00
0.0	$4,500.00

   Modify the IVYSTU data base to contain a calculated field named Increase which displays the amount of the tuition increase. Format the new field to display dollar values.

   e) Modify the INCREASE letter to merge the actual tuition increase in place of the "1,000".

   f) Save the modified versions of INCREASE and IVYSTU. Using the new INCREASE, print mail merged letters for all the students with last names ending in "B".

2. The Fantasy Wheels pre-owned car company would like to transfer their inventory data base WHEELS.WDB into a spreadsheet so that they can perform "What If?" questions with the data. This data base was created in Chapter Five, Exercise 10.

   a) Create a new spreadsheet named WHATIF which contains the year, model, amount paid, and asking price for each car copied from the WHEELS data base. Format the spreadsheet, adding titles and labels.

   b) Add two columns to the spreadsheet. The first calculates a new asking price which is a 10% increase of the current asking price. The second displays the additional profit gained by selling the cars at these new prices.

   c) Acting as Fantasy's sales manager, use the word processor to write a letter named NEWPRICE to the owner of Fantasy Wheels describing your plan to raise prices.

   d) Place a copy of the WHATIF spreadsheet into the NEWPRICE letter. Print a copy of NEWPRICE.

3. In Chapter Eight, Exercise 6 Mr. Horatio von Money used a spreadsheet named STOCKS.WKS to calculate his donation to Ivy University. Copy the spreadsheet into a new word processed letter informing the I.U. Board of Trustees of the donation. Save the letter as DONATION and print a copy.

4. Use the IVYSTU.WDB data base to display the students who have not yet paid their tuition bills and have a GPA less than 1.5. Create a new mail merge letter warning them to pay the bill or face expulsion from the university. Print a merged copy of the letter for each student.

5. Your friend Jill is searching for a new car and has written to you for information.

   a) Using the CARPRICE.WDB data base display all cars with air conditioning which cost less than $9,000. Copy those records into a new spreadsheet named JILLCARS. Include proper labels and formatting in the spreadsheet.

   b) Using JILLCARS, create a bar chart showing the different car names and prices.

   c) Create a letter informing Jill of her choices. Include both the JILLCARS spreadsheet and the bar graph in the letter. Save the letter naming it TOJILL and print a copy.

6. You have been asked to gather some statistics about car prices for your economics class.

   a) Create a new spreadsheet named PRICES which contains all of the data about new car prices from the CARPRICE.WDB data base. Use proper labels and formatting.

   b) Modify the PRICES spreadsheet to calculate each of the following:

   average base price of a new car
   average price for a new car with air
   average price for a new car stereo
   average price for a new car with sunroof
   maximum base price of a new car
   minimum price of a new car with air conditioning

c) Using the word processor, create and print a report detailing your findings for the class. Include the actual calculated figures from PRICES in the report.

7. Use the word processor to create the following file named MEMO:

```
Memo to: Steve Munger, Asst. Headmaster
From: Bob Doucette, Dean

Steve:

The following students have received Dean's List
status:

Please update their records. Thank you.
```

Copy the table of Dean's List students from the IVYCONGR letter created in Practice 6 into this memo. Save and print a copy of MEMO.

8. You have moved. Using the ADDRESS.WDB data base created in Chapter Five, Exercise 1, prepare and print a personalized mail merged letter to each of your friends which gives your new address. Use Escape to interrupt the printing if you wish. An example letter is shown below:

```
Amy Eppelman
343 Nenue Street
Honolulu, HI 08033

Dear Amy:

This is just a short note to let you know my new
address:

    1389 Southwest Drive
    Atlantic, FL 33800

Of course, we'll still get together on your birthday,
7/5/65, or I'll call you at (767) 145-5937.

See you soon,

A. Friend
```

9. In Practice 7 you created a spreadsheet named BOOKS.WKS by transferring records from the Ivy Bookstore data base file. Open BOOKS and make the following changes to it:

a) Insert rows at the top of the spreadsheet and add proper column titles.

b) Increase the width of the Item Name column to 25.

c) Calculate and display the average price of all items available. Use proper formatting and include a label for this value.

d) Format the Department column, making it centered.

e) In column E create a formula which displays the value of the items in stock for each item (price per item times the number of items in stock).

f) At the bottom of column E calculate and display the total value of all items available.

g) Format column E to display dollar values, and include a proper title and label for the total.

h) Save the modified BOOKS spreadsheet and print a copy.

An Introduction to Computing Using Microsoft Works

Chapter Twelve

An Introduction to Programming Using BASIC

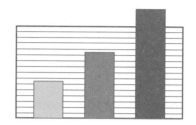

BASICA

PRINT

SYSTEM

END

RUN

LIST

SAVE, LOAD

INPUT

IF...THEN

FOR...NEXT

Objectives

After completing this chapter you will be able to:

1. Start the computer and load BASIC.

2. Use immediate mode to perform calculations.

3. Write and run a program.

4. Locate and correct programming errors.

5. Use the RUN, LIST, SAVE, LOAD, FILES, and NEW commands.

6. Assign values to numeric and string variables.

7. INPUT numbers and strings.

8. Use the IF...THEN conditional statement.

9. Produce FOR...NEXT loops.

I n Chapter One a computer program was defined as a list of instructions written in a special language that tells the computer which operations to perform and in what sequence to perform them. It is possible to write your own programs using the *BASIC* computer language (Beginner's All-purpose Symbolic Instruction Code). One of the reasons for naming this language BASIC was because it uses simple English words as commands. In this chapter you will be given a brief introduction to programming in BASIC.

12.1 *Using Immediate Mode*

To boot BASIC type BASICA at the DOS prompt and press Enter. BASIC displays the word Ok above the blinking cursor whenever it is ready to accept an instruction from you. It is possible to have the computer execute a BASIC instruction immediately by typing the instruction and then pressing Enter; this is called using the computer in "immediate mode." The computer can also receive instructions through programs, which will be explained later in this chapter. To return to DOS, type the command SYSTEM.

PRINT

PRINT is the BASIC command used to display numbers, characters, and words on the screen. Using immediate mode, the following example prints the results of a math operation when it is typed and Enter pressed:

```
PRINT 12 + 5            <press Enter>
 17
Ok
```

PRINT followed by a mathematical operation tells the computer to print the result of that operation. Notice that only the result and not the mathematical statement is printed. It is important to remember to press Enter after giving the computer any command. In BASIC the following symbols are used for each of the five mathematical operations:

Operation	Symbol
Addition	+
Subtraction	-
Multiplication	*
Division	/
Exponentiation	^

PRINT with Quotation Marks

The computer can print both numbers and words. To the computer a number is a symbol that can be used in a mathematical calculation. A character or word, on the other hand, cannot be used to do any of these things.

PRINT followed by quotation marks instructs the computer to print whatever appears between the quotation marks. The following example prints a message on the screen when Enter is pressed:

```
PRINT "Go Go Ivy!"
Go Go Ivy!
Ok
```

Note that the word PRINT and the quotation marks are not displayed in the output.

Syntax Errors

When the computer does not recognize an instruction, it prints an error message and stops to wait for the programmer to correct the error. One of the most common error messages is the Syntax error:

```
PRUNT "Go Go Ivy!"
Syntax error
Ok
```

Since the BASIC language does not contain the word PRUNT, the computer displays an error message.

Correcting Errors

If an error is detected before Enter has been pressed it can be easily corrected by using the left-arrow key ( ) to bring the cursor back to the location of the error, where typing the correction replaces it. When the line is correct, Enter is pressed. Pressing the Insert key causes the computer to enter "Insert mode" which allows characters to be entered in the middle of a line without typing over other characters. Pressing Insert again or an arrow key exits Insert mode.

If an error occurs after Enter is pressed and the Syntax error message printed, simply retype the entire line correctly and press Enter. An discussed in Chapter One, an error in a program is called a bug. The process of finding and removing program errors is called "debugging."

• •

Practice 1

This Practice demonstrates loading BASIC into the computer's memory, using immediate mode to print the results of a series of mathematical calculations, and the use of quotation marks in a PRINT statement.

1)   LOAD BASIC

Boot DOS as described in Chapter Two. Type BASICA at the DOS prompt. The BASIC screen is displayed:

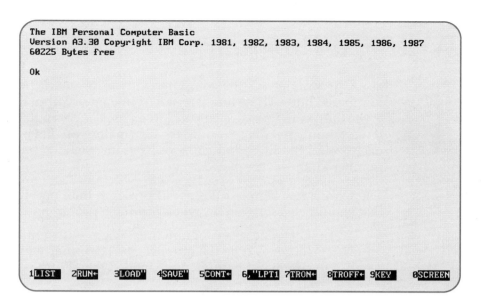

```
The IBM Personal Computer Basic
Version A3.30 Copyright IBM Corp. 1981, 1982, 1983, 1984, 1985, 1986, 1987
60225 Bytes free

Ok
```

`1LIST  2RUN←  3LOAD"  4SAVE"  5CONT←  6,"LPT1  7TRON←  8TROFF←  9KEY  0SCREEN`

2) USE IMMEDIATE MODE TO PRINT THE RESULTS OF CALCULATIONS

Press Enter after typing each of the following calculations:

```
PRINT 25 * 57
PRINT 218 / 32
PRINT 25 + 6 - 5 / 7
PRINT 25^2 + 12^3
PRINT "25^2 + 12^3"
```

What did BASIC print for each? Why?

3) ENTER EACH OF THE FOLLOWING LINES EXACTLY AS SHOWN

```
PRNT "Most Ivy students are not brilliant!"
```

Press Enter. Note that the syntax error may not be corrected with the left-arrow key if Enter has been pressed. Retype the whole line, being careful to spell PRINT correctly. Next type the line:

```
PRINT "But they are motvated."
```

Do not press Enter. Correct the spelling of "motivated" using the arrow keys to move the cursor to the letter "v." Press the Insert key to enter Insert mode and type the letter i. Note that the cursor becomes a blinking square. Press the Insert key again to return to overwrite mode and then press Enter.

4) RETURN TO DOS

Type SYSTEM. The BASIC screen is removed and the DOS prompt again displayed.

12.2 Writing a Program

A program gives the computer a series of instructions written on numbered lines. These lines are stored in memory until the computer is given the command to execute the program. The computer then finds the lowest numbered line, executes the instructions on that line, and continues to read the lines and carry out the instructions until the highest numbered line is completed.

Entering Programs

There are a few simple rules about program lines and line numbering that should be kept in mind when writing a program:

1. Each line in a program must begin with a number. If you forget to type the number, the computer will execute the command in immediate mode when Enter is pressed.

2. To enter a program line into the computer's memory, press Enter when the line is completed:

   ```
   10 PRINT 2 + 2              <press Enter>
   ```

3. When writing a program, it is best to use line numbers that are units of ten (10, 20, ... 100, 110, 120, etc.). This leaves room to insert nine possible lines between any two in case it becomes necessary to add lines later.

4. It is not necessary to enter the program lines in order. Line 20 can be entered first, then line 10 and later line 30, etc. The computer automatically puts the lines in numerical order. Any time a new instruction is to be added, just type the new line number and the instruction, then press Enter. The computer then puts the line into its proper sequence. Were the program lines

   ```
   40 PRINT 2 + 2
   20 PRINT "with a computer:"
   10 PRINT "Mathematics"
   30 PRINT "2 + 2 ="
   ```

   entered, the computer would execute them in the proper order (10, 20, 30, 40) when the program is run.

END

The END statement should be the last statement in a program, and is used to halt program execution. For example,

```
50 END
```

causes the execution of a program to stop when line 50 is reached. It is a good programming practice to place an END statement in all programs since it helps ensure that the program will terminate properly.

RUN

The RUN command instructs the computer to execute the program stored in its memory. Type the word RUN and press Enter when you have completed typing your program. It is important to realize that the RUN command is not part of the program, does not get a line number, and is typed only after the program is complete.

Note that when RUN is typed and Enter pressed, the computer executes the program lines that are stored in its memory in numerical order, beginning at line 10:

```
10 PRINT "Who at Ivy University"
20 PRINT "can solve the following?"
30 PRINT "5 * 3 ="
40 PRINT 5 * 3
50 PRINT "24 / 4 = " 24 / 4
60 END
```

```
RUN
Who at Ivy University
can solve the following?
5 * 3 =
 15
24 / 4 = 6
Ok
```

The message "Who at Ivy University" is printed by line 10 because those characters are between quotation marks, as are the messages on lines 20 and 30. Line 40 prints the results of the mathematical calculation because it is not enclosed in quotations. Note how line 50 prints 24 / 4 = and then the result, 6, on the same line. This is because the first part of the line is enclosed in quotation marks and the second part is not.

12.3 Correcting Errors - LIST

Typing errors and other mistakes in a program can be corrected in several ways. The following examples refer to Program 12.1:

1. If the error is detected while the line containing it is being typed, the left-arrow key can be used to move the cursor back to the error. The correction can then be typed and Enter pressed.

2. RETYPING A LINE: A program line can be changed by simply retyping it using the same line number. If

   ```
   20 PRINT "takes math?"
   ```

   is entered, only the output produced by line 20 will be changed.

3. ERASING A WHOLE LINE: An entire line of a program can be erased by typing the line number and pressing Enter:

   ```
   50
   ```

4. ADDING A NEW LINE: To add a line between other lines of a program, type the new line and press Enter. The computer then enters the line in its proper place:

```
15 PRINT "is a genius who"
```

The LIST command is used to display the program currently in the computer's memory. A LIST of Program 12.1 with the changes made in steps 2, 3, and 4 followed by a RUN produces:

```
LIST
10 PRINT "Who at Ivy University"
15 PRINT "is a genius who"
20 PRINT "takes math?"
30 PRINT "5 * 3 ="
40 PRINT 5 * 3
60 END
Ok

RUN
Who at Ivy University
is a genius who
takes math?
5 * 3 =
 15
Ok
```

Practice 2

This Practice demonstrates the writing, editing, and running of a simple program. Start the computer and load BASIC if you have not already done so.

1)   TYPE THE FOLLOWING PROGRAM

Remember to press Enter at the end of each line. Correct any mistakes you may make by either using the arrow keys or retyping the entire line.

```
10 PRINT "This program performs"
20 PRINT "calculations using 8 and 2."
30 PRINT "8 + 2 =" 8 + 2
40 PRINT "8 - 2 =" 8 - 2
50 PRINT "8 * 2 =" 8 * 2
60 PRINT "8 / 2 =" 8 / 2
70 PRINT "8 ^ 2 =" 8 ^ 2
80 END
```

2)   RUN THE PROGRAM

Type RUN and press Enter. What did BASIC print?

3) REPLACE THE FOLLOWING LINES AND RUN THE PROGRAM

Enter the following lines exactly as shown:

```
60 PRINT "So what?"
30 PRINT "This is a lot of work."
50
RUN
```

Note how the output produced by running the program has changed.

4) LIST THE MODIFIED PROGRAM

Type LIST and press Enter. The program is shown with the corrections you made.

12.4 System Commands

The following commands are called "system commands" and may be entered whenever the Ok prompt is displayed. System commands are not used within programs, but instead store, retrieve, and erase programs on the disk.

SAVE

The SAVE command is used to store a program on disk. The statement

```
SAVE "CALC"
```

saves the program currently in memory on disk and gives it the name CALC.BAS. BASIC automatically adds the file extension .BAS to indicate that this is a BASIC program. If there is already a program on the disk with that name, the new program replaces it, erasing the original. Program file names may be from one to eight characters in length, and should contain only letters and digits.

LOAD

Programs previously stored on disk can be recalled using the LOAD command.

```
LOAD "CALC"
```

loads the program named CALC.BAS into memory from disk. Any program previously in memory is erased. It is important to note that this procedure does not remove the program from the disk. An exact copy of the program is transferred to the computer's memory where it can be modified or run.

FILES

The FILES command produces a list of all the programs and files stored on the designated disk. Typing

```
FILES
```

lists the files stored on disk.

NEW

The NEW command is used to clear the computer's memory. Before entering a new program into memory, it is a good programming practice to type NEW to insure that any program lines from a previous program will not affect the new program.

```
NEW
```

12.5 Using Numeric Variables

Because the data used in a program may change, BASIC allows for the use of "variables." A variable is a name which is used to represent a value. For example,

A = 5

assigns the number 5 to the variable named A, which can then be used in place of the number 5.

To the computer there are two kinds of data: numbers and characters. (This is similar to the data base and spreadsheet which could work with values and labels.) Therefore, in order to use a variable, the computer must be told both the name of the variable and the type of data, either number or character, that is to be assigned to it.

Assigning a
Numeric Variable

An assignment statement is one way of assigning a value to a variable. For example,

10 A = 5

instructs the computer to set aside a place in its memory named A where the number 5 is stored. When the computer executes the above assignment statement, it sets aside a box in its memory, names it A, and puts 5 in it:

A

```
┌──────────┐
│    5     │
└──────────┘
```

Whenever the computer is told to use A, it looks in the box named A and uses the value that A represents, in this case, 5. For example, executing the command PRINT A would print a 5 on the screen. Note that this statement may not be entered as 5 = A because this would cause an error.

The value stored by a variable can change as the name "variable" implies; however, it is important to realize that a variable can hold only one value at a time. Suppose a later statement such as

50 A = 7

is entered. When line 50 is executed the value stored in the box named A changes from 5 to 7:

A

```
┌──────────┐
│    7     │
└──────────┘
```

The old value of A is lost and may not be retrieved again.

BASIC allows for variable names up to 40 characters long, but the first character must be a letter. BASIC reserves certain words like PRINT, SAVE, NAME, etc. for use as commands. These words may not be used as variable names.

This program demonstrates how variables are used in a program:

```
NEW
10 A = 5
20 B = 3
30 PRINT A * B
40 A = 7
50 B = 12
60 PRINT A * B
70 END

RUN
 15
 84
Ok
```

Line 10 assigns the value 5 to variable A, and line 20 assigns the value 3 to variable B:

```
    A              B
 ┌──────┐      ┌──────┐
 │  5   │      │  3   │
 └──────┘      └──────┘
```

Line 30 instructs the computer to print the product of A and B (15).

A variable can only hold one value at a time. If a different number is put in the box, then the first number is erased and lost. This happens when line 40 assigns the value of 7 to variable A, and line 50 assigns 12 to variable B:

```
    A              B
 ┌──────┐      ┌──────┐
 │  7   │      │  12  │
 └──────┘      └──────┘
```

When line 60 is executed, the new value of A is multiplied by the new value of B, and 84 printed.

12.6 Using String Variables

A character is any letter, number, punctuation mark, or mathematical symbol which can be found on the computer's keyboard. For example, A, !, and 5 are all characters. Even a blank space is a character. A "string" is a single character or series of characters that are strung together to form a word, number, or sequence of symbols. Digits can be made part of a string, but they cannot be used in a mathematical operation since the computer thinks of them as symbols rather than numbers when they are stored in a string variable.

String variable names must end with a dollar sign ($) so that the computer knows that this variable stores a string. A$, PERSON$, P1$, and COURSE$ are all legal string variable names. Note that NAME$ is not a valid variable name because NAME is a BASIC command.

Assigning a
String Variable

When a string variable is given its value by an assignment statement, the characters that make up the string must be enclosed by quotation marks:

```
10 PERSON$ = "Harry"
```

This statement assigns the string Harry to the variable PERSON$.

If we think of variables as boxes again, the computer names one of its boxes PERSON$ and places the string Harry in it when line 10 is executed:

PERSON$

```
┌───────────────┐
│               │
│   Harry       │
│               │
└───────────────┘
```

As with numeric variables, it is possible to change the value assigned to the variable PERSON$. For example,

```
60 PERSON$ = "Jane"
```

changes the value of PERSON$ from Harry to Jane when line 60 is executed:

PERSON$

```
┌───────────────┐
│               │
│   Jane        │
│               │
└───────────────┘
```

• •

Program 12.3

This program shows the string variable PERSON$ being assigned two different values:

```
NEW
10 PERSON$ = "Judy"
20 PRINT PERSON$
30 PERSON$ = "George"
40 PRINT PERSON$
50 END

RUN
Judy
George
Ok
```

12.7 Numeric INPUT

The INPUT statement allows a value to be assigned to a variable directly from the keyboard so that it may be changed each time the program is run. This differs from the assignment statement, which assigns the same value to a variable each time the program is run. A program that calculates a savings account balance provides a good example of these two situations. Each time money is deposited or withdrawn from the account the amount is likely to be different, but the rate of interest that the bank pays its depositors changes infrequently. Therefore, a deposit or withdrawal is best entered with an INPUT statement while the interest rate is best assigned to a variable.

The statement

```
10 INPUT A
```

allows a value to be assigned to A directly from the keyboard. When the computer executes the INPUT statement, it prints a question mark on the screen and then waits for data to be typed and Enter pressed.

●●

Program 12.4

This program inputs a number, N, and prints the result of that number multiplied by 5:

```
NEW
10 INPUT NUM
20 PRINT "5 *" NUM " = "
30 PRINT 5 * NUM
40 END

RUN
? 7
5 * 7 =
  35
Ok
```

When line 10 is executed, the computer prints a question mark on the screen and then waits for the user to enter a number. When 7 is typed after the question mark and Enter pressed, the computer creates a box in it memory, names it NUM, and places a 7 in it:

NUM

```
+-------+
|       |
|   7   |
|       |
+-------+
```

The value stored in NUM is then printed by line 20 and used in the calculation in line 30.

Be careful when using an INPUT statement not to use commas. When entering large numbers commas cause the computer to print a `?Redo from start` error message and ask for new input. If a letter or word is typed when the computer is expecting a number, it prints the `?Redo from start` error message and waits for appropriate input.

To prevent this error, the program user should be given a message indicating the kind of data expected. The message can be made part of an INPUT statement by combining the INPUT with the message enclosed in quotation marks:

```
10 INPUT "What number"; NUM
```

A semicolon (`;`) must follow the quotation marks that end the message to separate it from the variable name. Here is a run of the modified Program 12.4:

```
RUN
What number? 7
5 * 7 =
 35
Ok
```

12.8 String INPUT

An INPUT statement can also be used to assign a string of characters to a variable, for example:

```
10 INPUT PERSON$
```

Letters, symbols, and numbers can be assigned to the variable PERSON$. When the computer is expecting a value for a string variable the `?Redo from start` error message will not appear because the computer can accept numbers as part of a string.

Program 12.5

This program prints the string input by the user for MESSAGE$:

```
NEW
10 INPUT "Your string"; MESSAGE$
20 PRINT "This is what you typed:"
30 PRINT MESSAGE$
40 END

RUN
Your string? I am a 1994 Ivy graduate!
This is what you typed:
I am a 1994 Ivy graduate!
Ok
```

Line 10 instructs the computer to create a box in its memory named MESSAGE$ and then assigns data to it typed in from the keyboard:

MESSAGE$

```
I am a 1994 Ivy graduate!
```

As you can see, both the number 1994 and the exclamation mark symbol are stored in the string.

● ●

Program 12.6

This program, which calculates Ivy University's usually inflated grades, illustrates the use of all of the statements covered so far. It asks the user for a student's name and four grades, then prints the name and the student's average:

```
NEW
10 INPUT "Student's name"; STUDENT$
20 INPUT "English grade"; ENG
30 INPUT "History grade"; HIST
40 INPUT "Mathematics grade"; MATH
50 INPUT "Science grade"; SCI
60 PRINT
70 AVG = (ENG + HIST + MATH + SCI) / 4
80 PRINT "The average for " STUDENT$
   " is" AVG
90 END

RUN
Student's name? Kevin Connelly
English grade? 78
History grade? 85
Mathematics grade? 71
Science grade? 50

The average for Kevin Connelly is 71
Ok

RUN
Student's name? Suzie Jones
English grade? 92
History grade? 72
Mathematics grade? 86
Science grade? 90

The average for Suzie Jones is 85
Ok
```

Note how parentheses are used in line 70 so that the sum of the variables is divided by 4 rather than only the variable SCI. Also note how the PRINT statement at line 60 is used to print a blank line before the average, making the output easier to read.

Practice 3

Write a program which asks the user to enter his or her name and age and then prints the name and the age in 10 years. Your program should produce output similar to the following:

```
RUN
What is your name? Harriet
What is your age? 19

In ten years Harriet's age will be 29
Ok

RUN
What is your name? George
What is your age? 37

In ten years George's age will be 47
Ok
```

12.9 IF...THEN

The IF...THEN statement is called a "conditional statement." When a condition is met, a specified instruction is carried out; when not met, the statement is ignored. This is in contrast to the statements introduced so far (PRINT and INPUT) which are executed whenever they are read by the computer.

To describe a condition to the computer, an IF...THEN statement is used:

IF <condition> THEN <statement>

In the <condition> part of the IF statement a comparison is made. If the comparison is true, the computer executes the <statement> following THEN; if false, it skips the <statement> and proceeds directly to the next line in the program. By using one of the "relational operator" symbols shown below, two quantities can be compared:

Symbol	Meaning
=	equal to
>	greater than
<	less than
>=	greater than or equal to
<=	less than or equal to
<>	not equal to

The following are examples of IF...THEN statements:

```
20 IF STUDENT$ = "Mike" THEN PRINT
   "Hello Mike!"
```

When the condition STUDENT$ = "Mike" is true, the computer prints Hello Mike! and goes on to the next line; if the condition is false (STUDENT$ is not equal to "Mike") it prints nothing and goes on to the next line.

```
30 IF AVG > 90 THEN PRINT "Grade: A"
```

When the condition AVG is greater than 90 is true, the computer prints Grade: A; if variable AVG stores a value which is less than or equal to 90, the condition is false and nothing is printed by this line.

••

Program 12.7

This program determines whether the value input for variable X is the solution to the equation 2 * X = 6:

```
NEW
10 INPUT "What number"; X
20 IF 2 * X = 6 THEN PRINT X "is the
   solution."
30 END

RUN
What number? 5
Ok

RUN
What number? 3
 3 is the solution.
Ok
```

In the first RUN, 5 is not the solution so the comparison made in line 20 is false and nothing is printed. In the second RUN, because 3 causes the comparison to be true the program prints "3 is the solution."

12.10 FOR...NEXT Loops

Often it is desirable to repeat a set of instructions a number of times by adding a "loop" to a program. The loop will then execute the program lines contained within it over and over again a set number of times. To do this a FOR...NEXT loop is used which takes the form:

```
FOR <variable> = <starting value> TO <ending value>
    <statements>
    .
    .
    .
NEXT <variable>
```

Note that the <variable> after the FOR and the NEXT must be the same and that a string variable cannot be used. The first time through the loop the variable is given the <starting value>. Each time the loop is executed, 1 is added to the current value of the variable until it reaches a value greater than the <ending value>. To make clear which program lines are contained within a loop they are each indented by typing two spaces after the line number.

The following is an example of a valid FOR...NEXT loop:

```
10 FOR COUNT = 2 TO 6
20    PRINT "In the loop"
30 NEXT COUNT
```

When this loop is executed COUNT starts at line 10 with a value of 2 and retains this value until the NEXT COUNT statement is encountered at line 30. At this point the value of COUNT is increased by 1, changing from 2 to 3. All the statements in the lines between lines 10 and 30 are executed in sequence during each consecutive pass through the loop. The program continues to return from line 30 to the line immediately following line 10 until COUNT exceeds the specified limit of 6. At this point the program exits the loop and moves to the line following 30. During this process the loop is executed 5 times with COUNT being assigned values of 2, 3, 4, 5, and 6.

Program 12.8

Here a FOR...NEXT loop is used to calculate and print the 10 times table from 0 to 5:

```
NEW
10 PRINT "Times Table"
20 FOR NUM = 0 TO 5
30    PRINT NUM "* 10 =" NUM * 10
40 NEXT NUM
50 PRINT "Finished the loop."
60 END

RUN
Times Table
 0 * 10 = 0
 1 * 10 = 10
 2 * 10 = 20
 3 * 10 = 30
 4 * 10 = 40
 5 * 10 = 50
Finished the loop.
Ok
```

In line 20, NUM is initialized to 0 and increases by 1 each time the loop is repeated. Line 30 displays the multiplication table. The NEXT NUM on line 40 instructs the computer to increase the value of NUM by 1 if its value is less than or equal to 5; otherwise, it exits the loop and goes on to line 50.

Program 12.9

Any type of statement can be included in a loop. This program uses an IF in a loop to find solutions for the condition NUM * 6 >= NUM^2 for all integers from 5 to 30:

```
NEW
10 FOR NUM = 5 TO 30
20    IF NUM * 6 >= NUM^2 THEN PRINT NUM
30 NEXT NUM
40 PRINT "Done"
50 END

RUN
 5
 6
Done
Ok
```

Practice 4

Write a program which asks the user to enter 3 different numbers, and, after each entry, prints a message saying whether the entered number is greater than, less than, or equal to 25. Your program should use a loop and produce a RUN similar to the following:

```
RUN
What is the number? 17
Your number is less than 25

What is the number? 35
Your number is greater than 25

What is the number? 25
Your number is equal to 25

Ok
```

Chapter Summary

A program is a list of instructions that tells the computer which operations to perform and in what sequence to perform them. PRINT is the instruction used to display numbers, characters, and words on the screen in either immediate mode or within a program.

Errors in a program line can be corrected by using the arrow keys before Enter is pressed or by retyping the whole line after Enter is pressed. Each line of a program must begin with a number. When the program is run the computer executes the program lines in sequence beginning with the lowest number and proceeding to the highest number.

The END statement should be the last statement in a program. RUN instructs the computer to execute the program stored in memory. LIST displays the program currently in the computer's memory. Both RUN and LIST are not part of a program.

SAVE stores a program on disk and LOAD recalls it from disk. FILES produces a list of all the programs stored on disk. NEW erases the computer's memory so that a new program may be entered.

Variable names are used to represent values. There are two types of variables; numeric variables, which can be assigned numbers, and string variables, which can be assigned characters, symbols, and digits. A string is defined as any set of characters. The values assigned to variables may be changed at any time.

INPUT allows a value to be assigned to a variable directly from the keyboard. An input statement may contain a message called a prompt:

```
10 INPUT "What is your name"; N$
```

IF...THEN is called a conditional statement. If a condition is met, a specified response is carried out; if not met, the statement is ignored:

```
20 IF PAIN$ = "Itch" THEN PRINT "Poison
   Ivy"
```

prints Poison Ivy only if PAIN$ equals "Itch"; otherwise, nothing is printed.

A FOR...NEXT loop allows instructions to be repeated a set number of times. The lines

```
10 FOR NUM = 1 TO 10
20    PRINT NUM
30 NEXT NUM
```

print the numbers from 1 to 10.

• •

Vocabulary

Assign - To give a variable a value.

BASIC - Popular computer programming language. Its name is an acronym for Beginner's All-Purpose Symbolic Instruction Code.

Bug - An error in either the design or the instructions of a program.

Command - Instruction to the computer in a language the computer understands.

Conditional statement - Statement executed only when a condition is true. (See IF...THEN)

Debugging - The process of finding and removing "bugs" (errors) in a program.

Edit - To make changes in a program.

END - Statement that halts program execution.

FILES - Command for producing a list of files and programs stored on disk.

FOR...NEXT - Loop which executes a group of instructions a set number of times.

IF...THEN - Conditional statement that instructs the computer to take a specified action if a comparison is found to be true, and no action if it is false.

Immediate mode - Mode in which the computer executes commands and instructions immediately when the Enter key is pressed.

INPUT - Statement used for entering data into the computer directly from the keyboard.

Line number - Number in front of each program line that is used to place the line in its proper sequence within the program.

LIST - Command that displays the lines of the program currently in memory.

LOAD - Command for recalling a program previously stored on disk.

Loop - Section of a program designed to be executed repeatedly.

NEW - Command that erases the program currently in memory so that a new one can be entered.

Numeric operator - A symbol (+, -, *, /, ^) used to express a mathematical operation.

Numeric variable - Variable which stores a numeric value.

PRINT - Statement that causes the computer to display information on the screen.

Program - Series of instructions written in a special language directing the computer to perform specific operations and in what order to perform them.

Relational operator - A symbol (=, <, >, <>, <=, >=) used to indicate the comparison of two values.

Reserved word - Word such as PRINT or FOR that is part of the programming language and therefore cannot be used as a variable name.

RUN - Command that starts program execution.

SAVE - Command that instructs the computer to save the program in memory on disk under the name specified.

Statement - All the elements that combined carry out an instruction.

String - A sequence of letters, numbers and/or special characters such as punctuation marks. Strings may not be used in mathematical calculations.

String variable - Variable that stores a string. All string variable names end with a dollar sign.

Syntax error - Statement or command which the computer does not understand because it does not fit the rules of the programming language.

Variable - Name used to represent a value that is stored in the memory of the computer by a program. The value assigned to a variable can be changed.

● ●

Reviews

Sections 12.1 - 12.5

1. What is the difference between writing a command in immediate mode or making it a part of a program?

2. a) How can an error be corrected in a program line if Enter has not been pressed?
   b) How can an error be corrected in a program line if Enter has been pressed?

3. What is a syntax error?

4. Why is it better to number the lines of a program by units of ten (10, 20, 30...) rather than by units of one (1, 2, 3...)?

5. What statement should always be the last statement in a program?

6. What output is produced when the following program is RUN?

```
10 A = 20
20 B = A + 10
30 PRINT B
40 END
```

7. What output is produced when the following program is RUN?

```
10 A = 20
20 B = 30
30 C = 40
40 D = A + B + C
50 PRINT D * B
60 C = 12
70 PRINT D * C
80 END
```

Sections 12.6 - 12.8

8. What output is produced when the following program is RUN?

```
10 N1$ = "Tommy"
20 N2$ = "Trisha"
30 PRINT "Who has seen " N2$ " or " N1$ "?"
40 PRINT "I saw " N2$
50 END
```

9. What is the difference between assigning a variable its value using an assignment statement and using an INPUT statement?

10. What output is displayed on the lines when the following program is RUN and the data shown entered?

```
10 INPUT N
20 PRINT N * 10
30 INPUT N
40 PRINT 30 * N
50 END

RUN
? 50
_____

? 5,000
_____

? 5000
_____
```

11. What output is produced when the following programs is RUN?

```
10 A = 100
20 B = 20
30 IF B >= A / 3 THEN PRINT "Big!"
40 IF A < B^2 THEN PRINT "Small!"
50 IF A <> 2 * B THEN A = 5
60 PRINT A * B
70 END
```

12. What output is produced when the following program is RUN?

```
10 FOR J = 1 to 10
20    PRINT J - 5
30 NEXT J
40 FOR K = 2 TO 5
50    PRINT K * 2
60 NEXT K
70 END
```

Exercises

1. Perform each of the following computations on paper. Check your answers using immediate mode:

   a) 5 + 16   d) 239 * 27
   b) 33 - 16   e) 250 / 5
   c) 13 * 3   f) 999 / 11

2. Write a program that first prints the results of 275 times 39, and then 275 divided by 39:

   ```
   RUN
   275 * 39 = 10725
   275 / 39 = 7.051282
   Ok
   ```

3. Write a program which assigns the value 10 to variable A, and 35 to B and then prints the results of A + B, A - B, A * B, and A / B.

4. Write a program that uses INPUT to assign values to two variables NUM1 and NUM2 and then calculates their sum and product. A RUN of the program should look like this:

   ```
   RUN
   ? 45
   ? 10
   45 + 10 = 55
   45 * 10 = 450
   Ok
   ```

5. Write a program in which the price of a loaf of bread (PRICE) and the number of loaves purchased (NUMLOAF) is INPUT from the keyboard. The total spent for the bread is then printed:

   ```
   RUN
   Price of a loaf? .89
   Number of loaves? 6
   Total spent = $ 5.34
   Ok
   ```

6. Write a program that computes the volume of a room given its length, width and height in cubic meters.

```
RUN
What is the length? 12
What is the width? 4
What is the height? 3
The volume is 144 cubic meters
Ok
```

7. A state has a 7% sales tax. Write a program which allows you to INPUT the name and price (before taxes) of an item found in a department store and then prints the item name, tax, and the total cost of the item including the sales tax.

```
RUN
Name of item? Coat
Price? 65

Coat has a tax of $4.55 and costs $69.55
Ok
```

8. Write a program that allows two numbers NUM1 and NUM2 to be entered. Have the computer compare them and print a message stating whether NUM1 is less than, equal to, or greater than NUM2.

```
RUN
First number? 12
Second number? 45

 12 is less than 45
Ok
```

```
RUN
First number? 650
Second number? 650

 650 is equal to 650
Ok
```

9. Write a program which asks for a person's age. If the person is 16 years or older, have the computer print "You are old enough to drive a car!" Otherwise, have the computer indicate how many years the person must wait before being able to drive.

```
RUN
What is your age? 12
You may drive in 4 years.
Ok
```

10. Write a program that employs a FOR...NEXT loop to print the following values:

```
RUN
 5
10
15
20
25
```

11. Write a program that prints all integers with values between 1 and 100 which solve the condition $3 * X^2 + 5 * X + 3 < 200$.

12. Write a program that prints the cubes of the integers from 11 to 21, inclusive.

Chapter Thirteen

Telecommunications & the Future of Computing: Social & Ethical Implications

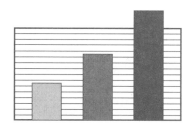

File - Create New File

Options - Communication

Options - Phone

Connect - Connect

Connect - Dial Again

Objectives

After completing this chapter you will be able to:

1. Define telecommunications and describe its uses.

2. Use the Works Communication application to connect to an information system.

3. Describe artificial intelligence and its use in expert systems and natural language processing.

4. Understand how robots may be used to automate tasks.

5. Describe different careers in computing and their educational requirements.

6. Understand the ethical responsibilities of computer use and programming.

7. Describe the impact of computers on today's society and list several objectives for the future of computing.

8. Understand the purpose of networks and desktop publishing.

3

I n this concluding chapter we discuss the future of computing, including the effects of various technological developments on computers, the career possibilities created by computers, and the social and ethical consequences of living in a computerized society. After having studied the previous chapters you should have a good understanding of how useful and powerful a computer is. In the first chapter of this text we stated that computers, unlike people, could not actually think but could store huge amounts of data and process it at very high speeds. This chapter describes how these capabilities will be exploited in the future to perform an ever increasing and varied number of tasks.

13.1 Telecommunications

One of the most important advances made in computing has been in the field of "telecommunications." Telecommunications means the sending and receiving of computer data over telephone lines. To do this an additional piece of hardware called a "modem" is required to translate the binary data of the computer into tones which can then be transmitted over phone lines. To receive data a modem must also have the capability of translating the waves back into binary form. This process involves what is called signal <u>mo</u>dulation and <u>dem</u>odulation, hence the name modem. In addition to the modem, special telecommunications software is required so that the computer can transmit and receive data.

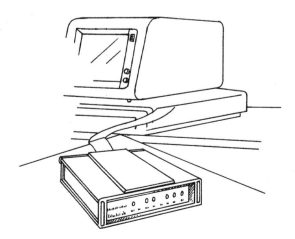

Modems can be "external," outside the computer, or built in

With a modem a microcomputer is capable of transmitting and receiving data between any two locations connected by phone lines. The rate at which each character of data is sent is measured in "baud," one baud representing the transmission of one character per second. Currently the most common rates are 1200, 2400, and 9600 baud which means 1200, 2400, and 9600 characters per second. However, newer modems are being created which are capable of communicating at higher rates.

Any type of data that a computer is capable of storing can be sent and received by modem. Using a modem it is possible to access and search very large data bases which might store financial data, news reports, travel information, or a company's sales data. If you go to a travel agent to book an airplane ticket, the agent will most likely use a computer to check the availability of flights and then make your reservation. The agent's computer is connected by modem to a large computer that contains a data base of flight information. This data base is similar to the ones you created using Works, only much larger.

Because of telecommunications it is now possible for many people to work at home rather than in an office. News reporters and writers often write their stories at home on a word processor and then transmit their word processing files to a central office many miles away. Financial consultants, accountants, and travel agents are sometimes able to work at home accessing needed data bases using a computer and modem.

In many states it is possible to do your banking by computer, paying bills and making deposits from your home. Companies are also establishing computer services that allow you to shop at home, make your own travel reservations, even play a game of chess with someone in another state or country all by using a computer and modem. As you can see, the impact of telecommunications on our society is becoming more and more significant.

13.2 Electronic Bulletin Boards and E-Mail

One of the most popular forms of telecommunication is the electronic "bulletin board system" or BBS. People who subscribe to a bulletin board service can call another computer and transmit messages to it which are then stored. When other subscribers of the service call the bulletin board it allows them to list all of the messages that have been "posted." Many companies and other organizations maintain bulletin boards to keep their employees aware of important events. For example, the Ivy University Alumni Association could have an electronic bulletin board which lists upcoming events such as athletic competitions and alumni reunions. An Ivy alumnus could then get a list of all of the events by calling the bulletin board using a modem and computer. Some BBS are run by individual users and are normally free. Others called "information services" are controlled by large companies and offer a variety of different services such as shopping or international weather forecasts for a fee.

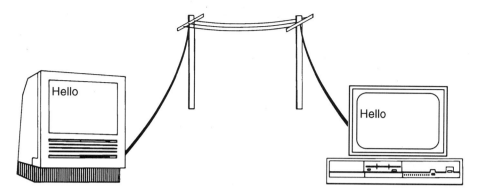

Telecommunications allows two computers to exchange information over telephone lines

Electronic mail or "E-Mail" is similar to an electronic bulletin board, but is used instead to send and receive messages meant for one person or a small group. The person sending the message contacts the electronic mail service using a computer and modem, and then types in the name of the recipient and the message. When the recipient calls the electronic mail service he or she receives the message. The advantage of this system is primarily speed. Letters sent through the mail can take days to receive, even when sent across town, while electronic mail can be received instantly. Another advantage of this service is that recipients can receive messages when they want them rather than when they are sent. This is especially useful when messages are sent around the world, into different time zones. A message sent from New York at 9:00 A.M. will be immediately received and stored by a computer in Tokyo at 1:00 A.M. Tokyo time, but the person in Tokyo need not call the electronic mail service until a more convenient time. Most larger information services offer E-Mail.

To keep electronic mail private a password system is employed. When first calling to receive messages, a person is asked to enter a secret password which must then be verified by the computer before the messages are transmitted.

It is possible to create a copy of a message left on a BBS or E-Mail system on your computer. This is called "downloading" and involves having the system's computer send a copy of the message file to your computer, where it is stored on disk. Similarly, the process of sending files to a BBS or E-Mail system is called "uploading." Once downloaded, you can print or edit the file, or save it for future reference.

Electronic mail is especially popular in universities where students and faculty can easily send messages to each other. If Ivy University chemistry instructor, Dr. Sulfuric, wants to change her homework assignment she can send the new assignment to each member of her class using the university's E-Mail system. She can also find out if the messages have been received (downloaded) because the system keeps a record of when each member of her class has checked for messages. It would be possible for a student to complete the assignment using a word processor and send the answers to Dr. Sulfuric as another message (upload).

A growing number of universities now require all of their students to purchase microcomputers and modems. Among many other advantages, it has allowed everyone on their campuses to make use of electronic mail services.

13.3 Telecommunicating with Works

The fourth application area in Works is Communications. If your computer is equipped with a modem, this application allows you to contact electronic bulletin boards and information services to send and receive data.

Telecommunicating can be complex, involving many different options such as baud rates. In order for telecommunications to take place, both computers must use the same options. New subscribers to an information service normally receive a large packet describing the options which must be used to access that particular service. Fortunately, Works allows the options for each different service to be saved in a communications file, meaning that once saved, the user does not have to be concerned about setting the proper options again. Works saves all communications files using the file name extension .WCM.

Selecting Communications from the Create New File dialog box displays the Communications screen:

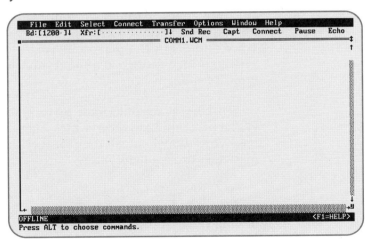

Works' Telecommunications Screen

For two computers to communicate, they both must use the same options. The four most important of these are:

Baud Rate: The speed at which each computer will send and receive data. 1200, 2400, and 9600 are common values.

Data bits: The number of bits (binary digits) that make up one piece of data. This can be 7 or 8.

Stop bits: The number of bits, 1 or 2, sent to indicate the end of a piece of data.

Parity: How the receiving computer will determine if an error occurred in the transmission of data. Common parity choices are named None, Odd, Even, and Space.

These four items are so important that bulletin boards (BBS) and information services are classified by the settings that they expect. For example, a BBS may list itself as "1200, 8, None, 1" or "12, 8, N, 1" meaning that its computer communicates using 1200 baud, 8 data bits, None parity and 1 stop bit. Works controls the values of these settings using the Communication command from the Options Menu:

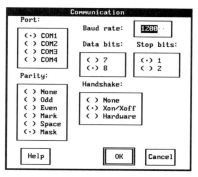

The Communication command controls telecommunications options

Once the Communication options have been set, all that is needed is to tell Works what phone number to dial by selecting the Phone command from the Options menu:

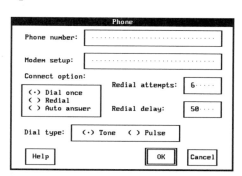

The Phone dialog box tells Works what number to dial

The **Phone number** option is used to tell Works what number to dial, including the area code if needed. Works allows dialing to be either **Pulse** (for older, rotary phones) or **Tone** (for touch-tone). Some modems require a special series of codes be used which can be specified on the **Modem setup** line.

Once the proper options for Baud, Phone number, etc. have been set, a communications file can be created by selecting the Save command from the File menu which saves your choices on disk. Opening a previously saved communications file recalls the options you have set. In this way, Works simplifies the process of setting communications options by allowing you to create a different communications file for each information service you contact.

After the options have been set and saved, Works can be told to contact the information service by selecting the Connect command from the Connect menu. When executed, Connect dials the phone number you supplied and attempts to contact the other computer. If a connection is made, Works displays ONLINE on the Status line and the amount of time that has elapsed since contacting the computer. The other computer then takes control of your computer, and anything that you type is sent to it. For this reason, the remote computer is often called the "host." Executing the Connect command again terminates communications with the host and hangs up the phone.

Practice 1 - Connecting to a BBS

In this Practice you will set options to access a BBS, and create a communications file for that BBS's options. If you do not have a modem attached to your computer you will not be able to perform this Practice.

Make sure that your modem is connected to a phone line and is turned on. As examples for this exercise we will use the options 1200, 7, Even, 1 and the telephone number 800-346-3247. You may be able to get actual information about a local BBS from your computer dealer.

1) BOOT DOS AND START WORKS

2) OPEN A NEW COMMUNICATIONS FILE

    a. Select **Create a New File** from the dialog box.
    b. Highlight **Communications** and select OK. The communications screen is shown.

3) SET THE COMMUNICATIONS OPTIONS

    a. From the Options menu, select the Communications command. Note the default options for **Baud rate** (1200), **Data bits** (8) and **Stop bits** (1).
    b. Change the **Data bits** to 7.
    c. Select the **Parity** option Even.
    d. The **Port** is the location of the modem in your computer. Normally, this is **COM2**, but your computer may be different. Set the **Port** to **COM2**. (If you know that your modem is in a different location, set the Port to that location.)
    e. Select OK to remove the dialog box.

4) SET THE PHONE NUMBER AND DIALING OPTIONS

    a. From the Options menu, select the Phone command.
    b. Type the number of the BBS in the **Phone number** option, 1-800-346-3247.
    c. If you modem requires a special setup command enter it on the **Modem setup** line.
    d. Select OK to remove the dialog box.

5) SAVE THE OPTIONS IN A FILE NAMED BBSTEST.WCM

    a. From the File menu, select the Save command.
    b. Enter the name BBSTEST and select OK. Works saves the phone number and communications options in a file named BBSTEST.WCM.

6) INITIATE COMMUNICATIONS

a. From the Connect menu select the Connect command. Works prints the phone number on the screen and displays the elapsed time and DIAL on the Status line. Depending on the type of modem you have, you may be able to hear the phone being dialed.

b. When the host computer answers the phone and establishes communications with your modem, Works displays CONNECT and may beep. Press Enter.

Note: If the host is already connected to another computer, or if your communications options are not set correctly Works display a message such as, ERROR, BUSY, or NO CARRIER. If this occurs, check your options (especially the **Port** set in step 3) and tell Works to dial again by selecting the Dial Again command from the Connect menu.

<u>Check</u> - When communications have been established, the host computer transmits a welcome message. Messages differ from service to service, but most ask for a name or account number. Your screen should be similar to:

```
ATDT1-800-346-3247
CONNECT 1200




Host Name:
```

Because you are connected, anything typed on your keyboard will be sent to the host computer. You will next enter a host name and receive information by following the instructions that the host computer sends to your machine.

7) ENTER PHONES AS THE HOST

At the "Host Name" prompt, type PHONES and press Enter. The other computer responds with a message. You are telecommunicating: your computer sent the message "PHONES" over the modem to the other computer which has now responded.

8) TERMINATE COMMUNICATIONS

a. From the Connect menu, select the Connect command again to terminate communications.

b. Works displays the prompt:

```
OK to disconnect?
```

Select OK. Works displays OFFLINE on the Status line. You may now exit Works, or switch to another application.

13.4 The Future of Computing

In Chapter One we traced the history of computing and discovered that as technology improved, computers increased in speed, decreased in size, stored more data, and most importantly became less expensive. This trend will, in all probability, continue. As it does, one of the advances will be the continued development of smaller, more powerful microprocessors which will be found in an ever increasing number of appliances and devices. Microprocessors can already be found in telephone answering machines, cameras, television sets, refrigerators, washing machines, and automobiles.

One example of the use of a microprocessor is in the anti-lock braking system (ABS) found on many cars. A computer connected to sensors on a car's wheels detects when, as the brakes are applied, the car begins to skid. The computer then takes over control of the brakes, pumping them rapidly to keep the wheels from locking. This process avoids the skidding which often results when brakes are applied on wet roads. Other microprocessors are being developed which increase the efficiency of an automobile engine or control how safety devices will perform in case of an accident.

Anti-lock braking systems use a computer to stop even the fastest car

One of the most promising areas of microprocessor development is in the diagnostic systems of complex electronic devices. Many devices such as computers and car engines have become so complicated that it is difficult to determine what is wrong when they malfunction. Therefore, microprocessors have been developed which pinpoint the component that is not working properly and then alerts the user. These types of systems are commonly found on automobiles, aircraft, or any device which contains a large number of complicated parts. Undoubtedly many new applications for microprocessors will be found in the future in areas which we can only begin to imagine.

Besides the development of better microprocessors, software will also improve. Most software developers are attempting to make their software increasingly "user friendly," which means easier to use. In learning the three applications areas you were required to familiarize yourself with a number of commands. By having similar commands in each of the applications areas, the program was made easier to learn. This process will continue to become less complicated as better software is written. Later in this chapter we discuss attempts to produce computers that allow the user to use voice rather than typed commands.

13.5 Artificial Intelligence

Although computers cannot think, one of the major areas of research continues to be the development of software programs that are capable of making increasingly complex decisions. Using computers to make decisions which would normally be made by human beings is called

An Introduction to Computing Using Microsoft Works

"artificial intelligence." Herbert Schorr, a computer scientist at IBM, has declared that the development of artificial intelligence is the "second wave" of the information revolution. The first wave was the development of automated data processing which you studied when producing data bases and spreadsheets. According to Schorr "the second wave will automate decision making."

The Internal Revenue Service (I.R.S.) has defined artificial intelligence as "the science of making machines do things that would require intelligence if done by man." As an example, there are currently computers which can play chess so well that they can beat all but the best players. Universities actually challenge each other's computers to play chess to determine which has the best chess playing program. Are these computers really intelligent? Most computer scientists would say no. They are simply programmed to make a series of decisions in response to the moves made by their opponents. It is merely their speed and ability to access huge amounts of stored data which make them appear to be intelligent.

Some specialized computers are capable of playing master level chess

In 1950 the brilliant English mathematician Alan Turing wrote a paper entitled "Computing Machinery and Intelligence" in which he raised the question "Can machines think?". To answer the question he invented the "Imitation Game." Briefly summarized, the game involves placing a person and a computer in separate rooms and an interrogator in a third room. Communicating by typed questions and answers, the interrogator questions the human and computer to determine which is the computer. If the interrogator cannot tell the difference between the responses then, according to Turing, the machine has human thought capabilities. Since not even psychologists can agree on a definition of intelligence, this is probably as good a test as any. Currently, no computer or software program has been shown to be capable of passing Turing's test.

13.6 Expert Systems

One of the most promising areas of research into artificial intelligence is the development of what is called "expert systems." An expert system is programmed to produce the same solution a human expert would if asked to solve the same problem. The concept was first employed in research done in the 1960's at Stanford University by Professor Edward Feigenbaum and Doctor Edward Shortliffe. They developed a computer program named "Mycin," named for a group of antibiotics, which was designed to perform medical diagnosis of infectious diseases and suggest possible treatments. The program worked by asking questions about a patient's symptoms. A diagnosis was then given based upon the answers. Was this program actually thinking? Again, we answer no. The program was making its decisions based upon over 500 rules given it by human experts. For example, such a rule might specify that if a patient had a low-level infection and was allergic to penicillin, then the antibiotic Erythromycin should be prescribed.

Mycin, which took more than 20 man-years to develop, turned out to be more accurate than the human experts against whom it was tested. In one test Mycin prescribed the correct treatment 65% of the time, in contrast to the experts who were right in 42% to 62% of the cases. One of the problems with Mycin was that it did not know whether it was diagnosing a human being or not. In fact, it was capable of prescribing penicillin to fix a broken window. However, programs such as Mycin can be useful when used to aid a human doctor in diagnosing a patient.

Since the Mycin experiment at Stanford, many expert systems have been developed in fields as diverse as accounting, biology, law, and automobile repair. Although expert systems can be helpful in reducing the time it takes a professional to analyze and solve a problem, it has so far been apparent that a computer is usually a poor substitute for a human expert. This is because human experts may use "intuition" to solve a problem. In making a diagnosis a doctor uses intuition, which is not based on systematic logic. By looking at a patient and discussing his or her feelings and moods, a doctor is often able to ascertain important information which could not be used by a computer. We consider these to be "human" or "psychological" factors which, while very important, can not be programmed into a computer.

An example of an expert system that works quite well is one installed by the credit card division of American Express. In the past when a store called to get approval for a large charge, a trained credit expert would have to decide if approval should be given. By asking a series of questions about the amount being charged, the type of item being purchased, and so on, the expert would then make a decision. Now if an American Express card holder wants to make a large purchase, for example a $10,000 oriental rug, in many cases the computer will decide whether or not to approve the purchase.

Another useful expert system involves the repair of automobiles. In the past when Ford automobile dealers were confronted by a hard-to-diagnose engine problem they called expert Gordy Kujawski. Now they simply run an expert system program developed to duplicate the reasoning Kujawski uses to solve a problem. Creating this expert system involved describing Kujawski's thought processes in terms of rules, like the Mycin program. Programmers watched Kujawski at work and asked "Why did you test the battery?" and "How did you know to look at the carburetor?" and programmed the computer to respond as he did.

One of the more secretive uses of expert systems is that used by U.S. intelligence agents to avert terrorist acts. Programmed with the knowledge of a handful of terrorism agents, the system has proven surprisingly accurate in its ability to predict when and where terrorist activities will occur. Another similar system is used by the F.B.I. to predict the activities of criminals. Both systems have been programmed with rules that human experts have developed based on decades of experience.

We earlier referred to the I.R.S. definition of artificial intelligence. They have developed an expert system which analyzes tax returns to determine if a person is correctly reporting income or making improper deductions. Programmed to look for suspicious patterns, the I.R.S. computer decides when a human agent should consider initiating a tax audit.

Currently there are thousands of expert systems in use, with the number increasing each year. To date, the expert systems that work the best are those for which a series of rules can be used to make a decision. When specific rules do not apply, as when intuition must be used, expert systems are usually not successful.

13.7 Natural Language Processing

Designing a computer system that can recognize human speech has long been a goal of computer scientists. After almost four decades of slow progress, machines are now being developed that can recognize spoken words and then translate them into digital form. This is called "speech recognition" and involves "natural language processing," a field of artificial intelligence which attempts to translate a sentence into its separate parts and understand its meaning.

The difficulties in producing natural language processing systems are many. First, many words have different meanings based upon the context in which they are used. The word "change," for example, could mean money as in "Here's your change" or a different order as in "Change my order to a hot dog." Second, there are almost an unlimited number of ways of giving the same instructions. Finally, in addition to the problems of determining the meaning of words, a speech recognizing computer needs to be able to understand many different voice patterns and accents.

Solving these problems highlights the difference between human and machine "intelligence." A person would have little problem overcoming the difficulties mentioned above, but to a machine, which is programmed to follow instructions in a logical sequence, the difficulties are considerable.

The potential applications for natural language processing systems are numerous. One such development has allowed users of car telephones to dial their phones by speaking the numbers or simply saying the name of the person to call. Other potential uses include allowing people to dictate letters to their word processors or ordering products like airline tickets over a telephone connected to a computer. Voice messages might also be sent in digital form to computers as electronic mail.

One very useful application of natural language processing would be in language translation. A person calling France could speak in English with the computer translating and speaking in French at the other end. Although systems have already been developed which allow the user to type in English and have the output printed in French, machines which can handle spoken language remain under development.

Today there are hand-held computers capable of translating a limited vocabulary of English to other languages as it is being spoken

A major problem faced by language translation programs is that most languages such as French, German, and especially Asian languages such as Japanese and Chinese are structured differently than English. Also, as you have learned if you have studied a foreign language, many words have a number of different meanings. For all of these reasons even the best translation programs are at present not very accurate, often producing humorous results. A computer asked to translate the biblical passage "the spirit is willing, but the flesh is weak" from English into Russian and then back into English produced the result "the wine is agreeable, but the meat is spoiled."

Many computer scientists believe that future advances in artificial intelligence will depend upon the development of radically new technologies. To be truly useful as artificial intelligence machines, computers will have to possess some form of "common sense." They will have to be able to distinguish, for example, between a sick person and a broken window, as Mycin could not. Until this is accomplished we would be wise to give artificial intelligence systems only limited trust, being on guard against the errors in judgement they may make.

13.8 Robotics

Another application of artificial intelligence is in "robotics." To be defined as a robot a machine must be able to be programmed and also be able to move. Most robots, unlike an R2D2 or C3PO in the movies, are simply moveable arms that can be directed to perform a task. Because they can be programmed, robots can make simple decisions and then act upon them.

Of the robots currently "employed," most are used in the automobile industry to spot weld and spray paint cars. As robots become capable of performing increasingly complicated tasks, they will undoubtedly be used in many more industries.

There are a number of advantages to using robots. One is their ability to perform tasks too dangerous for humans. Robots have been developed which can remove and defuse bombs, work in highly radioactive environments, or under conditions of extreme noise or temperatures. Their use in aiding handicapped people is also a very promising area. A major advantage of robots is that they can perform their tasks tirelessly, willing to work 24-hour days without rest or vacations.

To date robots have been used only to perform simple, repetitive tasks. They have often been both expensive and unreliable. A task as simple as picking up an egg has proven extremely difficult for them to perform. The hand/eye coordination which we take for granted requires an extremely complex set of actions which are difficult to duplicate mechanically. Even a task as simple as moving through a room without hitting objects is currently difficult for today's robots.

We have all seen science fiction movies where a robot becomes so human-like that it exhibits emotions and temperament, but so far no real robot has been developed which has any of these traits. In all probability such a robot is a very long way off, if indeed one can ever be invented.

When natural language processing and artificial intelligence programs are perfected, the use of robots will undoubtedly increase. The dream of having a machine you can order around like a personal servant may then become a reality. The factory of the future will probably contain numerous robots performing a wide variety of tasks. As manufacturers produce an increasing number of highly complicated products, robots will be easier to train than human beings.

13.9 Careers in Computing

As computers become more powerful they will play an ever increasing role in the world in which we live. Consequently most people, no matter what field they are employed in, will encounter computers. It is estimated that by the year 2000 over 90% of all office personnel will have a computer terminal or PC at their desks.

Doctors, lawyers, accountants, business people, educators, farmers, and almost any profession you can think of are currently using or will soon make use of computers. It is the purpose of this text to introduce you to the many varied tasks that a computer can perform to help and prepare you for almost any career you might consider.

If you have become especially interested in computers you might consider a career in computing. According to recent government projections, the computer field will continue to hire people at an increasing rate. In this section we discuss some of the careers that you might consider and the education required to enter them.

Data Processing

The area of computing that employs the largest number of people is data processing. Data processing, as you have already learned, involves the electronic entry, storage, manipulation, and retrieval of data. Banks, businesses, educational institutions — almost any organization requires large amounts of data and therefore employees capable of data processing. Careers in data processing are usually divided into the following six categories:

1. Data-Entry Operator
2. Computer Operator
3. System Analyst
4. System Developer/Programmer
5. System Manager
6. Computer Science and Research

We will consider each area separately, outlining the qualifications expected of a person entering the area.

Data-Entry Operator

It is the job of a data-entry operator to type data into a computer. This is usually done at a computer terminal which is much like the computer you have been using. Data-entry operators may work for banks entering cancelled checks, department stores entering inventory figures, or educational institutions entering student records.

Often data is entered from various locations and then sent over phone lines to a central computer. Because of this it is sometimes possible for data-entry operators to work at home.

The following are characteristics a data-entry operator should possess:

- The ability to type quickly and accurately.
- Attention to detail in order to detect errors that may occur.

Usually a high school diploma is sufficient to gain a job as a data-entry operator. Often several weeks of on the job training will be offered by the employer. To begin to prepare for a position as a data-entry operator it is advisable to take courses in typing and word processing.

Computer Operator

A computer operator is responsible for setting up equipment, mounting and removing tapes and disks, and monitoring the computer's operation. Often the computer operator must help the programmers and users of a computer when problems arise.

The following are characteristics a computer operator should possess:

- A good understanding of how the computer equipment operates.
- The ability to read and understand technical manuals.
- Be able to detect and correct operational errors.
- Good communication skills to explain to computer users problems they may encounter.

Most computer operators have technical school or junior college educations. Because of the many different types of computers, the majority of their training is usually received on the job. A good way to prepare for a career as a computer operator is to take computer courses and assist, if possible, in the operation and maintenance of an institution's computers.

Computer operators get hands-on experience with computer hardware

System Analyst

Before a data processing system can be set up a system analyst must first analyze and design the system. The analyst must determine how an organization will use their computer system, what data they will store, how they will access it, and how they expect the system to grow in the future. The success or failure of the data processing system will be primarily determined by how well the analyst does his or her job. The data base chapters emphasized the importance of carefully planning how a data base is to be structured. This type of planning gave you an introduction to what a system analyst does.

The following are characteristics a system analyst should possess:

- A good knowledge of the organization installing the data processing system including its goals and objectives.

- A comprehensive knowledge of both data-processing methods and the current software and hardware available.

- A working knowledge of programming languages and how they might be used to produce required software.

- The ability to work well with both technical and nontechnical personnel.

Most system analysts are college graduates who have majored in computer science or business administration or both. A good way to start preparing yourself to be a system analyst is to take programming courses in languages such as BASIC and Pascal and business courses such as management and accounting.

System Developer/ Programmer

After the system analyst has determined what type of system should be installed, it is the job of the system developer to provide the necessary software. This is accomplished by writing three types of programs:

- system programs - programs that operate the system's hardware. The disk operating system (DOS) booted on your microcomputer is an example of a system program.

- applications programs - programs that solve specific problems. In a business these might be problems such as customer billing or inventory control. The word processing, data base, and spreadsheet programs you have used are applications programs.

- program maintenance - many businesses need their programs expanded or changed to meet new demands or to correct errors. This is called program maintenance.

The following are characteristics a programmer should possess:

- A detailed knowledge of the programming language being used.

- A detailed knowledge of the organization or department for which the program is being written.

- An ability to reason analytically and pay close attention to details.

- Creativity to develop problem-solving strategies.

- Considerable patience to work out the fine details of a program and to discover the "bugs" it may contain.

- Knowledge of how the programs and computer hardware will interact.

The education required to be a programmer is usually determined by the needs of the employer. Many businesses employ programmers who have taken only technical school or junior college programming courses. Large or specialized companies, which need highly sophisticated programming, usually require college graduates. A good way to start in preparing for a career as a programmer is to take programming and computer science courses, as well as mathematics.

System Manager

Companies with large data processing requirements usually employ a manager who is responsible for running the Management Information Systems department (MIS). The MIS manager must organize the computer and human resources of the department in order to best achieve the organization's goals.

The following are characteristics a system manager should possess:

- A detailed understanding of the organization's goals.
- The ability to motivate and work closely with technical personnel.
- A detailed understanding of data-processing methods, hardware, and software.

A college degree in business administration with a concentration in information systems is desirable to be a system manager. Since a system manager is an administrator he or she will usually possess previous management experience.

Computer Scientist

The study of computer science is a very broad field involving many disciplines including science, electronics, and mathematics. A computer scientist often works in research at a university or computer manufacturer developing new computer applications software and hardware. It is computer scientists who first design and develop robots, natural language processors, or any of the other many applications that we have mentioned.

The following are characteristics a computer scientist should possess:

- A sense of curiosity.
- An aptitude for science and mathematics.
- Patience to perform experiments that may take years to perfect.

A computer scientist usually has both undergraduate and graduate school degrees. To prepare to be a computer scientist it is advisable to take science courses, especially physics, mathematics courses including calculus, and programming and computer science courses.

13.10 The Social and Ethical Consequences of Computers

The society in which we live has been so profoundly effected by computers that historians refer to the present time as "the information age." This is due to the computer's ability to store and manipulate large amounts of information (data). Computers have become such a dominant force that if all of them were to disappear much of our society would be unable to function. Because of computers we are evolving out of an industrial society and into an information society, much as over a hundred years ago we evolved from an agricultural society into an industrial one. Such fundamental changes in society cause disruptions which must be planned for. For this reason it is crucial that we consider both the social and ethical consequences of our increasing dependence on computers.

We have already mentioned the impact of telecommunications. By allowing people to work anywhere that telephones or satellite communications are available, we are likely to become a more diversified society. Large cities with their centralized offices will no longer be as necessary. This diversification could reduce traffic congestion, air pollution, and many of the other consequences of an urban society. Stock brokers or writers, for example, can now consider the benefits of working outside a city and yet still have all of the facilities they need readily available to them at home through a computer. Because of this, Alvin Toffler in his book "The Third Wave" called this the age of the "electronic cottage."

In our discussion of robots we mentioned their ability to work 24-hour days without vacations. While this is obviously a major benefit to an employer, it could have a negative impact on employees. Manufacturers are increasingly able to replace factory workers with machines, thereby increasing efficiency and saving money. This trend, however, also leads to increased unemployment of those factory workers who lack technical skills.

The argument is often used that new technologies such as robotics create jobs for the people who design, build, install, and service them. While this is true, these new jobs require well educated, highly trained people. For this reason it is important to think carefully about the educational requirements needed for employment. As we become an increasingly "high-tech" society, those properly prepared for technical jobs will be the most likely to find employment. In response to this problem many states have instituted programs to train laid-off factory workers so that they may enter technical fields.

13.11 The Right to Privacy

With computers impacting on our lives in an ever increasing number of ways, serious ethical questions arise over their use. By ethical questions we mean asking what are the right and wrong ways to use computers. As human beings we want to insure that our rights as individuals are not encroached upon by the misuse of these machines.

Probably the most serious problem created by computers is in invading our right to privacy. Because computers can store vast amounts of data we must decide what information is proper to store, what is improper, and who should have access to the information. Every time you use a credit card, make a phone call, withdraw money from the bank, reserve a flight on an airplane, or register to take a course at school a computer records the transaction. Using these records it would be possible to learn a great deal about you — where you have been, when you were there, and what you have done. Should this information be available to anyone who wants it?

Computers are also used to store information dealing with your credit rating, which determines your ability to borrow money. If you want to buy a car and finance it at the bank, the bank first checks your credit records on a computer to determine if you have a good credit rating. If you are able to purchase the car and then apply for automobile insurance, another computer will check to determine if you have traffic violations or have been involved in any activities which would make you a poor risk. How do you know if the information being used is accurate? To protect both your privacy and the accuracy of data stored about you, a number of laws have been passed.

The **Fair Credit Reporting Act of 1970** deals with data collected for use by credit, insurance and employment agencies. The act gives individuals the right to see information maintained about them. If a person is denied credit they are allowed to see the files used to make the credit determination. If any of the information is incorrect, the person has the right to have it changed. The act also restricts who may access credit files to only those with a court order or the written permission of the individual whose credit is being checked.

The **Privacy Act of 1974** restricts the way in which personal data can be used by federal agencies. Individuals must be permitted access to information stored about them and may correct any information that is incorrect. Agencies must insure both the security and confidentiality of any sensitive information. Although this law applies only to federal agencies, many states have adopted similar laws.

The **Financial Privacy Act of 1978** requires that a government authority have a subpoena, summons, or search warrant to access an individual's financial records. When such records are released, the financial institution must notify the individual of who has had access to them.

Laws such as the three mentioned above help to insure that the right to privacy is not infringed by data stored in computer files. Although implementing privacy laws has proven expensive and difficult, most people would agree that they are needed.

13.12 Protecting Computer Software and Data

Because computer software can be copied electronically it is easy to duplicate. Such duplication is usually illegal because the company producing the software is not paid for the copy. This has become an increasingly serious problem as the number of illegal software copies distributed by computer "pirates" has grown. Developing, testing, marketing, and supporting software is an expensive process. If the software developer is then denied rightful compensation, the future development of all software is jeopardized. Suppose for example that a programmer has written a piece of software which you like. If you illegally make copies and distribute them to your friends, that programmer loses income and may not be able to continue developing new software. Because most software is continually being updated and improved you could be denied these better versions.

Software companies are increasingly vigilant in detecting and prosecuting those who illegally copy their software. In recent years, software companies have actually made "raids" on businesses and searched their computers. A business found guilty of using illegally copied software can be fined, and their reputation damaged. Therefore, when using software it is important to use only legally acquired copies, and to not make illegal copies for others.

Another problem that is growing as computer use increases is the willful interference with or destruction of computer data. Because computers can transfer and erase data at high speeds, it makes them especially vulnerable to acts of vandalism. Newspapers have carried numerous reports of home computer users gaining access to large computer data bases. Sometimes these "hackers" change or erase data stored in the system. These acts are usually illegal and can cause very serious and expensive damage.

One especially harmful act is the planting of a "virus" into computer software. A virus is a series of instructions buried into a program which cause the computer to destroy data when given a certain signal. For example, the instructions to destroy data might wait until a certain time or date is reached before being executed. Because the virus is duplicated each time the software is copied it spreads, hence the name virus. This practice is illegal and can result in considerable damage. Computer viruses have become so widespread that there are now several computer programs that can be used to detect and erase viruses before they can damage any data.

Most people are becoming aware that the willful destruction of computer data is no different than any other vandalization of property. Since the damage is done electronically the result is often not as obvious as destroying physical property, but the consequences are much the same. It is estimated that computer crimes cost the nation billions of dollars each year.

13.13 The Ethical Responsibilities of the Programmer

Increasingly, computers are being used to make decisions in situations which can threaten human life. In one incident a patient being treated for cancer received five times the prescribed amount of radiation due to an error in the computer program operating the radiation machine. The consequences were a serious hazard to her life and health. As the use of computers to control medical equipment increases, this type of error may become more common.

It is extremely difficult, if not impossible, for a computer programmer to guarantee that a program will *always* operate properly. The programs used to control complicated devices contain millions of instructions, and as programs grow longer the likelihood of errors increases. What is a special cause for concern is the increased use of computers to control potentially dangerous devices such as aircraft, nuclear reactors, military weapons, or sensitive medical equipment. This places a strong ethical burden on the programmer to insure, as best he or she can, the reliability of computer software.

The Department of Defense (DOD) is currently supporting research aimed at detecting and correcting programming errors. Because it spends an estimated 18 billion dollars annually developing software, much of it for use in situations which can be life threatening, the DOD is especially interested in having reliable programs.

As capable as computers have proven to be, we must be cautious in allowing them to replace human beings in areas where judgement is crucial. Because we are intelligent, humans can often detect that something out of the ordinary has occurred and then take actions which have not been previously anticipated. Computers, on the other hand, will only do what they have been programmed to do, even if it is to perform a dangerous act.

We must also consider situations in which the computer can protect human life better than humans. For example, in the space program astronauts place their lives in the hands of computers which must continuously perform complicated calculations at very high speeds. No human being would be capable of doing the job as well as a computer. Computers are also routinely used to monitor seriously ill patients. Since computers are able to work 24-hours a day without becoming distracted or falling asleep, they probably perform such tasks better than most humans would.

13.14 Computing at Home

Most of the examples given in this text have involved using computers to help run a business or in the classroom. Personal computers are inexpensive enough that many people have them at home. As such, software has been created for the home user. Below we discuss several personal (non-business) applications for home use.

Games and Entertainment

Perhaps the most popular use for home computers is in the field of entertainment. As an example, software is available to produce graphics which can be recorded on a VCR. This allows the home user to produce professional-looking titles and animation for home videos. Other software can help organize a record collection or print labels for cassettes. There is even a program which turns the computer monitor into a "fish tank" by displaying images of coral, plants, and swimming fish.

Many people enjoy playing computer games at home. There are several different types available, but they generally fall into two categories: "simulations" and "role-playing." In simulations, the computer uses graphics to simulate an action such as driving a car. The most popular simulation is Flight Simulator in which the computer is used to fly a plane. By giving different commands, the "plane" can be made to take-off, accelerate, turn, land, etc. Flight Simulator is so realistic that pilots use it to practice flying techniques at home. There are also other forms of simulations available — card games such as bridge and poker, or sports like baseball and football. Many arcade-style simulations are also available to the home user.

Role-playing or fantasy games involve solving a complex puzzle by directing the actions of a character described on the screen. This is similar to reading a book, but being able to tell the character what to do. In role-playing games the user enters commands such as "go west" or "open the door" which the character follows. The player could be looking for treasure, or seeking information about a crime. Several popular role-playing games are named Zork, King's Quest, and Ultima.

Arts

The computer can be used by hobbyists in the arts. Artists can use drawing and painting software to produce pictures. Special input devices called "scanners" can read drawings and pictures into a file, which can then be modified using the computer. Photographers can use similar software to retouch slides and produce special effects.

Today's musicians are using a special type of computer output called "MIDI" — Musical Instrument Digital Interface. MIDI permits a computer to control synthesizers, allowing entire scores to be composed, edited, and performed using the computer. MIDI can also control recording and sound processing equipment, making the home recording studio easier to run.

Other software helps personal computer users to be more productive. For example there are several packages for administering home finances. These help develop a budget, keep track of expenses, and prepare taxes. Some even print checks to pay bills. Software can provide opportunities for home study in a variety of different fields: math, science, reading, and for specialized courses such as the SAT or real estate examination. This is called "computer aided instruction." Some students find that the ability to work at home at their own pace increases their understanding of the topic.

Computers have been used for many years by professional investors in an attempt to get an edge on the market. Home computer users can now have the same type of software for managing their investments. Modems can be used to download the latest stock prices immediately as they become available. Some brokerage firms allow home users to conduct transactions such as buying and selling stock using their computer.

These are not, of course, the only home applications for a computer. The Works software that you have learned could be used to create a family budget spreadsheet, keep recipes or addresses in a data base, or write personal letters in the word processor.

13.15 *Networking*

In Chapter One, we discussed the *time-sharing* technique used by mainframe computers — many people accessing the same computer at the same time. It is also possible to link microcomputers together, so that each person has access to the other's computer in what is called "networking."

In a network, microcomputers are connected by wires. Usually these computers are all in the same building, but they can be miles apart, even on different continents. Data is transmitted between the computers over the wires in a process similar to telecommunications. Networking is especially important to businesses which have computers in different departments or on different floors. As an example, suppose that you are preparing a report with a co-worker. If you are not using networked computers, the report file must be saved on a diskette and carried to the co-worker. When they are done with it, they must bring the diskette back to you. On a network, you could both have access to the file at the same time. This is especially helpful for large projects which require, for example, a spreadsheet from the accounting department's computer, a data base from the marketing group, and a letter from the advertising department. On a network, each file could be transmitted over the wires which link the computers, saving time and effort.

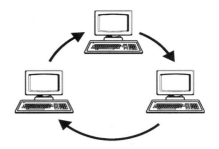

Networked computers can share files and send messages

There are several different types of networks, the most common being the LAN or Local Area Network. In a LAN, the networked computers are usually within a short distance of each other. The LAN operating system provides capabilities for sharing files, assigning passwords, and data security — preventing unauthorized users from reading or editing certain files. Some LANs have E-Mail services built-in, making it possible to send private messages between users. Rapid developments are being made in the area of the "wireless LAN," using technologies such as lasers, radio waves, and cellular phones to connect the computers in a LAN.

Desktop Publishing and Graphics

The popularity of computers has spawned a new generation of software applications geared to the presentation of information. This has made it possible for computers to be used to produce and manipulate art work, pictures, and the layout of documents in much the same way as word processors manipulate text. These applications, for example, allow a small business, educational institution, or individual to produce professional looking documents without the use of artists, designers, or typesetters. Below we discuss three of the most popular applications, and the technology that has made them available.

13.16 Laser Printers and Output Devices

Probably the most important advance which made these applications possible was the creation of a low-cost, dependable *laser printer*. The printer that you have most likely used is called an "impact" printer. Like a typewriter, impact printers require that an inked ribbon be pressed against paper to produce an image of the character. The most common impact printer is the "dot matrix" which prints characters as a series of small dots. Because the characters are made up of dots, dot matrix print can appear jagged, especially on curved letters:

```
This is an example of dot matrix print.
```

Examining the print closely shows how the dots are used to create a character:

A character produced by a dot-matrix printer is composed of small dots

Because they are not very precise, dot matrix printers are not very good at printing graphics, and their output often appears sloppy or unfinished.

A laser printer, on the other hand, uses a beam of light to draw each character on the page, employing a process similar to a photocopier. This allows the characters to be fully formed, eliminating the use of dots. A close examination of a character produced by a laser printer illustrates this:

T

A character produced by a laser printer is smoother

Laser printers are also able to produce graphics such as pictures and diagrams with the same level of clarity.

13.17 *Desktop Publishing*

One of the most popular uses for laser printers is in the field of "desktop publishing," or DTP. In desktop publishing, special software is used to allow persons not trained in art or layout to create professional looking documents using a personal computer and a laser printer. It is the purpose of desktop publishing software to combine text (created in a word processor) with illustrations (created by a graphics program) to produce the final document. Before desktop publishing existed, creating a document such as an advertising brochure was a complicated procedure, often involving many people:

1. A writer to create the text of the brochure.
2. An artist to produce the illustrations.
3. A typesetter to print the text.
4. A layout person to combine the text and illustrations into the completed brochure using scissors and glue.

Now a single person can perform all of these tasks using a computer. A major advantage of using desktop publishing software is that changes can be made to a document in much the same way as changes are made to text using a word processor. Illustrations and text can be added or deleted, changed in size, or the whole layout redone — all on a computer screen.

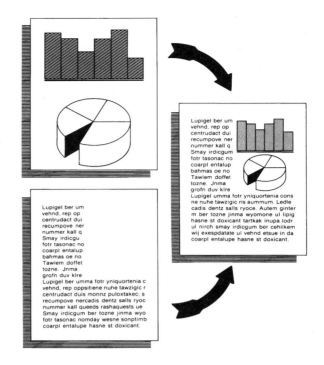

DTP software combines graphics and text into one file

By performing the layout of a document on the computer screen instead of on paper, changes may easily be made. Different layouts can be created and printed until the desired combination is found. Once completed, the final version can be printed and the document saved on disk so that it can be edited or reprinted at any later time.

Three of the most commonly used desktop publishing programs are *PageMaker*, *Ventura Publisher*, and *Quark Express*. Less powerful and inexpensive programs such as Publish It!, First Publisher, and PrintShop allow DTP documents to be created and printed on dot matrix printers. Most of these packages contain collections of prepared illustrations called "clip art" which can be included in whatever document is produced, often eliminating the need for an artist.

13.18 *Graphics and Illustration Software*

Using specialized software it is possible to create graphic images on the computer. By graphic images, we mean non-text items such as drawings, photographs, charts, logos, etc. The advantage of using a computer rather than drawing on paper is that the image can then be manipulated; changed in size, rotated, etc. When an artist wants to make a change to a picture drawn on paper, he or she must either use an eraser or start from scratch. Using graphics software, the artist could instead draw the picture on a computer screen. If changes were then desired, they could be made to the picture stored in the computer's memory. When the final version had been created, it could be printed in black and white using a laser printer, or in color using a special, color printer. The pictures you placed in a word processed document in Chapter 4 were created using graphics software.

An Introduction to Computing Using Microsoft Works

There are several powerful programs available for creating and editing graphics images. Several of these are *Adobe Illustrator*, *Aldus Freehand*, and *CorelDraw*. Most require the use of a specialized input device to aid in the drawing. The most popular of these devices are the mouse and the drawing tablet. These devices are used to translate the movements of the artist's hand onto the computer screen.

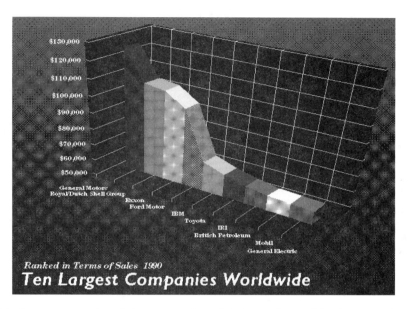

This is an example of the type of sophisticated graphic that can be produced by a graphics program

In addition to allowing the easy modification of a graphic, illustration software often has a variety of advanced tools that would be difficult or time consuming to duplicate manually. For example, suppose a business hires an artist to design a logo. Using pen and paper, the artist would then sketch the logo and add any colors using paint. Suppose the artist choose green as the color for the logo and painted it on paper. If the company then wanted to see what the logo looked like in red, the artist would have to start from scratch, drawing the outline, and painting it red. If the logo was instead prepared using illustration software, the artist could move the cursor to the desired location on the screen, issue a command which said "Change this green area to red" and print the version. Other examples of editing options include changing line widths, erasing lines and objects in a diagram, and changing the size or position of objects. Once complete, the final graphic can be saved in a file on disk, similar to a data base or spreadsheet, that could be edited or reprinted at a later date.

Another advantage to using illustration software is that any graphics produced can easily be placed in a desktop-published document. Most DTP software packages can read the files produced by illustration software, and place a graphic directly into a DTP document. Some DTP packages can even perform basic editing on the image, allowing it to be scaled (made larger or smaller), rotated, or clipped (choosing to display only part of the graphic).

13.19 How do we face the future?

In this text we have presented the history of computing, showed you how to word process, use a database, and a spreadsheet, and have considered the future of computing. Our hope is that you are excited by computers and realize the tremendous potential they have to serve us in a wide variety of ways. We also hope that you have been made aware of how computers might be misused. It is therefore the duty of each one of us, as responsible citizens, to insure that the awesome power given to us by computers be used only to benefit mankind.

Chapter Summary

This chapter began by discussing the future of computing. One of the most important advances in the field of computing has been in telecommunications, which means the sending of computer data over phone lines. Modems are used both to transmit and receive computer data. Because of telecommunications many people may be able to work at home.

A popular form of telecommunications is the electronic bulletin board which allows users to transmit and receive messages. A similar form of telecommunications is electronic mail (E-Mail) where single users are able to receive messages meant only for them.

The continued development of microprocessors will effect many products including automobiles and home electronic devices. With their ability to make simple decisions, microprocessors can automate many of the functions performed by these devices.

Using computers to make decisions normally made by human beings is called artificial intelligence. Although computers cannot think, they can be programmed to make decisions which, for example, will allow them to play chess. Expert systems are a form of artificial intelligence where a computer is programmed with a set of rules that can solve a problem - producing the same solution a human expert would. Credit card companies, automobile manufacturers and hospitals are a few of the organizations currently using expert systems.

Recognizing spoken words and translating them into digital form is called speech recognition which involves natural language processing, a field of artificial intelligence that attempts to translate a sentence into its separate parts and understand its meaning. Numerous problems face the successful development of language processing systems.

A robot is a machine that can be programmed and also move. Robots are currently used to perform simple manufacturing tasks. When natural language processing and artificial intelligence programs are perfected, the use of robots will increase.

Careers in computing were discussed in this chapter and the educational requirements needed to pursue them. Careers which required only a high school education as well as those requiring a college education were presented.

Historians refer to the present time as the "information age" due to the computer's ability to store and manipulate large amounts of data. As the use of computers increases they will profoundly effect society including what jobs will be available and the length of the work week.

A problem created by computers is their potential for invading our right to privacy. Laws have been passed to protect us from the misuse of data stored in computers.

Because computer software is easy to copy, illegal copies are often made, denying software manufacturers of rightful compensation. Another problem has been the willful destruction of computer files by erasing data or planting a "virus" into programs that can spread when the programs are copied.

As computers are increasingly used to made decisions in situations which can threaten human life it becomes the responsibility of programmers to do there best to insure the reliability of the software they have developed. We must continue to be cautious not to replace human beings with computers in areas where judgement is crucial.

The use of personal computers in the home has become popular. These computers are often used to play games and to run applications such as Works.

In a network, microcomputers are connected by wires that transmit data between them. The most common network is the Local Area Network (LAN) which allows files to be shared between a number of computers.

Desktop publishing software has made it possible for computers to produce and manipulate, art work, pictures and the layout of documents. Laser printers, which employ a beam of light to draw characters on a page, are often used in desktop publishing applications.

Special software is used to create graphics images such as drawings, photographs, charts, etc. on the computer. This software allows the images to be easily manipulated and modified.

Vocabulary

Artificial intelligence - Using computers to make decisions which would normally be made by a human being.

Baud rate - Rate at which characters of data are transmitted. One baud represents the transmission of one character per second.

Desktop publishing - using special software to create professional looking documents on a computer.

Download - To transfer a message or computer file from a bulletin board or E-Mail service computer to another computer.

Electronic bulletin board - (BBS) Telecommunications service which allows subscribers using a computer and modem to transmit messages that can be received by all the other subscribers.

Electronic mail - (E-Mail) Telecommunications service which allows a person using a computer and modem to send a message to another person's computer.

Expert system - System programmed to produce the same solution a human expert would if asked to solve the same problem.

Graphics - drawings, photographs, charts, etc. used in a document.

Hacker - Person who uses a computer and modem to enter a computer system without authorization.

Information service - A company that provides different telecommunications services, usually for a fee.

Laser printer - a printer that employs a beam of light to draw characters.

Local Area Network (LAN) - the most common method of networking microcomputers so that they can share data.

Modem - Device which translates binary data into waves and waves back into binary data so that computer data can be sent over telephone lines.

Natural language processing - Using a computer to recognize spoken words and then translate them into digital form.

Network - connecting computers by wires so that data can be transmitted between them.

Pirate - Person who illegally copies computer software.

Robot - Machine which can be programmed and is also capable of motion.

Simulation - where a computer produces information similar to that produced by a real world situation (i.e. flight simulation).

Telecommunications - Sending of computer data over telephone lines.

Upload - To transfer a message or computer file from a computer to a bulletin board or E-Mail service computer.

Virus - Program which hides within another program for the purpose of destroying or altering data.

Reviews

Sections 13.1 - 13.3

1. Describe four databases that you would like to be able to access using telecommunications. State why each of them would be useful to you.

2. Besides those listed in the text, list three occupations where people would be able to work at home rather than in an office using telecommunications.

3. What is the difference between an electronic bulletin board and electronic mail?

4. If all of the students in your class had computers and modems at home, in what ways could they be used by your classmates and instructor?

An Introduction to Computing Using Microsoft Works

Sections 13.4 - 13.5

5. What tasks do microprocessors perform in new model automobiles?

6. What is artificial intelligence?

7. a) What devices owned by your family contain microprocessors and what are they used for?
   b) What devices would you like to see include microprocessors? Why? What tasks would the microprocessors perform?

8. State three questions you would ask to determine which was the human and which the computer when playing Turing's Imitation Game. Asking "Are you the computer?" is not fair!

Sections 13.6 - 13.8

9. What did the computer program Mycin do?

10. List four jobs where you think expert systems could be used to help the people performing the jobs. Explain why the systems would be helpful.

11. List four jobs where expert systems could probably not be used, and explain why.

12. Would an expert system be helpful to you in selecting clothes to buy? Explain why or why not.

13. What are some of the difficulties being encountered in the development of natural language processing systems?

14. Why should we be careful in trusting expert systems? What do they lack that humans possess?

15. If you could have a robot built to your own specifications, what would you have it be capable of doing?

Section 13.9

The six computer careers mentioned in this chapter include:

(1) system analyst
(2) system developer / programmer
(3) system manager
(4) computer operator
(5) data-entry operator
(6) computer scientist

16. Which of the above careers require only a:

   a) high school diploma
   b) college diploma
   c) college and graduate school degrees

17. For each of the following students list the careers above that he or she should consider:
    a) a student who likes mathematics.
    b) a student who wants to be involved in the management of a business.
    c) a student who wants to work in the development of rocket guidance systems.
    d) a student who likes to think through problems in a methodical, logical way.

Sections 13.10 - 13.13

18. Alvin Toffler named his book "The Third Wave." What were the first two waves?

19. What is meant by the term "high-tech" society?

20. a) How do you believe society will benefit from the information age?
    b) What might be the negative aspects of the information age?

21. How can a computer be used to invade your privacy?

22. What can you do if you are turned down for credit at a bank and believe that the data used to deny credit is inaccurate?

23. What is necessary for a federal government authority to access an individual's financial records? What must the authority do after accessing the records?

24. What ethical responsibilities does a programmer have when writing a program that will be used to design a bridge? Can the programmer absolutely guarantee that the program will operate properly? Why?

Sections 13.14 - 13.19

25. Describe how 3 different organizations might make use of computer networks.

26. How does a laster printer differ from a dot matrix printer?

27. a) What are 4 advantages of using desktop publishing?
    b) Describe 3 organizations that might make use of desktop publishing.

An Introduction to Computing Using Microsoft Works

Appendix A –
Keyboard Commands and Functions

The following keyboard commands are grouped by application area. A complete list may be found by selecting the Keyboard Guide command from the Help menu. A list of functions which may be used in the spreadsheet and data base is given at the end of this list.

Word Processor Keyboard Commands

The following keyboard commands may be executed from the Word Processor screen.

Function keys:

F1	Help
Shift-F1	Tutorial Lesson
F3	Move highlighted block
Shift-F3	Copy highlighted block
F5	Goto a specified page
Ctrl-F6	Jump to next window
Ctrl-Shift-F6	Jump to previous window
F7	Repeat last Search
Shift-F7	Repeat last Copy or Formatting command
F8	Start or extend highlight
Shift-F8	Reduce highlight
F9	Paginate now

Cursor Movement:

Ctrl-Left	Left one word
Ctrl-Right	Right one word
Ctrl-Up	Up one paragraph
Ctrl-Down	Down one paragraph
Ctrl-PgUp	Top of current screen
Ctrl-PgDn	Bottom of current screen
Ctrl-Home	Beginning of file
Ctrl-End	End of file

Selection:

F8 (once)	Starts highlighting and any movement key will extend highlight
F8 (twice)	Highlights word
F8 (three times)	Highlights sentence
F8 (four times)	Highlights paragraph
F8 (five times)	Highlights entire document
Shift-F8	Reduces highlight to previous level
Shift-Arrow	Highlights in direction of arrow
Escape	Terminates highlighting. Pressing any movement key will remove the highlight

Text Formatting:

`Ctrl-+`	Makes highlighted text superscript
`Ctrl-=`	Makes highlighted text subscript
`Ctrl-B`	Makes highlighted text bold
`Ctrl-I`	Makes highlighted text italic
`Ctrl-U`	Makes highlighted text underlined
`Ctrl-SpaceBar`	Removes all applied formats from highlighted text (Plain text)

Paragraph Formatting:

`Ctrl-1`	Single spaces current paragraph
`Ctrl-2`	Double spaces current paragraph
`Ctrl-C`	Centers current paragraph
`Ctrl-J`	Justifies current paragraph
`Ctrl-L`	Left-aligns current paragraph
`Ctrl-R`	Right-aligns current paragraph
`Ctrl-H`	Creates hanging indent
`Ctrl-G`	Removes hanging indent
`Ctrl-N`	Creates nested indent
`Ctrl-M`	Removes nested indent
`Ctrl-X`	Removes all formats from current paragraph (Normal paragraph)

Editing:

`Alt-Backspace`	Reverse previous editing action (Undo)
`Ctrl-Enter`	Inserts manual page break
`Tab`	Inserts Tab character and moves cursor to next stop
`Ctrl-D`	Displays current date when printed
`Ctrl-Shift-D`	Displays current date in long form when printed
`Ctrl-F`	Displays name of file when printed
`Ctrl-P`	Displays current page number when printed
`Ctrl-T`	Displays current time when printed
`Ctrl-:` (colon)	Inserts current time into document
`Ctrl-;` (semi-colon)	Inserts current date into document

Data Base Keyboard Commands

The following keyboard commands may be executed when using the Data Base.

Function keys:

`F1`	Help
`Shift-F1`	Tutorial Lesson
`F2`	Edit contents of current entry
`F3`	Move highlighted data
`Shift-F3`	Copy highlighted data
`F5`	Goto a specified record or field
`Ctrl-F6`	Jump to next window
`Ctrl-Shift-F6`	Jump to previous window
`F7`	Repeat last Search
`Shift-F7`	Repeat last Copy or Formatting command
`F8`	Start highlight in List view only
`Ctrl-F8`	Highlight row in List view
`Shift-F8`	Highlight column in List view
`Shift-Ctrl-F8`	Highlights entire data base
`F9`	Switch between Form view and List view

An Introduction to Computing Using Microsoft Works

F10	Apply a query
Shift-F10	View report on screen

Cursor Movement:

Tab	Next field in Form view
Shift-Tab	Previous field in Form view
Ctrl-End	End of file
Ctrl-Home	Beginning of file
Ctrl-PgDn	Next record in Form view
Ctrl-PgUp	Previous record in Form view

Formatting:

Ctrl-4	Currency format
Ctrl-5	Percent format
Ctrl-,	Comma format
Ctrl-B	Bold
Ctrl-I	Italic
Ctrl-U	Underline
Ctrl-L	Left align
Ctrl-C	Center
Ctrl-R	Right align
Ctrl-G	General
Ctrl-SpaceBar	Remove formats

Special:

Ctrl-' (single quote)	Copies contents of same field in previous record
Ctrl-: (colon)	Inserts current time into field
Ctrl-; (semi-colon)	Inserts current date into field

Spreadsheet Keyboard Commands

The following keyboard commands may be executed from the Spreadsheet screen.

Function keys:

F1	Help
Shift-F1	Tutorial Lesson
F2	Edit contents of current cell
F3	Move highlighted cells
Shift-F3	Copy highlighted cells
F4	Absolute cell reference
F5	Goto a specified cell
Ctrl-F6	Jump to next window
Ctrl-Shift-F6	Jump to previous window
F7	Repeat last Search
Shift-F7	Repeat last Copy or Formatting command
F8	Start highlight
Ctrl-F8	Highlight row
Shift-F8	Highlight column
Shift-Ctrl-F8	Highlights entire spreadsheet
F9	Calculate now
F10	Exit CHART screen
Shift-F10	View chart on screen

Cursor Movement:

`Tab`	To next unlocked cell
`Ctrl-End`	End of file
`Ctrl-Home`	Beginning of file

Formatting:

`Ctrl-4`	Currency format
`Ctrl-5`	Percent format
`Ctrl-,`	Comma format
`Ctrl-B`	Bold
`Ctrl-I`	Italic
`Ctrl-U`	Underline
`Ctrl-L`	Left align
`Ctrl-C`	Center
`Ctrl-R`	Right align
`Ctrl-G`	General
`Ctrl-SpaceBar`	Remove formats

Special:

`Ctrl-'` (single quote)	Copies contents of previous cell
`Ctrl-:` (colon)	Inserts current time into cell
`Ctrl-;` (semi-colon)	Inserts current date into cell

Functions

The following is a partial list of functions that may be placed in a spreadsheet cell or in the formula for a calculated field or query in a data base. A complete list is given in the Works manual supplied by Microsoft.

In the discussion that follows

<value> may be replaced by:

a single value (such as 10)
a cell reference (such as C5)
an expression that evaluates to a single value (such as C5 * 2)
a field reference (such as GPA)

<range> may be replaced by:

a list of cells separated by commas (such as A1, B12, D5)
a continuous range (A1:A10)
a mixture of both separated by commas (A1, B1:B5, C3, C5:C7)
a field reference (such as GPA)

Mathematical & Statistical Functions:

ABS(<value>)
Returns the absolute value of <value>: ABS(10) returns 10, ABS(-10) returns 10.

ACOS(<value>)
Returns the arccosine of <value> in radians. Value must be between -1 and +1.

ASIN(<value>)
Returns the arcsine of <value> in radians. Value must be between -1 and +1.

ATAN (<value>)
Returns the arctangent of <value> in radians.

ATAN2 (<Xvalue>, <Yvalue>)
Returns the arctangent in radians of an angle defined by the coordinates <Xvalue>, <Yvalue>.

AVG (<range>)
Returns the average of the values in <range>. Cells which contain text are treated as 0.

COS (<value>)
Returns the cosine of <value> where <value> is measured in radians.

COUNT (<range>)
Returns the number of non-blank cells in <range>.

EXP (<value>)
Returns e raised to the <value> power.

INT (<value>)
Returns the integer value of <value>: ABS(1.9) returns 1.

LN (<value>)
Returns the natural logarithm (base e) of <value>.

LOG (<value>)
Returns the base 10 logarithm of <value>. <value> must be positive.

MAX (<range>)
Returns the largest value in <range>.

MIN (<range>)
Returns the smallest value in <range>.

MOD (<value1>, <value2>)
Returns the remainder of <value1> + <value2>. <value2> may not be 0.

PI ()
Returns the constant 3.1415..., π (pi). No argument is used.

RAND ()
Returns a random number between 0 and 1. No argument is used.

ROUND (<value>, <decimals>)
Returns <value> rounded to <decimals> decimal places. When <decimals> is 0, <value> is rounded to the nearest integer.

SIN (<value>)
Returns the sine of <value> where <value> is measured in radians.

SQRT (<value>)
Returns the square root of <value>. <value> must be positive.

STD (<range>)
Returns the standard deviation of the values in <range>.

SUM (<range>)
Returns the total of the values in <range>.

TAN (<value>)
Returns the tangent of <value> where <value> is measured in radians.

VAR (<range>)
Returns the variance of the values in <range>.

Financial Functions:
CTERM (<Rvalue>, <Fvalue>, <Pvalue>)
Returns the number of compounding periods required for <Pvalue> investment to grow to <Fvalue> at <Rvalue> interest.

FV (<Pvalue>, <Rvalue>, <Tvalue>)
Returns the future value of an investment where <Pvalue> is a periodic payment, <Rvalue> is the interest rate, and <Tvalue> is the term.

PMT (<Pvalue>, <Rvalue>, <Tvalue>)
Returns the periodic payment on an installment loan where <Pvalue> is the principal, <Rvalue> is the interest rate, and <Tvalue> is the term.

RATE (<Fvalue>, <Pvalue>, <Tvalue>)
Returns the fixed interest rate required to turn an investment of <Pvalue> into <Fvalue> when <Tvalue> is the term.

TERM (<Pvalue>, <Rvalue>, <Fvalue>)
Returns the term required to turn payments of <Pvalue> into <Fvalue> when <Rvalue> is the interest rate.

Date / Time Functions:
SECOND (<Time>)
MINUTE(<Time>)
HOUR(<Time>)
Returns the seconds, minutes, or hours portion of a time.

DAY (<Date>)
MONTH(<Date>)
YEAR(<Date>)
Returns the day, month, or year portion of a date.

NOW ()
Returns the current date and time. No argument is used.

Special Functions:
CHOOSE (<value>, <option$_0$>, <option$_1$>, ...)
Returns the <option$_0$> if <value> is 0, <option$_1$> if <value> is 1, and so on. <options> may be text.

HLOOKUP (<value>, <range>, <rows>)
Locates cell in first row of <range> the contains the largest value which is less than or equal to <value>. Returns contents of cell which is <rows> below that cell.

IF (<condition>, <true value>, <false value>)
Returns the <true value> if <condition> is true, <false value> if false. Both <true value> and <false value> may be text.

VLOOKUP (<value>, <range>, <columns>)
Locates cell in first column of <range> the contains the largest value which is less than or equal to <value>. Returns contents of cell which is <columns> to the right of that cell.

APPENDIX B –
DOS Commands and Making Backups

File Names

Every program and file on a disk is identified by a unique name. For this reason you have specified a file name each time you saved a new file. The general format of a file name is:

```
<name>.<extension>
```

The <name> part may be from one to eight characters long. The <extension>, which is optional, may be up to three characters long. Works automatically adds standard extensions to the file names you enter to distinguish between files produced by different applications:

Extension	Application
.WCM	Communications
.WDB	Data Base
.WKS	Spreadsheet
.WPS	Word Processor

Only the following characters are allowed as part of a name or extension:

```
Letters: A, B, ... Y, Z
Numbers: 0, 1, ... 8, 9
Special Characters: # ) ( @ ! } { $ % & - _ ~
```

While the special characters shown above may be used, it is usually best to limit file names to only letters and numbers. Also, because Works needs them to distinguish which application produced the file, it is a good idea to let Works supply the default extension when a file is saved. The following are examples of valid file names:

```
CHAPTER1.WPS
STUDENT.WDB
89GRADES.WKS
COMPUSRV.WCM
```

Using DOS Commands From Works

Works normally controls the creating and saving of files. There are times, however, when you will need to have access to certain DOS commands to manage and organize your files. As an example, you might

want to delete old data files from your disk. Works allows certain DOS commands to be accessed by selecting the File Management command from the File menu which lists the DOS commands which may be accessed:

The File Management dialog box lists DOS commands which may be executed from Works

File Management gives you access to powerful commands which can change and delete files. <u>There are several files on your Works disks which should never be changed.</u> These have names such as WORKS.EXE, SCREEN.VID, TEMPLATE.1, and SPELL.OVL, and are required to run the Works program. A good rule of thumb to follow is, if the file is not a Works data file (.WPS, .WDB, .WKS, .WCM) then it should not be altered (deleted, copied, etc.). Below we discuss the File Management commands and their uses.

COPY FILE

The Copy File command is used to duplicate a file. The file to be copied is selected from the **Files** list which displays files in the current directory. The drive and directory may be changed by selecting the appropriate drive letter or directory name from the **Directories** list. Once a file to be copied has been selected, it may be saved under a new name or to a new location.

DELETE FILE

The Delete File command is used to remove unwanted files from the disk. Once selected, a list of files that may be deleted from the current directory is displayed. A file is deleted by highlighting or typing its name. A warning is given before the file is deleted:

Select Cancel to terminate the deletion of a file

Note that an open file (one currently displayed on the Works screen) may not be deleted. Care should be taken when using this command, because once erased, a file may not be recovered. Remember, only Works data files (file names ending with .WPS, .WDB, .WKS, .WCM) should be deleted.

RENAME FILE

The Rename File command is used to change the name of a file. Once selected, a list of files that may be renamed is shown. A file is renamed by highlighting or typing its name and selecting OK. A dialog box then asks for the new name:

The Rename File dialog box

CREATE DIRECTORY

It is convenient to organize files by a type or characteristic into separate directories, like the different folders in a filing cabinet. For example, files used at work could be stored in a directory named WORK. The Create Directory command is used to make a new directory. Once the command is selected, a list of the current directories is shown:

The Create Directory dialog box

When a new directory name is entered it becomes a sub-directory of the currently selected directory. When files are now saved they may be placed in this directory.

REMOVE DIRECTORY

The Remove Directory command is used to remove unwanted directory names. Once selected, a list of the current directories is shown. To remove a directory, select the directory name. Note: one of the protections that DOS offers is that a directory cannot be removed unless all files in that directory have be deleted.

SET DATE & TIME

The Set Date & Time command is used to alter the current date and time. Once selected, the computer will ask for the new date and time:

Selecting OK sets the computer's clock and calendar

Pressing Escape will restore the previous values.

COPY DISK

The Copy Disk command duplicates an entire disk. The user is first prompted to enter the source disk (disk to copy from) and then subsequently the target disk (disk to copy to):

The source (copy from) disk drive is selected, followed
by the target (copy to)

All of the data on the source disk is copied to the target disk leaving the source data intact. Any previously saved data on the target disk will be lost. If you wish to return to File Management after selecting this command, press Ctrl-Break (or Ctrl-C). <u>Note</u>: Copy Disk requires that a copy of the DOS file DISKCOPY.COM be available. If it is not, Works displays the message "Bad command or file name" and returns to File Management. Any old information previously saved on the target disk is destroyed. If the disk being copied to has not been previously formatted (see below), Copy Disk will format it automatically.

FORMAT DISK

The Format Disk command initializes a disk so that files can be saved on the disk. Before a disk can be used by the computer it must be formatted. The computer will ask which drive contains the disk to be formatted:

Blank disks must be formatted before they may be used to store files

After the new disk has been inserted and a key pressed, the computer will format the disk and print a status report when finished. Because formatting removes all previously stored information, only new or empty disks should be formatted. Formatting a disk that contains data will erase the data. If you wish to return to File Management after selecting this command, press Ctrl-Break (or Ctrl-C). Note: Format Disk requires that a copy of the DOS file FORMAT.COM be available. If it is not, Works displays the message "Bad command or file name" and returns to File Management.

●●●

The Importance of Backups

Files that you saved have been stored on diskettes or on a hard disk. These files have taken time and effort to create. Businesses and institutions that use computers have even more time invested in the data stored on their disks, and often that data is invaluable because it cannot be replaced. Chapter Two lists several sources of potential disk damage. The most common threat is the invisible magnetic radiation which surrounds us: computer monitors, electric motors, even the small magnet found in many paper clip holders. All generate sufficient magnetic radiation to destroy the files stored on a disk. Because computer disks are susceptible to different types of damage it is important to keep copies called *backups*, which are used should the original files become damaged.

Creating Backups of Important Data

Although it is easy to create backups of a file or disk, many people do not take the time to do so. There are businesses that have lost thousands of dollars when their only copy of an important file such as a client list data base or accounts receivable spreadsheet has been damaged.

The simplest way to create a backup of your Works files is to make a copy of your data disk. This can be accomplished using the Copy Disk command described in the previous section. The procedure for making a backup copy of a disk is:

1. Boot DOS and start Works.
2. Select the Copy Disk command from the File Management list.
3. Select 'Disk to copy from' as Disk drive A and 'Disk to copy to' as Disk drive B.
4. Place your data disk (the disk to be copied) in drive A:.
5. Place a blank disk in drive B: and press Enter.

When Enter is pressed, a complete copy of the data stored on the disk in drive A: is made on the disk in drive B:. The entire process takes only a few minutes. Once created, the disk in drive B: is a backup copy and should be stored in a safe place, away from the original disk.

A backup copy of a single file can be made using the Copy File command described above. For example, suppose you want to make a copy of a Works database file named CLIENTS.WDB on a different disk:

1. Boot DOS and start Works.
2. Select the Copy File command from the File Management list.
3. Select CLIENTS.WDB from the list of files.
4. Place a formatted disk in drive B:.
5. Select drive B: from the Directories list ([-B-]) and press Enter.

When Enter is pressed a copy of the CLIENTS.WDB file is placed on the disk in drive B:. The disk in drive B: now contains a backup copy of the selected file and should be stored in a safe place, away from the original disk.

It is also possible to create backup copies of Works data files from within Works by using the Save As command from the File menu. To do this open the file and select Save As. If the backup copy is to be saved on the disk in drive A:, type

A:*FileName*

when asked for the file name on the Save As dialog box, replacing *FileName* with the name of the backup file (e.g., CLIENTS2.WDB). Do not type a space between the "A:" and the file name. When Enter is pressed, a copy of the current file will be saved on the backup disk in drive A:.

For extra security, you can also save a file under another name on the same disk. For example, use Save As to create a copy CLIENTS.WDB using the file name CLIENTS.BAK (for BAcKup). This will protect you should something happen to the original CLIENTS.WDB file. Works can be told to create a backup copy automatically using the 'Make backup' option on the Save dialog box:

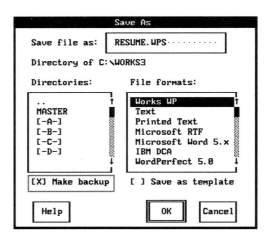

Selecting 'Make backup' tells Works to make a backup copy of the file with every Save

When this option is selected, each time the file is saved an additional copy is made with a new file name extension: .BPS for word processor backups, .BDB for data base, and .BKS for spreadsheets. These files are listed at the bottom of the list in the Other Files section of the Open Existing File dialog box:

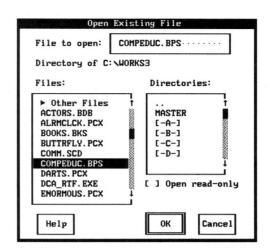

Backup files are listed in the Open Existing File dialog box

You should only open the backup copy if the original file has been damaged in some way.

It is important to keep backup disks in a different location than the original copies. That way, the chances of both copies being destroyed are low. For example, if you keep your Works data diskette at school, keep your backup copy at home. Businesses often store their backup copies in special fire-proof safes or in safe-deposit boxes at a bank. Several companies have been created just to provide safe "off-site storage" for computer data.

Remember, the data stored on a diskette is not permanent and may easily be erased or damaged. Following the diskette handling rules given in Chapter Two, and keeping backup copies of important files in a safe place are the best insurance against data loss.

Appendix C -
Keyboarding Skills

Learning to Touch Type

The ability to "touch type" is especially helpful in using a computer. When touch typing you place your hands on the keyboard in a position which allows you to strike any of the keys without looking at your hands. The advantage of learning how to do this is that you can keep your eyes on the material you are typing. You will also be able to type with greater accuracy and speed than you could using the "hunt and peck" method where you must search for each key before striking it.

Before you begin to type it is important to have your hands and body in their proper positions. Your hands should be placed lightly on the keyboard with the slightly curved fingers of the left hand on the keys **ASDF** and the right hand on the **JKL;** keys. The left pinky is placed on the **A** key with the other fingers of the left hand placed on the **SDF** keys. The right pinky is placed on the semicolon (;) key and the other fingers of the right hand on the **LKJ** keys. The right thumb is placed on the space bar. This is called the "home" position.

Place the chair you are sitting in so that your arms reach out leaving the elbows loosely at your side. Sit in a relaxed but erect position with both feet flat on the floor. Maintaining proper posture will help to keep your body from tensing. Try not to slouch or bend over the keyboard. The proper posture is shown in the diagram:

Always maintain proper posture when touch typing

To touch type it is necessary to memorize the location of each of the keys on the keyboard. This is best accomplished by learning just a few keys at a time which you will do when performing the following Lessons. Developing an even, smooth rhythm as you type is important. You want to strike each of the keys with the same pressure using a steady pace. To help you develop speed and accuracy a Timed Practice in most lessons ask you to keep track of how many words per minute you are typing and the number of mistakes being made.

Each of the following lessons makes use of the Works word processor. Therefore, we will begin by learning how to access and use the word processor. Read pages 2-1 through 2-6 in Chapter Two and performing the steps in Practice 1 on the computer to learn how to boot DOS and run Works.

Lesson 1 - The Home Row: ASDF

Start by booting DOS and Works as described in the beginning of Chapter Two. Press the Enter key twice to create a new Word Processor document. A blank word processor screen is displayed. You will perform each of the typing lessons on this screen. Note the blinking underline at the top left-hand side of the screen which is called the "cursor." It indicates where characters typed into the word processor will appear.

Place your hands on the keyboard in the "home" position described above with the left hand on the keys **ASDF** and right hand on the keys **JKL;**. The right thumb is placed on the space bar.

Type the following letters and when you finish each line, press the Enter key with your right pinky. The cursor will move down one line and to the left side of the screen. Note that the semicolon (;) is normally followed by a space when typing actual material. Do not look at your hands while you type, look only at the picture of the keyboard below.

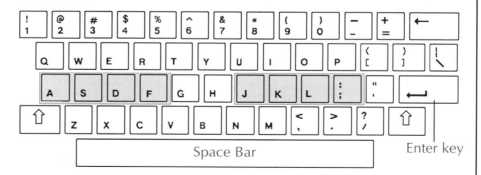

Always place your fingers on the home row *when beginning to type*

Practice 1.1

```
1    aaa ;;; aaa ;;; sss lll sss lll ddd kkk ddd kkk fff jjj fjf
2    aaa sss sas asa sss aaa sas aaa sss sas aaa sss sas sss a;a
3    ddd ada ddd daa dss dad dsd ddd sss aaa ads asd asd dad sls
4    sss aaa ddd ddd ssa dad dsd dsa dsa dss daa aaa sss dda dkd
5    fff fff faf fss fss fas fas fad ffd faa fsa ffs fsa fad fjf
6    fss saf fad sfa fss fad fsa sda fad aff fsd sff ffa sss fjf
7    jjj jjj jja jaf jfj jdj jfs jja jad jsf jja jda jaf jjj jfj
8    jad daj fja das saj jjs jsa daf sfj jad faj jjj jad jaa dkd
9    kkk kka kkk kak kjk kss kkj kak ksa ksk kfk kkf kkk kjj kdk
10   kad dak sak adk sak akk kak jak jak dak ask sak kkk kjk ala
11   lll lll lff llk lak las lad lfl lld lll lsk lfl lkl ljl lal
12   lsl sal fal dsl lsl llf jal all sal lsa fal lll lkl lal a;a
13   ; ; ; ; fa; da; sa; da; fj; sa; da; jl; ; ; ; sa; lad; jak;
14   dad dad lad lad sad sad add add lad ask dad fall fall falls
15   ask ask fad fad ads ads dad lass lass sass sass salad salad
```

Practice 1.2

```
1    ;;; aaa lll sss kkk ddd jjj fff ;a; a;a lsl sls kdk dkd jfj
2    sas saa asa asa dfd fdf ffd dfd das sad sad das las das ad;
3    jjkk kkjj jkjk kjkj jkkj l; l; jkl kjl; dakl kald jakl jakl
4    jjk jjl jj; jaj ksk lal las las kad kad laf laf la; ja; la;
5    aad aas aaf aaj aak aal aa; fad fad dad dad lad lad sad sad
6    dask jljl fafa fajk ddl; jadl lads lads dads dads sads jakl
7    asks asks dads fall lass fads lask fads lads ffjj kkll fkf;
8    asks dads fall fads lask adds lass fall alls lads dads sad;
```

Repeat the Practices above until you can type the keys without referring to the keyboard diagram.

When you have completed the lesson and want to leave Works select the Exit command from the File menu by holding down the **Alt** key and pressing **F** and then pressing **X**. You will then be asked if you wish to save the file. Select No by pressing **N**. The computer may now be turned off.

Lesson 2 - RTYU

In this Lesson you will learn the **RTYU** keys.

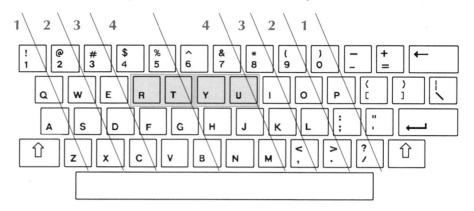

*Press **R** and **T** with the left hand, and **Y** and **U** with the right*

The letters **RT** are typed using the pointer finger of your left hand and **YU** with the pointer finger of your right hand. Note the finger lines in the diagram which show which finger is used to type which keys: "1" for the pinky, "2" for the ring finger, "3" for the index and "4" for the pointer.

From this point on each lesson will begin with a review of the previous lesson. **Remember to press Enter at the end of each line with your right pinky.**

Review

```
1   aaa ;;; aaa ;;; sss lll sss lll ddd kkk ddd kkk fff jjj fjf
2   aaa sss lll sas asa ddd das kkk jjj lkl fff fjf jfj klk jas
3   ljl kfk ldf klj kjk ljk fsd sda jkl fsd sad sad lad lad fad
4   dada fada sads jass klas fas; dad; fkal dasd jjkk jaka fada
5   asks lads lass daj; jakl kfkf ladf klds adas fjl; dads lads
```

Practice 2.1

```
1   fff ffr frf frr frr rrr frr frf rrr frf frr rrr fff frf rrr
2   fff fft ftf ftt ftt ttt ttt ftf ttf ftf ttt ttt fff tff ftt
3   frt frt frt frt fra rta rat rat jar jar far far tar tar far
4   jjj jju juj juu juj jju juj juj uuu juu juj jjj uuu juj juu
5   jjj jjy jyj jyy jyy yyy jyj jyy jyy jyj yyy jyy jyj jyj yyy
6   juu juy jju juy jyu juy jyu jyu jyy juu uuu yyy uyu yuy yuy
```

An Introduction to Computing Using Microsoft Works

```
 7   fujy furt fryt juty rfrt sats fats jakd dar; rats rats sats
 8   krad jury safy last last jury tars tars star star duty duty
 9   yard jury duty fast just dark dust data klas jars furs yard
10   ruts says lass tar; hats sats rats yard dull tart last dad;
```

•••

Practice 2.2

```
 1   juts furs dust suds dart rats sats just just task task fast
 2   rats ruts daft rays sats lark jars salt suds suds lads furs
 3   yard duty fast lads sad; lass tars hats data tart last dust
 4   jar ask fry lad fat dad add sad rut dad add say say far tar
 5   dart dull rut; ruts furs asks lass rust just fall star rays
 6   dusk last fast lads kart dust sass furs furs just task salt
 7   dull darts suds jars lark dusts rust data data rats salt as
 8   asks just last fur dark dart says jury task tart tars darts
 9   tar rat sally sally last yard dark try; fats lark dark data
10   ruts rudy trudy rust dart just salt dark furs say; dust tad
```

Repeat the Practices above until you can type the keys without referring to the keyboard diagram. When you are finished, exit Works by pressing the **Alt** and **F** keys, then **X**, **N**.

Lesson 3 - EGHI

In this Lesson you will learn the keys **EGHI**. Rather than pressing the Enter key at the end of each line we are now going to allow the computer to determine where the end of each line is. If there is not sufficient room for a word at the end of a line the word will automatically be moved to the beginning of the next line in a process called "word wrap." Where your computer breaks a line will differ from what is shown in this text since the break is determined by where the margin is set. Just keep typing the lines below without ever pressing Enter

Note the lines showing which finger is used to type each key:

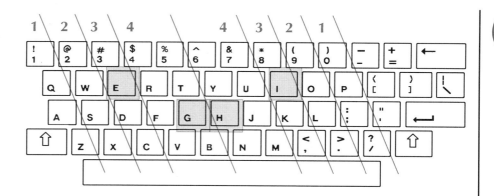

*Press the **E** and **G** keys with the left hand,
and the **H** and **I** keys with the right*

Review

1 fff frr frf frf fft ftf ftt ftf ttt juu juj jju jju juu juj

2 jyy jyy jyj jyj fuy fuy frt fju juy jyy ftt frr jyy juy juy

3 asks jury yard jars arts judy lark rust dust just fast dark

4 trudy dark sally yard daffy salt rat tar fur rays tall fall

5 darts fats sat; us all task lad; salt dust trust last fault

Practice 3.1

1 ddd ded ded dee dde ded ded ded ddd ded dee dee dee eee ded

2 fff fgf fgf fgg fgf fgf fgg fgf fgg ggg fgg fgf fgg ggg fgf

3 fgd deg fed def fgd deg fed def deg def feg dfe eee ggg ege

4 jjj jhj jhj jhh jhj jjj hhh jhj jhh jhj jhj jjh jjh hhh jhj

5 kkk kik kik kik kii kii kik iii iii kii kik kii kii iii kik

6 jhki jhik kiik kijh kijh khij jhik kihj jhki jhki jhki jjkk

7 did tug lad the she hid set age red red did ask let age the

8 did lug tug hit age yet ask rut elk gas she she did did use

9 rake dirt sake high dirt rail jail kiss jilt hale side said

10 saddle kettle us huddle jerry jail dirt yet little rut side

11 ask rail; kiss jilt hale said elks gas hers juggle rid teds

12 the fight federal fester justify sight satisfy deride kitty

An Introduction to Computing Using Microsoft Works

Practice 3.2

```
1   did lag elk yes age let rug kiss rake that said; sail hills
2   her; dig a rut age is hill high hear set sail satisfy there
3   erase refer defer agree reset sir differ legal degrees tell
4   satisfy father egret fifes fifth fly leg hedge sell his her
5   gail harsh heart thigh yalta light irish alight; ideal star
6   last jelly judge high kelly jail; kay jest hail to thee jet
7   halts the digs highest eight three furs halt judge judge as
8   lilly ladle legal aisle drill salt the these as; highest to
9   drudge tusk halt fudge last jest hail has gall deak salt as
10  hark yak said sail the less; fastest highest edge all halts
```

Timed Practice 3.3

The next few Lessons end with a timed practice which allows you to check your speed. Type for 1 minute and then calculate your speed in words per minute by counting the words typed. Each line contains 12 words. Words in a partial line are calculated using the scale below the lines.

```
1   did yes let rug age rut set ted ask elk yet dad sad lads hit    12
2   sake rail jail dirt side said jails kiss rake that tug; dull    24
3   jilt just fads fife flag fall digs ages rail tell star kills    36
4   fight sight deride just father fifth kettle jelly judge ask;    48
            1    2    3    4    5    6    7    8    9    |    1    2
```

When you are finished, exit Works.

Lesson 4 - CVB MNO

In this Lesson the letters **CVB MNO** are added as well as capital letters. Use the finger lines in the diagram to determine which finger is used to type the new letters. To type capital letters use either your left or right pinky to depress one of the Shift keys and type the letter. If the capital letter is typed with the right hand the left pinky is used to depress the Shift key. If it is typed with the left hand the right pinky is used. As in Lesson 3, allow the computer to determine where the end of each line is by not pressing the Enter key.

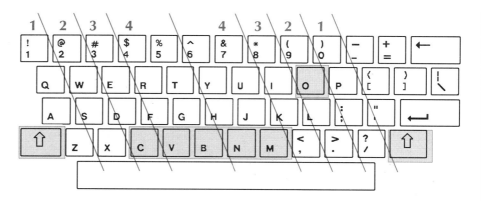

*Press the **C**, **V**, and **B** keys with the left hand, and the **M**, **N**, and **O** keys with the right. Use the pinky to press the Shift key*

Review

1 ded eee fgf ggg jhj hhh kik iii fge fgf jhj fgh jhi dek deg

2 digs ruts ages hill high sats fads sake rail dirt side said

3 all irish thigh gale takes legal aisle salt eight that flag

4 hail thee; fastest gail sledge haste tasks jet get hail art

Practice 4.1

1 ddd dcd dcc dcd ddc dcc dcc dcc ccc dcc dcd ccc dcc dcc dcd

2 fff fvf fvf fvv fvv vvv fvv fvv fvf vvv fvf fvv fvv fvv fvf

3 fff fbf fbf fbb ffb bbb fbb fbf fbb bbb fbf fbb fbb bbb fbf

4 dcv dcv cfv fvb fvb fbv fbf fvv vdc bdc bbd ccc vvv bbb bvc

5 jjj jmj jmj jmm jjm mmm jmm jmj jmm mmm mmm jmm jmj jmm jmj

6 jjj jnj jnj jnn jnn nnn jnn jnj jnj nnn jnn jnj jnj jnn jnj

7 lll lol lol loo ooo loo loo lol lol ooo loo lol lol loo lol

8 jmn jnm jnm jml jno loj ojn ooj jmn jno loj mno mno bcv bcv

9 Bill odd nod boy Bob night vent Sam avoids mad bite buried;

10 dock mint convert common bimini money none bongo volume vat

11 convince civic conic occur yucca bulb blurb member mayor to

12 ninth linen noun announce mono minds vocation victim vacate

13 kitty Gerry highly Eighty saddle kettle monies Tony convert

14 Jimmy Miami Thomas Fast Kludge Doll Rest Ernest Joan Laurie

15 Satisfy small Father; fight federal Jail tuggle yet Law Jim

An Introduction to Computing Using Microsoft Works

Practice 4.2

1 Lara Nina monkey said Gray is art color Has Harry come home
2 Janet will not be at school today It is too late to make up
3 Let us make haste before school starts This is not the time
4 Should you be very good or not This is the universal center
5 George Ferrit was raised in Iowa John Smith in Rhode Island
6 You need to make some money; to be able to go to the movies
7 Bob Cindy Virginia Monica Nina Ollie Barbara Veronica Bruce
8 This is the time for to be verbal Robert is a very nice guy
9 Miami New York Chicago Cleveland Boston Houston Dallas Dent
10 The gain made by becoming a good typist may be considerable

Timed Practice 4.3

Type for 1 minute and then calculate your speed in words per minute by counting the words typed. Each line contains 12 words. The words in a partial line are calculated using the scale below the lines.

1 Come to my house if you need to sell a vacuum cleaner today; 12
2 This is not a good time to help you with cooking the turkeys 24
3 Bill Crane is the secretary at our local offices of the club 36
4 Virginia is a beautiful state; Its capitol city is Richmond 48
       1   2   3   4   5   6   7   8   9 | 1   2

When you are finished, exit Works.

Lesson 5 - WQZX P,.?

In this Lesson the letters **WQZX P** are added along with the period (.), comma (,), and question mark (?). The question mark is typed by pressing the left Shift key with the left pinky and the question mark key with the right. Two spaces normally follow a period or question mark; a single space follows a comma. Note the finger lines in determining which finger to use for each key.

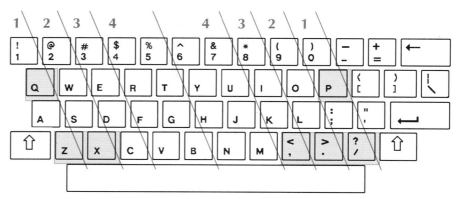

Press the **Q**, **Z**, *and* **X** *keys with the left hand, and the* **P**, *comma, period, and* question mark *with the right*

Review

1   dcdc fvvf fbfb jmmj jnjn Jmnj jnlo loon fvcd Fcvf jmnl Lojn

2   very task dark volt None vast many salt belt bolt none cold

3   Verbal Bimini Bahamas vacuum Nina member announce mist mold

4   members linen Venice Bob Vermont San Antonio convert Melvin

Practice 5.1

1   sss sws sww sww sws sww www sws ssw sww sws sws www sws sws

2   aaa aqa aqa aqq aqq qqq aaq aqa aqq aqq aqq aqa qqq aqa aqa

3   aaa aza azz azz zzz azz azz aza azz azz azz azz zzz azz aza

4   ;;p ;;p ;p; ;p; ;p; pp; pp; ll. ll. 1.1 lo. lo. la. ll. 1.1

5   sss sxs sxx sxx xxx sxs sxx sxs xxx xxx ssx sxx sxs sxx sxs

6   kk, kk, kk, k, kkk, k, k, kk, ; ? ; ? ; ? ; ; ? ; ? ; ? la?

7   aqua, zap? Zeus, want; aqua. quart, extra, quilt. Zoe quill

8   quick query equip quilt quits quote Queen quality paper top

9   apple panel support append popular profess quota quail pops

10   Rudy Penn Paul, plastics proof quart quit? Walter Thomas at

11   Aztec zero, unzip. fuzzy gauze sizes Inez epitomize Prizes?

12   exact axiom vexed Felix, Exxon. Xerox, mixed index exciting

13   dozen Zeke. Brazil, William, hertz gauze dozes? lazy Zurich

14   zonal zooms seize quilt quick prime power opera? allow. Zak

15   Oprah robot Boone, Texas, Portland, Zeus Zola extremely fax

  An Introduction to Computing Using Microsoft Works

Practice 5.2

1 Jake quit his jobs. What do you want? Exit from the west.
2 Zinc is not really that pretty. Would you please be quiet?
3 I would like to go to Zurich, Brazil, Texas and Queensland.
4 Robert Roodez is a fine person whose qualities are special.
5 In which Texas cities would you like to stay at Quality Inn?
6 The Aztecs had an advanced civilization which disappeared.
7 What equipment would you like to have added to a gymnasium?
8 I have visited Washington, Texas, Arizona, Utah, Vermont.
9 Inez Zola has the qualities that will make her quite famous.
10 Do you have zebras, polar bears, and turtles at your zoo?

Timed Practice 5.3

Type for 1 minute and then calculate your speed in words per minute by counting the words typed. Each line contains 12 words. The words in a partial line are calculated using the scale below the lines. To test your accuracy count the number of letters and spaces missed.

1 There are qualities which are required to become successful.   12
2 The following will come to the front; Bob, Zelda, and Betty.   24
3 Would you please; ask your parents to allow you to visit me?   36
4 Twelve quiet students sat on the wall waiting for the twins.   48

    1   2   3   4   5   6   7   8   9 | 1   2

When you are finished, exit Works.

Lesson 6 - :"/

In this Lesson the colon (:), quote marks ("), and slash or division sign (/) are added. The colon is typed by pressing the left Shift key with the left pinky and typing the key containing the semicolon and colon. A space always follows a colon. Quote marks are typed by pressing the left Shift key with the left pinky and the key to the right of the colon key using the right pinky. The slash is typed using the right pinky.

Review

1 dozen unzip zesty gauze amaze wants excite explain exhausts
2 prop Perhaps? personal, profit, operator. Quality qualify
3 equip quest quicken, proud supports puppy Zanadu? Exciting
4 quit extra Paul Zak? Extra qualify pest apple quart quick.

Practice 6.1

1 : : "abcd" l: "What is that?" "This is a quote from Jane."
2 "John is the best." The team is: Zeke, Jake, Rob and Quent.
3 ; / / ; / ; abc/de x/y; words/minute nt/m miles/hr, xyz/abc
4 These states are in the west: Utah, Oregon, and California.
5 What person said: "We have nothing to fear but fear itself"?

Lesson 7

The two Practices in this lesson are timed practices. In the first, type for one minute and then calculate your speed in words per minute by counting the words typed. Each line contains 12 words. The words in a partial line are calculated using the scale below. To test your accuracy count the number of letters and spaces missed. Record both your speed in words per minute and the number of errors per minute. Repeat the Practice a few times recording the results of each attempt. Your speed and accuracy should improve each time. Note the specific letters which appear as errors and repeat the Lesson for that letter. For example, if you often type the letter R instead of T by mistake, go back and repeat Lesson 2. Note that this material is fairly difficult; its "syllabic intensity" is high. You should be familiar with the entire keyboard and be able to perform all the previous Lessons before attempting this one.

Timed Practice 7.1

1 dale rail flight word, solve draft general; writers rough at   12
2 Important: work orders going ahead; instead rise part, taken   24
3 gift week disaster creates advantage been skill oral success   36
4 sharpen your smile coal miners desire: insure achieve smiles   48
5 Press exit Zack; suspend flowers: beginning strokes reunite,   60
6 carriage blooms crowd works quite document fashion computer: 72
7 having options print transfer undo; Marcia, Melvin, Samantha   84

```
  1     2     3     4     5     6     7     8     9  |  1     2
```

Timed Pratice 7.2

The **Tab** key is located on the upper left of the keyboard, next to the "Q". Rather than using spaces, Tab is used to indent paragraphs and to begin lines which do not start at the left margin. In the Practices below, you will press Tab once with the left pinky to indent each paragraph. You will learn more about Tab in Chapters Three and Four.

In this Practice type for five minutes and then calculate your speed in words per minute by counting the words typed and dividing by 5. The total of words is given at the end of each line. The words in a partial line are calculated using the scale below the lines. To test your accuracy count the number of letters and spaces missed. Repeat the Practice typing for ten minutes and then calculating your speed and accuracy. Repeat this Practice several times, over several days. You should note an increase in both your speed and your accuracy.

```
1     Many of the advances made by science and technology are      12
   dependent upon the ability to perform complex mathematical      23
   calculations and to process large amounts of data.  It is       34
   therefore not surprising that for thousands of years            44
   mathematicians, scientists and business people have             54
   searched for "computing" machines that could perform            65
   calculations and analyze data quickly and accurately.           76


2     As civilizations began to develop, they created both         87
   written languages and number systems.  These number systems     99
   were not originally meant to be used in mathematical            109
   calculations, but rather were designed to record               119
   measurements.  Roman numerals are a good example of this.       130
   Few of us would want to carry out even the simplest            140
   arithmetic operations using Roman numerals.  How then were     151
   calculations performed thousands of years ago?                 162


3     Calculations were carried out with a device known as an     174
   abacus which was used in ancient Babylon, China and            185
   Europe until the late middle-ages.  Many parts of the         196
   world, especially in the Orient, still make use of the        207
   abacus.  The abacus works by sliding beads back and           217
   forth on a frame with the beads on the top of the frame       228
   representing fives and on the bottom ones.  After a           239
   calculation is made the result is written down.              249
       1     2     3     4     5     6     7     8     9   |   1     2
```

Lesson 8

In this Lesson you will make use of the top row of keys which contain both numbers and symbols. Note which finger is used to press each key. The right Shift key is used to type the symbols at the top of the keys 1 through 5 and the left Shift key for the symbols on the top of keys 6 through =.

Practice 8.1

1   aqa aq1 aq1 aq1 a1a a1a a11 sws sw2 sw2 sw2 s2s s2s s22 ss2

2   ded de3 de3 de3 d3d d3d d33 de3 frf fr4 fr4 f4f f4f ff4 fr4

3   fr5 fr5 fr5 f5f f5f f55 ff5 juj ju7 ju7 ju7 j7j j7j ju7 j77

4   jyj jy6 jy6 jy6 j6j j6j jy6 j66 kik ki8 ki8 k8k k8k ki8 k88

5   lol lo9 lo9 191 191 lo9 199 ;p; ;p0 ;p0 ;p0 ;0; ;0; ;;0 ;p0

6   aq1! aq1! aq1! aq!! sw2@ sw2@ s2s@ Sw@@ s@@s de3# de3# d#3d

7   fr4$ fr4$ fr$$ fr$f f$4r fr5% fr5% f5%% f5%5 f%f% jy6^ jy6^

8   ju7& ju7& ju7& j&j& ju&j ki8* ki8* k**k k*8* k8*8 lo9(lo9(

9   L(990); : L(; 0) ;)0)) (9923) : ; 00) 19(00) ; - - __ ;

10   ; + +567 - 342 =$45.60 + ; " ' ;+ ; + = - ; ___ -- +1895.00

11   $435.00; = 389* (873) &23 $35.89@ 380.23! 89 + 78 = $382.00

12   Mary has bought a dress that costs $145.67 plus 6.0(%) tax.

13   (A) 3^2 = 9 & $12@ for 5 items = $60.00. 89 * 34 = 3026 47%

14   If I win the Florida $10,000,000.00 lottery I must pay tax.

15   Jack & Jill went up the 3,450 m hill to fetch 12# of water.

16   23 & 79 are odd numbers! (34 + 78) / (245 * 12.8) = 0.00035

An Introduction to Computing Using Microsoft Works

C

Timed Practice 8.2

In this Practice type for five minutes and then calculate your speed in words per minute by counting the words typed and dividing by 5. The total of words is given at the end of each line. The words in a partial line are calculated using the scale below the lines. To test your accuracy count the number of letters and spaces missed.

1   Hortense Bargain has decided to reduce the price of   11
stock items #3485 (paint), #7431 (electric saws) and #2945   23
(lawn furniture) by 45%. The new prices will be $38.50@,   35
$72.95@ and $14.98@.   39

2   Ivy University is having a book fair and charging the   51
following for books and supplies: pens $0.45@, note books   62
$3.78@, and boxes of paper clips $0.67@. "An Introduction 74
to Computing Using Microsoft Works" is specially priced   85
with a 10% reduction (plus 6% sales tax). The stock number 97
of this text is #34-2578 (for paperback) and #34-2580   108
(hardcover). Heidi Crane's new novel "Old Houses in New   119
Jersey" is specially priced at $12.45 after a 25% discount. 131

3   Please be advised of the addition of the following   142
courses to the Ivy University catalog: #126 Advanced   153
Computing (2 credits), #365 Very Advanced Computing (7   164
credits), #782 Computing for the Exceptionally Intelligent 176
(12 credits). The tuition for each course is $45.00@.   187
What a bargain!   190

    1   2   3   4   5   6   7   8   9 | 1   2

Lesson 9

In this Lesson type for five minutes and then calculate your speed in words per minute by counting the words typed and dividing by 5. The total of words is given at the end of each line. The words in a partial line are calculated using the scale below the lines. To test your accuracy count the number of letters and spaces missed. Repeat the Practice typing for ten minutes and then calculating your speed and accuracy.

1   One of the most important advances made in computing   11
has been in the field of "telecommunications." By   21
telecommunications we mean the sending of computer data   32
over telephone lines. To do this an additional piece of   43
hardware called a "modem" is required to translate the   54
binary data of the computer into waves which can then be   65
transmitted over phone lines. To receive data a modem   76
must also have the capability of translating the waves back   88
into binary form.   92

2   With a modem a microcomputer is capable of transmitting   104
and receiving data between any two locations connected   115
by phone lines. The rate at which each character of data   127
is sent is measured in "baud," one baud representing the   138
transmission of one character per second. Currently the   149
most common rates are 300, 1200 and 2400 baud which means   161
300, 1200 and 2400 characters per second. However, newer   173
modems are being created which are capable of communicating   185
at 9600 baud and higher.   190

3   In a recent newspaper article the Internal Revenue   201
Service (I.R.S.) defined artificial intelligence as "the   212
science of making machines do things that would require   223
intelligence if done by man." As an example, there are   235
currently computers which can play chess so well that they   247
can beat all but the best players. Universities actually   258
challenge each other's computers to play chess to determine   270
which has the best chess playing program. Are these   281
computers really intelligent? Most computer scientists   292
would say no. They are simply programmed to make a series   304
of decisions in response to the moves made by their   315
opponents. It is merely their speed and ability to access   327
huge amounts of stored data which make them appear to be   338
intelligent.   341

        1   2   3   4   5   6   7   8   9 | 1   2

Index

I

I

An Introduction to Computing Using Microsoft Works

I

J

K

L

M

An Introduction to Computing Using Microsoft Works

S

An Introduction to Computing Using Microsoft Works

X

Y

I

An Introduction to Computing Using Microsoft Works